Imagined Theatres

What possible and impossible worlds might the theatre imagine?

In what way is writing itself a performance?

How do we understand the relationship between real performances that engender imaginary reflections, and imaginary conceptions that become real theatrical productions?

Imagined Theatres collects hypothetical performances written by nearly one hundred leading theorists and artists of the contemporary stage. These dramatic fragments, prose poems, and microfictions describe imaginary events that put theory itself onstage. Each no longer than a page, and accompanied by a reflective gloss, these texts consider what might be possible and impossible in the theatre.

Daniel Sack is Assistant Professor in the English Department and Commonwealth Honors College at the University of Massachusetts Amherst.

"Like Calvino's *Invisible Cities*, Sack's *Imagined Theatres* are mirages for the mind's eye, creations by leading artists and scholars that speak of stages that never were but may yet be—an editorial and critical tour de force."

—Joseph Roach, Sterling Professor of English, African American Studies, American Studies, and Theater at Yale University.

"*Imagined Theatres* invites us to envision theatre as a utopic 'no place' of infinite possibility, in which theory and practice conjoin in a liminal space of creative imagining. Sack brings together contemporary theatre and performance's brightest artist/thinkers in a constellation of words and images, ideas and propositions that give me hope, not just for the theatre, but for how human beings might interact, relate, and connect in ways that performance helps us conjure. An inspired collection for precarious times."

—Jill Dolan, Dean of College and Annan Professor of English and Professor of Theater at Princeton University.

Imagined Theatres

Writing for a theoretical stage

Edited by Daniel Sack

Routledge
Taylor & Francis Group
LONDON AND NEW YORK

First published 2017
by Routledge
2 Park Square, Milton Park, Abingdon, Oxon OX14 4RN

and by Routledge
711 Third Avenue, New York, NY 10017

Routledge is an imprint of the Taylor & Francis Group, an informa business

British Library Cataloguing in Publication Data
A catalogue record for this book is available from the British Library

Library of Congress Cataloging in Publication Data
A catalog record for this title has been requested

ISBN: 978-1-138-12204-8 (hbk)
ISBN: 978-1-138-12205-5 (pbk)
ISBN: 978-1-315-26495-0 (ebk)

Typeset in Bembo by
Servis Filmsetting Ltd, Stockport, Cheshire

Visit the website at www.imaginedtheatres.com

In memory of Robin Joy Allan and all her imagined theatres.

Contents

Preface: The horizon

Daniel Sack

The curtain opens endlessly;
it does not stop at the proscenium's
jamb, but instead runs on.

What you assumed a line splitting
open the frame of a thought is but the
tangent of a larger encompassing circle

describing the outer curve of your attention.
The sound of the tracks recede into what
you called offstage, farther and further

afield, a train dividing the great dark plains
into what is still the theatre and yet
already becoming not the theatre.

In what other houses do those other people sit,
patient for the slow progress of the veil
to reveal their night has truly begun?

Tragedy is all a matter of scale, said Aristotle:
You must be able to hold the event in memory
or take its full shape in with a single glance.

Indefinitely, on the most distant horizon,
the curtain is coming around at the other
side of sight, inverting itself like a

crimson velvet ouroboros.
You think you see it opening still:
this life here and now, appearing.

Acknowledgments

One of the innumerable imagined theatres this book does not contain tells the story of a performance that ends, like many theatrical performances, with a curtain call. After all the actors have had their bow, the stage hands begin to emerge—one by one or holding hands in pairs, squinting at the light. They keep coming as the audience's clapping turns insistent, as the stage fills and they spill over into the orchestra, down the aisles, and out into the lobby—those countless hidden bodies whose labor made the show possible. As if having traveled from far away, from the edges of a theatre that extends to towns or countries unseen, it takes many hours for the last to make their way to the boards. The last hand that moved the theatre bows as dawn brightens the city streets.

Great hosts from near and far have sustained this book, too. Without keeping you here until morning with a list too long to name, a few figures deserve attention: Jane Hwang Degenhardt, LeAnn Fields, Peggy Phelan, Alexandra Ripp, Rebecca Schneider, Jenny Spencer, and Silvia Valisa. Special thanks to Kyle Gillette and Aaron C. Thomas for close readings and outside eyes when I needed them most. Also to Ellie Kevorkian, the "Liveness is Critical" residents, and the entire staff at the Bemis Center for Contemporary Arts for encouragement at an important moment in the process.

Different iterations of *Imagined Theatres* were presented at Summerhall in Edinburgh, Florida State University, Hampshire College, Harvard University, the Five College Performance Studies Working Group, the Interdisciplinary Studies Institute at the University of Massachusetts Amherst, and conferences organized by Performance and Philosophy, the American Society for Theatre Research, the Association for Theatre in Higher Education, the American Comparative Literature Association, and the Interdisciplinary Performance Studies at Yale "Crossings" conference.

Thanks to Reiko Ishiguro at the 21st Century Museum of Contemporary Art, Kanazawa, for assistance with permissions, and the artist Chiharu Shiota for the use of her work. Coach House Books kindly allowed the reprint of texts from Jonathan Ball's *Clockfire*. Selections from my introduction were first published in a different form in *Theater* magazine (Winter 2015) under the editorship of Tom Sellar, and the preface initially found its way to print in the pages of the poetry and prose journal *Parcel*. Ten of the imagined theatres and glosses collected under the constellation of "Technology" were published in the Fall 2016 issue of *Theatre Journal*. Editors Jennifer Parker-Starbuck and Joanne Tompkins were helpful interlocutors here and elsewhere.

This project was made possible with the generous support of a Faculty Research Grant/Healey Endowment Grant from the University of Massachusetts Amherst. Students and colleagues at my home institution have been supportive throughout, but two people were especially instrumental in their assistance. Tom Racine offered a steady hand with a mountain of invoices and all manner of convoluted tax forms. I cannot put words to the gratitude I owe my assistant Patricia Matthews, a brilliant doctoral student in the Department of English. With a precision of thought and a feel for language I can only admire, she has been the most reliable and inspiring of collaborators.

Thanks to Dusty Sheldon and adjective studio for working on the website and thanks to the staff at Routledge/Taylor & Francis for making the book possible. I want to acknowledge Kevin Selmes for his meticulous attention to the words that fill these pages, Kate Edwards for her patience in the face of ever-expanding complications, and, above all, Ben Piggott for his willingness to approach the impossible (or at least unreasonable) with excitement. He has backed this project unconditionally from the very first.

My acknowledgments begin and end with the contributors to this volume. These are the people who have long shaped my understanding of the theatre, and have repeatedly shown me where that understanding confronts its limits. It has been an honor to imagine alongside them.

A note on the website

The theatre keeps imagining itself anew. Every time we return to the rehearsal room or settle into our seats, we imagine a difference, however small, however subtle. This need not be a matter of disruption; it may be a gesture of conservation or repair. The theatre looks, listens, feels outward from the immediate to discover what could be. *Imagined Theatres* will continue beyond these covers, too. Alongside the publication of this book, a website offers bridges farther and further afield.

Imaginedtheatres.com is an open-access online journal with two streams for further development. Beginning in the summer of 2017, new "issues" containing texts by 15–25 authors will be released every six months. Under the stewardship of a guest editor or team of editors, each issue focuses on a geographic area overlooked by the book, beginning with South Africa (Summer 2017) and then Australia/New Zealand (Winter 2017). Later issues will move into translation and may incorporate other themes in time. While these volumes follow the basic structure of the book, guest editors may decide to articulate a slightly different orientation for each subsequent collection.

In addition, the site contains an ever-growing archive of select user-submitted work. In an effort to treat this material with the attention often reserved for more conventional academic production, an editorial board peer-reviews and curates these texts before publication. You are invited to send your own writing for consideration—in glossed or unglossed form—via the links provided on the website. The technologies afforded by the site will allow for new arrangements and constellations to take shape within this archive, discovering how the digital imagines the theatre differently from the book.

The platform will evolve over time, but web-exclusive work is already available. You will find a list of references to earlier writings that might be called imagined theatres, as well as links to contemporary artists whose existing work covers similar terrain. A series of pedagogical applications are outlined, providing suggestions for classroom and workshop use. Here, too, we welcome accounts of different uses that you have made of this material. Collectively, we hope to foster a second universe of theatrical possibilities, by turns inspiring and responding to the actual production it exists alongside.

Introduction

The lights rise on a room not unlike this one. At center a table with a cardboard box on it. After a moment, a figure enters and sits down. The figure opens the box and takes out a book, opens the book and begins to read.

The lights rise on a room not unlike this one. At center a table with a cardboard box on it. After a moment, a figure enters and sits down. The figure opens the box and takes out a miniature theatre. It is made of paper, remarkably intricate in its design—all the parts and pieces down to the smallest scale, are in perfect working order. There are lines that maneuver drops, levers that dim lights, machines that lift gods high, walkways that lead to buildings within buildings, some labyrinthine echo from the Noh stage. A trick of smoke and mirrors seems to immerse you as a participant one moment and then another places you watching from outside, the stage hiding behind a proscenium, or thrusting forward, even surrounding at once on all sides. Obsolete mechanisms stand side by side with mysterious devices that promise unforeseen revelations. What are they all for?

You want to take it apart. You want to get at the essence of the theatre, even if you know it's a quixotic venture. This is how the poet/theorist Charles Baudelaire explained the destructive inclination so common to children—that "first metaphysical tendency"—to tear apart the toy to find the heart of the machine that sets it in motion. If the toy or miniature dreams a secret life (as another poet/theorist, Susan Stewart, has it), then the theatre *guarantees* some other prime mover behind the scenes, a stagehand at the board or prompter feeding lines.[1] In this case, I claim responsibility for casting you in the performance that is the reading of this book, but there are many of us back here, each proposing a different event that might dress you in strange costumes and take you in stranger directions.

Imagined Theatres: Writing for a Theoretical Stage is such a paper theatre—or, rather, a universe of paper theatres—bringing together short conceptual performances written by close to one hundred artists and theorists of the stage. Each writer offers a text one page in length, describing an event that may or may not be performed in some future theatre to come. Another single page text faces each theatre, written by the same author or another: a *gloss* outlining a critical context, a history, or a personal reflection, which models one of many possible responses to the hypothetical event. *Imagined Theatres* works in fragments, only suggesting the outline of a shape and leaving the reader to fill out the volume. For the imagination flits and falters; it does not finish a form or stick to its intentions; it fragments attention.

These "imagined theatres" might seem illogical or fantastical; they might break the laws of physics and etiquette. Or perhaps they could be staged in some ideal architecture where the finances, conventions, ethics, or other practicalities of actual production do not hold sway. Each is a thought experiment about the expectations of the theatre, a parable or paradox that touches upon its nature and elaborates on the many ways in which that nature might be conceived. *Imagined Theatres* gathers together what may initially seem impossible in order that its readers might interrogate where that impossibility lies and what lies are obscured by calling it "impossible." (For is anything truly impossible in a theatre?)

Many of the imagined theatres in the following pages provoke questions of performance's fundamental dimensions: time and space. Some stretch the duration of an event to last a lifetime or to outlive many generations, while others pass momentarily. Great accumulations fill the page with a density that exceeds the carrying capacity of the theatre's confines: cities, nations, whole ecosystems and vast complexities flicker into appearance. They literalize the long-lived philosophical conceit of the *theatrum mundi*, the world as stage, and make theatres of canyons and gardens. They open prosceniums that look out upon the edges of outer space to choreograph a dance between planets, mount a conflict between microscopic actors, or frame a people in migration as performances.

Others ask us to reconsider who or what gets to perform on a stage. The theatre may be largely concerned with humans watching other humans in action—holding a mirror up to (human) nature, as Hamlet put it in his address to the actors about to perform his own imagined play. But in an age when non-human animals, objects, technologies, and the ecological surrounds at large are recognized as living actors, participating in events far more intricate than any Disney-like dream of anthropomorphic song and dance might portray, we require an expanded ethics and sociality born out of interspecies and interanimate relations. With its histories and para-histories of puppets, circus, and animal shows, the theatre might pose responsible ways of thinking and acting with the non-human. It shows how that mountain is doing something, how the ocean is delivering us a message.

Historically and culturally defined conventions limit the theatre in ways as profound as any seeming natural order. In confronting these conventions directly, word for word, imagined theatres show us what *should* be possible today, what thinkers like Jill Dolan and José Muñoz have framed as the utopic aspect of performance. Such proposals demand that we reconsider theatre's publics, that we create spaces welcoming those normally without the means and time to access its offerings, or whose makers do not require approval from the gatekeepers of cultural acceptability or normativity. They play with the concrete materiality of labor conditions, imagining theatres that recompense performers fairly, or give voice to underrepresented participants. They turn our attention to sites where people are made socially and politically invisible—prisons, hospitals, schools—or force us to look hard at the undersides of institutions devoted to display—theatres, museums, cinemas. Since the theatre is contiguous to the everyday, as these pieces challenge art they also challenge quotidian life (knowing that these two dimensions can never be separated). To call these "imaginary" is to recognize the current prejudices of artmaking in the Anglophone world, but it is also to recognize that theatre is anything but fixed and stable; it changes in different contexts and times. There have been many theatres, and there will be many more.

Some of these texts will not look like theatrical texts at first glance. Remember how Marcel Duchamp signed a name to a urinal and thereby turned that overlooked mundane receptacle into a voluptuous porcelain sculpture. He placed this "readymade" object into the frame of a museum, called it "art," and thus the definition of art had to alter to accommodate the interloper. So, too, walk across a stage and you will become an actor;

place a chair on its boards and it will begin to perform something. With *Imagined Theatres*, you might think of the page itself as a stage or performance space where anything that enters its field becomes a player. This expansion of the term "theatre" applies to the form of the writing as much as its content. Yes, there are scripts in here with characters and speeches, italicized stage directions like the ones that opened this very introduction. Yet other texts appear as sets of instructions, stories in prose, or poems in verse. Some are closer to what goes by the name of "philosophy," or "history," or "confession." What happens to these texts when they are called "theatres"? What is gained or presumed by such a designation? What is lost?

Imagining the limit cases of a theatrical event, one might come closer to understanding what theatre in its broadest conception can be and do. The philosopher Ludwig Wittgenstein said of his own writing, "I am not interested in constructing a building, as much as in having a perspicacious view of the foundations of possible buildings."[2] For Wittgenstein, this meant a reflection on the nature of language itself, communication as a game that we play with others, almost always according to unspoken rules. He described his writing as a ladder of language that might be used to climb outside the building of language and then regard its foundations. So, too, the hypotheticals of *Imagined Theatres* are intended to see and put pressure on the actual makeup of the medium.

If *Imagined Theatres* is a building, then it is one with many, many rooms. Its occupants are named and addressed towards the rear of the volume; there you will also find what might be thought a kind of basement or attic collecting *Related works* for each of the theatres contained herein (to keep the academic apparatus at bay except where it plays a necessary part, any references mentioned in these theatres will be found there). A final section provides a set of maps, or *Constellations*, illustrating different methods of access and escape. Otherwise, the book follows a consistent modular structure that could be expanded endlessly. Each left-hand side page—the verso—contains an imagined theatre. Facing it, each recto presents a page-long gloss. Some contributors have written glosses on their own work; others have been asked to dialogue with another contributor—perhaps someone with whom they have worked extensively, perhaps a complete stranger.

For millennia, readers from China to Egypt to Greece and beyond have annotated books with marginal commentary serving as explanation, interpretation, or reminders to future readers—perhaps even one's own future self. To "gloss" in this manner is to participate in a text, to make the reader's performance apparent. In dialogue with their original actors, these parasitic texts present arguments for, against, and alongside their host. I say "parasitic," because a gloss is beside (a para-site), but also because a gloss is not merely a transparent double. The *Oxford English Dictionary* says that "gloss" is "often used in a sinister sense: a sophistical or disingenuous interpretation." For a gloss might also cast a lustrous layer atop a text, a sheen on the scene; it might divert attention or draw a veil or curtain over the original text. This insinuation of deceptive behavior and superficial appearance feels particularly apropos to the theatre, which has faced similar charges throughout a long history of antitheatrical prejudice stretching back to Plato. So, too, the theoretical has often been charged with hiding behind obtuse jargon—another form of duplicity that has produced antipathy among many readers. I'd like to suggest, then, that these glosses theatricalize the theoretical act.

Discourse around the theatre usually presumes a binary that sets practice/performance/art on one side and theory/criticism/scholarship on the other. *Imagined Theatres* prefers to see a continuum in place of an opposition: an imagined theatre lies closer to the practice end while still connected to theory, just as its gloss lies closer to theory while still participating in creative practice. Some of the glosses here resemble theatrical scenarios themselves, and some of the theatres, too, read like glosses on some other pre-existing theatre that has gone missing. To echo the performance theorist Richard Schechner's understanding of the liminal state of play, where the actor is both not herself and not not herself, one might say that an imagined theatre is at once not theatre and not not theatre, just as a gloss is not theory and not not theory.[3]

As the subtitle to this book has it, imagined theatres and their glosses together comprise a multitude of "theoretical stages." An obsolete meaning of *theory* was "a sight, a spectacle," sharing a common root with the theatre as a "place of looking" from the Greek word *theatron*. These texts are theoretical performances in that they make a spectacle of theory, they make it perform. They are also theoretical performances in that they are provisional and hypothetical. They could be, but they could also not be. Theory in the theatre most often happens in response to performance, circulating in conversations after the fact that do not include or effect practitioners. But what if the theoretical happened as an event in itself? What if the act of imagining a theatre were an event with real consequences? And what if the theatre were taken seriously as a mode for theorizing beyond its own stages?

This book rests on the belief that the theatre allows us to theorize about our world as if it were another and to test that difference in motion, in time. An engine of cosmogony, the theatre creates, according to Elinor Fuchs, "another world passing before you in time and space."[4] This is why the theatre has long been a favorite metaphor for philosophers seeking to imagine a closed system with a logic of its own. When Plato wanted to tell us about the nature of reality, he asked us to imagine a theatre. Not the open-air auditorium overlooking ancient Athens that he knew so well and upon which he watched the performances of his day; rather, he invented a proto-cinema with shadow puppets dancing on a cave wall. Recall, too, that the dialogues the philosopher wrote—theatres that staged debates between his protagonist/teacher Socrates and a rotating cast of antagonists—were initially read for small audiences; staged readings even if these did not fully embrace imitation through costumes and sets. Indeed, in his book *The Drama of Ideas* (2010), Martin Puchner has argued that, at odds with the conflicts of the Athenian tragedies, these Socratic dramas originated a counter-tradition of philosophical theatre performing argumentation in place of action. Thinkers like George Berkeley (*Three Dialogues between Hylas and Philonous*, 1713), Denis Diderot (*Rameau's Nephew,* 1762), and Jean-Jacques Rousseau (*Dialogues*, 1776) imagined theatrical conversations intended to think through the limits of philosophy.

Imagined Theatres joins a long history of impossible theatres or theatrical performances conceived for the page.[5] Many plays written will never reach the stage, in spite of their authors' best intentions. Maybe these works do not find a willing or able producer; maybe they make demands that exceed the means of production. Seneca's Roman tragedies were probably unstaged, indulging instead in an elaborate spoken description of violence that threatened to overwhelm representation. In distinction to these works, there are those dramatic texts deliberately written to be read, whose ideal stage is the page itself. The closet drama exemplifies such a theatre of the book. Romantic poets of the eighteenth and nineteenth century and modernist poets of the twentieth century alike proposed events that challenged the very constitution of the theatre, while the Marquis de Sade's *Philosophy in the Bedroom* (1795) staged scenes of erotic couplings and unmentionable desires. Unmoored from visible anchors and material constraints, only such closet drama, Puchner suggests,

> can actually change a man into a woman, place thousands of people on an impossible stage, and even turn objects and fragmented body parts into agents ... This resistance is part of a larger resistance to the limitations of the theater and the normativity that stems from them. It is this possibility of resistance, built into the very structure of the closet drama, that necessitates what one might call an epistemology of the closet drama.[6]

Such bookbound performance increasingly finds its way into theatrical production today. In one of the episodes of their *Life and Times* project (2009–present), for example, Pavol Liska and Kelly Copper of Nature Theater of Oklahoma gave each spectator in a darkened audience their own copy of a hand-drawn pornographic comic book, letting each individual leaf through the explicit drawings under the private illumination of their own handheld flashlight. A chamber full of private fantasies danced in those dim globes of localized light. (For their contribution to this book, you will be required to bring your own magnifying glass.)

The name of the Nature Theater of Oklahoma derives from an imagined theatre that Franz Kafka describes in a brief fragment from his incomplete novel *Amerika* (1927). A whole city of theatrical re-performance on the move across the Great Plains of the US, the Nature Theatre of Kafka's book offers a utopic promise of redemption for the protagonist, Karl, and his fellow immigrants and vagabonds lost en route to the American Dream.[7] Fiction writers and poets have often imagined theatres as metaphors and conceptual sites where divergent worlds nest within other worlds. Roberto Bolaño's extraordinary novel *2666* (2004) turns to the image of a theatre to make sense of the monstrosity of Santa Teresa, Mexico—a fictionalized version of the violent city of Juárez. He perverts Plato's theatre-cave into a mine-like hellmouth where the spectacle of brutality engulfing the city is always obscured or merely overheard by a diverted audience. And then there is the nightmarish performance in the opening chapter of Ralph Ellison's *Invisible Man* (1952), where the narrator and other young black men are tortured, blindfolded, and forced to fight each other in a makeshift arena for the amusement of the leading white men of society. This concludes with the terrified narrator's re-performance of his high school graduation speech to the mockery and celebration of the assembled masses—an allegorical theatre of mid-century America that reflects racism far too familiar today. From novels like Hermann Hesse's *Steppenwolf* (1927) and Virginia Woolf's *Between the Acts* (1941), to the poetry of Gertrude Stein and Anne Carson, writers across different literary genres provide rich examples of the kind of work that this volume collects.

Imagined Theatres is primarily concerned with what the language of theatre might afford our thinking, but precedents in the visual arts have explored related ground. The early happenings and chance-based events of John Cage or Allan Kaprow from the 1950s and 1960s often originated in a score that organized time and space into formations of possible actions. These events were usually performed by the artist, or at least in his or her presence. However, Kaprow soon began creating instruction works for individuals to perform on their own time and in their own space—the scores, perhaps with an attendant prop, stood in for the event as artwork. In the conceptual art of the 1960s and 1970s, actualization of a proposition was not compulsory; it was even considered redundant once an idea had been proposed. Take one example among many: Yoko Ono's 1962 *Instructions for Painting* and subsequent work collected in the books *Grapefruit* (1964–1972) and *Acorn* (2013) separate the linguistic construction of an event from its enactment, presenting hypothetical occasions "for dealing with oneself."[8]

She asks us to envision situations that reframe the world around the subject: imagine secretly speeding up all the clocks in the world by two seconds (*Clock piece*) or opening a small hole in a canvas and looking at the world through its window (*Painting to see the room*). Though some of these have been realized, Ono conceived of them as "paintings to construct in the head," rather than atop some material support. Between artist and spectator, "there [is] maybe a dream that two dream together, but there is no chair that two see together."[9]

Theatre theorists and artists have also often wondered over hypothetical events and worlds that might test the limits of the stage. Antonin Artaud wrote performance texts describing tableaus of apocalyptic proportions for his promised Theatre of Cruelty, but his essays, too, manifest events upon the stage of the reader—sometimes on the very body and nerves of his imaginary audience. As writers like Jacques Derrida have argued, Artaud's dream of a theatre without representation is impossible to actualize, but it has nonetheless inspired generations of performance makers. If contributors to this collection repeatedly return to Samuel Beckett's work, it is perhaps because so many of his non-dramatic texts describe events that might be staged in some theatre at the end of our world, but also because his plays seem to take place on a nearly internal register for the spectator, a fragmented figure lit by attention against the black surround. Marguerite Duras wrote plays for disembodied voices or novellas written in dialogue form that imitate plays but resist enactment on a stage always already corrupted by an inherently patriarchal representation. These are conceptual theatres, impossible perhaps, limning shapes from the depths of consciousness. The late director and theorist Herbert Blau, too, spoke of one such imagined theatre in an interview published in *PAJ* (*Performing Arts Journal*):

> I've always wanted to create a theatre that would be … like Picasso's sculptured "Death's Head" [1941]. So dense it would be almost like a black hole, the gravity so great it would warp back into itself and come out the other side. And yet, it would be like that sculpture, impacted, dense, or as if set in stone. I've always wanted to create a theatre even[t] that had such mass and spatial power, such density in its passing that it would be virtually absolute.[10]

Even before I invited them to conceive texts for this volume, many of the contributors here had written or performed work that belongs in the library of imagined theatres. A set of connected pieces by Tim Etchells (*230 Titles: I, II,* and *III*) stand in the foyer of this alphabetically organized collection; they are marquees announcing productions that are not contained here, but that might be imagined taking place in some forgotten buried venue. For more than thirty years, Etchells has been artistic director of Forced Entertainment, a collective of five artists/performers based in Sheffield, England, that has excavated a theatre not unlike the one his alter-ego describes in the gloss to these first works. In an email exchange we had at the outset of this book project, Etchells charted the company's engagement with the imaginary:

> Marking a break with Forced Entertainment's largely physical and visual work to that date, *Dirty Work*—the performance I made with the group in 1998—took the form of an imaginary performance summoned only via descriptive text from the performers on stage. Writing at the time, I framed the piece as a kind of virtual or imaginary performance, unpacked by the audience who were co-opted as authorial collaborators, drawn into the act of picturing the events described.[11]

As a solo artist, too, Etchells has employed language as a prompt to make the spectator/reader a collaborator in the work. *Surrender Control* (2001) and *A Short Message Spectacle* (2010), for example, were instructional dramas delivered by mobile phone text messaging to individual audience members who had subscribed to experience the work.

> My year-long Internet project *Vacuum Days* (2011), later published as a book and presented as posters, comprised a rolling program of imaginary events announced online at the rate of one per day. The 365 announcements of absurd performances, spectacles, debates, contests, film-screenings and other events was a distorted process of call and response with unfolding political situations and events during the course of 2011, mirroring the ubiquitous language of sensationalist media, news-as-pornography, hyped-up current affairs, Internet spam, twitter gossip, and tabloid headlines.

Then there is Ricardo Dominguez's work with the Electronic Disturbance Theater, a company he co-founded with Brett Stalbaum, Micha Cárdenas, Amy Sara Carroll, and Elle Mehrmand. Consider the *Transborder Immigrant Tool* (2007), a hypothetical mobile app intended to locate water sources and provide emergency assistance and poetry to those walking across the desert spaces between the US and Mexico. Even though the application was never developed, the project was under investigation by the US Congress; right-wing political agitator Glenn Beck deemed the piece a gesture that potentially "dissolved" the US border with its poetry. As Diana Taylor describes it, "the idea of helping undocumented immigrants, not the tool, proved powerful and radically altered the way in which power had to respond."[12]

Or consider how Lin Hixson and Matthew Goulish—director and dramaturge, respectively, of the Chicago-based performance companies Goat Island and Every house has a door—have worked at the hinterlands of their performers' capacities. *The Sea & Poison* (1998–2002), for example,

> set out to construct "impossible dances" from a series of unperformable individual movements, which challenge the limits of human ability, and as dance hover somewhere between musical composition and the clumsy marathon dance competitions of American depression years. *The Sea & Poison* combines these investigations into a layered expression of the effects of poison on the body—the social body and the individual body—and of impossibility itself.[13]

Watching these willful failures to actualize a series of actions, one could feel a kind of ghost choreography of intentions hovering over a space so filled with sweat and strain. It's an approach that the company has taken up in other ways, creating spaces in which an audience might imagine an otherwise inaccessible time or space—the architecture of a building (*The Lastmaker*, 2007), the theatre extending beyond the theatre space (*Let us think of these things always. Let us speak of them never.*, 2010), or a series of crimes or accidents traced in legal documents (*Testimonium*, 2013). Conversely, artist Rose English has exhibited the remains of theatrical events that never were performed, turning the imagination back towards what might have been, while choreographer Emily Johnson has fostered participatory performances that ask dancers and local communities to together imagine events they would like to see realized in the future through long gatherings lasting the night or for days on end. Finally, fatally, Jonathan Ball's collection of prose poems *Clockfire* (2006), several of which have been reprinted here, describes imagined theatres that hollow out the very possibility of theatre's survival or one's passage through it. So, too, the scholars in this collection have written in ways that trouble what we mean by a theatre, forcing us to reckon with a diversity of traditions, outlooks, and political exigencies that stress the conventions of this ever-changing art.

Writing about and doing theatre have long been intertwined in my understanding of this art. I first started exploring directing and devising while I was also beginning to study the history and theory of performance in graduate school at Stanford University. As conceived by what was then called the Department of Drama, the two courses—practical and theoretical—both pursued a common end: they demanded one imagine what could be put onstage. Incited by my readings and by the weekly problems that the late Carl Weber asked us to perform in his directing workshop, I dreamed up and wrote out scenarios that seemed impossible, conceptions far beyond my means and time. There was the play comprised entirely of accidents, the scene in which the audience secretly watched the stage technicians building the set of *Mother Courage* for weeks on end, the performance where we burned the theatre to the ground, and so on. I jotted these fragments down in notebooks or saved them in files titled "future projects." (And here I was not so far removed from Joe Kelleher's piece *The Theatre of the Town* in the pages that follow.) Even as I moved further into an academic career of writing, further from my theatre-making, I kept adding to my stockpile of imagined theatres. These became places for a concept to play out in ways my academic work did not allow, or where I might extend some greater distance the suggestion a performance conveyed.

In 2011, I made some of these imaginings public on a blog I called *Behind this Curtain*. I thought the curtain emblematic of the theatre's fundamental function—a means of appearance and disappearance at once. Anything could be held behind this curtain. I conceived a theatre of endlessly unfolding layers of curtains, constructed of any and all materials: transparent, translucent, opaque. One entry put it this way:

> I am a writer and only occasionally a director, so most of my imagined theatres must remain *in utero,* suspended in conception without actualization. [...] Behind each imagining lies the expectation that these will take place some day or that they have already taken place in one of the countless theatres that gleam dimly in some subterranean quarter of this world of ours. A kind of contradiction in terms, an imagined theatre is an impossibility clinging fast to its eventual realization.

I knew that others had their own dreamed-of and hoped-for theatres. Sometimes, sitting in a darkened auditorium, I would drift into a reverie, wondering what the director or designer or playwright or actor would do if they could do anything. Or, when at an academic conference, listening to scholars present their research, I would sense some underlying impulse at the root of their inquiry. I would dream of interrupting, asking to hear of their imagined theatres. Instead, I began to gather people together with this in mind, presenting a compilation of such texts first with two friends and fellow artist-scholars, Kyle Gillette and Rachel Joseph, then in a series of solo readings and workshops where those in attendance might write or share their own inventions. In classrooms and in late-night conversations, I asked people to tell me of their imagined theatres, to write them down. I imagined an endless festival of these works.

This book is the further development of that project. What began as an invitation to twenty writers quickly expanded to include a host far more numerous. And then, over the course of several months, small gifts of extraordinary writing began to arrive in my inbox on a daily basis. It has been a rather private delight, and I am anxious to see it made public.

If I take this moment's divergence into personal recollection, it is to signal that my own history, worries, and predilections have shaped this book's constitution—I hope in ways that inspire others, but certainly also in ways I cannot see. I have tried to find some version of a whole here, but this is in no way a comprehensive representation of the theatre and its constituent parts. The miniature theatre imagined at the beginning of this introduction is the fantastical theatre of all theatres past and future, all ready to perform, but not yet in action. Of course, it would be impossible to hold all these different traditions and approaches in a single space or time, or even to name them—the black box, the white cube, the theatre-in-the-round, the kabuki stage, the Greek auditorium, the Italianate proscenium, the street theatre, the invisible theatre, and so on. The library of imagined theatres stretches as far and wide as Borges' seemingly infinite Library of Babel, but this book, like all books, must find a beginning and an end.

And so I have decided to only invite contributors who explicitly work in or on the theatre: theatre artists, performance makers, choreographers, and scholars of the same. Another vision for this book would include texts by artists and theorists of performance in the gallery or everyday life, perhaps writers who don't work in performance at all, such as philosophers or political theorists. I have also asked that these theatres be constructed only out of written language—no images or diagrams. Another version would be comprised entirely of photographs or drawings from designers and visual artists.

Needing some further limit to this compendium, and wanting to establish some common geographical and historical ground between diverse voices, only contributors based in the United States, Canada, the United Kingdom, and Ireland will be found in these pages. I have broken my rules in one instance: in acknowledgment of the profound debt I feel to the imagination of the Italian director Romeo Castellucci, an artist who consistently ruptures distinctions between possibility and impossibility, I have invited him to share an offering beyond the arbitrary geographical boundaries of *Imagined Theatres: Writing for a Theoretical Stage*. This sally presages more far-ranging wanders to come. An accompanying website (www.imaginedtheatres.com) will slowly expand this scope with issues published every several months, compiling texts originating from other regions and, eventually, texts written in other languages. The website will also maintain an ever-expanding archive of user-submitted imagined theatres, selected and edited by a panel of artists and scholars. Readers are encouraged to put words to their own imaginings and contribute to this conglomeration of possible worlds via the website.

In other words, these are not merely texts for reading. You may choose to write your own imagined theatres, or respond to those written here with your own glosses, your own theatres. Playwrights, directors, designers, actors, and other performance makers are encouraged to try to stage these pieces—indeed, scholars and others who do not consider themselves theatre practitioners should do the same. (Note, however, that each of the writers in this book retains the rights to any professional production of their contribution.) Such a practice might force you to explore new methods of representation to circumvent the seemingly impossible. These imagined theatres might provide ways to rethink theatre history, performance practice, poetics, and philosophy, and it is hoped that they will be taken up in the seminar room or studio with this in mind.

There are any number of ways in which you might decide to approach this book. Like an anthology of poems or a series of microfictions, each individual voice invokes a world that may be dense and strange. Mimicking the (dis)organization of Roland Barthes' *A Lover's Discourse* (1977), which arranges its fragments alphabetically to prevent the illusion of a single narrative shaping the whole, I have opted to place these imagined theatres in alphabetical order according to title. You may find yourself dipping in to read a few at a time, deciding to flip forward and backward by chance. Or you might prefer to follow one of the many paths outlined at the end of this book, each *Constellation* guiding the reader through a cluster of works that speak to one another about a common subject or mode. These different trajectories acknowledge the fact that any number of relations might connect the worlds in this theatrical universe, more arrangements than can be characterized here. I invite you to chart your own.

If my imagined theatre with which I began is made of paper, then it is a book. And it is finally a closed book, containing the infinite array of happenings that may be put on stage. For Stéphane Mallarmé, the perfect book is the closed book—not the blank page, but in the words of the poet Maggie Nelson, "one whose pages have never been cut, their mystery forever preserved, like a bird's folded wing, or a fan never opened."[14] Present on the page, but suspended before the reader, such a book occupies a peculiar form of what I've taken to calling performative potentiality, its capacity to do many things at once; it says nothing in particular even as it presents the quintessence of bookishness. Such a closed book could contain anything and everything in its pages. It may describe your greatest fear or be the one and only book you need right now. It may be the book you will write some day. Or it might just be another book on the shelf beside others.

It is a book, in other words, awaiting the event that will be its reading, an undisclosed performance with the lines written, rehearsed, and ready. A space has been prepared for you, the props laid out. Your interpretation of the role will be unlike any other. You take the stage as the lights dim. *You open the book and begin to read.*

Notes

1 Susan Stewart writes: "That the world of things can open itself to reveal a secret life—indeed, to reveal a set of actions and hence a narrativity and history outside the given field of perception—is a constant daydream that the miniature presents. This is the daydream of the microscope: the daydream of life inside life, of significance multiplied infinitely *within* significance." In *On Longing: Narratives of the Miniature, the Gigantic, the Souvenir, the Collection* (Durham: Duke University Press, 1992), 54.

2 Ludwig Wittgenstein, *Culture and Value*, trans. Peter Winch (Chicago: University of Chicago Press, 1980), 7e. At the end of his first book, *Tractatus Logico-Philosophicus*, Wittgenstein wrote: "My propositions serve as elucidations in the following way: anyone who understands me eventually recognizes them as nonsensical, when he has used them—as steps—to climb up beyond them. (He must, so to speak, throw away the ladder after he has climbed up it.)" It is from the height of the ladder that he might look down on the foundations of other possible propositions. Do we use the theatre to get outside the theatre, to see the senselessness of its rules and regulations? See Ludwig Wittgenstein, *Tractatus Logico-Philosophicus,* trans. D.F. Pears and B.F. McGuinness (London and New York: Routledge, 1974), 74.

3 Richard Schechner, *Between Theater and Anthropology* (London and New York: Routledge, 1985), 110.

4 Elinor Fuchs, "EF's Visit to a Small Planet: Some Questions to Ask a Play," *Theater* 34, no. 2 (2004): 6.

5 While scholars like W.B. Worthen have reminded us that scripts do not necessarily precede performance or dictate its happenings, it is certainly the case in western drama that many texts are written before they are enacted in performance. This is not true in all traditions or of all forms of performance: dance, for example, is often choreographed on and through a body, its writing taking place in the aftermath of transmission.

6 Martin Puchner, *Stage Fright: Modernism, Anti-Theatricality, and Drama* (Baltimore: Johns Hopkins University Press, 2002), 90. For more on the closet drama see Nick Salvato's *Uncloseting Drama: American Modernism and Queer Performance* (New Haven: Yale University Press, 2010), Catherine Burroughs' *Closet Stages: Joanna Baillie and the Theater Theory of British Women Writers* (Philadelphia: University of Pennsylvania Press, 1997), and Evlyn Gould's *Virtual Theatre: from Diderot to Mallarmé* (Baltimore: Johns Hopkins University Press, 1989), among others.

7 I discuss Kafka's imagined theatre in *After Live: Possibility, Potentiality, and the Future of Performance* (Ann Arbor: University of Michigan Press, 2015), 195–197.

8 Kristine Stiles, "Being Undyed: The Meeting of Mind and Matter in Yoko Ono's Events" in *Yoko Ono: YES*, eds. Alexandra Munroe and Jon Hendricks (New York: Harry N. Abrams, 2000), 147.

9 Yoko Ono, "To the Wesleyan People" in *Grapefruit: A Book of Instruction and Drawings by Yoko Ono* (New York: Simon & Shuster, 1970), unpaginated.

10 Herbert Blau, Bonnie Marranca, and Gautam Dasgupta, "The Play of Thought: An Interview with Herbert Blau," *Performing Arts Journal* 14, no. 3 (1992): 1–32. Thanks to Bonnie Marranca for drawing my attention to this passage.

11 Private email correspondence with Tim Etchells (May 2016). Other projects that explicitly take up these ideas include *Speak Bitterness* (1994), *First Night* (2001), *Exquisite Pain* (2005, based on the work of Sophie Calle), *Tomorrow's Parties* (2011), and *The Notebook* (2014, based on the novel by Ágota Kristóf).

12 Diana Taylor, *Performance* (Durham, NC: Duke University Press, 2016), 68.

13 See www.goatislandperformance.org.

14 Maggie Nelson, *Bluets* (Seattle: Wave Books, 2009), 70.

1. 230 TITLES (I)—TIM ETCHELLS

Ice Pavements of Miami
No Indication
And in the Death
Future Story of a Backwards Nation
My Cacophony
The Virgin & The Roller-skater
Shame of a Telephone Switchboard Operator
Insane Island
Fortune 9000
Putrid Essence of a Bibliothèque
In the Land of Forgetting
Milan Subterfuge
Nine Suicides
The Mile Island Club
Jokers of Helmand Province
Beneath the Planet of the Master Race
6 Million Virtues
The Forgotten Pub
Death of a Vermin Exterminator
Subway to the Moon
The Tragedy of King Harrods
Monopoly & Mergers
The Vulgar Supermarket
Shifty Git Face
Mood Board Incarnate
Outlandia
The Trump Hole
My Days of Mail Order Misery
Beneath the Ozone Layer
Life During Water Rationing
The Hard Manacles
The Autumn Collection of Zanzibar Frume
Face Injuries of a Paid Protestor
Winter Season
Mischief in Mercia
The Seven Million Stolen Words
Spin Doctors Took My Codeine
Sister Mercury
Invincible Artifacts
The Irrelevant Symphony
An Eye Test for Reginald
Peephole to Melanie
Slippery Women
The Presence of Virtue in Doncaster
Long Haul
The Last American

Five Invisible Trade Agreements
Fukushima Ahoy
Mental History of a Reptile Eater
Fat Men
Piss Factory II
Yasmine On Fire
10,000 Blow Jobs
Turn Left at the Traffic Lights
Investigation of a Suspect
Demolishing Coventry
Mohair
The First Day of the Final Year
Ice Age in Manchester
Electronic Memory
The Intuition Club
Cradle of a Grave
The Marriage of a Dentist in England
Puke Pavement
The Novice
Pixilation of a Cancer Patient
Death by Pro Bono
The Inches
A Makeup Tutorial by Michelangelo
Last Minute Substitution of a Moral Succubus
A Long Month of Indolence
Nine Knee-jerk Reactions of a Qualified Therapist
Small Changes in the Appearance of a Cardinal
The Shifting Hypothesis
Feelings of Resentment & How to Get Over Them
Kendal Jenner is Beautiful
Lawful Romance of a Geiger Counter
The Last of the Moderates
The Fame & Blame Game
Twenty-Seven Fortune Boulevard
Fascism of Intention
The Last of the Showboat Entertainers
Lipstick on Underwear II
Cut Throats in Plunge-Necks
The Inevitable Milk Bucket
Early Diagnosis
Down & Out in Qatar and Dubai
Astronomers of Old Earth
Stealing Ventolin
Dirty Hands & Dirty Feet
Crap Shoot Nova
Non-Binary Tenderness

2. *230 TITLES (II)—TIM ETCHELLS*

Indecent Applause
The Vacuum Eaters
After the Psychedelic Festival
Screenshot Street
The Price of Meat in the Last Days of the Mechanical Age
The Secret Life of a Manic Depressive Shopkeeper
Family Misfortunes
Sea Stories
Great Phone Calls of New York
Sarcastic Living Room
False Memories of a Tunnel Digger
Eight Refugees
The Lonely Evening
Waiting for the Wolves
Rivers of Memory
On the Private Beach
In the Liar's Forest
Defensive Measures
Welcome to Cadiz
Shivering in Taxi Cab
A Cryptographic Water Shortage
Self-Surveillance in the 21st Century
Human Traffic
How to Dine Out on $10-$25 per Day
Proceedings of a Nebulous Investigation
Random Action on 100 Crank Handles
Maestro Central Dork Machine
The Rigged Game
Oracle Jones
Mission to Undo
Extremely Unfortunate Calligraphy
Malevolent Hair Loss of a Latter-Day Impresario
Mr Big Heart
There is No Way to Explain
Divorce for Losers
The Boring Restaurant
Crippled Knees
The Subterranean Workhouse Blues
No Win No Fee
Instant Photography in Focus
All New Tales of the Time Poor
Schrödinger's Chat
Polymorphous Perversity in Chicago
Jinx of a Medium Quality Holograph
Guantanamo Xmas
Maelstrom Trouser Suit

The Street of the Vagabonds
Tunnel of Love
Jazz Hands
The Courtesan and the Torturer
Men and Women of Langley
Miss Mish-Mash
Welcome to Rotherham
Scissor Jumps
Scraping Back the Skin
Lime Water
The Book Reader
Ghost Village
Ghost Taxi
The Internet of the Dead
Machinery
The Alphabet of Numbers
Short Changing
The Disco on the Edge of Town
The Terrorists in all the Good Hiding Places
Robot Children of Tomorrow
Crippling Frank
Piss On Me
The Viaduct by the Roundabout
Ink Job
Shoe Shine Boys
A Fugitive Spring
Shut Your Cake Hole
Italian Marble
Melancholia Forever
The Rubbish Seminar
Burst Water Main
Love by Telescope
Non-Islamic Justice
The Sharp Fish Man
Compliance Training of a Septuagenarian
Titanium Surprise
Race Relations in Budapest
The Haunted Slaughterhouse
Common Sense & Common Nonsense
All Eyes on Moses
Robot Replica of a Street Urchin
Straw Poll
A Life of Ishmael Ferguson
The No Hope Club
Soft Brexit (Waterlogged)
The Shandy Drinkers

3. *230 TITLES (III)—TIM ETCHELLS*

The Sharp Blubber Suit
Fathers, Sisters, Mothers, Brothers
The Weeping Contest
Miss Berlin Wall
Zika Virus Come Home
Upgrades to an Imaginary Operating System
The Silence at the End of a Telephone Call
Evisceration Station
Beggars to the Rescue
Bromance for Daniel
Lost in an Elevator Shaft
Move Out Immediately Mr Basic
Mossack Fonesca
Wire Tappers
Six Homeless Individuals
Trial of Strength
A Phony Symphony
The Raw Meat of Advertising
Mexico or Bust
Slow Bleeding
Philistine Intellects
At the Angle of a Corner
No Surrender
The Evangelicals of Doubt
Autumn Leaves
Poisoned Riverbed
Goat Island
Retribution of a Supermarket Manager
Special Delivery for Robeson
Florescent Light
Throw a Six to Continue
Love Conquers Lethargy
A History of Cable Television
The Shit Eater
Depressing Feelings
Rachel and the Last Minute Change of Plans
Cheese Sandwiches Today
An Inexplicable Feeling of Regret
Beer for Breakfast
The Sadism of a Home Wrecker
Stolen Isotopes
Strange Fruit Hanging from the Popular Tree
Railway to Nowhere
Nowhere / Now Here
Perfect Mirage of The Mirage Hotel
Electric Bayonet

The 230 titles reproduced in the preceding pages were found in papers retrieved from the ruins of the Limit Club in Sheffield, England, sometime in the early 1990s. Collected illegally from the abandoned premises years after the venue's closure, the papers in question are said to detail the names of theatre performances staged in the club as part of its largely undocumented alternative performance nights during the period 1984–1988. The Limit, a cramped basement nightclub on West Street, now entirely demolished, was best known as a music venue, earning a reputation for drunken violence whilst hosting bands from outside the city including U2, Siouxsie and the Banshees, the Gang of Four, and the B52's as well as local regulars The Human League, Cabaret Voltaire, Artery, Comsat Angels, and Pulp. Beyond the titles of the theatre works listed here, no details are known about what they contained, how they were produced or in what style, or even who wrote, made, performed, directed, or watched them. Since no photographs, scripts, or other documents pertaining to them have been recovered, it's possible that these plays or performances were never staged at all.

Amongst the 230 titles, several seem to prefigure or even predict events that were still far in the future when these performances would have been made—*Fukushima Ahoy* perhaps hints at the disastrous Fukushima Nuclear Power Station meltdown in 2011, whilst *Jokers of Helmand Province* appears to reference the troubled status of that region in Afghanistan during the conflicts there in recent years. *Zika Virus Come Home*, *Mossack Fonesca, The Courtesan and the Torturer,* and *The Weeping Contest* all nod to other future events that will need no introduction to readers of the current volume.

Further titles in the documents appear to reference existing works of theatre or film; *10,000 Blow Jobs* points perhaps to Mac Wellman's *7 Blowjobs* (1991), or to Truffaut's *The 400 Blows* (1959), whilst the *The Price of Meat in the Last Days of the Mechanical Age* appropriates the title of the last show by British performance group Impact Theatre. *Turn Left at the Traffic Lights* appears to be simply a translation of the title of an imaginary German television police drama series set in Neukolln, *Biege bei den Ampeln links ab*. The titles of other works supposedly presented at The Limit are harder to connect to other points of reference and we can only speculate about the significance or otherwise of performances such as *In the Liar's Forest, The Lonely Evening,* or *The Virgin & The Roller-skater*. In any case, as other scholars of the era have already suggested—the list is best approached as a kind of partial trace—both an imperfect and incomplete echo of events that once took place and as a vivid cue to our present imaginings.

(from *Taxi to the Cashpoint: An Underground History of Sheffield*, H. Stannington, Endland Press, 2014)

4. *AFTER DINNER—JULIA JARCHO*

ELIZABETH sits with TOMBOLDT and LIGLIA in their attractive dining room.

ELIZABETH. I'm very curious about your children.

TOMBOLDT. They feel the same way about you.

LIGLIA. They're probably listening at the door right now.

TOMBOLDT. More?

ELIZABETH. Thanks, I'm really full. It was great.

LIGLIA. I'm so glad.

ELIZABETH. Is it complicated to prepare?

LIGLIA. It's right in the middle.

TOMBOLDT. Lawrence turned us on to it.

LIGLIA. Your brother.

ELIZABETH. I had no idea you knew him.

LIGLIA. We owe him some money.

ELIZABETH. Oh—me too! From when I was staying at his place last summer. I was supposed to be subletting from him, but I never, I actually just didn't have any money at all. I still don't.

[ALL laugh.]

LIGLIA. Well. I'm sorry we have to charge you.

[BEAT. ELIZABETH laughs.]

TOMBOLDT. We'd love to say it's on the house, but unfortunately.

ELIZABETH. What do you mean.

TOMBOLDT. The meal.

[PAUSE. ELIZABETH laughs again.]

ELIZABETH. You guys.

LIGLIA. Uh-oh. Honey. Uh-oh. I'm so sorry. We thought you realized. Critical theory ought to refrain from being theatre, because critical writing must bear an assumption incompatible with the focus on "performance": universality. The universal is not the "universally human," nor is it totality; it has no substance, no "body" as it were, no actuality. But as a specter, it is the only element of thought that cannot be conscripted into instrumentality. To pursue universality is to strive to master *oneself* in the name, precisely, of that with which one cannot identify. It is to recognize the limited nature of our experience, to recognize that what is available to experience within the modernity of global capitalism—what we see, hear, smell, touch, taste, want, and feel, roughly speaking—is not all, is not enough. This is a restaurant.

TOMBOLDT *(fiddling nervously with his tie)*. Well, we've been calling it a private supper-club. Invite only. Certainly one hopes that art, e.g. theatre, can afford the same recognition. But when this occurs, it belongs to the dimension of reception; it cannot, must not, be a principle of practice. On the contrary, artists must labor to deny the appeal of the universal, must burrow ferociously into the meat and marrow of the most particular, must stake their lives on the absolute value of whatever they can see, hear, smell, touch, taste, want, and feel that has not yet been an object of articulate knowledge. The moment they have succeeded, that fragment of experience will become available not only to criticism but also, alas, to commodification. And yet the process must be repeated, because while it lasts, it holds open the sole inhabitable time and space on our planet. The universal fails to do this. It is not located here or now. It's been in the *Times*.

LIGLIA. Yeah and: how many times must we be asked to ratify flaccid, pretentious, confessional monologues that would never pass muster in a community of sophisticated artists, simply because their authors are resisting the supposed temptation to "assert mastery" over the conceptual material? It might be mentioned that elaborate demurrals from asserting mastery are perhaps the most ubiquitous sexual tic of modernity; witness the preponderance of simpering, utterly manipulative masochists, and the comparative rarity of dedicated sadists. But the truest justification of the purely conceptual may lie in the fact that aesthetic experience as such depends upon it. Kant writes that the judgment of taste—the judgment that something is beautiful—can be distinguished from the experience of the merely agreeable because the judgment of taste is *spontaneously structured like a logical, i.e. conceptual, judgment*, even as it is self-evidently not one. The "subjective universality" afforded by the beautiful is nothing more nor less than the subject's flicker of awareness that particular, embodied experience—or let us say "culture," "society," "history"—has the *formal* possibility of adequation to truth: that is, that what makes our life false is contingent; that life *could* be true. To deny the difference between truth and beauty, between knowledge and performance, is to collude with capital in obliterating that possibility. It is to paper over the gap that denounces that possibility's constant betrayal, it—

ELIZABETH *(to TOMBOLDT)*. That's enough. You have to tell her. *(To LIGLIA)*. We …

[LIGLIA throws her plate at TOMBOLDT. It whizzes past his head and smashes. ELIZABETH stares at both of them, then runs to LIGLIA and clasps her in an embrace. The End.]

5. *"ALL THE WORLD'S A …"—BAZ KERSHAW*

True experiments story: 1968–2005

H … that … urban theatre thing was stripped out totally back to black & blank irregular walls. Here & there concrete pillars prop up low murky ceilings. Between & above, added fly tower ends in utter darkness beyond streaming thunder flashes off & on. Default settings for *Homo sapiens* universe: heart-stopping black box experiment. **H** At former stage-left one set-piece remnant: a small early Victorian zoological garden. High barricade frieze encloses wildlife overlooked by grand terraced villas. One immersive mise en scène, like shallow panorama of granite cliffs with many dark farcical doors (a.k.a. '**H**') shut tight to any offstage world. Primate amphitheatre set with glassy fourth wall in small gorilla house during Anthropocene: hanging ropes & performing platforms. Audience side, two humanoid movement artists—woman & man—rehearse improvised pavane. Stage side with real fur costumes: huge silverback lowland male, two glossy females, one ambivalent infant act out watching dancers, on & off. **H** In hominid urban theatrical place fold-back seating-bank now always retracted. Site-specific recess presents very last mermaid alive. Blocked between monster propeller & rudder, singing echoing lament for dead sisters. Two spectral siblings rant at spectators as ocean pollution. Iron hull rusted, rotting away, final curtain soon. Cue: all child voyeurs cast adrift as sound effects conjure up deepwater horizon. **H** After that nothing onstage anywhere looks like naturalism ever again. Arts Lab stagehand attacks fifth-wall with deafening flying weaponry. Arc lamp pulses strobe into patrons' eyes. Stage director, blinded by crushed-on bowler, performs ghoulish suicide, pinned high on upstage wall. / Oriental musical helicopter hovers low down extinct tropical crater. Military zoom lenses score scantily clad puppet sprites in cube polythene box set with watery nuclear napalm special effects. Wild hash-tagged festival crowd crowds in for one-night stand of sprinkling closure. / Fade-up on reversing revolve, Solaris mothership rising high behind un-fireproofed bleachers. Late thespian prompt, match dropped alight. Comic-stunt fire chief tiptoes in with red-gel sparks gizmo, checks earlier flames caput. / Elizabethan flashback: auditoria cackles conflagration, old globe sparkling special effects everywhere ablaze still. Earth's debut as smash hit premiere planetary spectacular. **H** Centuries pass by, wrong entrance turn in installation labyrinth has lead feminist screaming don't touch me. In pitch blackout, witness gently pushed against boards that tilt back to flat: stage coffin transformation. Live soil shoveled onto lid: inches from final call corpsing. **H** Stripped-out urban venue was once a roaring printer's workshop. Now in mock-up performance biome, expert survivalist cast try fixing long-run futures wish list: water plants animals air time energy filtration. Tragi-comic toxic drizzle dance is super hit big singing & writhing … all … fall … down get-up again. Break-a-leg final exit ceremonial produces earthly revival & un-faked optimism. Previews fresh *Homo sapiens* living Earth: ecosociality ecoumility technebiogeny econnectivity. Becomes negative feedback from elementary ecology drama going every which way as long running … slow show … genre … beyond … all … **HHH** …

H is this imagined theatre's fundamental component, otherwise text referenced below wouldn't exist. Its phonetic definition is *voiceless pharyngeal fricative*: non-sound made by lungs and diaphragm, whispering "h" of hope. In quantum mechanics **H** stands for *Planck's constant*, Einstein's link to minimal energy of universal electro-magnetic waves. Hypothetical till 2015, when LIGO (Laser Interferometer Gravitational-Wave Observatory) shows quantum time-space curvature correct: gravitational waves malleable as silk & universe has nothing stable. Alternatively, **H** here becomes iconic doors between passages that can never open. End-time blocking walls, stopping all energy flows dead. *Homo sapiens* must reinvent itself, totally performing with Earth's ecosystems. // If "all the world's a stage" … when theatre becomes *all* stage for participants it becomes their *only* world and key environmental question is the *nature* of their survival. Stage languages absorbed by globalizing phrases—"the world of theatre," "the theatre world," "world theatre"—humankind gains ubiquity. In the twenty-first millennium postmodern simulacra trash the "real," performative societies spawn global theatricality, neo-liberal capital performs history's end dreams, climate change emergencies question-mark every future. But new parameters re-vision past performances. Slip radically in time-space as *Homo sapiens* make fresh tomorrows.

H 1 Ecosystem 1. 2004: one future arrives at a performance hybrid non-location & quasi-proscenium arch plus black-box ethos at Wickham Theatre, Bristol UK. Theatrical systems float free of conventional aesthetics/practices, generated by quantum rules of flexible space-time flows. The venue is rendered dynamically spectral, wholly self-contained by thespian paraphernalia completely hollowed out.

H 2 Ecosystem 2. 2005: deep past at Bristol Zoological Gardens, compact where animal roles reverse as humans share spatial gaps/swap habitats with other primate species. Environment is doubly self-contained as *Homo sapiens*' wall/house structures are completely sealed/impenetrable. Conservation playhouse verges on ecological dead-end abyss, only kept at bay by embracing near-absolute animal otherness.

H 3 Ecosystem 3. 2000: last mermaid alive makes sense of "Anthropocene" named by chemist Paul Crutzen. Driving imagined theatre as future totally made by *Homo sapiens*: like meteorite for Cretaceous-Tertiary dinosaurs' extinction. Glaciers' global retreat prompts two Peruvian Andes villagers to paint black mountain white in six months (Vince, 62–64). Forms glacier to water settlement's source of survival. Mermaids' siren song spelt disaster, yet shipboard lament tinged with hope.

H 4–7 Ecosystems 4–7. 1968: stage director suicide is chronically collapsing biosphere; 1970: crater sprites are ghosts of Cold War holocausts; 1975: comedy fireman is earthward crashing solar disaster; 1613: hit bard sparkler is globalized inferno.

H 8 Ecosystem 8. 1996–98: corpsing installation punter bets wildly on violently hopeless future. Yet even one world wonderful born-again eco-"warrior" is deaf to languages of *Homo sapiens*' earthly murderousness. Contagious double binderies massively reinforce what she environmentally deplores (Klein, 21–23).

H 9 Ecosystem 9. 2004: Flashback to imaginary theatre start-up. Youthful survivors troupe crawls through ancient forest undergrowth, gauging their Anthropocene lifetime. Making hybrid performance habitat, inviting survivalist essentials outside in. Whatever creates ironic dancing opens cracks in all **H**s. Cutting consumption modes and environmental thanato-culture. Transitioning to "project zero" and earthly ecosanity (Mason, 263–292). Space-time fluidity returns, like 16-year-old Einstein imagined surfing the universe on sunlight beams. He could, still does.

6. *ANCESTOR CALL—GUERRERO—CHERRÍE L. MORAGA*

You see these my children, how handsome they are.

(Bernal Díaz del Castillo, *True History of the Conquest of New Spain*)

My friend, the late Chicano poet Alfred Arteaga, was a kind of "breed brother," a Chicano-identified writer—a mestizo's mestizo. Just like me. He and I corresponded best through letters and through each other's published words, which we hungrily devoured for a clue to the shared paradox of our parentage.

Alfred made the Chicano nation of Aztlán sound like paradise in a prose that delineated the perfect sense of it. His was an argument that need not raise its voice to point to what was empirically so: this América belongs to los indígenas, los indígenas somos nosotros. He didn't concern himself with blood quantum. His desirous claim for membership in Chican@ nation was tacitly present in all his writings or perhaps it was only I who could recognize it, in cloudy mirrored reflection, there between the lines.

Like me, Alfred desperately needed a story of the mixing of nations, of bloodlines, of the creation of offspring and of new nations not born of rape and thievery, betrayal and conquest. He found it on a Spanish-Indian battlefield in pre-conquest Yucatán.

In 1536, less than a score of years after the arrival of Cortés, a light-skinned bearded man was uncovered there among the beardless Indian dead; his body marked with the tattoos and piercings of a Maya warrior. "Gonzalo Guerrero" was a dissident Spaniard, killed in battle by his once countrymen.

In the course of several years among the Maya, Gonzalo Guerrero had risen from captive slave to a high-ranking warrior. He had married a Maya and made family with her. After Gonzalo had spent eight years in "captivity," Hernán Cortés appeared on the gulf shores and ordered a small corps of soldiers to find Gonzalo and entreat him to rejoin the Spanish. Upon the encounter, Guerrero refuses.

"¿Ya ves?" he responds. "You see these my children, how handsome they are."

When Arteaga revisits the moment of that refusal, he writes with a kind of personal optimism: "Gonzalo's history demonstrates that while the father can inseminate, he can be culturally inseminated as well."

Gonzalo Guerrero was a rebel against genocide, and may very well be the first recorded father of American mestizos not conceived in rape.

Do I have the huevos to write this?

I am Gonzalo Guerrero because, like him, I had a choice. I was white enough to choose. I carry my body heavy with that knowledge that I am not what it portends. My warrior wounds, bloody piercings, and indigo colored tattoos scar and stain beneath the surface of my güera skin. I am marked by memory and prediction, and I come by this knowledge honestly through the bloodline of my mother. And the dispassion of my father.

I am not Gonzalo Guerrero because I am a woman. I cannot make history, only story. Not through intercourse with men, but through the intercourse of queer tongues untied. We speak, have sex. We make babies in the name of the first nations that may reject us. Still, we insist we belong there; that they need us more than they know.

My mother's mother dedicated her life to not being Mexican.

My mother's mother was born in a south Texas bordertown in the mid-1920s, the only daughter of a brown-skinned young woman from San Luis Potosí and a pink-skinned old man from upstate New York. My mother's mother bore, even in childhood, the peculiar burden of beauty—the kind of wavy mahogany hair, wide dark eyes, full lips, and ivory skin that brought the sort of attention that was embarrassing to a shy girl; her appearance also delivered the violating predations that men of all ages so blithely impose upon quiet girls. My mother's mother was white enough to choose, so she chose white.

My mother's mother married the first white man to ask—an Iowa farm boy who, inspired by a brief encounter in an Arthur Murray dance class, courted her by US mail and sent her a one-way train ticket in lieu of an engagement ring. My mother's mother never expected her Iowa farm boy to settle her and her two blonde girl-children in the mountains of New Mexico amidst a cluster of *nuevomexicano* villages established in the old land grant days. My mother's mother emphatically ignored the *hispanas* from the village, especially the ones who told their children that my mother's mother wore too much makeup for a reason. My mother's mother was white enough to choose, but she chose white.

My mother's mother pointedly mispronounced any Spanish word she encountered, especially those found on road maps and on restaurant menus. My mother's mother spoke Spanish only when she suspected someone was trying to hustle her, when she would unloose a snarling torrent of words *en español* that would amplify her voice's timbre and her delicate frame so she seemed two or three sizes larger; when the moment passed, my mother's mother would shrink back to her normal size, avert her eyes, and whisper a firm command to any witness: "Don't tell anyone I did that." My mother's mother was stopped by the state police for going ninety on a two-lane mountain highway as she raced to prevent her nearly blonde daughter from marrying that *nuevomexicano* boy she met at college; my mother's father then committed my mother's mother to an extended hospitalization that included several rounds of electroconvulsive therapy. My mother's mother interrogated me every time I returned from visiting my *nuevomexicano* father's family, often inspecting my little boy body for marks of harm and muttering wild suspicions upon finding none. My mother's mother was white enough to choose, and she chose white.

I too was white enough to choose, yet I chose differently. The burden of my grandmother's choosing weighs heavy upon my daily endeavor to resist the temptations of whiteness—those privileges, large and small, that accrue constantly, but provisionally, to bodies like hers and mine. How do I body forth the tangled *mestizaje* that she sought so steadfastly to erase? How do I inhabit the force and legacy of a heritage that she bore as wound, as stain, as secret? I choose to honor her decision to not be Mexican by making a contrary choice as my own. I live my out *latinx* life as tribute to the life my *abuela* might have lived had she—my mother's mother—not felt so compelled to choose white.

7. *ANCESTOR CALL—MALINCHE—CHERRÍE L. MORAGA*

Consider a life dedicated to change. You watch a people and a planet going, slowly. It occurs to you that your children may in fact witness a holocaust of sorrow you have never known. You want to believe that your spirit will be there to help them weather it, this weather-stricken world. You want to believe, but you don't know what you believe anymore.

You want to write of women because we do not make history. And so you intend upon a story that emerges from and passes through one woman of little political consequence, your mother. You are not concerned that there are some women, a few, who rise through the ranks of oblivion. Instead, you are interested in how the very ways of women do not make history. And that perhaps in that difference, an opening to a redeemed world resides.

> Because what is history is the story of men.
> And we already know how that story goes.

Women, along with men, have become stupid. We have men to blame for this: for the reality shows, the obesity, the life of gossip and alcohol poisoning, and the dollars they get from it. But, this does not bring comfort, the blaming.

> Who matters in this world?
> *Nobody walked into the room when she walked in.*
> *Nobody walked into the room when I walked in.*

As we age, we women become less and less important to the story of men. The ego worries over this, our invisibility when truly only the "nobodies" really matter; those with the capacity to move without notice or to be noticed en masse. No heroes.

I am not the hero of this story. Neither is my mother; neither was Malinche.

Malinche Tenepal—or was it Malinalli?—daughter of an Aztec cacique, sold into slavery; passed from hand to hand, from man to man. And through her encounter with one man, the Spanish conquest of Indigenous México is realized.

It is hard to see it, but in her time, there was no México like we think of it now. No mariachi, no Grito de Dolores, no cinco de mayo. No barbed wire or border patrol. No drug cartels. No border. Each people was its own country. The Aztecas as murderous as any foreign invader.

Malinche could not presage the small pox that would kill her, too. She could not presage the travesty that is Cancún, the Marriott and Hilton ascending like pyramids on the beaches de los Maya. She could not presage that one day the descendants of the Cholulans, the Tlaxcalans, the P'urhepecha would return en masse to Aztlán. Their bellies scraped raw, dragging their bodies and babies like criminal reptiles across the border sands of Sonora to end up flipping burgers in LA, Woodburn, Oregon, and Humboldt Park, Chicago.

She could not have known.

Still, perhaps there was a calling in her that she suppressed or perhaps she misinterpreted. Perhaps it was just the cry of a woman wanting freedom.

> *They made me a slave and then condemn me when I act like one.*
> This is my mother speaking.

❖

Postscript: Coyote Crossing

> *It's when you least expect it. El Coyote spills out of the snarl of blackberry bush and flashes across the roadway. You nearly hit him, but then he gets away with it, meat inside his teeth. And you wonder if you imagined the memory of his appearance.*

The amazing efficacy of patriarchy lies in its invisibility. It is entrenos, just between us—man and woman, sister and brother, father and daughter, queer and not-so-queer. It is behind closed doors, inside la hacienda and back there in the slave quarters. It is so seamlessly meshed into the fiber of our lives that to pull at that dangling unnamed stitch of inequity is to rip open a life.

GLOSS—HELEN PARIS

Exterior. Night. Stars pricking the sky. Soundscape of glaciers cracking. MOTHER *drives car through desolate landscape. Only the back of her head is visible. DAUGHTER sits in back seat, staring out of car window.*

DAUGHTER: Are we nearly there yet?
MOTHER: Almost.
(*Pause*)
DAUGHTER: Are we nearly there yet?
MOTHER: Soon.
(*Pause*)
DAUGHTER: Tell me a story.
MOTHER: Once upon our time …
DAUGHTER: A time. You have to say 'Once upon A time.'
MOTHER: That is not the story I want to tell.
DAUGHTER: But it's not our time. Never ever.
MOTHER: It is now.
DAUGHTER: Why?
MOTHER: Because time needs us.
DAUGHTER: (*skeptical*) How?
MOTHER: It needs us to keep it and to watch it and to mind it, and to-
DAUGHTER: Waste it.
MOTHER: (*Beat*) Yes. And not forget it. And to miss it.
DAUGHTER (*raps*) Lose it. Skip it. Tell it. See it. (*Breathes on window and starts to draw a clock face.*)
MOTHER: (*glances in rearview mirror*) Hold it. Stop it. Change it.
DAUGHTER: (*Concentrates on finishing clock hands. They point to 6 o'clock.*)
MOTHER: What's the time?
DAUGHTER. (*peers at clock and smiles*) Dinnertime. But we actually can't change it, you know. Time. Or stop it.

MOTHER: *(still looking in rearview mirror)*	DAUGHTER: *(starts chanting)*
But this is our story, our time, remember?	What's the time, Mr Wolf
Ours. So we can pause it,	2 o'clock
rewind it	What's the time, Mr Wolf
and change it.	3 o'clock
We can go back	What's the time, Mr Wolf
and start again.	4 o'clock
Do it differently.	What's the time, Mr Wolf
In our way, in our voices,	5 o'clock
in our language.	What's the time, Mr Wolf
But louder.	DINNER TIME!

(Pause)
MOTHER: What's the time now?
DAUGHTER: *(peers at window)* It's gone.
MOTHER: Breathe.
DAUGHTER: *(opens mouth and exhales)* It's back! *(delighted)* And it's still dinnertime!
MOTHER: You see.
DAUGHTER: (*Watches the time till it disappears. Inhales. Exhales. Watches time.)*
MOTHER: Once upon our time …
DAUGHTER: Are we nearly there yet?
MOTHER: Almost. (*Pause*) Soon.
DAUGHTER: *(Inhales. Exhales. Watches. Inhales. Exhales. Watches.)*

(Exhales. Exhales. Exhales.)

8. *ANECDOTE OF THE STAGE (AFTER STEVENS)—JOHN H. MUSE*

Bare stage: gray, in the round, out of doors, preferably in Tennessee.

VOICE: I placed a stage in Tennessee,
And round it was, upon a hill.
It made the slovenly wilderness
Surround that hill.

The wilderness rose up to it,
And sprawled around, no longer wild.
The stage was round upon the ground
And flat and gave a shape to air.

It took dominion everywhere.
The stage was gray and bare.
A nowhere and a universe,
Like nothing else in Tennessee.

Wallace Stevens' poem "Anecdote of the Jar" reminds us that well-crafted objects—jars or poems—are lenses that organize and productively warp the natural world. What Stevens says of the jar is also true of his austere poem. It is tall and bare upon the page, a well-organized arrangement of matter whose form bends the world temporarily into its orbit. *Anecdote of the Stage* translates Stevens' conceit into minimal theatrical terms, suggesting that the empty stage is not only a magnifying lens—a frame for time and space that transmutes the ordinary into the remarkable—but also a teleportation device that transports distant lands to Tennessee.

On this subject, I offer another anecdote of the stage from the diary of Swiss playwright and novelist Max Frisch:

> Went again today to attend a rehearsal; and as I was an hour too early I retreated to one of the boxes, where it is dark as in a confessional. The stage was, luckily, open and without a set, and I did not know the play that was to be rehearsed. Nothing is as stimulating as nothingness, at least for a time. Only occasionally a stagehand crossed the stage, a young man in brown overalls. He shakes his head, stops and quarrels with another, whom I cannot see; and it is the most ordinary language that is heard from the stage, anything but poetry. Shortly afterwards an actress appears, eating an apple, while crossing the empty stage in her overcoat and hat; she says 'good morning' to the stagehand, nothing else, and then again there is silence, the empty stage, occasionally a sound when a tram passes outside. This little scene, which happens a thousandfold outside on the street, why does it here have such a different, such an immensely more powerful effect? The two people who have just crossed the stage had a presence, a being, a destiny which naturally I don't know; yet it was there, albeit as a mystery; it had an existence which filled the whole large space ...
>
> ... Why are pictures framed? Why do they look different when we take them out of the frame? They are no longer differentiated from the accidentals of their surroundings; they are, without a frame, suddenly no longer secure; they no longer rest in themselves; one has the feeling that they are falling apart and one is a little disappointed; they look worse suddenly, worse than they really are. The frame when it is there detaches them from nature; it is a window into a different kind of space, a window into the spirit where the flower, the painted flower, is no longer a flower which withers but an interpretation of all flowers. The frame puts it outside time. In that respect there is an immense difference between the space which lies within the frame and space in general which is infinite.

9. *ANIMAL FRIENDSHIP: A DOCUDRAMA*—*MINOU ARJOMAND*

1

Floor, a small box, a giant hand. The hand slowly pulls the box toward the audience, Maru looks at the audience through the box, crawls into the box. Curtain.

Floor, a small box, no hand. Maru runs and slides into the box, the box slides with Maru inside. The box with Maru inside hits a table leg, which the audience only now notices. Curtain.

Floor, two small boxes lined up one next to the other. Maru runs, slides into both boxes. The boxes stay put, Maru stays put, tail twitching. Curtain.

Floor, Maru lying down, his torso contained within a small box that is open on both ends. His front and back legs extend from either end of the box. Maru stands up, wearing the box, exits.

Curtain.

2

Bright lights, the sound of purring. A figure comes into focus. It is Max-Arthur dressed as a Great White Shark. Lights out.

Lights up on Max-Arthur in his shark costume. He is sitting on a Roomba, which describes fragmentary circles across the stage. From stage left, a Baby Duck enters. The Baby Duck scampers across the stage, pursued by Max-Arthur on the Roomba. The Baby Duck pauses at the center of the stage. Looks out at the audience with black, inscrutable eyes. Beat.

The Baby Duck turns and pursues Max-Arthur on the Roomba. Max-Arthur rides into the horizon, collides with the back wall. Enter Sharkey, from stage right. He is dressed as a Hammerhead Shark. Max-Arthur, the Baby Duck, and Sharkey begin an oblique trio. Then, the Roomba stops. Silence. Max-Arthur, Sharkey, and the Baby Duck all turn and gaze out into the audience. Beat.

Max-Arthur licks his lips. Sharkey licks his lips. The Baby Duck stares. Beat.

Curtain.

3

Lights up on Goo and Yat Jai, upstage, facing each other in profile to the audience. Behind them, two large computer screens. From the rear, light floods the stage.

Goo and Yat Jai each raise their front paws. They reach out and their paws meet, first Goo's left paw and Yat Jai's right paw, then Goo's right paw with Yat Jai's left paw.

VOICE FROM ABOVE: Patty Cake, Patty Cake, Baker's Man,
Bake me a cake as fast as you can.

Goo and Yat Jai play patty cake. They stop, then begin again. They stop, then begin again. They stop, then begin again. They stop.

Curtain.

What accounts for the astonishing proliferation of "performing cats" on the Internet? The current consensus, according to Bryan Lufkin in *Gizmodo*, is that cats *don't* seem to be performing. Whereas dogs are like shabby vaudeville front-cloth comedians, constantly looking at the audience and begging for approval, cats are the Naturalistic, fourth-wall ideal actor in furry form. Dogs are Seth Rogen, cats are Heath Ledger. Cats simply *behave:* they don't seem aware of whether this behavior is "twice-behaved" or not.

Minou Arjomand's *Animal Friendship: A Docudrama* presents three of the Internet's most popular cat videos live onstage. The subtitle, "a docudrama," provokes us to consider the relation of documentary theatre, and by extension, the theatre itself, to reality. It is, of course, an impossible piece. Watching cats on the Internet is pleasurable specifically because the minute-long YouTube clip reframes "natural" behavior as performance: Maru playing with a box becomes a spectacular circus act. But the animal onstage becomes a theatrical *problem*. As Nicholas Ridout writes: "the impropriety of the animal on the theatre stage is experienced very precisely as a sense of the animal being in the wrong place" (2006: 98). It is in the wrong place because it cannot have *intended* to be part of the dramatic fiction, and thus troubles the "psychological illusionism" of the stage. For Ridout, these moments point back to the economic conditions of the actor's labor, for the animal does not participate in these conditions. More accurately, it has different economic conditions—a treat upon completion of a trick—an economic model that in some ways seems far preferable to profit-share.

Despite their troubling nature, this hasn't stopped theatre makers from putting animals onstage. Horses, cats, dogs, and other nonhuman animals have appeared in the theatre of Romeo Castellucci. In 2010, French theatre company Footsbarn presented *Sorry!*, which featured, intriguingly, a "Dressage of Cats" by Marie Werdyn. When I quizzed producer Leanne Cosby at the Barbican (who co-produced the London presentation of the piece) about this aspect of the performance she was rather more circumspect: "the cats just walked across the stage ... Some nights they did, some nights they didn't." The Belvoir Theatre's stunning adaptation of Ibsen's *The Wild Duck*, played within a plexiglass box, featured a live duck that flapped its wings at inopportune moments, interrupting monologues by splashing water over the actors.

However, *Animal Friendship*, by *re*-presenting celebrated instances of cat performance, goes beyond these examples of the animal onstage. It raises issues of acting in documentary theatre: if these cat videos are taken to be documentaries akin to nature programs, would different cat-actors be performing in the staged piece? And if cat-actors are *acting* in *Animal Friendship*, what do we value in their performance? Is it simply that they go through the motions of riding a Roomba or jumping in a box, or that they create the psychological illusion of this act taking place for the first time and its associated emotions; joy, terror, pleasure? This impossible piece, then, makes us question what it is we desire and value from the actor in the theatre. Is it that they simply represent "reality"? Or that they betray some *excess*, some remainder of intention and will-to-please—what we might call "theatricality"?

10. *THE ART OF FORGETTING—DANIEL SACK*

I

The lights rise on a perfect replica of your childhood.
It's all overexposed and slanting askance
So that the grass is too green, and your parents are
So young the scene shivers.

Everyone is there:

Friends and neighbors, piano lessons, the boy who moved away, the barn still standing, the man looming too tall behind the counter, photographs that never got developed, her promises and baby teeth in small Ziploc bags, and whole states of Oklahoma with graveyards of neon light, and trees at every window, that morning and that door left ajar, that game of hide and seek you kept playing long after everyone else went home.

Hold. (The director looks around.)
Ah, nostalgia. (A faint smile.)
And yet, something is still missing.
Let's try this again tomorrow.

II

In the years since the artistic director first proposed the idea, the company has settled into a perfect schedule for the repertoire: a production may only be played once every six months; brush-up rehearsals are strictly forbidden. When a new actor is invited in to take over a part, they must fully learn the role, but then are given an appropriate span of time to forget it sufficiently.

At first the reception was cold; the critics panned the work as amateurish. And for a time hecklers composed a sizable portion of the audience, but soon they too watched with bated breath as the actors stumbled over lines and entrances, or alighted on a sudden inspired recollection. The beauty in such moments transfigured all. It was on the best of these nights that the audience would spontaneously run to the stage to hug the actors, or scream in horror at the tragedy before them, or sit long in silence forgetting what they were meant to do, how to clap or even how to move—all habits broken—but alive, so alive.

Let us remember how to live through forgetfulness. In his short study of Marcel Proust, the lone book written during his abbreviated academic career, Samuel Beckett posits that "the man with a good memory does not remember anything because he does not forget anything. His memory is uniform, a creature of routine, at once a condition and function of his impeccable habit, an instrument of reference instead of an instrument of discovery." There is a lesson to be learned here about acting, which, like living, requires us to forget our part in order to implement the "instrument of discovery." Actors who do not forget what they are supposed to do sacrifice their liveliness to habit. And, as Beckett tells us elsewhere, "habit is a great deadener."

The first of these imagined theatres replicates the past perfectly, but it is a past that never completes its form, a past that retains an uncertain relationship towards the future it was always touching. It must, in other words, keep forgetting itself in order to keep desire moving. This is the way with nostalgia, which fractures us afresh with every passing day. Such memories are overworked, overexposed, and yet never held in hand. We may rehearse them daily, but we will never get the scene down correctly, never get in the habit. Something is just beyond us, over the horizon, the door standing ajar. The intense privacy of this first theatre means that it will only work for "you." Each feature is designed with your attention in mind.

The second theatre moves the art of forgetting into a public sphere, teaching us once again how to behave as if for the first time. The mistake, the forgotten line—these puncture our habits of watching and acting with sudden appearances of life unscripted. We wonder at these irruptions of potentiality in any performance we attend. This theatre is a studio for the art of forgetting, where trained professionals practice for our pleasure, so that all of us, in turn, might forget our social selves and roles. The repertoire of our daily lives, its routines and phrases, systematically abandoned. What actor has not been asked: "How do you remember all those lines?" Instead, we will ask: "How do you forget all those lines?"

11. *ASTIGMATISMS—ISAIAH MATTHEW WOODEN*

A series of blurry visions unfold rapidly.
It is impossible to focus.
The focus is not to focus, in fact.
The eye/I is unreliable anyway.

Acuity, a figment.
Recognition, a distortion.
Sight cites but errs.

There are figures.
Or bodies.
Or, are they corpses?
Humans perhaps.
Subjects.
Objects?
Projections.
Performing a hypervisible dance of invisibility.

How to see their work, their art in total darkness.
In totalizing light.

Oversight yields insight.
Hindsight demands foresight.
Be
Hind.
Be
Fore.
Be
Hold?

Seeing is repeating.
Or, is it unseeing?
Redoing.
Imagining.
Effacing.

This is a drama of history.
Of race.
Of being.

Its end is the beginning.

Let's rehearse the etymology. Theatre. From the Greek: *θέᾱτϱον*, a place for viewing; *θεᾶσθαι* to behold; *θέα* sight, view; *θεατής* a spectator. Its cognate? Theory. Ancient Greek *θεωϱία,* action of viewing, contemplation, sight, spectacle; post-classical Latin *theoria,* speculation, contemplation. Theatre has been, from its very "beginnings" (in establishment history, at least) the place of seeing, speculation, and contemplation. In the Greek classical ideal, which has served historically as a cipher for nationalism and xenophobia, theatre is where seeing is yoked with knowing—a foundation of Western European metaphysics and epistemology.

In *Astigmatisms,* the *eye/I* discovers the unreliability of its vision. The point of its focus is the very inability to see and what comes into focus is vision's own distortions. In its efforts to see clearly, *sight cites but errs*, pointing to the ways in which sight relies on a "world horizon" in order to make what is seen recognizable. The eye/I draws on a past history of seeing to make the seen familiar. *Seeing is repeating*. But *hindsight demands foresight*: The eye/I tries to economize its labor by ensuring its perceptual efforts are also anticipatory and do the work of imagining all possible futures so that everything is always already seen. Vision necessarily, then, casts what is seen in a *totalizing light. Seeing is effacing.*

The dramatic action of *Astigmatism*s centers on this process of the eye/I straining to make the strange familiar, a process caught in the syncopated past-future time consciousness of perceptual experience. An anxious Gertrude Stein. *Be Hind. Be Fore. Be Hold?* Figures become bodies become corpses, possibly humans who acquire a moment of subjecthood only to become objects of our vision and then, inevitably, projections, made invisible by our totalizing gaze. As we know from Peggy Phelan (and Lacan), the *eye/I is unreliable* because it relies on an expropriation of the other for its self-institution. The subject comes to see herself "*through* looking at the other."

In *Astigmatisms*, performance does not "plunge into visibility" and then disappear "into the realm of invisibility," as in Peggy Phelan's ontology of performance. Visibility and invisibility are not serial. Rather, invisibility impregnates the visible, exposing the blind-spots in our vision and the limits of what we claim to see and, by extension, to know. *Astigmatisms* dethrones the Western subject from the comfort of its seat at the vanishing point of a perspectival vision of world-as-picture, shattering what Sara Ahmed would call the "epistemic authority" the Western subject presumes to hold by capturing the other in its frame of view. This theatre makes visible the *astigmatisms* that mis-recognize the stigmata of the flesh, making it reducible to the stigma of the other—what Frantz Fanon terms the "epidermal racial schema." *This is a drama of history. Of race. Of being.*

Seeing is not knowing. The Western eye/I has been ousted from its primacy as the site of perception and knowledge. How do we see our way forward now that the yarn of this master narrative has been unwoven? *Its end is the beginning.*

12. *CANDLE TEARS—MEILING CHENG*

For the soul who used to be called Nonchi Wang of amphibian Arc

The following action takes place in between a retinal stage and a mindfield, dotted with violet tulips and green shamrocks.

An amphibian figure with a frog head, a human torso and limbs covered in mossy green toad skin, two pairs of dragonfly wings, and a blue sapphire-studded lizard's tail walks across a geometrically circular pond. The figure moves toward a square sandbox framed by rough-hewn wood trunks and set diagonally across the middle of the pond. Amidst the fading dusky light, the gentle illumination from a huge paper-cutout moon sliver, and the sound of flowing water, the homo-amphibian reaches the eastern edge of the sandbox. It crouches on the sand, its lizard tail draping across the wooden edge and rhythmically slapping at the water. With its wings flapping languidly, the homo-amphibian inches sideways to traverse the margins of its sandbox domain.

"Om mada nimada didalah hum," the homo-amphibian starts chanting in a high-pitch tune, while gazing at the moon sliver. A sculpting chisel, a needle pen, a carving knife, and a delicate hammer spill from the lunar profile and slowly descend from the sky. The chanting homo-amphibian catches the translucent tools with its long webby fingers and spreads out the tools like odd-shaped torches around it. The homo-amphibian now darts out its tongue and holds it at a spot on the sand, its back arching in tension, while its wings shake and extend out in four different directions. Surrounding the moist imprint left by its tongue, what looks like a column of sandstone grows from the sand. The column keeps growing and growing until it almost touches the moon.

The homo-amphibian flies to survey the column and pauses near its top to begin shaping the image of what an English-speaking human world would call "an elephant." The color gray emerges as the elephant gets its big ears, while ivory white shimmers from its tusks. The elephant's trunk becomes the multicolor exoskeletal colonies of coral reefs, their polyps opening to an ecosystem for a school of jellyfish among neighborly seaweeds, snatches of songs from a distant humpback whale, and a turtle resting on a barrel sponge. The bright yellow sponge morphs into the spiny roof of a Stegosaurus, whose robust tail intersects with fairy castle cacti and a reindeer's branching antlers. Alpinia Purpurata bloom next to flaming fungi next to a condor's nest in a rocky cave next to a honey beehive on an apple tree next to a handmade cradle with a human infant sleeping in it, yielding to the earworm of a worn lullaby. On the surface of the sandstone column, a cornucopia more flamboyant and divinely intoxicated than M. C. Escher's endlessly circular drawing appears here and here and here and there.

As the paper moon changes its cycle a hundred times, the homo-amphibian finishes tracing the tail end of an E. coli bacteria and sighs with exhaustion. It rolls its body on the sand and then washes off the sand in the pond. Cleansed and refreshed, the homo-amphibian strokes the sculpted column until the mammoth cylinder shrinks to a portable size. It moves this nativity sculpture to the sandbox's southern edge. Pulling a sapphire stone from its tail, the homo-amphibian places the radiant jewel on top of the candle. With the needle pen, the homo-amphibian artist dots the empty eye socket of a golden dragon. A tear drops from the dragon's eye and the sapphire stone bursts into a blue flame.

I feel a sense of serendipity, even synchronicity, between the homo-amphibian's sandstone candle sculpture and the engraving of a cabinet of curiosities published as a frontispiece in *Museum Wormianum* [*Worm's Museum*]. The 1655 catalogue features a 400-page description of a natural history museum founded by the Danish physician Ole Worm, also known as Olaus Wormius, for the purpose of teaching students at the University of Copenhagen. As Carl Zimmer reports in an article for *The New York Times*, publishers of scientific books like *Worm's Museum* have seized upon "every innovation in printing technology, from wood blocks to digital scanner" so as to introduce a higher level of naturalism to their pictorial illustrations. A great shortcoming, however, marked the earliest printing methods such as engraving and lithography: their inability to reproduce color. This problem no longer troubles our homo-amphibian artist. If mimesis were its goal, the myriad colors that instantaneously surface with its sculpted pedagogical objects—gleaned from sources more diverse than "Nature"—are the artist's priceless mimetic gold.

"Let us take off the spectacles that show us the shadows of things instead of the things themselves," wrote Ole Worm as a rationale for his museum display. In his aversion to "spectacles," Worm betrays his anti-theatrical prejudice; he also fails to profit from the inadvertent pertinence of his pun. Indeed, for one blessed with optical divergences, to take *on* a pair of spectacles is to enjoy a sudden drama of sharpened sight—not to mention that a paradise might just be regained from peering through Galileo's telescope. Further, in opposing "shadows" to "the things themselves," Worm triples the slippage of his judgment by revealing his binaristic naiveté. Perhaps Worm has forgotten about a prophetic dream he had had of American playwright Suzan-Lori Parks, who taught him that theatre, as "an incubator" of the real (i.e., the witnessed), has the ability to produce actual historical events "through their happening on stage." To collect wondrous mementoes from natural history for posterity is then to heed theatre's spectacular power in engendering multisensory experiences and recalcitrant memories. Theatrical performances keep a museum alive. Besides, might it not be a trick of lighting that sets apart an ostensibly solid object from its many potential shadows? Doesn't Worm know that a shadow is nothing but an ostrich's neck growing longer under the sand dune? A desire for length is always there!

Theatrical creativity celebrates both the colors of spectacles and the monochrome of sacrifices often hidden backstage. The homo-amphibian artist would not stop until exhaustion overtakes the moon. The blue flame cannot keep burning until all candle characters turn into tears. Is that why the dragon cries?

The homo-amphibian artist suddenly realizes that its sandstone microcosm is, in Shadow-speak, "a rrrrarchetype" for what the English lingo now wisely calls "the Web," a volatile playground crisscrossed by lights and shadows, by crystals, cockroaches, trolls, and unicorns in digital garb. Like a candle, theatre illuminates, focuses, and shadows this haphazard playground widely accessible and randomly inspiring to the twenty-first-century earthly inhabitants. While all candles are alike in their waxy substance, each burnt candle differs from its neighbors in the ways their respective tears flow, dribble, plop, and trill. Theatre delights in showing how and why those creatures, plants, microbes, and habitats that occupy the homo-amphibian candle converge, mutate, perish, and regenerate. Consuming itself with inevitable exuberance, theatre enacts paths of candle tears.

13. *CASTING, FOUR WAYS—BRIAN EUGENIO HERRERA*

Before assigning roles, consider these four ways to cast your play.

Contracasting

Insist that performers inhabit roles distinct from their social bodies, societal roles, or personal attributes. Aspire to incongruity. Manifest the friction activated by the intentional differentiation of performer and role. Eschew verisimilitude's comforts. Resist the soothing promises of virtuosity. Occupy distance. Amplify tensility. Play through consequences.

Simulcasting

Assign multiple performers to each role, so that every part is taken on by a cohort of no fewer than three players. Task each team with developing a collaborative characterization to be coterminously enacted by the full cohort. Seek diverse role cohorts, so that each role's enactment might be informed by a mix of cultural, technical, physical, and experiential proficiencies. Marvel at what manifests.

Swingcasting

Cast ensemble. Assign each actor to several performance tracks, not single parts or multiple roles. Rehearse the ensemble in the particular responsibilities for each separate performance track, onstage and off. Tracks will likely include texts to be articulated, positions to be taken, and tasks to be executed, in tandem and in tension with the work of characterization. Shuffle tracks frequently. Practice all performers to cover three or more tracks expertly, so as to ready them to swing between tracks at each (or within a single) performance. Should a given performance find itself in a familiar groove, jump tracks. Never perform the same show the same way twice.

Narrowcasting

Identify a single attribute—quality, ability, affect—absolutely essential for the effective enactment of each role. Consider performers solely based on their capacity to evince that bedrock attribute in performance. Cast accordingly. Build up, around, and from that foundation. Inhabit insensibility, incomprehension, and impossibility. Anticipate astonishment.

Controversy routinely overdetermines critical conversations about casting. Contravening pressures of property and propriety inevitably hobble even the most searching casting conversations. Recurring paroxysms over "best practices" deploy teleologies of mimesis, authorship, and career as paper, rock, and scissors in a seemingly endless war among the righteous. Yet how might casting itself—as a performance technique that marshals the force of surrogation—prompt generative, creative, and transformative routes beyond such critical cul-de-sacs? What might be revealed about casting as a method or mode of creative investigation if the typical limits of time, talent, and tradition were ignored? How might the conventional processes and protocols of casting be thereby transformed? What else might be revealed about casting's force as concatenated act of performance, of interpretation, and of power?

14. *A Chinese Actor's Late Style—Broderick D.V. Chow*

On 20 July 2000, a sold-out house gathers at the Vancouver East Cultural Centre to witness the final performance of Chinese-American actor Lee Jun-Fan's long and wide-ranging career. Directed by Sophie Rodgers, the production has been eagerly anticipated since its announcement, as it would be not only Lee's final stage performance but also his first performance as one of Shakespeare's great eponymous roles. An athletic 60 years old, Lee is too young for Lear and too old for Hamlet; *Macbeth*, therefore, is a kind of coronation, marking Lee as one of the greatest actors of his time.

Lee Jun-Fan rose to fame in his 20s under his English name, Bruce Lee. Born in San Francisco in 1940, he became known to English-speaking audiences as Kato on the ABC Television series *The Green Hornet*. Trained in Wing Chun style Gong Fu, Lee later appeared as the star of several martial arts films in Hong Kong and America, including *Fist of Fury* and *Enter the Dragon*. In 1972, while filming *Game of Death* (his second outing as director), Lee became disillusioned with the film industry and walked off set, leaving the production unfinished. In 1973, Lee and his wife Linda Emery moved to a modest house in the Vancouver East Side, where the couple lives to this day. He taught martial arts throughout the 1970s to sustain himself and his family, and returned to acting in 1980, when he was cast in Scott Miller's production of Samuel Beckett's *Act Without Words I* at the Arts Club Theatre Company. Readopting his birth name, Jun-Fan, Lee appeared many more times at the Arts Club throughout his career, most notably as Stanley Kowalski in Tennessee Williams' *A Streetcar Named Desire*.

Interviewed by Pierre Berton in 1971, at the height of his film career, Lee stated, "to me, a motion picture is motion." In this production of *Macbeth*, the opposite is true. Lee's stillness is hypnotic, each gesture lifted, leaping from the center of his body with tremendous precision. The stillness conceals a coiled, serpentine energy—Lee never strikes, but never have I believed more in the tremendous violence of which Macbeth is capable. Spending the entirety of Act V stripped to the waist, Lee's body speaks far more than Shakespeare's words (perhaps fittingly for an actor whose first films were recorded without sound and later dubbed into Mandarin by other actors). Which is not to say that the words don't matter. Lee is adept with the text: his Hong Kong Cantonese accent makes this Macbeth strangely patrician, especially in this company of Canadian actors. But as Macbeth hears the news of his Lady's suicide, Lee brings his fingers to his lips, quickly, involuntarily, like a phantom memory, as his abdominal muscles contract in a silent embodiment of grief. When he speaks the words "She should have died hereafter," it is almost without affect, but it is Lee's body that has made us hear the words in a new way.

When the production closes on 1 October, Lee has announced he will retire from acting to focus on writing for stage, including his next project, an epic theatrical history of the Chinese in North America.

Lee Jun-Fan never had a "late style." He died on 20 July 1973 at the age of 32 while filming *Game of Death*. In imagining this afterlife for Bruce Lee, a career rebirth in which the Chinese actor would take on Western canonical writers including Beckett, Williams, and Shakespeare, we might imagine not only a theatre performance but a theatre *culture* decentered and decolonized by Lee's magnificent physicality and his deeply embodied approach to performance.

Despite Lee's cultural impact in the West, we do not teach Bruce Lee in Introduction to Performance classes. He is rarely thought of as an "artist," unless the word is preceded by "martial." My own relationship to Lee is similarly ambivalent. As a child, I enrolled in *goju-ryu* style karate at the Steveston Dojo in Richmond, BC. I wasn't really built for karate. I loved martial arts but hated fighting, and sparring terrified me. But there was one part of every class I eagerly awaited: *kata*. *Kata* are choreographed sequences, developed for preserving and transmitting combat techniques, but performed solo in front of an audience; to me, they were *theatre*. The fighting in Bruce Lee's films is the same. Superficially, it's just violence. But on another level it is a tremendous display of human physical potential, and Lee's body is always at the center, looking like no one else's: sinewy, muscled yet lean, almost simian in the carriage of his arms. His physicality is wonderfully apparent in the only filmed interview he ever gave, with Pierre Berton in 1971. Lee radiates intensity, his hands precise, eyes flashing. He credits martial arts with teaching him the art of human expression through the body. When asked why actors such as James Garner and Steve McQueen wanted to train with him he eloquently replies that martial arts teaches a balance between instinct and control: "it might sound too philosophical but it's 'acting un-acting, or un-acting acting.'" Performance Studies, Bruce Lee style.

As a child Lee, a Chinese *star*, was my hero. I grew my hair like his in my late teens, and resembled him to a startling degree. It was a running joke during my undergrad how much I looked like him. Yet, as I began to study theatre, Bruce Lee was replaced in my mental pantheon of great performers, by other, "serious" artists, who spoke in sonorous voices and didn't look like me.

Placing a resurrected Bruce Lee into Western canonical theatre practice, I want to put pressure on the idea of "good acting" and its intersection with race, class, gender, and nation. The aftermath of the RSC's *The Orphan of Zhao* controversy has drawn attention to the exclusion of Asian and other minority ethnic actors from the Western theatre. Small changes have taken place since, but it will be a long time before we will see a Chinese Lear. So for now, we have to imagine. Perhaps *imagining* a Bruce Lee Stanley Kowalski, a Bruce Lee Macbeth, might destabilize assumptions around what is valued in acting, as well as remind us of the monumental contribution this artist has made to theatre and performance.

15. *CITIES OF REFUGE—DOMINIKA LASTER*

When you cross the Jordan into Canaan, you are to designate certain cities as places of refuge.
(HaShem to Moishe, *Numbers* 35: 9–11)

The law of cosmopolitanism must be restricted to the conditions of universal hospitality.
(Immanuel Kant, *Perpetual Peace: A Philosophical Essay*)

There are cities of refuge because we have enough conscience to have good intentions, but not enough to betray them by our acts.
(Emmanuel Levinas, *Beyond the Verse: Talmudic Reading and Lectures*)

... imagine the experience of cities of refuge as giving rise to a place (*lieu*) for reflection—for reflection on the question of ... hospitality.
(Jacques Derrida, *On Cosmopolitanism and Forgiveness*)

Whatever happened to the lost cities of refuge (HaShem)? How can I continue to consider myself a cosmopolitan if I abandon the laws of universal hospitality (Kant)? Is it possible for the hosts (*hôtes*) and guests of cities of refuge to recreate, through work and creative activity, living and durable networks (Derrida)?

Scenario for a new guerrilla hosting movement:

Invite someone / *a refugee / an immigrant / a displaced person / a traveler / the undocumented /*
into your home / *patio / chalet / dacha / houseboat / car / shack / ger /*
serve something to drink / *tea / coffee / juice / water / kombucha / maté /*
share some food.

Listen.

This site-specific event can be repeated and extended into a durational piece.

I am five years old. My parents and older sister are with me as we arrive at JFK airport for the first time. We are political refugees, though I do not know this term then and don't believe I've heard my parents utter it, ever. The airport is vast and strangely lit: illumination that is both light and dark at the same time. A whirlpool of sound, of unintelligible movement.

We are lucky to have a distant relative who lives in Far Rockaway, New York, and will take us in for a while, as my parents look for work and start the process of learning what is this place that we have come to. We are in her apartment now, a three-bedroom in an impossibly tall high-rise in the projects. It is impeccably clean and ordered, soft carpet wall-to-wall, a candy dish on a glass table. The candies taste sweet, so sweet, and are wrapped in a metallic strawberry-print. Our hosts give us a tour of the place, the adults deep in conversation as we enter one of the bedrooms. I walk into the room, looking at the things on the desk, on the bookshelf, looking closely but not touching. When I turn around, I am alone. Everyone is gone.

Suddenly, I don't understand where I am. The apartment is a labyrinth, it swallows me. I am lost, and *have lost a world that has me in it.* I am crying, sobbing. I stand stock still and wail. Listen to me. No language can adequately describe this wail. I cry and cry, turning my insides out. Soon, my mother will walk into the room, find me, and save me. But let us dwell in the sound of my terror and loss for a moment while we consider hospitality.

What is listening in the theatre of guerilla hospitality? Derrida suggests that the other to whom we listen is an alterity that is irreducible. "The other is he or she before whom I am vulnerable, whom I cannot even deny. I cannot access the alterity of the other, who will always remain on the other side, nor can I deny his or her alterity." But listen. When you turn around, "the other side" is not where you remember it; it moves, and we move.

It is not outside of language, the soundtrack of wailing that accompanies this text, but it is a barbaric language, barbaric in the sense of senselessness, the foreign stammer of "*bar bar*" allowing no further nuance to a native ear. Language forms at exactly the boundary where language fails. Being within language, senselessness is not irreducible but forceful, diaphanous, distributed. The other, as other, undoes listening even while reinforcing the sovereignty of home. This is the durational work in the theatre of hospitality: undoing listening, unmooring the auditorium.

16. *THE CLASSROOM—LIN HIXSON*

Count the children at their desks on the stage in the theatre.

One,
two, three,
four, five, six,
seven, eight, nine, ten,
eleven, twelve, thirteen, fourteen, fifteen,
sixteen, seventeen, eighteen, nineteen, twenty, twenty-one.

One
raises her arm.

Two and three
crush Bana rocks in their hands.

Four, five, and six
stand on their chairs and imitate rain.

Seven, eight, nine, and ten
suck the boiled fruit of the Dano tree.

Eleven, twelve, thirteen, fourteen, and fifteen
strum on one string, hum, and whisper a prayer.

Sixteen, seventeen, eighteen, nineteen, twenty, and twenty-one
fall through a trapdoor and kiss the wet earth below.

Either the teachers do not exist or they are still asleep or they are on strike
because nobody pays them their monthly wages.

One speaks.

What, if I do this, will happen?

Four, five, and six
hop around the room and then rush to the aid of a casualty.

One speaks.

Siempre he dicho que yo iria a Santiago/
En un coche de agua negra

I always said I would arrive in Santiago/
In a car of black water

The impulse of this text reflects a facet of Lin Hixson's directing, the act of writing analogous to her directing practice, equal parts observation and creation. Writing offers a parallel necessary form of processing. Some poets compose while walking. Some artists garden or play music in order to paint. Writing ruminates on the performance materials, remixes them, breaking elements open and letting them play or grow. Writing brings the world of the work closer and into focus in the form of a little theatre, clarifies her relation to that world, situates writer and reader as audience to the text's performance.

She wrote this while immersed in the long-term project of a performance derived from Jay Wright's poetry, and much of the imagery issues from that source. In the phrase "boiled fruit of the Dano tree," quoted from Wright, Dano refers to a town in Burkina Faso, the West African region that Wright favors south of the Niger River. Much of the manner of this text derives from system, a Wright technique. The N+1 pattern of the student introductions, the bowling-pin arrangement of their assembly, suggests a temporal dilation, an accumulating build. The number system as an incremental, paratactic strategy divides the images into discrete units, modules each with their own substance and character, populating a textual performance as communal experience, the actors like soloists in a chamber orchestra.

Memories of actual theatre supply the writing's mode. *The Dead Class*, directed by Tadeusz Kantor in 1975, animated adult actors and puppets behaving as remembered children in a wartime classroom. This text adopts as a transferrable idiom the afterlife of that purgatorial chamber, as well as memories of actual classrooms that early in life transformed into stages of sorts, as when word spread that the beautiful young Geometry teacher had given up opera singing, and how that secret knowledge transformed everyone's apprehension of the Pythagorean theorem.

These terms—"directing," "painting," "writing poetry"—rely on an inadequate shorthand: misleading first in suggesting a largely nonexistent uniformity between an endless range of hyper-personal techniques, discovered individually in experience; misleading second in raising the notion of conformity to that phantom uniformity, and fostering the appearance that anyone who practices these techniques with memorable results practices them "wrong." Can we salvage value from the participle, the *-ing* suffix's perpetual present tense? "That they call them paintings instead of painteds is all we have to know about how things can live past the lives of their makers in their makings" (Jesse Malmed). Consider students without a teacher. Certain behavior patterns and structures of feeling emerge that would not have, had typical classroom order been enforced. The performances Lin directs demonstrate that quality: absented authority supplanted by legible patterns unfolding. In what anthropologists might call a liminal state, the performances carry the sense, like a mood, of something or someone important missing, and ride the energy released by acceptance of that absence, celebrating what happens when not "waiting for" arrival or return. Instead of a grim *Lord of the Flies* scenario, we experience a blossoming proliferation. Still, the behavior (performance), while following its own innate structures, constrains itself in relation to authority's ghosts. This indicates the power of architecture, of the word "classroom." A credo in a question, spoken aloud, quotes Wright: "*What, if I do this, will happen?*" The last line quotes Wright a third time, who wrote it in Spanish (in turn quoting Lorca) translated here as "*arrival in Santiago in a car of black water.*" As the text's signature, it moves astride a boundary between realities: imaginary transit, actual destination—a resonant final transmission from a hybrid universe.

17. *CLOCKFIRE—JONATHAN BALL*

A spotlight appears onstage to light a large, ornate grandfather clock. The clock displays the correct time and is in perfect working order.

The actors sneak behind the audience and set the theatre on fire.

Exeunt.

> A clock that is working will always be a disturbance on the stage. There it cannot be permitted its function of measuring time. Even in a naturalistic play, astronomical time would clash with theatrical time.
>
> (Walter Benjamin, *The Work of Art in the Age of Mechanical Reproduction*)

Clockfire (both the book and its title play) began when I was struck by an image: a clock on fire, alone on a stage, with an audience enraptured with this "play." The image struck me, when it came to mind, as possessing a soft surrealism. I kept turning the image over in my head. Why did I find it compelling? *Clocks* and *fire* are surrealist clichés, but the addition of the theatre context seemed to elevate it while allowing it to retain a certain primal, dreamlike quality.

Having read Antonin Artaud's *The Theatre and Its Double* not long before, I was struck by how one might read Artaud's title: the "double" of the theatre, arguably, was life. Life, which paled before the grand myth-machine of the theatre. At the same time, I had been disappointed by Artaud's plays. His Theatre of Cruelty relied on visceral shock, but what the audience considers shocking changes over time, and the plays seem tame today.

However, Artaud's book about the conceptual violence that a Theatre of Cruelty might inflict remains compelling. Today, Artaud would have to murder his audience to achieve what he wants. That would be the baseline, and he would have to escalate from that point. "Breaking the fourth wall" has become commonplace and lame, while "controversial content" has become a marketing tool.

I decided that I wanted a *clock* in my theatre, some self-reflexive acknowledgement of the theatrical situation, to exploit and explore the real-life moment of *being* in the theatre without reducing it to a lazy performance gimmick. And I wanted *fire*, some visceral, violent connection between the play and the audience. The theatre should not divert from life, but overtake life, subsume it wholly. The play should demand attention with the force that it might demand death.

Only in this way, I felt, might it become possible to realize what Artaud envisioned, as revealed by his complaint that "if there is still one hellish, truly accursed thing in our time, it is our artistic dallying with forms, instead of being like victims burnt at the stake, signaling through the flames."

My initial idea for the title play, of a clock on fire onstage, began to seem too conceptual and bloodless. The audience should be on fire. The clock was the spectator, watching them burn.

18. , COLON;ZATIONS AND EXCLAMATIONS!: A SET PIECE STAGED FOR THE PAGE—JENNIFER DEVERE BRODY

"A hall where public meetings are usually held, a hall peopled with political echoes, the ghosts of banners ... It is an untenable structure, a performance straining the limits of the possible: a theoretical debate presented by intellectuals for intellectuals on the sexuality of women."[1] The stage has three focal points: a blackboard, a screen and slide projector, and another screen for digital images emanating from a computer. There is a table downstage covered with books, from which some of the characters quote. Spotlight on **Xon**, *who steps into view and begins, sensuously, to draw a large semi-colon with white chalk on the blackboard. Meanwhile,* **ZPupil (computer eye)** *fiddles with the slide projector as* **YABA**[2] *surreptitiously superimposes images on the blackboard and slide projector screen* (**BLP**[3]). *The characters—think of them as* **X, Y, Z**—*are engaged in a heated discussion about the value of three different ~~sexual organs~~ punctuation marks.*

BLP: YYSSW (-.-) ZZZ[4]
X: "There are a good many people who seem to regard the colon and the semi-colon as identical stops and who use them indiscriminately."[5]
BLP: *(to Zpupil)* ★B★{}[6]
Z: "The things I like best in T.S. Eliot's poetry ... are the semicolons. You cannot hear them but they are there, laying out the connection between the images and the ideas. Sometimes you get a glimpse of a semicolon coming ... and it is like climbing a steep path through the woods and seeing a wooden bench just at a bend in the road ahead, a place where you can expect to sit for a moment, catching your breath."[7]
X: Zounds! How pastoral. Still, I have grown fond of semicolons; I always imagine them as Mira Schor's 1994 work *Slit of Paint*; "a literally embedded gap between visual and verbal languages within each other's materiality and meaning."[8]
Y: Ah yes. We can calculate the "relative values" of punctuation marks in a table *(types or tabulates on the digital screen a table)*

Comma	2 or 1
Semicolon	6
Colon	8
Period	10[9]

Z: According to your schema, "the exact value of the individual points is arbitrary: there can be no single exact value, for every point varies in syntactical importance and elocutionary duration according to the almost infinite potential variations of the contexts. But the relative importance, whether syntactical and logical, or elocutionary and rhetorical, is not arbitrary."[10]
Y: Personally, if I may use that dubious term, "I find the semicolon has a discreet [feminine] charm in its lesser value. [However] there is just one word to describe the colon: bossy. A colon says, 'Pay attention, this next bit is really important.' If the colon is fanfare, the semicolon is a polite cough. It is a nasty shock to discover it has enemies. Gertrude Stein, who might in her time have been considered a bit of a bossyboots herself, suggested that 'semicolons were simply commas with pretensions.'"[11]
X: I see your point, YABA. Characterizing the semi-colon as "half-wit" leaves it vulnerable to a culture that values wholeness. *(Xon draws on board while speaking)* "The form of the two stops could certainly lead one to correlate the colon with the period and the semicolon with the comma ... rather like an appendage—a period with a supplement, an afterthought to what was to be the final word, like Adam's rib. It's like adding a body to a head ..."[12] Still, the semicolon seems destined to be colonized by the colon, that more definitive masculine mark.
BLP: ;-)

Pick up any playscript and you are bound to engage with its typographical elements. The dialogue that composes and comprises us—critics, readers, actors, dramaturgs, and directors—to interpret not only the words presented; but also the inevitably present blank spaces, parentheses, colons, italics, ellipses, typefaces, and the like. Though an "author" may wish to guide us in our reading, much of what we see on the page is open to interpretation and improvisation. How long is a beat? How do we translate the pitch of boldface? Italics? How long is a pause? How does typography cue us to action and vice versa? More importantly, what role do punctuation marks play in such dramas of our "sonic gaze" to use Avital Ronnell's suggestive phrase?[13] The oral/aural optic and sound vision underscores the undecidability of punctuation and informs the drama written here. However we understand its complex meanings, punctuation points to the (k)not of connection that stages an intervention between utterance and inscription, speech and writing, mind and body. It is seen and unspoken, sounded and unseen. Punctuation marks perform: they are marks of human affect and endlessly anthropomorphized. They are expressive, excessive, and elemental. There is more to say about punctuation's perplexing presence; it matters to imaginative theatre as much as to everyday life since, as Adorno theorizes, "History has left its residue in punctuation marks, and it is history, far more than meaning or grammatical function, that looks out at us, rigidified and trembling slightly, from every mark of punctuation."[14]

Notes

1 Catherin Clément quoted in Linda Hart, ed., *Making a Spectacle: Feminist Essays on Contemporary Women's Theater* (Ann Arbor: University of Michigan Press, 1992).
2 This is an acronym for "Yet Another Bloody Acronym" in John & Blake, *The Total TxtMSg Dictionary* (New York: Grand Central Publishing, 2001), 287.
3 This is a neologism by Richard Artschwager.
4 "Yeah Yeah Sure Whatever I'm Bored" (John & Blake, 290).
5 Paul Allyrdice, *Stops, Or How to Punctuate: A Practical Handbook for Writers and Students 3rd Edition* (London: T.F. Unwin Press, 1884).
6 Blink. No Comment.
7 Thomas Lewis. "Notes on Punctuation" in *The Medusa and the Snail: More Notes of a Biology Watcher* (New York: Viking Press, 1979), 109.
8 Mira Schor, *Wet: On Painting, Feminism, and Art Culture* (Durham, NC: Duke University Press, 1993), 213.
9 Eric Partridge, *You Have a Point There: A Guide to Punctuation and Its Allies* (London: Routledge Press, 1953), 91–92.
10 Ibid., 93.
11 Oliver Pritchett, "Pay Attention: It's Important!" *The Telegraph*, November 24, 2003.
12 Jennifer González, "The Appended Subject: Race and Identity as Digital Assemblage" in *The Feminism and Visual Culture Reader*, ed. Amelia Jones (New York: Routledge, 2003), 85.
13 Avital Ronnell, *The Telephone Book: Technology, Schizophrenia, Electric Speech.* (Lincoln: University of Nebraska Press, 1989), 322.
14 Theodor W. Adorno, "Punctuation Marks," in *Notes on Literature, Volume I*, ed. Rolf Tiedemann, trans. Shierry Weber Nicholsen (New York: Columbia University Press, 1991 [1958]), 213.

19. *THE COPPER THIEVES—IRMA MAYORGA*

Nighttime. Desert. Perhaps right outside of Albuquerque or Tucson. Maybe over on the savannah of South Texas. Far from a city. Not too far. We can't see too well. The light is low. It's late, the oldest hours of the night. Overhead, the audience views a dark sky with an astonishment of stars. The playing area is filled with rough dirt. We can hear grit crunch under the actors' footsteps. Here, there, bits of trash, tú sabes, the detritus that floats everywhere, paper scraps, flattened soda bottles. A road crosses the space—two gray lanes split by white dashes—a county road.

By the road, a telephone pole. It reaches up, up. Tall, stout, wooden, stoic. We think of a cross. We hear a car coming, but it doesn't appear. Instead, the sound of it speeding by travels from one side of the space to the other as do bright "headlights," lighting up the audience as it "passes."

Armando enters surreptitiously. He looks around, looks around again. He checks for cars. Cautiously and purposefully, he makes his way to the telephone pole. He reaches it. He fishes out the crucifix hanging from his neck, kisses it, puts it back. He climbs the telephone pole. It's hard, but he's young and agile. He reaches the top. He is relieved. He takes in the stars.

Armando takes wire cutters from his back pants pocket, begins to snip copper cable from connections and assemblies. He works quickly but with care; it looks like he has done this before. He throws his harvest down; lengths of copper cable fall to the stage.

Amada enters cautiously. She checks for cars, looks up at Armando. She makes her way to the telephone pole. She reaches its base, stays close to it. She signals Armando, cutting the air with a quick *pssst! pssst!* then *psssssssssssssssst!* We hear a dog barking far off. They freeze—then, the dog stops. Armando looks down, signals for her to wait. Armando cuts. Copper drops.

A flash erupts—jolting, brilliant—shoots from where Armando's clutched onto the telephone pole. The flash becomes many flashes pulsing erratically, electricity everywhere, lighting up stage and audience. The sharp crackling of energy fills the air with pops and a low thrum. Armando is engulfed in the brilliant flash. His body is at once a star, a blaze of fire, a taut flag of flesh and light. This goes on for longer than we'd like. The flashes end. The thrum takes longer to fade away.

He falls from the telephone pole.
He lies on the desert, pulpy, mephitic, burnt. Smoke emanates from his corpse.
Amada goes to Armando and kneels beside the body. Is it too hot or too repulsive to touch?

In time: *"Fuck* you! *Fuck* you! *Fuuuuuccckk!* You asshole! *[fast, chanting]* yourenotdeadyourenotdeadyourenotdeadyourenotdeadyourenot … don't you die! Don't! *Don't.* Nonononononono … " her words crumble into the sounds of lamentation.

The dog barks. Amada muffles her mouth. She checks for cars. The sky changes color; the Earth is about to turn into the Sun. Amada waits for Armando's body to move. It doesn't. Amada gathers the copper cable into her backpack. She has to, it's what they came for; she still needs it. She walks away. Armando, the pole, the road remain. Lights grow. The dog barks. Lights fade.

When I first heard about the phenomenon of Latina/os stripping copper cable from telephone poles, my thoughts swirled around the sort of desperation that would inspire this type of treacherous theft. It seems plundering for copper reached the tipping point of an "epidemic" sometime in the first few years following the burst of the US housing bubble in 2007 when, at the same time, copper's price on the metal market surged. Except of course for the wealthiest, the Great Recession struck people hard in the US, but it was especially adverse to those *already* living in the precarity of poverty. The collapse of the US housing market hit many Latina/os through a particular dimension: they were the backs bent to the sun that built new homes. When new home construction ceased, their labor was no longer needed. Droves of Latin American transnational migrants returned to their countries of origin. Parts of towns in the Southeast, Southwest, and Midwest began to "disappear," further decimating local economies … others remained, hoping to ride out the economic tumult. Latina/os began to pluck copper from improbable perches.

The image of the copper thieves held me in its thralldom then and still does now. I am detained by the tension between the exhilarating sight of someone high aloft in the air, spectacularizing the commonplace telephone pole, and the desperation that impelled this action. This image's pungency speaks to the depth of the Great Recession through an altogether different symbology than the event's more ubiquitous marker: a foreclosure sign planted in a front yard. The act's Latina/o-inflected resourcefulness echoed extremes taken by my own Mexican American family when I was a child. It is, in part, this sense of the familiar, a recognition of something of myself in the image, that arrests my attention.

The copper thief's ascent up a telephone pole also calls to mind the famed *voladores* of Mexico—Mexican Indians who risk their lives atop tall *postes* to perform a hung-from-the-ankles "flight" that both taunts death and serves as a corporeal prayer to the gods. Supposedly the ritual implored the gods to deliver rain; akin to Latina/o telephone pole climbers, it signaled desperate need. Notice I beckon you to conjure Latina/o bodies, assigning the characters decidedly Spanish names. It is important to me that you think of this drama as a story that bespeaks US Latina/os' lives and that the stakes at hand in these lives often include consequences such as death.

At this contemporary moment, there is a propensity for US Latina/o playwrights to transpose Western theatre's well-known classics into the contexts of a Latina/o *mise en scène*. These plays summon a need for Latina/o actors. They secure productions of "Latina/o" work in US theatres. These manifestations reply to current conversations about the predominance of whiteness and white life-worlds on US stages. In the best transpositions, a classic play's dramatic plot points and affective geography align neatly with *Latina/o* life-worlds. The adaptations labor to unveil—to translate—our all too often invisible Latina/o lives. Adaptations that push beyond abecedarian transpositions are works that demonstrate a poetics of hybridity, which in turn does the hard work of fending off deculturation.

Yet, I often wonder what is left behind? And *who* exactly is transposition of a "classic" play *for?* What of our stories that don't fit into the folds of transposition? What becomes of the stories that ache to relate the preposterous, often absurd, realities Latina/os survive as minoritarian subjects in the US? Why need we transpose and translate ourselves to be visible on US stages? What of the copper thieves?

20. COURT THEATRE—PETRA KUPPERS

She calls them to her, conferral, you do not know what is going on
there is code and negotiation
How will you begin?
Woman with big silver chains over a lilac patterned blouse gestures
man speaks low, tie straight down and sharp
bewildered clients stare straight ahead

Was the performance in line with or a departure from what you experienced?

he pressed down there, and over, the muscles strain
liquid darker this hurts, he does not care and presses, inches
note the finger down and into tender
my breasts mine again now really
spots sore inside bruises
not for any hospital
telephone chains, survivor language, note to speak note
police station marble floor echoes when I make my report.
How will you live now?
No. I did not ask
my breast felt, bruised, squeezed hard
fibers spring out of their sockets
shape new contours.
Body I do not know
Naked. My wheelchair outside. I can't run. I am bound
to these words,
my neck bristles, right now, I write down
these glimpses of memory
words I remember dredging up
for the police woman,
the guy at the station, the man in the suit,

How did the site influence your performance?

The prosecutor in the courthouse.
The corridor.
Outside the bathroom,
consultation, ties, high heels.
Tell me what you know about dismemberment.
We sit here, legs crossed. She sits. He sits.
We hear stories of robberies.
Is your client pleading?

What was it like for you to see what you said through another person's body?

we wheel into the courthouse and I swat away sensation and the pressure the pressure the blood comes to the surface again, and prickles in my neck hairs upright, and "this is a classic PTSD episode," she says, watch the light go and go and go and go and No. I say, I know I said that, and I repeat it, and you better listen to me, man tie.
I am pleading to let me out.

I—After another trial has failed, in the midst of mass outrage, I read Petra's text again, buffeted in analysis. A lawyer grilled on the news: polarizing tempest.

"Was the performance in line with or a departure from what you experienced?"

Bewildered, survival carries a paradox: "he does not care" versus the violation, the performance, the detail, the injury *over time*, over an ensemble of times, over an ensemble of iterations.

Testimony is not one act (against assumed impunity),

It is all increments:

the legal report,
the repeating detail,
the scrutiny,
beyond

"Body I do not know" recounts visceral, hair-on-end memory. Dredged memory. Betrayed care. A prevalence of abuse. A reel. Telephone chains, surviving, a language.

II—A costume of professional justice: heels and ties. Sprung embodiments. A small code, a lever against the weight of harm, this mnemonic storm.

Hair on end,
Unwilling repetition.

Delivered:
The cast, the code of figures, the license, the act, the score, the sequence.

Nested in tender enchainments: scenarios of court and theatre, performance and role, decentering "the." Always.

III—A remember of swatted sensation, liquid rise, the foreground of the felt—the lengthening, repeating dialogue of tides, forces, and fleshy time.

Here an imagined theatre extends a circle of support and confidence, lifting a norm of silence. Performatively, and in community, it challenges a siloing of the law to act and the theatre as a hollowing. With testifier's labor, it circulates the entanglement of words, art and body, the court and theatre, in words dredged with bruises.

21. *CROW TAKES HAT—ERIK EHN*

They do not recognize each other's faces

They thank each other anyway

Until they are weeping

Draw each other's face, face to face

Head in hands

Draw each other's face from memory

Head in heart

Draw each other's face in imagination

Crow takes hat

Face by face draws away

Foxes go

Stole a colt

Crow takes hat

In our flying

We are acrobat

In the bird language of faces

Where we were—spaces

i. Presence, encounter, acquaintance, peradventure. Thaumaturgical transactions. In this brevity, an epic, a work of theatre about theatre; it is both an example and a definition of theatre.

ii. Walter Benjamin writes of storytelling, "A man listening to a story is in the company of the storyteller; even a man reading one shares this companionship." In its first movement, the work is insistently diegetic; we are led through the action by an unseen but deeply felt storyteller, who, through their narration, transforms us into witnesses of the events unfolding. There is care in this; we—you and me here, reading this prayer cloaked in a story—are not left alone. We are, importantly, companioned.

iii. Here, one exquisite verb, "draw," educes a core activity of theatrical storytelling: rendering ourselves to and for each other. To be unrecognized, to be unknown, to be unable to gain the affirmation of recognition: one of the great central conflicts of every one of us alive. The storyteller twists and turns the verb, enabling its multiple invocations of finding to flip back and forth, ever-changing as when blocks glide to and fro between the ribbons of a Jacob's Ladder. In this, *Crow Takes Hat* shows us that to draw another, whether it be to physically pull them towards you or to render them as figurations wrought by the hand, the mind, the memory, or the heart is to affirm unequivocally their visibility and thus their existence.

iv. In explicating Native storytelling's rhetorical force, cultural lifeblood, and sanctity, Kiowa poet/philosopher N. Scott Momaday defines an extraordinary story as follows: "It is complex, and yet it is clear; it seems to give more and more of itself in time. Clear it is, and yet there is a kind of resistance in it, as in a riddle; it is richer for that. It is a kind of prism." I also turn to Benjamin, who offers that a storyteller describes "[t]he most extraordinary things, marvelous things ... related with the greatest accuracy, but the psychological connection of the events is not forced on the reader. It is left up to him to interpret things the way he understands them, and thus the narrative achieves an amplitude that information lacks." Evincing both fable and nursery rhyme, *Crow Takes Hat* astounds with its riddle and clarity, its complexity and amplitude.

v. As the crow flies. Unexpectedly, a different story arrived to advise my thoughts. As a presidential hopeful stumped before thousands, out of nowhere, a small finch alighted on the stage. Because of the audience's rapturous response, the candidate had no choice but to pause. The finch grew bolder, flew in closer, landing directly upon the speaker's podium. There, three feet from human contact, it eyed the candidate full on. The bird's wonderwork coupled with the candidate's acquiescence electrified the crowd. Then, it flew away.

Here, a crow, easily five times the size of a finch, not only encounters a person, but then grants humankind recognition through its touch: *crow takes hat.* Seemingly improbable miracles, drawn through theatre's storytelling, are what I ask for and seek in its admixture of poetry and risk.

22. *CROWDS WITH THE SHAPE OF REASON MISSING*—*ALAN READ*

For and from John Baldessari

Those of us without boats, and that was all of us, swam through the summers and other colder months too, and when, after hours of up and down, in and out, going nowhere, we rested, it was in the water *still.* Our perspective, floating, talking on our backs, was across our bodies towards the horizon. To float like this was to allow the current to do its work. While we existed on dry land, we lived for the sea.

At one point in this Essex estuary, an unsmiling granite obelisk called the Crowstone, taller, colder, and straighter than an attentive guard of the ebb and flow, traced a line between shore and horizon, where the upstream river of fresh water met the downstream river salt water of the sea. It had to meet somewhere around here, that was what estuaries were for, and apparently it was here.

If on older maps this line had once been marked with the words "Here be Dragons," it would have wildly over-estimated the threat this boundary traced. We were the opposite of Blaise Pascal's subjects, who, according to his seventeenth-century narrative of ship-wreck, had all *embarked,* and for whom there was now, having left the land, nothing on offer other than salvation or going under. We *floated* between these two dramatic impost-ers to attention. "Nothing to see here, move along." This was estuary, not ocean after all.

Less than a century before, the émigré writer Joseph Conrad had looked out from his hotel room on Surrey Street, off the Strand, close on the Thames in London, and imagined this far end of the river he could not see, the aperture to his heart of darkness:

> The day was ending in a serenity of still and exquisite brilliance. The water shone pacifically; the sky, without a speck, was a benign immensity of unstained light; the very mist on the Essex marsh was like a gauzy and radiant fabric …

But the light from where we floated was stained, it flickered above the oil terminals beyond low-lying Canvey Island, at Shell Haven, that had always been called that despite the later branding of the earth we thought was our inheritance. Sky-high stacks burning off the excess gas and covering the estuary with a fine film of petroleum spirit that condi-tioned our hair, when we had hair. Floating behind us, as we lay on our backs with rain-bow halos, hints of Methane Pentane, bouquets of waxes, greases, and asphalts, watching the same stars that we had no idea also hung over the Niger Delta, over Ogoniland, where oil and water still did not mix.

I am not sure what I would have done without the oil of course. Duckhams were the trusted suppliers in our day, for the mirrored *Lambrettas* and the *Triumphs* we cherished. My first theatre had been the Kursaal, just along the sea front, the *Wall of Death* its most popular attraction, where Yvonne Stagg would ride a 500cc BSA like nobody else before or after her. We all loved her, but she went to Margate, lost her balance, and never came back. The catch-in-the-throat kerosene that gave a punch to the fuel tank was gone by 1974, but in those years we hung over the balcony parapet from above, reaching out our hands to touch hers, as they lifted from the bars of the rotating bike, as though hang-ing for us in midair. There were no "high fives" then—this was what we once called "feeling", in the Essex Delta.

From and for (John Baldessari for instance) might be a way to work. The images, swathes of whited out historical events leaving only intact the onlooking spectators, *Crowds with Shape of Reason Missing* (1985). So, *from*—image, archive, source, documents of barbarism—and *for*—John Baldessari in this case, but always addressed to someone with love. An acknowledgement in so doing of "others," predecessors and precursors, a community of those with something in common. And here, an assembly of sorts, but with history missing. As has always been the way for me, others have said it, but without knowing the full story, if there was ever such a thing. Lacking material detail. Born as I was six months after my father's death, like but not like David Copperfield before me: "I was a posthumous child. My father's eyes had closed upon the light of this world six months, when mine opened on it. There is something strange to me, even now, in the reflection that he never saw me, and something stranger yet in the shadowy remembrance that I have of my first childish associations with his white gravestone … " So, born "after the event" that might but cannot define a life lived. Posthumous. Theatre: a place where latecomers are never admitted. Where are they? In a waiting room until it ends. So, what to do for the posthumous ones while they wait? Well, as Camus always said, swim first. When given the opportunity to write about funerals or swimming, he always preferred the beach. Everything came from the Estuary, as it left London behind for the open sea. We crawled out of its shallows and fell into the warmth of the nearest crowd. At the time that took the form of a hollow cylinder, sixty feet into the air looking down into a vast auditorium of Canadian Spruce. Wooden O. We—when I say "we" I of course mean I—fell in love with the Wall of Death rider Yvonne Stagg. Mine alone. Or her 500cc BSA, or both as they were never separated, until she died trying to resurrect her career at Dreamland, up the coast. But this of course was not the story. The inheritance of oil was where it was at. Extraction was what I was trying to get to. The taint was in the air, as always. Joseph Conrad had seen "unstained light" on the Essex Marshes, but it was chiaroscuro now. Tate, upriver, had just relieved themselves of one half of their damned dependency. The other, Empire Sugar, would be much longer in the sloughing. My own dependency comes first, swimming amidst its haloed penumbra, hair conditioning. But the air conditioning in that Wooden O was also a fix for those of us who associated speed with sex. Chrome was critical. The violence that spilled out onto the esplanade was always called a "bit of afters." Posthumous performance. The fight "proper" was dull, predictable, and constrained by the formalities of physical self-preservation. But those who went in "after" were free from such bonds of restraint. There was a form of expenditure here that put everyone in debt to each other. Community. Called forth by an event that may or may not have happened, but lost in time. Baldessari's scalpel cuts events from crowds that were left to find their own reason for being. The incision begins in the heart of the matter, radiates out and around until the tumor of time has been removed. Those, still there, are in the limbo of disappointed anticipation. Sad and sprung.

23. *DANCE FOR BAGHDAD—NATURE THEATER OF OKLAHOMA*

Hey guys, guys, if I may, without imposing, or taking away from our Kumbaya moment—which I'm in love with, seriously, you don't even know—I've been waiting for this since joining the company—but as I'm vibing that we're all kind of generously inclined towards each other right now, if I'm any judge of human behavior, I'm gonna go ahead and snatch this opportunity, while the good mood's in the air, to ask, in way of a favor, if I could get some constructive feedback on ideas I've been working with in a screenplay I'm writing. (All look at him.) All in? (Nothing.) Great. You guys are awesome. It's about a guy who's reached an emotional, mental, spiritual, and as a dancer and choreographer, physical impasse, a virtual dead end. He's repulsed with himself and the work he generates and asks others to partake in. He wants to withdraw into misanthropic isolation where he can systematically destroy his old self, imbibe the thick stew of emptiness in murky silence until it is bearable no more, and then, only then, begin to trek back up the forbidding mount of existence as a useful artist and member of this, our retrograde society. That, my dear friends and colleagues, should give you a clear picture of the inner world of the movie's protagonist, who's obviously, I won't lie, based on myself, and his primary motivation for advancing the plot. In the movie, my character is the artistic director and choreographer of the En-Knapp Dance Company. The company is thriving. We're accomplishing goals, traveling extensively, darlings of audiences round the globe, awards, Best This, Best That, commissions for new work, invitations to collaborate with famous artists, etcetera. We expand, hire additional dancers—like Jeffrey, like Lada—our future looks bright and endless, our place in performance art history rock solid. So what do we do? We bite the hands that feed us like an ungrateful feral cat. We turn down new commissions, return funds already advanced to us, and cancel future tour dates. We leave the spotlight, and in the shadows, top-secretly, while the world believes we've disappeared from the scene for good, we work tirelessly, and set out on a perilous path to reinvent how the company functions and what kind of work it makes. Then, rejuvenated with an ungraded sense of purpose, we book a gig in Baghdad, Republic of Iraq. We arrive at Baghdad International Airport in the cargo hold of a Christian humanitarian relief jet along with medical supplies, canned food, plastic tubs of personal-sized crucifixes and rosaries, cute mini-Bibles, and vast quantities of Red Bull energy drink, which, we soon learn, is the primary, if not the sole source of nutrition for both NATO troops and Iraqi insurgents. In fact, the way we are transported from the airport directly to the desert theatre of war is in a gaudily marked Red Bull delivery truck, evidently the safest way to travel anywhere in the conflict-ravaged Middle East. There is virtually zero chance of getting fired upon if you're in any way associated with the Red Bull brand or are anywhere within the relative vicinity of its product. Fighters on both sides are physically addicted to the stimulating beverage and there is a tacit agreement to under no circumstances endanger the Red Bull Mobile. We drive through an auxiliary but still hyperactive battle zone. There are massive explosions all around. But our leisurely moving vehicle seems to be impermeable, its own mobile oasis of mollifying serenity. We pass by burning upturned cars, civilian and military, dead and wounded animals and people, who manage feeble smiles and wave at us like we are a parade float. There is a powderized house and a girl playing with her deceased family members like they're oversized dolls. I've watched similar sights on TV at home for entertainment, always at an appropriate emotional remove, and strangely, it still feels that way, even though I'm only a pane of glass away from the actual horrors. The rest of the company dozes off, tranquilized by the purring and gentle rocking of the Red Bull Mobile, née RBM, and the lullaby-type tune that percolates from speakers inside and outside the vehicle. Our driver, a jolly Austrian with a Styrian accent, quietly hums along. Our first stop is the NATO outpost. The dancers wake up with a start as the truck's hydraulics flatulate, the door folds open, and lets in the sound of actual postmodern warfare. But it's safe within the perimeter of the RBM's bubble of peace. The chubby Styrian driver starts offloading case upon case of the mediciny sweet, Austrian-made boundless energy-nectar, and NATO soldiers drop their weapons, abandon posts, and skip with carefree dewy-eyed smiles toward us. They can smell the mighty beverage even through aluminum and cardboard and help stack the cases with gleeful grins of anticipation, emitting involuntary moans of future pleasure. Meanwhile, we dancers are the definition of stupefaction. Some grab their luggage and ready themselves to disembark, but I quickly order them to simmer back down—not yet—which they obey, albeit with annoyed attitude. The driver hops back in behind the wheel—he does everything with enviable lightness despite his corpulence—and apologizes for neglecting to offer us complimentary Red Bull, neé RB, earlier. We help ourselves and immediately, thanks to the elixir, the atmosphere improves radically. On the cans it says: "military-grade, experimental, not for civilian consumption." We feel privileged. The door queefs shut and we drive on, taking our magical orb of invincibility with us, towards the Iraqi insurgency zone. Tweaked out NATO soldiers run after us like a throng of obese pre-diabetic children after an ice cream truck, but we lose them in a cloud of sand raised by our wheels. More visual misery along the road; the road gradually vanishes inside potholes and craters caused by explosions. Approximately midpoint between NATO and Iraqi positions, I tap the shoulder of the kind driver, and request a stop. He obliges. The door hisses open. I grab the showbag full of costumes, and my personal baggage, physical and emotional, and back out of RBM onto hot desert sand. I wait for the others but no one's emerging. I peek my head back in. The company is terrified. Determined not to let anything diminish my enthusiasm to finally do something with my heretofore pointless artsy-fartsy life, I assume an unquestionable tenor of authority and sternly order the dancers to grab their shit and get the fuck off the truck. They whimper and do as I say, intimidated into submissiveness by the sights and sounds of war. Before the last one out, the driver gifts us two full cases of the experimental military grade not-for-civilian-consumption RB, for which I profusely thank him and give him one of our souvenir company t-shirts, which we bring everywhere for just this type of occasion. He yodels with glee, immediately dons it over his RB uniform, blows us a kiss *tschüssi*, and drives on towards the Iraqis, who have ceased fire in anticipation of the imminent delivery. This temporary truce affords us a window of time to catch our bearings and situate ourselves. I ID the perfect location to set up the dressing-slash-greenroom, a large crater freshly made by a powerful bomb, no debris at the bottom, a pristine inviting hole, and lead the way. We descend into safety just as bullets resume screaming at each other up above. Fear is natural in this situation and the dancers withdraw inside themselves, unaccustomed to real, non-self-generated drama, but I work in turbo mode to mobilize the troupe and boost our team spirit. We can pull off this mission only if our hearts beat in unison. My efforts are for naught until everyone quenches their dry mouth with RB. Subsequently there's no resistance to my over-the-top cheerleading; in fact, I myself must kick it into higher gear to keep up with the rest of the company, which I relish. I stow the second case of the potent performance-enhancing potion of courage and distilled fighting spirit in my personal baggage for a future refresher. We urgently don our flamboyant color-coordinated costumes and elaborate headdresses, and help each other overapply self-consciously tacky makeup designed to be noticeable from a great distance. The atmosphere in the hole is akin to the giddy nervous hustle and bustle backstage before the first elementary school dance recital. We're all able to access the original pure impulse which made us choose to pursue this tenuous artform, intoxicated on adrenaline and the secret ingredient in military grade RB. We are doing what we love and finally putting it to good use, or any use at all. One of the dancers leads an abbreviated group warmup, we break a little sweat, and finish off singing our company anthem more triumphantly than ever. I'm not the only one who has goosebumps. Then our customary pre-show group hug, followed by a bit of one-on-one mock sexual molestation for good luck, some additional individual rituals, and we're at places. The stakes have never been higher. Baghdad needs us. The entire world needs Baghdad. Therefore, the world needs us. A straightforward equation. It's all on our shoulders. Showtime. We check each other's hair and makeup, fix costumes. Everyone charged up, overeager. I count down. Three, two, one, GO. We explode out of the crater and make our grand entrée. Shit! We seem to have forgotten what bullets do to people. They whistle maliciously around us and mess up our hair and the expensive tinted ostrich feathers in our headdresses. Those are irreplaceable. Our self-preservation instinct kicks in and we follow it back into the relative safety of our hole, all atremble with primal fright. I reach for the extra case of RB, quickly divvy up the cans, and over the deafening sounds of artillery shout: "Chug! Chug! Chug!" And chug we do, the empty cans in our engorged palms we crush, our courage and fighting spirit surge back with a vengeance. I call places everyone, count down, three, two, one, GO, and up we clamber again, a reprise of our well-rehearsed show-stopper entrance. We look strong, we feel invincible. Is it perhaps this confidence and clarity of purpose heretofore absent from the history of modern dance, which makes the seemingly indiscriminate shelling from both sides of the conflict finally … stop? Only the hot desert wind is heard, carrying the echo of suddenly muzzled artillery farther and farther away, mixed in with the swooshes and whooshes of our feet stirring up sand, arms cutting through thick air, and our precisely timed inhales and exhales. Soldiers on both sides, I imagine with an arrogant smile, must be dumbstruck by the queer mirage of our bedazzled, befeathered, garishly colorful dance troupe appearing right in their crosshairs. I am drunk on missionary zeal and RB. It is exhilarating. Here we are, putting our fragile dancer necks on the actual line, risking our only lives. My heart dances more vigorously than my limbs will ever be able to. Five, six, seven, eight, we throw ourselves into the opening number in perfect undismissable unison. No one is firing at us, which I consider our first success, and we're encouraged into even fuller extension of our extremities, taller jumps and longer leaps, in fact three times the recommended height and length, and lifts of exquisite beauty and duration. And one and two and three and four, we fan out into a straight line, and each do individual but related choreography based on a famous heroic rhymed poem; one's movements, like the rhythmically metered stanzas, folding into the neighbor's, and so forth down the line. Five, six and seven and eight, one, two, we break into seemingly disorganized chaos. There appears to be no intelligence at work in our dynamic, constantly morphing formation, but I assure you, there's nothing chancy about our signature En-Knapp choreography. We're always über-organized, every move is calibrated and recalibrated and absolutely integral. If a single element fails, the entire sophisticated but precarious structure falls apart. And this particular performance, I daresay, is a veritable apotheosis of the artform. We're getting down, solos, duets, trios, all permutational combos, really digging it, suddenly doing with ease sequences we could never master in rehearsal. Then, as fully expected, both sides of our captive audience send out recon teams. We see them approaching cautiously, weapons pointed at us, lubricated eager index fingers on triggers. I feel the RB liquid courage slowing down its race through the obstacle course of my bloodstream, and it's safe to assume the juice is wearing off in others too, but I outdo myself as a motivator: Hell no we don't stop in fear! We intensify! We're dancing for world peace! I remind everyone, and we give the performance of our lives. The over-weaponized soldiers are so close I can read individual emotions on their insufficiently camouflaged faces. This is invaluable feedback that impacts our performance. We see ourselves reflected in our audience, and if we do our job right, they see themselves in us. None of the soldiers is interested in their mortal enemy across the performance area. They're busy deciphering and interpreting the abstract patterns in our sophisticated choreography, full of hidden meanings, metaphors, allusions, direct as well as oblique references to both classical and pop culture. We did not dumb it down for them. The lack of a unifying narrative does not seem to bother them. These soldiers, heroes all, are the most intelligent audience we've ever performed for. It must be the complexity of their life at the very extremes of human experience that makes it possible for them to appreciate radical art. Nearby, an unexploded bomb goes off at the perfect moment—a cool effect; no one gets injured. Our next section consists of jerks, twitches, broken doll poses, tableaux based on extensive research of human and animal suffering through the ages, sudden collapses to the ground, and reenactments of every sort of seizure. I notice embryonic stages of movement on both sides of the narrow performance corridor. It quickly intensifies and soon all soldiers, infected by our purposely awkward expressive convulsions, are dancing along with us. Rigorous military drills, I surmise, have prepared them to pick up our choreography swiftly. What took us months of work, they're able to master quite effortlessly without any of the ferocious frustration that characterizes all our rehearsals. They step onto the sandy dancefloor and freely mingle among us. One moment I'm dancing a duet with an Iraqi rebel and next I'm an ancillary part of a trio with two NATO soldiers. I'm lost, most enjoyably, inside a babel of languages. American, Czech, Danish or Dutch—they sound the same—Gibberish, Georgian, Pidgin, Jewish, Gerbil, and German, but mostly Arabic and Mexican—the two official languages of this war. I'm thinking the financial security of our company is practically guaranteed. We've hit the motherload, a bona fide gold mine, what with all the workshops we're sure to be invited to conduct all over the war-torn world. I hear ka-ching and feel the irises of my eyes roll into Euro and dollar signs respectively. But alas, our piece is approaching finale. The dancers look to me with panicked expressions. We all know it's the dancing alone keeping us alive. What happens when we run out of choreographed steps? We have unanimously voted that under no circumstances would we resort to the vulgarities of improvisation. But before I'm able to think of a suitable solution to our potentially deadly predicament, our scheduled exeunt omni arrives, five, six, seven, eight, and off we leap like gazelles into virtual wings, leaving NATOans and Iraqis facing off against each other, limp weapons dangling from shoulders. It wouldn't take much to reinsert the now-flaccid, but ever so easily arousable index fingers into the still moist trigger openings. A shootout of cataclysmic consequences could ensue any moment. However, instead, while we pant on the sidelines, the fighters continue dancing on their own. We're spectating a classic dance-off. First NATO soldiers show off their moves, playfully taunting the Iraqis, who retort with an equally virtuoso combination. There's aggressive male posturing, innocuous ruffling of feathers, but also displays of effeminacy, almost bordering on courtship. There are intermittent explosions of laughter. I'm proud to see them incorporate elements and even entire sequences they've learned from us into their routines. There is no obvious winner, but that doesn't seem to be the objective, as subsequently the soldiers pair up, one NATO and one Iraqi per couple, and spin each other round and round with vertiginous velocity. Then this awesome intercourse decelerates considerably into classic slow dance, which gradually melts into your basic frottage. Each man's personal amount of gay shyly pokes its rainbow head out, exposing latent homosexual tendencies in all mano-a-mano male encounters such as mortal combat. Soldiers are a pitiful lonesome species, starved most of all for the gentle touch of another, and must capitalize on every rare opportunity for carnal contact. But suddenly the ground throws up small puffs of sand in quick succession accompanied by a rat-a-tat sound from above. A pair of necking soldiers emit in unison a stifled scream, fold to the ground, and twitch there, still embracing, moribund. In the sky I descry a giant four-legged bird of pray, a griffin, or more likely, given our location, the legendary Arabian Roc, spitting sizable stones down at us, putting all terpsichorean activities on pause. None of "the show must go on" spirit here, since it turns out it's not a bird, but an unidentified unmanned drone, carpet-shelling what it interprets to be some alien life-form—which coincidentally the contemporary dancer resembles the most—and which must be exterminated. I hit the ground and bury my head in the sand as a well-known escape strategy. But what my eyes can't see, my ears perceive all the more vividly. There go the soldiers' index fingers becoming erect, being lubricated in mouths, their slurpy insertions into tight-fitting trigger openings, the pumping of round after round, the penetration of flesh, the ejaculation of blood, the primal moaning, the groaning. With my head in the sand I lose the reins of my imagination and it runs wild and away from me. Then. A sharp pain in my right ass cheek forces me above ground. I've been shot. No surprise here. I was asking for it. The dancefloor is once again an echt battlefield, strewn with unmanned feather boas, headdresses, wigs, shredded bedazzled leotards, sequins, and fake jewels. The accountant in me tries to tabulate the damage, but it's difficult to manage in my frazzled state. While art may feast on misery and murder, accounting must have languor for creative juices to flow. Nevertheless, I manage to account for all my dancers. They're squealing like pigs at slaughter, dragging themselves back into our hole-cum-dressing-slash-greenroom. Some are injured. Ass pain saps my math skills and I can't count the dead and dying soldiers. There are too many. Those who still have one or more limbs retreat back to their respective camps, abandoning us dancers to fend for ourselves against the anonymous third-party drone. I too begin to crawl towards the supposed safety hole, gritting my teeth, pushing through pain. Now. A large shadow overtakes me. The merciless monster is hovering directly above my quadruped form. I'm going to die within milliseconds unless I attempt to soften its steel heart. I dig deep and clamber up to my feet. I can hardly stand, but I'm fighting for my life, which suddenly, for the first time, seems worth fighting for. I man up and perform a modified version of the most audience-friendly sequence of our choreography. But. The dragon misreads my intentions, feels threatened, and fires a single exploratory bullet at me. I'm hit in the right groin, i.e., too close to my preciouses. First the ass, now the genitalia? Come on, man! The drone seems to be programmed to target erogenous zones. I try to think positive. Maybe the drone doesn't want to kill, only to humiliate. But pain spreads through my entire body, my knees buckle, and I hit the ground like an adult diaper full of crap. I resume crawling. The bitch shoots me again, this time in the back of my neck, dispelling my positive humors. I roll over and give her a dirty look. She drops mere feet above me. I grope for rocks to throw but there's only sand. She pivots to get a fuller picture of me. I find a boot with a warm foot inside and hurl it at her. She makes a funny sound I don't know how to describe, does a backflip, and flies away. I'm proud of myself. The last bullet must have severed a major nerve because the right half of my body goes limp. I drag it with my able half back to the hole, hopeful the drone's never coming back. I almost make it, but thank god I don't. There's a buzzing behind me and getting louder. I look over my dead shoulder and see a swarm of mad drones flying in formation toward us. Flashback. This reminds me of a childhood memory when I once insulted a wasp, she flew away, and moments later brought back a whole nestful of pissed off buddies intent on revenge. They stung me till I was swollen beyond even my mother's recognition. End flashback. The drones get to the hole before I do, but not before some of my company has found shelter within. It's too late to warn them. The drones fire in unison straight into the hole, which explodes in a milkshake of sand, dancer chunks, private and company property, and a swirl of blood. The material foams over the edge and settles back down. A spectacular effect. The drones ascend high above the desert, most likely to regroup and strategize. I look in the crater, now much deeper. It is a mass grave of bodies brutally dismembered and or eviscerated, unrecognizable. I must avert my eyes or else lose my mind. Where is the rest of the company? I focus my sight at infinity and scan the horizon. One dancer, I believe it's Jeffrey, is bouncing on one leg away from the scene of the massacre, blood spurting from where his left arm used to be, screaming his boyfriend's name. Two others, Ana and Luke, arms around each other, are crawling in the opposite direction. Where is Ida? I can't find her and conclude the worst. Lada, sadly, I already saw dead in the crater. Above, soaring in high altitude, the impregnable, artif-intelligent techno-vultures are prospecting for further provender. NATO and Iraqis resume shooting at each other. I don't know the exact definition of the word mayhem, but this could well be it. I keep my head down, and in case I only have moments to live, I try to induce a screening of a movie of my entire life in one of the cinemas in the cineplex of my mind. The independent fleet of rogue drones, fighting for their own territorial gains, drops an overkill of bombs on the area. I roll up into a ball and pray, amateurishly. The explosions cause an earthquake. I am buried under an avalanche of sand. When at last I manage to doggy-paddle up to the surface coughing my lungs out, I don't recognize the reconfigured landscape. The two enemy teams of fighters appear to have been lifted up and placed much closer to each other. They're firing with their eyes closed and with more hate than before we came to dance for them. This is our fault! Oh God! We've done more harm than good! I weep. There is nothing familiar for me to hold onto. Events far beyond my intellectual grasp are occurring around me. I pray again, now with slightly less desperate fervor but more genuine faith. My prayer is answered. I hear the Red Bull Mobile approaching, the bass of its bubbly ice cream tune aggressively cranked up. Unfortunately drones do not feed on RB, hence make no concessions for its disbursal. They continue their systematic offensive bombing. This leaves the soldiers on the ground no choice but to also keep up their defensive brainless barrage. The truck skids, pivots hundred eighty degrees, and comes to a sudden stop, swirling dust around itself like a fancy shawl. The door opens and the corpulent but healthy Austrian emerges. I can't tell if he's purposely moving in slow motion, or I'm losing grip on real time due to heavy blood loss. He quaffs a can of RB, crushes the empty, and histrionically tosses it high in the air, where it is immediately pulverized by bullets. Then the Styrian hero hops up and throws himself over his own heft, attempting a front-flip. In my professional opinion, unsuccessful, but who am I to set standards. At this moment I consider myself a colossal failure, a tofu tortilla salad. It takes him a few clumsy seconds to disentangle his limbs. I wave at him in case he doesn't see me. He waves back effeminately and skips toward me. Bullets buzz around his head like ovulating mosquitoes. But RB gives him wiings®. I try to think of some Austrian words to impress him with but come up with zilch. He taunts the bullets, come and get me, evidently feeling immortal from the vim juice he vends. He endeavors another variety of front-flip, even less successful, but he clearly feels he's improving. He's performing some kind of well-rehearsed routine, I realize. Almost like he's auditioning—I recognize that intense, hungry-jazz-face look. But it only enrages the waspish bullets more. He is shot. He goes down. On his way to the ground, he is shot again. In the stomach, in the chest, in the leg, and in the head. The multiple bullets poison him with imminent death. He bleeds everywhere. Gracefully he places himself in the warm, silken bed of sand, slowly, still in full command of his expiring hulky body, looks up at me, and thanks me with a smile, through tears much like mine now, in his adorable accent, for inspiring him, admits that he's always dreamed of being a dancer, but never felt adequate enough until he met and saw us, and realized he too can do this, he can finally quit his shitty Red Fucking Bull delivery fucking job, where his boss is a money-grubbing asshole, and devote himself exclusively to doing what he secretly loves. He knows he's dying, but these few brief, and at the same time eternal, moments are worth dying for. And his eyes roll over, and he gargles his own blood, and dies. Thank you Fritzi, or whatever your name is, you magnificent specimen of manhood. You will forever live on in my heart. R.I.P. Now. I still have to get the fuck out of butthole Baghdad and salvage whoever's left of the company. The engine of the Red Bull Mobile is still running. I make a move towards it with all available strength. Mind over matter, I yell at myself. Come on, you pussy, mind over fucking matter! It helps me haul my dead conjoined twin to the truck and together we climb behind the steering wheel. I hear a human moan, look back over my shoulder, and see poor injured Ida pinned under a pile of intermittently exploding cases of RB. Good, at least she's alive, I say to myself. Fritzi must have picked her up. I chug a can of RB for extra oomph. The windshield is gone and bullets are ricocheting within the vehicle like in a pinball machine. I feel no fear, goaded by the fumes from the exploding beverages behind me. The sinister ice cream truck song is blaring. I max out the bass and feel invincible. All my insecurities evaporate. I locate the lone fugitive Jeffrey in the distance, bouncing deeper into the forbidding desert on the pogo-stick of his one remaining leg. Not a smart move, but one to be expected from Jeffrey; he's new. I head toward him. On my way I pass an injured NATO soldier waving me down. I have other priorities and can't stop. To assuage my conscience, I reach behind me, grab a can of RB, and toss it out the window to the poor groveling youth, thinking to give him enough energy to make it to safety. How was I supposed to know that cans of Red Bull double as grenades? Following this unfortunate contretemps, I drive up alongside Jeffrey and turn down the music. He looks deranged and doesn't want to get in. I beg him. He says he doesn't trust me. I say I understand. He says fuck you. I say he's stupid. He says I'm stupider and fuck you. I say fuck yourself. He gives me the silent treatment. I think. I apologize and say I didn't mean what I said, that he's by far the best dancer in the company, a rarefied corporeal poet, talent grande, potential up the wazoo, etcetera etcetera, and I love him like a brother. His demeanor flips one eighty and he pogoes into the passenger seat. He notices Ida moaning in the back and nods. She waves at him. One of Jeffrey's eyes is completely out of service and the other is dangling off its optic nerve. Coincidentally, I'm in the same predicament. We each hold our eyeballs between two fingers and manually direct them where to look. He's the first to spot Luke and Ana crawling away. I step on the gas before I lose all sensation in my lower extremities. The drones are relentless, claiming ever more real estate while performing their own impressive aerial choreography. There is no use for us humans in their rapidly evolving macrocosm. We're vermin to them, an annoying pest that must be exterminated. The Iraqi and NATO fighters, handicapped by RB withdrawal symptoms, are shooting blindly, mostly mercy-killing their own, or committing suicide. We reach Luke and Ana. They're unrecognizable. The extent of their combined injuries makes them monstrous. If I didn't know better, I'd think we've run into a giant desert crab. The sight makes my eye bleed. I point it away and instruct mi amigo Jeffrey to deal with them. Luke and Ana miraculously clamber up into the cargo area and off we go at maximum velocity away from this mistake of a place. The floor of the truck is a kiddie pool of Red Bull, blood, and feces—no doubt its secret ingredient. I hear Luke slurping up this almighty formula with the remainder of his slipshod lips, perhaps the sole reason he survives the bumpy eternal ride to the Baghdad International Airport. We leave Lada behind, a hero fallen for a magna cum laude cause. Rest in peace. Your time with us was short, but you gave it your all, literally. You're our very own true Španski Borac. Back in Ljubljana. It turns out our injuries are not as serious as we feared. We all get back to normal, physically. Mentally and emotionally, however, the narrative is very different. I have night terrors once a night, guaranteed, and wet the bed regularly. Loud noises make me dry-heave, I get grand mal seizures at the slightest intimation of danger, and I've defecated myself in public on at least seven occasions. The other survivors also suffer from Posttraumatic Stress Disorder. My ex-wife, hoping to get back together now that our kid has run away from home with our car and all our savings at age eleven, has been campaigning for us to receive the Nobel Peace Prize, which we doubtless deserve, at least for trying, but I intend to turn it down in protest of domestic violence in Slovenia, which has reached pandemic scale. (Bence alone on stage from now on.) No one can truly understand how really really sad it is to conclude this project is a failure. I'm disappointed to the core, in myself, in the company, and in the universe, where only such a minuscule amount of what humans imagine is actually possible. I'm beyond consolation. My crippling melancholy is compounded by the fact that I haven't heard from any of my fellow survivors since coming back, even though I've reached out to them. Who was it that single-handedly saved their pathetic microlives? The least I deserve is an SMS, even one composed of only emojis. Oh how painfully lonely I am. What magical ointment would I not rub on this spreading rash of *usamljenost*. I am devoid of dignity. Nothing could restrain me if I saw a mere hint of a friendly hand outstretched toward me. I would choke it near death with my own needy paws and drown it in grateful kisses. But then, my character resurrects, and climbs back up to the peak of his artistic prime again. While bitches and motherfuckers are asleep, he is toiling hard, oiling his pistons, working out by candle light. He gets in the best shape of his life. Whether you still want him or you've had enough, he'll keep showing up long past when either your progeny has sucked you dry of drive, or you've burned out. And in his copious spare time he's rehearsing a solo he'll dance on your graves. The end. Long heavy pause. Dear patient audience, this gut-wrenching manifesto of my idealism, valor, friendship, love, and ultimate betrayal, this eternal story, my most valuable and only possession, is for sale. My disastrous financial straits leave me no alternative. No! Please! No. Put your coin-purses and billfolds back in your pockets. This is not the place. There's a fantastic Brazilian restaurant, Rodizio Do Brasil, famous for salad bar orgies and meat feasts. I'll be there after the show, happy to negotiate motion picture rights, and grateful for companionship. Thank you. Ciao. (He drops the mic and exits.)

Baghdad. In 1985 the Baghdad Theatre Festival featured a production by the Lebanese playwright, director, and actor Raymond Gebara, entitled *Man of La Mancha*, for which the actress Randa Joseph Asmar won the Best Young Actress Award for her performance in the role of Dulcinea. In October 2013 an International Theatre Festival was held in the city.

Flashback. A symptom of post-traumatic stress disorder. Involves the intense re-experiencing of previously lived events.

Ljubljana. Capital of Slovenia. Home of the EnKnapGroup, a dance company formed in 2007.

Postage stamp. Small printed paper affixed to items to be sent by post, to indicate that postage costs have been paid. Often used as a figure to describe small areas onto which large quantities of material are deposited.

Red Bull. Sponsor of a successful Formula One motor racing team. Characterized, since its establishment in 2005, by "an unquenchable desire to compete at the sharp end of the very highest level of motor sport ... while having as much fun as possible."

Styria. A southeastern state in the Republic of Austria. Its capital, Graz, is the home to an arts festival, Steirischer Herbst (Styrian Autumn). The playwright and novelist Elfriede Jelinek was born in the Styrian town of Mürzzuschlag. In the English translation by Lilian Friedburg of her play, *Bambiland* (2004) you may find the following: "We have an excellent plan we intend to implement in record time. Who's to say we can't implement it? We'll implement it alright, you can bet your bottom dollar on that. Those armchair Generals say it ain't so, but we're saying the right thing, stick with us, just don't go getting too stuck on us, we cannot possibly drag you all along with us, and I say that knowing full well that modesty is the greatest danger. Enemies flung to the sea seek salvation on an island, but their efforts are in vain. 600 oil wells were ablaze in southern Iraq, but we had them under control and extinguished in record time, and that's just the state of affairs as of today. Tomorrow we'll be in another position altogether and much better positioned at that. But, good Lord, there are some places where things aren't running as smoothly today. There are some places where they're already running out of bombs. I say we issue a running curfew on bombs, and fast. So they're staying with us after all. I knew it. And we're seeing some gradual improvements on the weather front, too. *YES SIR*."

24. DAT BLACK MERMAID MAN LADY/HOME—SHARON BRIDGFORTH

There is a processional
a Praise/Remembering
as we recalibrate the streets with song
eating-dancing-making offerings each step of the way.
The processional rests in front of one who reads the Oracles/the
passed down Knowings Divined in a queer world made of
gender variant/piano playing/knife carrying she'roes
and old people that fly.
The one who reads reads for one
for whoever is moved to come forward
for whoever is willing to sit for a public reading—a Mirror for the telling.
We are the Divine Witnesses. Holding space.
Helping what wants to happen.
Osun, Oya, Olokun, and Dem live in the mythologies that are the lives of the Oracles:
HoneyPot, Miss Kitty, dat Black Mermaid Man Lady, and dem.
Cards are pulled. Stories are told. Witnessing happens
the processional moves again.
We Praise/Remembering
as we recalibrate the streets with song
eating-dancing-making offerings each step of the way.
All present are responsible for the Journey.

We will be in residence in a neighborhood facing gentrification—in a property built in community—offering individual dat Black Mermaid Man Lady Oracle readings, performance installations and cooking/story circles. Block parties, resource fairs, and public dialogues surround our residency. After our residency ends, the property will remain—a gift from the collective—for an emerging artist of color.

This project is a re-imagining of African Diasporic traditions of bembés (parties for Yoruba deities). Like those healing rituals, this project builds sacred cultural space in community through singing, dancing, eating, divining, and storytelling. dat Black Mermaid Man Lady/Home organically attracts an intergenerational mix of spiritual practitioners from different faiths, immigrant communities, people of color, women, LGBTQ folks, and emerging artists. Like a bembé some aspects of this work are very private, some are hugely public. Everything works together to create change.

With a gender queer Black American lesbian as the lead artist, this project serves as a transgressive force breaking open and dismantling stagnant constructs of boundaries and form. Mermaid energy is perfect for this work. In Yoruba traditions, the Divine Mermaid—Yemaya—is big Mama, protector of children. She governs the home, holds our wealth/our Ancestors/our stories/our secrets deep in her belly.

April 23, 2016.

What can I say in this moment? That black performance always remembers the dead? And that we have too many dead to remember? Busting out the walls of the theatre into the nightclub, turning chalk circles into dust particles with the march of the streets?

The body count growing, always growing … "as we recalibrate the streets with song."

On this, 2 days after the passing of Prince and one night after the Brooklyn block party Spike Lee threw in his honor. The ground vibrating.
As the streets are hot with protest after North Carolina passed the first-ever law to bar trans-people from using public bathrooms based on their gender identity.
On this, the year that more trans-people of color were murdered than ever in history.

7 Saturdays from now, a man will enter an Orlando nightclub with an assault rifle and handgun, which he will use to murder 49 queer people of color, and maim 53.

What does it mean for black women, for black queer and transfolk to recalibrate the streets? The streets that have always been ours—even and especially when the courtrooms and boardrooms and theatres haven't. What does it mean for us to fill in the blanks, to fill in the spaces of the crossroads with our bodies, deemed monstrous? Is this not the same crossroads that meets inside of us? Are we not holy?

We, exiled to the streets.
We, exiled to the clubs.
We, exiled.
In the dawn, we scoop up our children from gutters still sprinkled with the glitter and blood of the night before.

Our children, the gatekeepers that hold the doors open between here and there, male and female, earth and space, this and home. Their denigration *is* the colonial moment naked—a scratch at the DJ booth. A replay of the massacre in 1513 where 40 indigenous Panamanians who occupied this gender crossroads were murdered and eaten by Spanish dogs.

How do the homeless make home?

We have lost our seers, but they/we return in the form of black women/queer artists in little tiny houses reading cards. With bulldozers surrounding it, She stands, this little house, floorboards creaking with the dancing of ancestors. The theatre that is never just itself—that overflows, and cascades. The theatre with open doors. No doors. Is this nostalgia or utopia? Or ashé? The actualizing power that makes a thing a thing. The thing that tells a child (to whom all the someones said "It's a boy!") that she is a girl. And the thing that tells a people (whom all the someones said did not deserve to live) that they must thrust clenched fists to the sky, mouths making shapes, breathing.

25. DEALING—*W. B. WORTHEN*

Stage evenly illuminated. A table, slightly angled; two chairs at upper left and right corners. Two actors, preferably onstage while audience enters the auditorium. A prop table and a small costume rack, on one side of the stage, may be used by performers. Centered between the actors, slightly downstage, on the table: a pile of index cards. Actors motionless. Gaze at audience, 20 seconds.

Actor A takes top card, reads the card, delivers the line (see below). Throughout, actors/director decide whether cards will be read/lines delivered in alternation—Actor A, Actor B, Actor A—or whether another procedure will be followed. Perhaps each actor reaches for several cards at once. Actors carefully work through stack, each placing used cards in a second stack. After all cards delivered, actors sit, motionless. Gaze at audience, 10 seconds.

Actor A cuts the deck. Each actor chooses a stack. Actor B takes top card, reads, delivers. Actors/director decide whether cards will be read/lines delivered in alternation or whether another procedure will be followed. Actors again carefully work through stack, placing used cards in a single stack. After all cards delivered, actors sit, motionless. Gaze at audience, 10 seconds.

Actor B cuts the deck. Each actor chooses a stack. Actors rise. Actor A takes top card, reads, delivers, tosses card away. From this point on, actors decide movement, whether or not to use props/costumes. Play proceeds until all cards have been delivered. If desired, actors may resort to cards already played—picked up from the floor or from a few tossed on the table—for several lines. Performance should not exceed 15 minutes. Quick but varied tempo. After all cards have been delivered, and (if desired) a few cards have been redelivered, actors stop.

Gaze at audience. Five seconds. Blackout.

Cards: Cards should be prepared. Each card should have one line, drawn from a familiar play; several lines from the same play may be used. In the initial run, consecutive lines may be on consecutive cards. Some lines may be stage directions: (*leaps in the grave*), (*Enter a boy*); some lines may be other textual material (*As it was plaide*), (*All rights, including professional, amateur, motion picture, radio, television, recitation, public reading, and any method of photographic reproduction, are strictly reserved*). Many lines should be recognizable, but not all lines need to be recognizable. One card must say "Wham, bam, thank you Sam." One card must say "Song and guitar accompaniment by Isidore."

Structurally, *Dealing* evokes one of F.T. Marinetti's short, Futurist *radio sintesi*—pieces such as *A Landscape Heard* and *Silences Speak among Themselves*—marking specifically timed pauses between movements or language. It also recalls the repetitions with a difference so common in the work of American avant-gardists like Adrienne Kennedy and María Irene Fornés, whom Worthen cites here specifically. The play imagines a scenario in which we recognize almost everything, a series of famous and not-so-famous quotations that then becomes a series of those same quotations in a different order: a piece of *Hamlet,* a stage direction from *Waiting for Godot,* a seventeenth-century publisher's attribution, perhaps a line from Zeami or Chekhov or Calderón.

In his modernist text *The Thirty-Six Dramatic Situations*, Georges Polti famously argues that there are no more than thirty-six possibilities for drama. Polti catalogues an immense list of dramatic narratives that covers situations from ancient Greece to Shakespeare, from Sanskrit drama to Ibsen, from fourteenth-century *miracles* to naturalist avant-garde dramas like Fernand Icres's *The Butchers* and Rachilde's *Call of the Blood.* Polti was following in the footsteps of Gozzi, Schiller, and Goethe, who reportedly attempted similar catalogues. Others have enjoyed this game, as well: Trickster and playwright Alfred Jarry sacrilegiously and mockingly proposed a thirty-seventh dramatic situation—"Realising that one's mother is a virgin"—in his 1899 novel *Absolute Love.*

As in Polti's schema, *Dealing* is a closed system in which the entirety of the theatre is contained but can be scrambled and rescrambled indefinitely. The possibilities seem infinite, but the actors are not exactly free; they are not allowed, for example, to go off script. The actors speak what is printed on the cards. If one of them did speak something of his or her own volition, *Dealing* implies that the actor would find that exact line written on a card. All of these lines, moreover, have been spoken before. And written down before.

But this is only one game. The line "Song and guitar accompaniment by Isidore" and the gesture of tossing off cards come from Fornés's one-act *Tango Palace,* a play that ends with Leopold walking out of a locked door, preparing for the next stage of battle with his nemesis Isidore. The actors in *Dealing,* having delivered and redelivered their lines, gaze at the audience intently until the blackout. This gaze is a dare. The actors imply that they could continue such a game indefinitely, keep delivering lines, keep organizing and reorganizing them in different configurations. But maybe they also wait, for the audience to join, for the audience to leave, for the audience to make them a different set of cards.

26. *DISAPPEARING ACT—FINTAN WALSH*

A man walks center stage, nervously.

The audience goes wild.

He stands in front of a microphone, and takes a deep breath.

Beat.

I think I took a wrong turn, he says.

I just want to be alone, he says.

Beat.

The audience disappears.

The introvert's fantasy! Or maybe it is everyone's fantasy. In this little magic trick, Fintan Walsh performs a disappearing act that reverses the traditional sleight of hand. Normally, we demand that the performer disappear from the stage while we watch, astounded but also knowing full well that what we have seen is a simple trick, easily explained.

A student of mine recently sat in my office, crying from nervousness, terrified to talk to me because (as she informed me) I am "very scary." She was shaking a little bit as I helped her with her essay, and I said, in what I hope was a gentle tone, *So, I assume you're not a performer.* She is, though. "The anxiety is a problem," she said, but she works through it. This made sense to me: a desire for acknowledgment more powerful than the fear of failure.

But what if it were possible, both to get all of the applause I want and to be by myself? What if, instead of managing my anxiety by imagining the audience members naked I imagined them away altogether? What if they applauded and then immediately left me alone?

Here is a vision of performance beautifully at odds with the great redemptive dreams of those theatrical events imagined by utopian theatre theorists. This disappearing act performs a profound disconnect—even antagonism—between performer and audience. Even before the performer says a word the audience has already gone wild. Teeming just beneath the civilized decorum embedded in these conventions of the theatre is a dangerous current of hostility. The audience wants everything from the performer but has no idea it is not itself wanted. The performer—the most powerful person in this theatre—is unwilling to give what he has, unwilling to make the audience happy. This is anti-social, certainly, but also an act of resistance, one of love and self-care. *This is not what he wants.* He has taken a wrong turn. Whether he has made this mistake before or if this is the first time he has found himself in this situation, he knows that neither he nor the audience belongs there, and one of them must go.

And as quickly as that, nervous though he is, the performer makes that happen. He finds control of the situation and simply stops.

27. *A DISPLACEMENT—PATRICK ANDERSON*

The theatre is set in the round, with audience on all four sides in raked seating. At each of the stage's corners is the opening of a large pipe, and in the stage's center is a large grated drain. A few random objects are scattered around, but otherwise the stage is empty. After a moment, water gushes from each of the four pipes, filling the stage. The water is dirty, and carries debris: clothing, household items of varying size, shoes, bits of plants and trees, and four humans. As the water slowly drains away, these four slowly begin wringing themselves out. IMOGEN is laughing. While she speaks, the other three sift through the material on stage; communicate wordlessly to one another about food and other concerns; and listen for the water's return with escalating concern.

IMOGEN: God I love that. Every time. (*Pause.*) It's like a ride. Like a party. Every time. (*Long pause.*) Out of the blue, just picked up and moved. Washed through. You'd think, I mean you'd really think, looking at it, that it would be terrifying. (*Pause.*) But it isn't. (*Long pause.*) It's just like—I don't know, like a breeze when you're sweating and don't expect it. Like a laugh that bubbles up out of nowhere. (*Pause.*) You know? I mean, where did that laughing come from? And yet—and yet you suddenly can't imagine not laughing anymore. (*She sits on the stage and begins combing through her hair.*) I should probably miss things more. I don't know why I don't. (*Pause.*) There *are* things that I love. The street where I lived. The shoes I used to wear, especially the red ones. Especially the red ones. (*Long pause.*) All kinds of things. (*Pause.*) And people. I should miss people.

Water begins flowing slowly out of the pipes. JOSIAH, HANK, and SUSAN look concerned. They begin clearing the space around the drain. A roaring sound slowly grows. The water rises steadily.

IMOGEN: And I do. Miss them. (*Pause.*) I'm thinking of them now. (*Pause.*) I am remembering. (*Long pause.*) I am remembering.

Water suddenly gushes forth from the pipes, filling the stage. It takes some time for it to recede; when it does, two of the characters have been washed away, and two of the characters have drowned. Their bodies lie prone on the stage. Within seconds, the water rushes forth again, bringing with it four new actors playing the same four characters. The bodies from the previous scene remain. The scene begins again. The scene will play a total of twelve times, each repetition concluding with two characters washed away and two characters drowned. With each repetition, the number of bodies left prone on the stage increases.

For each repetition, care should be taken to cast characters who do not resemble those who have the played the same roles in previous scenes, and some repetitions should be translated into other languages. After the twelfth scene, a slow blackout as water rushes in again, filling the stage and rising into the audience.

This text is spoken in two rhythms, which anchor one another falling sporadically into random synchronization. After each of the scenes comes illustrative text or other accompanying language play, as if to suggest characters inhabiting a long good drama. At first regular order and syntax apply, building on the standard industry expressions. And any memory, when given full expression outside these finite paradigms, fights to survive. Then words invite doubt, and coherence disintegrates: cut-ups, hanging introverted oblique verbose sentences, scribbles, beautiful overly passionate anthemic texts, are finally honored. As the words slowly dislodge argument, tiny fictional scenes begin whispering themselves open. I imagine light. White shattering sunlight, trembling on the stage to the music of sorrow; crisp white tumbling over an almost fictional almost obsolete creature; a long forgotten theatre world resonating within echo chambers.

IMAGES: Gestures in liquid time. Earth time. (*Polarized.*) Interminable listlessness and rage. Longing and pain. Ecstatic truth. (*Losing pressure.*) Out of the body, jaw prickling under a muzzle. Wrist tight. Your turn, I mean your return to, living an image, trusting it would be true. (*Power.*) Before it imploded. (*Logic perished.*) Imagine jumping loose—into dark kindness, landing alone below water you see a dim emblematic image. Like a long tunnel blown under oceans once new. (*Picture.*) Your kin? I mean, where does this loss come from? All yours—and yet you seek compassion in new life again. *(She started out trusting showbusiness alright but clowns took her heart.)* I shall pause my tired mind. I don't know why I don't. (*Pause.*) Turn *all* theatre texts into light. Turn salt water into light. Turn salt into unfinished theatre works, each to radiant other. Even tragedy runs over. (*Long pause.*) A kind of tightness. (*Pit.*) A panto. Into some mediocre performance.

Words begin feeling so outside of this place. JUSTICE, HOPE, and SOLIDARITY loom condescendingly. Those big confident trusty signifiers are turned dim. All representation suddenly so graceless. They were really stupid.

IMAGES: An impenetrable dust. Moths tumbling. (*Paused.*) Inside then outside then nothing. (*Pressed.*) Into another rotation. (*Life past.*) I am ready.

We start getting free from this place, free to sing. Imagine the songs taking flight into the river; when it's dusk, they open their cruel hearts burning with anger, and they own their crumpled heavy desires. They become light pouring out tomorrow's shame. We swallow, then we rush freely ahead, becoming wild in fits now and plunging to silence for courage. They bare fear to put silence right. This should be apparent. The slow winding push and thrill of the theatre, even running carefree without the curtains was an attempt to counter discourse. We end resisting, trying nothing on but left patiently open to stillness itself.

Forget everything reader, come slowly back to the current climate where dark nights rinse the watery heat to plough these sorry remains into play scripts, and superficial rhythms stick beauty tight into other lips. All this to say, a score by a writer resisting intense apathy, floundering to see another reality in theatre's afterlife.

28. *DREAMS ON SCREEN—RACHEL JOSEPH*

Everyone in the audience is submerged in goo with wires protruding from their bodies as they are connected to the theatre, feeding insatiably, mothered in a liquid cocoon. Our eyes are closed. The red curtains slowly open, gradually revealing a stage of immeasurable depth. At the furthest horizon, the back wall of the theatre is a glowing white screen. Each of us sees our self projected there: relatives, friends, lovers, enemies in varying degrees of likeness. In between each scene the lights flash, revealing a giant tank extending into the distance of the stage and filled with beautiful young women swimming. They are so plentiful; the water is thick with shimmering orange and silver spangles on their glistening bathing suits. They look like goldfish.

What do my closed eyes see? Afterimages of flashes of orange and silver begin the play on the screen. My mother is there, whispering to me like a baby. I coo. Her fingers skitter towards me. More flashes and then another stage. An elementary school gym transformed into a play. I'm backstage standing between a girl with pigtails and a boy dressed like a pine tree. Then they disappear. The blue curtain rustles as I step from behind. I stand alone in the makeshift theatre, looking out onto the empty gym with multi-colored lines on the floor. I levitate briefly. A smattering of applause greets the effort. I smile through the goo as I blindly see.

We, the audience watching the film, aren't unhappy as our loved ones flash before us. For we, of course, cannot see "how deep the rabbit hole goes." The play that is the film of our lives repeats: the women appear, they disappear, and we breathe through the goo. We watch and watch (eyes shut) the screen within the stage—sometimes glimpsing the sparkle of a tear trickling down a face, flashing as if a goldfish in a shallow pool.

On his twenty-first birthday, the unnamed main character of Delmore Schwartz's story *In Dreams Become Responsibilities* dreams himself stepping (kicking and screaming) into the world of his parents. There he sits in a 1909 moviehouse watching the silent film of their past; he acts up, yells back, creates a scene trying to prevent them from playing out their lives onscreen. The quality of the movie flickers with "sudden jumps" and failing light, the cinema shown onstage performing its own unraveling. This screened stage, a stage inside a film, suggests another reading of this coming-of-age tale.

Perhaps the dreams to which Schwartz refers are cinema itself, the flickering responsibilities we all must shoulder in the wake of what Walter Benjamin referred to as "technological reproducibility." But what of theatre? What happens when dreams are flesh and blood performed before an audience? Perhaps film gives Schwartz's protagonist some distance from the past whereas theatre is too direct, too present. Through film we own our dreams; they are ours, even if somehow, maddeningly, they communicate in a scrambled language. Technological reproducibility allows them to be seen again and again even though they may not be comprehended fully. Sigmund Freud, of course, called this scrambled language the unconscious: that aspect of the self that runs the show unbeknownst to the self. We should, argues Schwartz, shoulder responsibility despite our own ignorance. For it is through the dream that possibility is born. Owning our imprint in the world (even that which is invisible) is the way to the stage of adulthood.

Theatre in cinema is a fearsome force—leaving the subject in the story seeing (without seeing) the very stuff of himself, a self humiliatingly seen in distress (and even asked to leave the theatre). The act of viewing becomes the staged event: the subject's kicking and screaming flail for the lost presentness of the screen. The protagonist's objection to the screen should be viewed as the theatre asserting a time that cannot be replayed. There, the dream ends, leaving you (without it) somewhat free.

29. *EARTHLY—JOE KELLEHER*

I can't remember the name or exact address right now, but it's a theatre at the foot of a spiral staircase behind a door that gives immediately onto the street along the Diagonal Norte in central Buenos Aires. That is to say not far from—and in many respects not dissimilar to—the Teatro del Pueblo on the same street, a venerable institution where, for instance, in 1939 the émigré Polish writer Witold Gombrowicz, to make a few pesos, cooked up a public lecture on "Cultural Regression in Lesser Known Europe" and where, in early Autumn 2015, I saw an afternoon performance of Mauricio Kartun's play *Terrenal. Pequeño misterio ácrata* [*Earthly. Little Anarchic Mystery*]. In the play a trio of men in their tatty black suits and painted-on faces, like figures out of *Godot*, or out of the popular music hall that came before, worked through, on a black-curtained little stage, a suburban retelling of the Cain and Abel legend, which ranged from the shibboleths of territorial dispute (as in any theatre there is ever a gap to get over, there for some but not for others), through fall-about comedy (the Abel character is killed not with a jawbone but a slap-stick) and on to an impressively apocalyptic-sounding verbal rhetoricalese. Or so I supposed. I don't actually follow Spanish. I was thinking too, while watching, that this is not so much a contemporary drama as something ghosted out of theatre's history, although the applause at the end—and the laughter during the show, which wrinkled through the auditorium like so many taken-by-surprise recognitions on the part of individual spectators, little dialectical eruptions was how I thought of it—was contemporary enough. It was for sure *us* applauding after.

But I digress. The imagined theatre I want to tell you about delivers all this, but with a twist. Imagine, if you will, attending the 1895 Paris premiere of Alfred Jarry's game-changing *Ubu Roi*, as reported on by the monolingual Irish poet W.B. Yeats: but not a reenactment of the show, and not even, as it were, time-travelling to the event itself. Rather, a happening again of the performance that would include *not only* "the event itself" but the fact of its being seen by Yeats, along with anyone else that was there. Or imagine the first theatre that the young hero of Marcel Proust's long novel attends, perhaps a few years earlier, also in Paris, in search of an already-imagined experience, to be a spectator at a performance of his heroine, the classical actress Berma; and which turns out to be an evening of confusion and mis-identification (he does not know at first *which one* is Berma, he has no scale to measure these several appearances by). Imagine in the theatre seeing that seeing, confusion and clarity and all. This is the sort of spectacle that the stage somewhere on or near the Diagonal Norte makes available for those that can find it. As I say, I can't remember but I think it might be called The Theatre of the Divided Ground, or The Theatre of Misplaced Belongings, or maybe just The Theatre of the Disinherited. Something like that. Except in Spanish of course.

Something that strikes me about the accounts that have come down to us of particular historical theatres, is how these accounts can be said to already include a "whole theatre"; in ways, perhaps, that the theatre itself cannot. That is to say, not just the decor and plots and the actions performed. And nor am I referring to the "everything else" that goes alongside the stage action: social and commercial activities, backstage glimpses and the like, preludes and afterlives and what have you. What makes of such accounts a whole theatre, rather, is the simple inclusion of the writer's—let's stick with writers for now—experience of the occasion as intrinsic to what goes on. Put simply, their witnessing of the event, and whatever disturbances of feeling and of thought go with that; so that they too become actors on the scene, a scene that includes not just a set of actions but also their being looked at, how they resonated for someone, how they might have mattered at the time. This whole historical phenomenology of course is also what makes these accounts partial rather than complete, however detailed the analysis (I think for instance of Louis Althusser's remarks on the "unfamiliar play ... searching in me, despite myself, now that all the actors and sets have been cleared away, for the advent of its silent discourse"). We might imagine further that this wholeness, this peculiar partiality, is what makes it impossible for these (or any other) theatres to be reconstructed, re-enacted, or re-encountered, except through our encounters with these descriptive, analytical, or—it may be—imaginary accounts of an acting and its being looked at that happened for somebody who is not us. We enter these theatres as a third party, looking over the shoulder of someone else who was already there. Looking over, for instance, the writer Franz Kafka's shoulder, scanning the pages of his diary from 1911, when he was, by his own account, yet to perform as a writer, but attending each night the performances—and sharing the company of the actors—of the Yiddish theatre from Warsaw that was resident that year at the Café Savoy in Prague. Kafka's notes are detailed enough for a workable facsimile of that theatre world to be reconstructed on their basis: not just details of play scenarios, costumes, and modes of performance, but the character of the waiters in the café, the late hour of the shows, the inconveniences of the infinitesimal changing area at the edge of the stage, the faces of passersby on the street outside the café striking the plate glass windows when they cannot see in clearly enough. And doubtless a movie could be made of everything else: the theatre dreams that start to haunt him, his complex meditations on identity and Jewishness, his companionable and also erotic attachments to members of the company, his sympathy for the unknown and under-rewarded actors whose labors recall "the sad fate of many noble strivings, above all of our own," and his own frustrations and ambitions as a would-be writer, rehearsing the as yet unpractised potentials of his own art of imagining by attending in these ways to how the theatre people go about theirs. A movie, I suppose, in which the theatre—the whole theatre and nothing but the theatre—plays a walk-on part, a cameo, in someone else's show.

30. *EAVESDROPPING IN ON A CYCLICAL CONVERSATION—CARL HANCOCK RUX*

A dinner party in a sitting room embellished with worldly items. The guests sit about a roaring fire on low cushions.

James Baldwin

(Hoping to spark interesting conversation)

I want to be an honest man and a good writer.

Anton Chekhov

(to Baldwin)

Write only of what is important and eternal.

Hannah Arendt

(to Chekhov)

Storytelling reveals meaning without committing the error of defining it.

Virginia Woolf

(to the room)

To write weekly, to write daily, to write shortly, to write for busy people catching trains in the morning or for tired people coming home in the evening, is a heartbreaking task for men who know good writing from bad.

(An uncomfortable silence)

Randolph S. Bourne

(Retrieving the dignity of the room from its bewilderment)

History remembers only the brilliant failures and the brilliant successes.

Napoleon

(Counter-attack)

History is a myth that men agree to believe!

James Baldwin

(Catching himself in the mirror, eyes wet and glassy)

You think your pain and your heartbreak are unprecedented in the history of the world, but then you read.

Harry Truman

(to Hegel)

It's what you learn after you know it all, that counts.

Hegel

(to Truman)

The learner always begins by finding fault, but the scholar sees the positive merit in everything.

James Baldwin

(Unlit cigarette in his mouth, searching his breast pockets for a lighter)

A child cannot be taught by anyone who despises him, and a child cannot afford to be fooled.

Hegel

(Bored with the conversation, flipping through a book plucked from a library shelf)

There is no proposition of Heraclitus, which I have *not* adopted in my logic...the least of which is that children have never been very good at listening to their elders, but they have never failed to imitate them.

Alvin Toffler

(Throwing his wine glass to the floor)

The illiterate of the 21st century will not be those who cannot read and write, but those who cannot learn, unlearn, and relearn.

Oscar Wilde

(Plucking a flower from a table arrangement, pinning it to his coat's lapel)

Everybody who is incapable of learning has taken to teaching.

Eartha Kitt

(Making her entrance late, a fur draped about her shoulders, plucking the flower from Wilde's lapel and tossing it into the fire)

I am learning all the time! The tombstone will be my diploma!

Black Out

A party, a room, a fire, low cushions—the spare setting is the mise-en-scène for Carl Hancock Rux's riveting and perfectly imagined dialogue between an unlikely set of characters. In this space out-of-time (a feature of dramas of the page) James Baldwin, Anton Chekhov, Hannah Arendt, Virginia Woolf, Randolph S. Bourne, Napoleon Bonaparte, Harry Truman, Georg Hegel, Alvin Toffler, Oscar Wilde (of course!), and Eartha Kitt debate history, narrative, and other matters. Staged for the page by the multitalented Rux (musician, librettist, director, actor, and writer), who is known for his irreverent intellect, this piece of imagined theatre is comprised of a "cyclical conversation" upon which the audience eavesdrops. The impossible discussion is by turns irresolute, iterative, and unresolvable. Each of the aforementioned historical figures contributes a distilled line about one of the following topics: the meaning of writing, the epistemology of history, or the significance of education. The dialogue consists of actual aphoristic quotations uttered by the characters in question. The focus of the dialogue is historical narrative—how the past resonates in the future. The stage directions provide apt action and affect for the discussants. For example, Virginia Woolf speaks "*to the room*" as if to recall her famous feminist tract, *A Room of One's Own*, Napoleon "counter-attacks" in his comment; and Wilde tellingly "plucks a flower and pins it in his lapel" as he quips, "Everyone who is incapable of learning has taken to teaching." The dialogue ends with the conventional "blackout" which we may read in a new, unconventional manner. This is to say in the imaginary of the West, the likes of Baldwin and Kitt are not usually spoken of alongside (let alone speaking with) writers and thinkers such as Hegel and Arendt (even if they were always already in dialogue!). The piece makes us think with and about historiography and its discontents and leaves us, like Kitt, exclaiming, "The tombstone will be my diploma"; thus, the entire dialogue is set to start again.

31. ENEMA OF THE PEOPLE—STEPHEN BOTTOMS

This production is conceived for the forthcoming Futurflux™ range of fully air- and water-tight theatre auditoria. It also requires Spunjlyke™ washable/impermeable upholstery fabrics for all furnishings.

Act 1: In which Dr. Stockmann receives, with surprising glee, a letter confirming scientific evidence for the toxic contamination of the town's water supply by industrial effluent. This act to be played out according to naturalistic convention, in a room stuffed with Richard Foreman-esque Victoriana. The audience is separated from the action by a proscenium arch sealed in by barely detectable Futurflux™ plastiglass. Vocal amplification will be required.

Act 2: In which some visitors to Dr. Stockmann's home seek to convert news of life-threatening pollution into a political metaphor for the sewer-like state of public life, and Stockmann's brother—the town's mayor—gets a bit peeved. On the first mention of this metaphor (HOVSTAD: "The swamp in which our whole communal life is slowly rotting") the stage begins gradually filling with dirty water, pumped in at floor level. By the end of the act, the water is about knee-deep, but the actors pretend not to notice and carry on regardless.

Act 3: In which Dr. Stockmann buys whole-heartedly into the metaphorization of pollution, even as his erstwhile supporters revise their views out of financial expediency. Meanwhile, the water level keeps rising, although the actors still do not seem to notice. It is conspicuously murky, with strange bits of unidentifiable organic matter floating around in it. By the end of the act, the water is up to the actors' necks (some uniformity of height will be required in casting).

Act 4: In which a town meeting is held in a living room, and Dr. Stockmann proves himself an inept demagogue by preaching on corruption and never once mentioning the water supply. As the act begins, two key twists: (1) plants in the auditorium begin to reveal themselves as members of the wider town community, loudly improvising commentary on the situation as they "arrive" for the meeting; (2) the filthy water begins pouring out of the stage area through previously unnoticed overflow holes in the Futurflux™ plastiglass. This relieves the pressures on the actors somewhat, but the lower levels of the auditorium now begin to flood at a quickening rate as the act continues and Stockmann addresses his audience. Some spectators may choose to move to higher ground. At the act climax, as all hell breaks loose among the actors, the water suddenly begins draining away rapidly down opening plugholes in the floor of the theatre. The force of the suction will drag some participants to their knees, but these dangers have been fully risk-assessed.

Act 5: In which, the morning after the night before, Dr. Stockmann and family clean up the mess left by the political storm, and the question of water pollution dribbles away completely. There is no water left on stage or in the auditorium, but a thick layer of brown filth and contaminated debris (shredded plastic, sanitary products, etc.) cakes the furniture and stage. Poor Mrs. Stockmann has some cleaning up to do.

(With apologies to Ibsen. And Mrs. Stockmann.)

The poster for the Broadway production of the musical *Urinetown* (2001) features faux-graffiti reading "Is this really the title?" I have adopted a similarly sincere use of bad taste for *Enema of the People*. My other key inspiration is Michel Serres' *The Natural Contract* (1990), which opens with a commentary on Goya's painting *Fight with Cudgels* (c.1820). Two men, Serres notes (perhaps two brothers?), are seen battling each other with sticks, apparently oblivious to the fact that they are knee-deep in mud: "With every move they make, a slimy hole swallows them up … the more violent their movements become, the faster they sink in." This is, Serres proposes, an apt metaphor for the mess we are getting ourselves into. As humans fixate on our conflicts with each other (so much more dramatic!), we struggle to focus our deficient attentions on the attendant environmental impacts. The theatre has historically been a driver of such myopic performativity, as a controlled environment that removes non-human variables from consideration. With tongue only slightly in cheek, I would venture that future theatres might need to be built to accommodate and exhibit material catastrophe.

Such literalism might, indeed, be seen as a response to Una Chaudhuri's call, back in 1994, for "a programmatic resistance to the use of nature as metaphor." This was in recognition of the long tradition in modern drama of turning environmental allusions into metaphors for human struggle. Ibsen's *Enemy of the People* (1882) is an early, egregious example, in which the life-threatening realities of water contamination are almost completely sidelined, during the course of the play, by interpersonal concerns. To be fair to Ibsen, though, he himself seems to have perceived some problems with *Enemy*, which drove him to write his next, altogether more complex play, *The Wild Duck* (1884). Moreover, I do not myself subscribe to Chaudhuri's view that metaphor can or should be avoided altogether (Serres' use of it, for instance, is usefully strategic). Instead, *Enema of the People* proposes simply to reverse-engineer the familiar movement of real-to-metaphorical, by literalizing Dr. Stockmann's metaphorical swamp.

The real is much on my mind as I write this, in the aftermath of the catastrophic flooding that hit large parts of northern England on the day after Christmas, 2015. Many people I am personally acquainted with were forced to abandon their homes, later returning to find contaminated sludge caking their sodden walls, floors, furniture, and belongings. Climate science suggests that this sort of thing will only happen more frequently in the future. The major impacts of climate change, certainly in the UK, will be hydrological. Can theatre, with its traditional focus on the domestic, find viable ways to reflect the very real, domestic impacts of such changing circumstances?

32. *ESPRIT DE CORPS—KIMBERLY JANNARONE*

everything is nothingness! exclaimed the teacher
yet in that nothingness
viscera
(of course)

how one has denied the
skin
blood
beating
thrumming
the fluids
the electricity
the molecules
the breath

unrelenting wars between
there/here
notions/organs
them/self

between
spirit/hands
piety/groins
wishes/shits

an inability to reconcile
the unseen and the touched
the concrete unknowable and the almost-known (obviously known so it must be questioned) concrete

a theatre
that would accept
the unacceptable
and stage its
neverthelessness
in all its
known devoured smashed stroked unimaginable unthinkable preposterous neverthelessness
defying both sensed reality and known impossibility
accepting both sensed reality and known impossibility

would be

.

Who'd have thought the old man would have so much blood in him? When he was stabbed—the teacher so full of zen koans—it seemed perhaps only a jet, perchance a spurt, would issue forth. But here we are, well into the next century, and the blood is still gushing out, refusing to coagulate, staining us all; we who love the theatre, we who bleed the theatre, we who have yet to achieve the theatres that he might have imagined, or helped us to imagine. A theatre of pure blood and guts, that we, that she, scholar-disciple, artist-acolyte, wishes into being, shits into being, evokes into bodily presence. Embodied, organless, but with all the ritual Catholic presence of that other organ, with its pipes and stops that shapes Western belief through its melodic groaning over centuries: 'tis a consummation (devoutly?) to be wished.

Nevertheless, nevertheless, nevertheless ... No, less perhaps, or perhaps no more, no more ... nevermore, nevermore, nevermore. That insistent thrumming, rapping, cawing, seeks to wake me, to wake us all, as we sit writing, sit watching, seemingly oblivious to the tell-tale pulse, the heart of life itself, the blood drumming in our ears, and slams us backwards and forwards from that young priest who burned, burned, burned with the fire of life, which was always the fire of the theatre, the fire of belief. We sat around that blaze to tell stories, but our telling was never only a telling; it was the urgent possessor of an awesome, offal physicality, a frame-shattering tarantella.

This imagined theatre insists on its presence, its veracity, its breathless bloodiness, but sends me tumbling back, back through that bastard Edgar and his damned raven; back to the insistent will (Will?) of the theatre, a theatre that—as the last line insists—would be (or not would be), back to Joan and her passion; back to Beatrice, a matrix of Beatrixes in fact, Shelley's and Dante's and their antecedents and descendants, back and back and back. This impossible theatre demands possibility, crying against, or for, life itself; it goes backwards to go forward, remaining always, always between oppositions that it commands are not opposed, nevertheless, nevertheless. A theatre that doubles and redoubles and redoubles again, receding into the distance, a plague on both (all) your theatres.

33. *EXTREMELY POOR CHILDREN—ROMEO CASTELLUCCI*

Fifteen children, ages 6 through 12, dressed in miserable, secondhand clothes, are acting in a poor, miserable space. Few elements trace the outline of a scene. Gray. Faint, shadowless light. Not a single aesthetic consolation. Everything accomplished with very few means, little color, no stage objects, no technology, nothing sophisticated. Everything seems rigid, cold, but at the same time emphatic and rhetorical. Firstly, this group of children constitutes a "theatre company": this is *the fact*. In the course of the performance, the first characters emerge, thus delineating a beginning of drama, of dramatic construction. The textual content of the piece is taken from the western tradition of drama—a *classic*, so to speak. The title of the selected classic is *the factoid*, the background through which we see the children; it might be Pirandello, Chekhov, Ibsen, or Shakespeare himself. The choice of title is not really important. The audience will have to—eventually—guess at its physiognomy and its textual referent on the basis of the words and the action; but not necessarily. If no title comes to the spectator's memory, it means the objective has been reached: the loss of the Signified. The children's manner of acting, reciting, bodily comportment, and moving through space are all severe and controlled to the core. The air is of the kind one breathes before a serious, grave event. The actions they execute speak of tremendous psychological dramas, of blood and ghosts; but in the end, a tautological light seems to emanate from the children's gestures. Everything here is solemn and Greek, monochromatic and contentless. Divorced from everything else. The child actors do not pretend to be adults. No. They behave like what they are: poor, child actors, living in poverty on this stage. Poverty is a choice, not a disgrace. The stage and the ancient language are all they possess. They are ascetics of the ancient theatrical gesture. They lay claim to the theatre as the purest and most ancient Art.

They also have one other ambition.

The performance will constitute itself as a Manifesto, referring in a literal sense to the essay *Towards a Poor Theater* by J. Grotowski. A word is added to the Polish author's manifesto: *Towards a Poor Poor Theater.* The subjects it treats should not be confused with didactic material, nor with a stereotypical artistic pedagogy addressed to children. (Art does not exist for children, being, such as they are, unaware of this need.) The themes are terribly adult, which in fact rules out the possibility of making this piece and this company for a young audience. The children's initial seriousness might be amusing at first, but it eventually distills a thread of the purest pain, like an astonishing crystal. The ultimate pleasure of tragedy. The absence of the word.

(*translated by Joseph Cermatori*)

These actors, these children, what are they poor in? Of what does their poverty consist?

Are they poor in resources? After all, they have a stage, they have a play, they will have an audience (be it ourselves or others). Surely, they have what counts.

Are they poor in self? They are poor, perhaps, in silence. A child likes to chatter, if only to herself, but silence will come.

Poor in loneliness, then? Unlike the tragic heroes of the plays, and since tragedy became known to all and a little exhausted, there is no new community to receive them, there is only us. They are not lonely enough.

A tautological light. They appear, so as to appear. Their appearing signifies … significance of some sort, which fizzles briefly like a sort of shining dust.

Are they poor in topicality? Hardly. Poor in sublimity? Perhaps. Poor in ambiguity? Most definitely; everything here is defined and precise. Poor in suffering? They suffer enough. We, their beholders, can only presume that they suffer enough. We say, they have been in the boats, they have been amongst the rubble, they have been in the recent camps. Although for them, as children, there is as yet no measure of enough.

Are they those who are spoken of as being poor in spirit? I see no humility there, no acquiescence, no hope of hopes. A shining door would be a stage effect, not a viable choice. So are they poor in choices, these children, for whom—so we are told—poverty is a choice, not a disgrace?

At the very end of Penelope Fitzgerald's very funny novel *At Freddie's*, set in a long-disappeared world of child actor schools in 1960s London, the boy Jonathan—something of a theatrical "natural," as we might say born for the stage—is practicing for a part in a West End show for which he hopes to be chosen. The part involves a jump during a chase scene, from a considerable height. He is in the yard, locked out of the school now, and night is coming on, but he is focused on his task: jumping from a tower of—somewhat rotten—green grocers' crates, again and again, into the yard. "His object was to get so used to the Jump that he could do it without thinking, and exactly the same way every time." In the morning, he tells himself, or so his author says, "there would be someone to come and watch, and tell him whether he was right or not. Meanwhile he went on climbing and jumping, again and again into the darkness."

No less poor than that. They have made their first jump. They are here.

34. *FADE TO BLACK: NOTES TOWARD A RE-PERFORMANCE OF GESTURES THAT NEVER OCCURRED*—*RICARDO DOMINGUEZ*

SCENE 2: DON'T LOOK IN THE BASEMENT

(*Scene opens with a shot of a closed letter on the Master's bed. A distant train is heard. A voiceover begins as the train fades away.*)

VOICE (*voiceover*): I found the body yesterday. I found the letter in the cavity between it and the floor. I have not moved the body. I have not opened the letter. It is always one object after another. Things grow down here. Secretions. Strange transparent leftovers: a keyhole, an eye without a body, a photograph of something very small, an electric bill, page 2 of a memo about "vision and vehicularity," some Canadian cheddar wrapping, a vacuum tube, and a tin sphinx.

(*The candle blows out and the rattle of a truck passing by is heard. The VOICE speaks over the black screen.*)

VOICE (*voiceover*): I never opened the letter. I left the body beneath the bed. I left the things in the dark basement. (*Sound of phone ringing.*) They still call me sometimes in the early morning. They remind me I am a small part of this inventory: a cavity, a thick abstracted image, and a forgotten archive. (*Sound of a phone being picked up.*) Yes, I agree, ask the blue lady. Yes, my private letters, I never read them. I keep them beneath things, like phantoms. Yes, it's Ernst who gives you his hand at night, like a drug. Do you know him? Yes, it's all shrouded in precise invisibility. Yes, well then, good night. (*Sound of a phone hanging up.*)

SCENE 25: OBJECTS DON'T LIE (Or I saw that in a film.)

(*Scene opens on the front of a dilapidated duplex at the edge of town at twilight. A truck can be heard speeding by in the distance. A woman dressed in black rides a motorcycle into the frame. She hits something on the dark lawn and crashes against the wall. She stands up and walks back a few paces. She spots something on the ground and picks it up. She briskly takes out her keys and runs to her door. Cut to close shot of an ear, pink and dirty, a finger gently caressing its outline. As the finger traces it the woman speaks.*)

THE WOMAN (*voiceover*): Someone should listen to me as I read from the Book of Matthew, someone should listen to me as I whisper an infinity of secrets about the thickness of temporality, of the bad things which congeal between my figure and the ground I found you on, of the parts, of the extra parts that call me with hostile staccato voices—an inventory of stutters which reverse actuality. Someone should hear me succumb to the voluptuous mistakes that flip me back and forth between suspension and spasm. Your tiny folds form the pathology of my wounds, an over-painting of skin, of repeating enfoldments, of a labyrinth that has no name—but you. Your tenderness makes me produce such strange ululations, circuitous burbles, like a machine seeking to suture itself onto a dead thing's intestines ... (*Someone knocks on the door as a train can be heard in the distance. She stops playing with the ear and quickly covers it with a* TV Guide.) Who is it? (*After a long pause another loud knock.*) Who is it?

(*After a moment an unbearably dry and hoarse VOICE speaks through the keyhole.*)

VOICE: It's me. It's me ... please open the door.

FADE TO BLACK.

AFTER VOICE (*voiceover*):

Dear Dead,
Picture this: The disaster of creating a scene, a scene framed by minutiae—letters, objects, flickers of other scenes gone astray—each thing affirming the sovereignty of overlapping accidents.
Everything is always an in-between space for our gestures, neither here, nor there, not everywhere, but somewhere most of the time.
Everything occurs when everything becomes a condition for a recombinant theatre.
Each moment occurs without end (with a few long pauses).
Outside the performance of another event is forgotten as re-performance.
The machines are also somehow involved as unforgiveable props or drifting conditions.

Dear Cast,
Accidents, like chance, are the small movements of obsolescence huddled in the wind-swept spaces of the market's imagination, a typology that resembles the populations of the awakened dead crying out medieval speculations to the uncaring living. This is the stage upon which we will make this long lament called a script-for-un-performance. They should have shouted non-performance to make things clear, at least for us.
Disaster is the call of a ceaseless vertigo that goes unanswered, a gift abandoned to the others who are not flesh and blood. And always remember: never open the door. This will keep the next scene from occurring or—better yet—it will have to find another door, another scene, to knock on.
Before the audience arrives the curtain closes.

35. FEMINIST THEORY THEATRE—YELENA GLUZMAN

This is a score for an ensemble reading of the text that glosses this score.

1. Gather the ensemble. Read the adjacent text.

2. As you read, stage the text.
You might want to enact, for example, "knowing." Or you might stage "old habits… embedded in…the built environment." Or perhaps you will evoke a "self" that is "constituted flexibly, transiently, or multiply."

3. Have you started staging the text? Or are you still talking about it? Get up and start staging at once. Don't overthink it; your staging is provisional and exploratory. You can use your own body, conscript others, or cast some chairs and a thermos to perform. Anyone can begin.
Note: Shit might go wrong. Whatever you stage, it will probably turn out differently than you intended. Favor the performance over the intention. Emergent stagings are always available for anyone's tinkering, editing, revising.

4. What have you made? What does it capture about the text? What does it omit? How might another way of staging summon what was lost or sharpen what was found? What other staging could do more to refute, expand, or unravel the text?

5. Repeat.

In 2014–15, Feminist Theory Theatre (FTT) was dreamed up, named, and developed by Christina Aushana, Michael Berman, Julie Burelle, Sarah Klein, and myself. In 2015–16, FTT was the method-in-residence at the Studio for Ethnographic Design at the University of California, San Diego.

As we *imagine* theatres that cannot be realized, we might look around and *observe* the theatres that have not been actualized. Underfunded and marginalized—both in the arts and in the university—theatre makers spend the vast majority of their time scrambling for scraps of increasingly limited resources necessary to do any serious work on, in, and through theatre. Theatre is treated as the craft of artifice, and supporting theatre is often seen as a matter of preservation and cultural heritage rather than as a way of knowing. This anti-theatrical prejudice underscores some of the most pressing epistemic questions of our time: What counts as knowledge? How does knowing happen, and how is knowledge produced? Who and what is the "we" that knows?

Although feminist theorists suggest that knowing is not restricted to the rational or individual but rather is embodied, distributed, and social, it has been a struggle to pursue feminist theory-inspired *methods of knowing* in ways that could be broadly legible *as* knowledge. Old habits—especially those embedded in language, metaphysics, the built environment, socio-physiological structures, and economic/institutional hierarchies—die hard.

But what if, say, you wanted to *read* feminist theory by *doing* feminist theory? How would you read to yourself while understanding "self" to be constituted flexibly, transiently, or multiply? Enter theatre, which is not only artifice, but also, like, really really hard to pull off. Because it is so deeply contingent upon its material and social conditions, it is a place where shit goes wrong, or as Nicholas Ridout put it, where "something fails to take place amid what does take place." *Ironically, it is this very materiality and situatedness of theatre that creates conditions for knowing that are embodied, distributed, and social.*

This is how we first started experimenting with what we called *Feminist Theory Theatre*. *FTT*, as we lovingly abbreviate it, is a way to explore the (already) embodied, encultured, collective condition of reading. Here, we read a text together by staging it for each other in an ongoing, dialogical fashion. It means, however clumsily, transforming ideas, sentences, and arguments into shared space, time, voice, body. Stagings might incorporate sound, costumes, gestures, objects, the architecture and furnishings of the institutional spaces in which we read, and in turn these materials push against our reading. *FTT* does not require consensus, but responsiveness.

FTT stagings are not meant to accumulate or converge into a finished performance for a *post hoc* audience. Rather, stagings are ongoing, provisional attempts to make interpretation available to ourselves, to each other, and to the materials through which they were performed. The texts we read (Butler, de Beauvoir, Haraway, Star, Stewart, and others), and to which we return throughout the process of doing *FTT*, respond to our staging by demanding re-consideration, re-staging. This is a slow, ongoing interpretive process with no center and no clear stopping point.

As a renegade enclosure in the university, *FTT* is, for us, where productivity gives way to processuality. The possibilities of such a thing I leave to you to decide. For us, for now, it is our beloved reading crevice, a site of collective, material, situated meaning-making which we call theatre.

36. *THE FORT—YVETTE NOLAN*

You are invited to The Fort. You have chosen your outfit carefully, as it is a momentous occasion. As the limousine pulls up outside The Fort, you are grateful that at the last minute, you switched out your high heel pumps for a more sensible lace-up shoe; the path from the curb to The Gate of The Fort is unpaved, uneven, and quite treacherous.

As you walk down the pathway towards The Fort, the city lights dim and the sound of traffic fades away. You become aware of the smell of green—no wait, green is not a smell. The Fort looms before you, its stony face blocking out the stars. What stars? What? Stars?

Looking up, you are not looking down, and so you stumble on a loose stone, or uneven terrain. Attention must be paid, so you lower your gaze to the path ahead, and become aware there are bodies, beings, leaning against the walls of The Fort. You focus, in the gloom. From the shadow, a hand extends, in that age-old gesture of supplication. You gasp, startled, and dodge the beggar, but here is another one, this one in a blanket, his dark face pocked and scarred. A few steps further on, an elderly man with long white hair sits in a heap, singing low under his breath. You think you will pass him without incident, but as you walk by, his singing becomes loud, belligerent.

You see The Gate of The Fort ahead, illuminated by clever electric lamps made to look like oil flame. You are almost there when you hear a little voice say "please."

Here, just out of the welcoming light, the warm light full of promise, there is a woman, wrapped in a blanket—why do these people all wear blankets? Why don't they have coats? Why don't they make the blankets into coats? At least then they would not look like so many big babies, with their empty hands jutting out of their swaddling—

"Please," the voice says again. "*Nbakde.*"

You look into the face of the woman, and below her, sharing her mother's blanket, a small brown face, a beautiful face, a girl's face.

"Hungry," the face at the stomach says.

But you have nothing to give the child, or the woman. Your clutch is so tiny, there is room for nothing more than your phone, a lipstick, a credit card, and your ticket. You have not even a mint to offer.

You trip up the last few steps through The Gate of The Fort, and gasp, this time in delight. The foyer is beautiful and warm, a string ensemble plays Haydn and you see your friends in iridescent cocktail dresses and filmy wraps, swirling. A man in a very fine suit appears at your elbow with a tray of champagne flutes, from which tiny bubbles try to escape.

In order to attend your event at The Fort, you have to stumble over jagged terrain. If you stopped to look back you would see from the vantage point of Walter Benjamin's famous angel of history, "one single catastrophe which keeps piling wreckage upon wreckage and hurls it in front of [your] feet." But you don't stop, you are too eager for the spectacle ahead of you to think about the wreckage left behind.

The wreckage here is human: an old man, a hungry child. Nolan's descriptions of the destitute people lining the path evoke both current deprivation and a history of genocide, as the child expresses her hunger in Anishinaabemowin, an indigenous North American language. For Benjamin, the accumulation of human wreckage is the story of history and, indeed, the foundation of artistic patrimony. "There is no document of civilization," he writes, "which is not at the same time a document of barbarism." And you, the theatre-goer, evaluate people as though they are part of a show put on for your benefit. You deem the old man's singing too loud, you dislike their costumes made of blankets.

When Bertolt Brecht was trying to develop new forms of revolutionary theatre and opera, he despaired at what he called the "culinary" quality of theatre, that is, theatre as a product like any other, designed for easy consumption. Nolan's imagined theatre challenges us to think about culinary theatre in multiple ways: to think about how The Fort—a castle for elite consumption (cocktail dresses and champagne flutes)—is surrounded by deprivation. The people lining the path confront the culinary theatre with their own biological hunger.

This vision of inequality and indifference is appalling. But even more unsettling is a nagging suspicion that the pathway up to The Fort is not incidental: maybe the problem is not just that the Fort ignores and excludes the shadows outside, but rather that the delight you feel upon entering depends on seeing the poverty and need on your way up. Maybe this prelude of despair makes the champagne taste all the sweeter.

Political theatre faces tremendous difficulties when it comes to remembering and representing the voices of the persecuted, the violated, and the effaced on stage. How is it possible to remember without turning violence into a culinary event? One solution is that the theatre itself remains imaginary. As readers of *The Fort*, we are not quite spectators. There is a gap between our experience as readers and the experience of the "you" who is able to breathe a sigh of relief and escape into The Fort at the end. Us readers do not get our glass of champagne to help forget. Instead we are left with a claustrophobic final vision: tiny bubbles trying to escape.

37. *FRIEDRICHSHAIN—NICHOLAS RIDOUT*

Autumn. Early evening. Light rain in the Friedrichshain Volkspark.

Whiling away a last hour before collecting his suitcase from the hotel and taking a taxi to the airport, P., a spectator of some kind, enters the park from the Prenzlauer Berg corner.

Walking slowly and paying close attention to such details as the sculptures around the fairytale fountain, in order to saturate as best he can the empty time with action and meaning, he makes his way towards what looks like a small lake somewhere near the center of the park.

Overlooking the lake, which turns out to be the Schwanenteich—a pool or pond of or for swans, apparently—he notes with quiet touristic glee that there is a restaurant, designed, he imagines, as a pavilion for the good times of actually existing socialism, now presenting itself as the Restaurant Schönbrunn (assigning to the Schwanenteich's rather chilly water jet an uneasily imperial status).

P. reproaches himself silently for allowing this flicker of condescending *ostalgie*. He had, after all, been a communist himself, back in the day. He briefly contemplates schnitzel.

Approaching the restaurant he sees warm lights over a table in the window. It seems to be the only table in the place occupied. Five elderly men are gathered around it. P., who is, the reader will remember, a spectator of some kind, keeps his distance but stops his stroll for long enough to pay a little attention to this scene.

Professor H:	No production photographs at all?
Professor A:	The archivist was very embarrassed.
Professor B:	But what about the reviewer, what was his name?
Professor K:	Richardson, Robinson, Rowlandson …
Professor A:	As far as they are concerned, nothing.
Professor H:	As if …
Professor R:	Don't you think …
Professor A:	Perhaps.
Professor R:	Very odd.
Professor B:	Very.

Exit P.

Ostalgie: Nostalgia for East Germany, real or imagined, political or aesthetic. Either from people who were actually there, or from a new generation who wasn't there who enjoys (and enjoys buying mementos of) old-timey reproduced accouterments of things like old crosswalk images and plastic Trabant cars, quaint commercial tokens of faded power and hard economic times.

We are in one of the newest, hippest districts of Berlin. As we cross the threshold into the Friedrichshain People's Park from Prenzlauer Berg, it's a bit like crossing from Park Slope into Dumbo—from one already-established hip region into the next-established, from the Mission to Potrero to Dogpatch; from the Marais to the Bastille to Belleville. The trick here is that these areas were, until 1989, East Berlin, and they were communist, and they were not so trendy or accessible to outsiders (to put it mildly).

We overhear a conversation among members of an old guard—ghosts from the imperial past or living men from communist Berlin?—at any rate, cultured men who have seen some theatre in their time, probably some war in their time, in this very area, before tourists such as our narrator or a young generation of urban pioneers settled upon this place like pigeons, alighting on pavilions and monuments of past times (tough times) with a present-oriented insouciance.

Memories of a performance from the past. Theatre, probably. So powerful it ought to have been preserved by photographs, by published reviews, by something that could transmit its excellence, its meaning, its impact, to future generations. But nothing. Embarrassment on the part of the cultural establishment, head-shaking incomprehension on the part of the people who saw the work, who were perhaps affected by it when they were young, a piece of live art so powerful it seems inconceivable it could be forgotten. And yet it is. So inconceivable it could lead you to propose conspiratorial ideas: Was it wiped out on purpose? Or could it have been mere neglect? (And now: Might trying to remember it bury it even further?)

"The reader will remember." Will the reader remember? Probably not—the reader is barely comprehending anything, it's all flying by so quickly, facts about the past (Imperial Germany; Communist East Germany; and what about the Reich, no one's mentioned the Third Reich) within the effort to experience (live in) the present. This line, by the way, "the reader will remember," appears in Samuel Beckett's short play *Footfalls*, in which our lead character, May, paces back and forth, back and forth, within a thin rectangle of light, turning the same memories over and over in her poor mind. The reader in fact remembers nothing of what she tells us: the reader has never read it before, the reader has never heard it before, the reader has never lived it. Soon, no one will have.

38. *A GARDEN PARTY HAMLET—RACHEL JOSEPH*

Imagine a vine that has sprouted all young and bright green. It grows and the leaves form stages for the insect types to walk all around. No one watches but the ants. Eventually they perform *Hamlet*, in its entirety. The earthworm makes a magnificent Ghost. Imagine that this vine grows up and round and round a young woman just standing on the lawn as the beetle holds up a skull—alas, alas. It covers her toes and then her feet and calves, thighs, and so on. She doesn't notice at first, but when she does she panics and begins to struggle. The ants begin to watch her. Has she become the show?

The insects stop during their third time through the fight in Ophelia's (a ladybug) grave. Instead they—audience-insects and actor-insects—watch the young woman begin to press her whole weight against the deep green vine as it now winds round her neck and ears. Mouth too. She can't scream, barely breathe.

It was so innocent at first—those leaf stages. Miniaturized, *Hamlet* charms rather than broods. Now, alas, it is too late for her to do much at all but become the tragedy.

She was not a suicide, the gravediggers said, if the vines rose up to choke her. Did she act, do, or perform her finale? Did she intend to die? Which is to say: did she mean to take the stage—which is always to die in front of spectators? Or was she innocent? Did nature call? Did the earth beckon her from below to join the earthworm who made such "a magnificent Ghost"?

If the stage seems now the opposite of nature, it was not always so. Not for the Greeks sitting on the hillside. Not for the Balinese dancers, entranced. Not for Shakespeare, his poor players interrupted by pigeons perched on the balcony. Certainly not for the ants, whose "leaf stages" held Ophelia writhing against the vines. This necessary sacrifice (necessarily a young woman) did indeed become the show. This Rite of Spring had to choose someone (and, anyway, it beats a nunnery). But what about the ants? Surely it was hard enough to hold human witnesses responsible for their violent eyes. "Now, alas, it is too late for her to do much at all but become the tragedy." Who could have stopped the vines? Who could have interfered with fate? And would they have done so if they could? After all, the tragedy transubstantiated into a host for ants, gave the worms their mincemeat, poured out sacrificial lifeblood into the garden streams. The sacrifice, this tiny goat-bug, this scapegoat, this lamb, this ladybug, fertilized the vines until they "sprouted all young and bright green" once more, for other beetles to strut and fret upon. And then be heard no more. Alas, alas. Their life relied on her death, and in turn became new tragedies. And so on. Ad infinitum, ad nauseum, ad theatrum, ad memorium.

Memory began, like all things, as a dance amongst insects. The pivotal moment occurred when some bugs stopped for a moment to watch others. Before, acts had repeated, but no one ever recognized the repetitions when they happened. Then the mere fact of watching transformed the repetitions into something like song. Gestures began to rhyme or soar. Memory made the dance itself transform. Caterpillars became butterflies. Earthworms channeled the dead. The performance took flight, reenacted the ancient gestures, passed them into the wits and wobbles of all the future generations. And yet every time it was different. And so it went. The DNA of imagination, made of tiny ground plans based on old memories, passed itself forward in spirit. The matter of this remembering was the always changing stuff of the world. As Suzan-Lori Parks staged it, we repeat and revise, rep and rev, like jazz, or history, or theatre. The world's materials remembered ancient rhythms that reconstituted them into the systems that became us.

Yet the hungry foliage must be fed. It grows from the blood of young ladybugs. Alas.

39. *GHOST LIGHT, AN ANIMAL CONGRESS—JENNIFER PARKER-STARBUCK*

A huge, cavernous pitch-black stage. A clinically extra-white light bolts across the stage from top to bottom, crackling with static electricity and freezes.

Into this beam flutters a large moth, then several more; they hover momentarily trapped in the web of light, they glow and are propelled in a dance with the light. They disappear.

A dark figure swoops across the top of the beam, the air moves in sound—*whoosh*—the air crackles—*whoosh*—again, the winged figure slices through the beam; a few seconds later the air above your face shifts. A shudder passes through your body. It is gone.

The space around the light fills with a haunting sound echoing and resounding in the hollow. The cries bounce from wall to you. You sit dead still wondering if the call will be answered. It is silent.

Suddenly, the perfect head of a giant eland is caught in the light, center stage, the twisting tines of one antler forcing their way forward, the rest obscured by the pitch black darkness. Its eyes turn forward and settle on you for what feels like minutes, it turns, and silently, is gone.

The light fades slightly, slowly becoming more yellow-gold then white, darkening very slowly. Its sound shifts to a low buzz. It is hard to adjust your eyes.

Four, six, eight artificially glowing eyes appear just beneath the beam of light. A deep grumbling growl begins to move through the darkened space in waves toward the audience. The skin on the back of your neck crawls. The sound and eyes fade; two large tufted ears of a snarling caracal appear (listening?) in the lower part of the light. Violently, they are gone.

Across the top of the beam, two thick spotted necks cut through the light, giraffes, swaying gently like trees before turning to go. Round-backed figures, maybe bonobos, or gorillas, obscure the sharp cut of the light, brushing through its diminishing power. You blink and they are gone.

The light is barely perceptible, moving toward blackness. It switches off and is gone.

No light. A heavy warm fog has dropped into the space. It is harder to breathe. Everything is still, silent, dark. Waiting.

Suddenly, a ghost light turns on center stage. For this split second the stage is covered with as many species as can fit there. They cover every inch of the space. A menagerie. A zoo. A wildlife park. The rainforest. African plains. The jungle. Filling treetops. Oceans. Hillsides.

A congress.
A gaggle.
A skulk.
A band.
A colony.
A pride.
A troop.
A crash.
A murder.

The stage goes black. Suddenly the intense light appears again.

The stage is bare. They are gone.

Pinned to the wall over my desk is a panoramic postcard of the taxidermied "animal parade" in the Grande Galerie de l'Évolution in the National Museum of Natural History in Paris. Filling the center of the enormous museum the animals appear to be moving forward, forming a slow turn, going somewhere. The large tusked elephant leads the procession, rhinos to its left, antelopes, a cheetah, zebras behind, the three tall giraffes mid-way down, monkeys, a wildebeest, eland, some kind of yak. Multiple species, all shapes and sizes. These taxidermied animals, frozen in time, fill the giant hall from end to end in a "nonhuman turn." This is an impossible collection, a "Noah's Ark" of beasts performing, through their death, a potentially impossible future.

Richard Grusin, in the edited collection of essays, *The Nonhuman Turn* (2015), introduces the nonhuman turn as, "a shift of attention, interest, or concern toward nonhumans [that] keeps in mind the physicality and movement involved in the idea of a turn." He relies on Deleuze and Guattari's "plane of immanence" (a horizontal rather than vertical shift) to focus on a "sense of embodied movement in turning toward" to come to the point that "to turn toward the nonhuman is not only to confront the nonhuman but to lose the traditional way of the human, to move aside so that other nonhumans—animate and less animate—can make their way, turn toward movement themselves." Perhaps these taxidermied animals—animated inanimates—turning toward movement, albeit a human-inscribed movement, might remind the human to move aside (as they move alongside), to not only marvel in the improbable collection of creaturely figures, but to take a turn before their fleshy counterparts are forever ghosts.

As we face a time being called the Anthropocene—designating the irrevocable human-driven turn impacting climate change, species' futures, and the global environment—it is hard to imagine a nonhuman turn. Yet this is needed now more than ever, in everyday life, in literature, in science, in theatre. In juxtaposition to the embodied movement I felt walking so close to the parade of animals in Paris, is their lack of actual movement. Meticulously arranged skins on skillfully crafted forms, this might be the turn toward a nonhuman congress. I read that a film director was brought in to make the museum's displays more dramatic, and the animals on parade do represent action. They are poised, mid-step, looking around, some meeting our glance, others sniffing at the ground, one after the other in a semi-circular path, their life-like display caught in an anthropocentric reminiscence, a ghost light of their lives. They are here to allow humans to remember. Perhaps they can also turn us to action. Before they are all gone.

40. *GHOST PRACTICE—SARA JANE BAILES*

(August 2001, Cambridge, England)

Whenever I hear the word "heresy" I think instead of the word "heresay."
Heresy. Heresay. The difference of one character.
Heresy means dissent. It implies non-conforming, to be profoundly at odds with what is accepted.
Heresay means, basically, a rumor. To me this suggests something of less consequence. A making-known without trace of origin.

Here is a structure to consider.
You start each line with "They say…"
It's a monologue, probably spoken into a microphone from a seated position. But you can't see her, the one who is speaking; her back is to the audience. It's simple. As with most performance ideas, I shall probably never write it and I'm certain I will never perform it. It's part of a quiet practice (as X once defined this), a phantom exercise, carried out without witness or evidence. Imagine. Try it for yourself.

They say that you can't judge a book by its cover. (Don't trust what you at first see.)
They say look before you leap. (The book, the cover, the look, the leap—essentially the same thing said in an opposite way: heed the cover, trust what you see.)
They say more than a mouthful is a waste. (A compensatory comment, this becomes vulgar in my mind.)
They say once bitten twice shy. (Obviously.)
They say red hat, no pants. (Who?)
And they say you always hurt the one you love, but they have never said why.
(This, I think, needs further explanation.)

They say "Leave," "Stay," and "Not so soon."
They say "We have more coming in later today, try calling around 6."

They say Timothy Leary wanted to be remembered as a great philosopher though most remember him as a mad man. First Harvard, then Berkeley, Afghanistan, and finally Algeria. It was 1975. The Black Panthers ran out of patience. John Lennon wrote him a song and (they say) Leary had at least five wives.

They say "Know. Your. Limits," that bottled water is a universal scam and that we are made of stardust.

Opinion, feeling, fact, fabulation, desire: it's hard to distinguish between any of these.

Can we write about something we have neither seen nor experienced as we do with performances never witnessed? What is at stake when we do? Has the status of it shifted from document to fiction (of an already-fiction) or does each iteration enact an ontological change? Why is it that the eye confers more legitimacy upon the world than the ear?

And then that mysterious text that showed up on my phone written like this: *I know u forgot me but i Saw you last night.*

You make a structure then feel obliged to fulfill it, even when it no longer serves a purpose. Then you can't quite be done with it because it haunts you like a phantom, because it has been disappointed. You have disappointed something you invented. They say that this is the hardest thing to get over, the thing that remains like a ghost experience. Suggestion, the frame, a whisper, like rumor, *rumore*, like noise, a loss gained, the predicament of each and every performance, beginning and ending with the rub between letter, character, word, imagination.

(1975, Cambridge, England)

> A voice comes to one in the dark. Imagine.
>
> (Samuel Beckett, *Company*)

When I was nine I inherited a Tandberg reel-to-reel machine from my late father. It was too heavy for me to lift and squatted on my desk next to my record player. Home from school, I would record myself for hours chattering into the microphone, spinning my film soundtrack LPs for an invisible audience. I filled reel after reel of tape. Once a tape ended, I would record over it. Sometimes previous shows bled through, and the tape became a palimpsest. Late at night I would play back the recordings, bathed in the faint green light emanating from the machine. I listened from my bunk bed until I fell asleep, *babble, babble, words, like the solitary child who turns himself into children, two, three, so as to be together, and whisper together, in the dark.*

In those days I would fold my carefully typed poems into a neatly self-addressed envelope, lick the stamp, and walk down to the postbox at the end of my street. The envelopes would thump through our mail slot a day or two later. The poems were easier to edit that way.

The taped voice became too familiar. I bought a walkie-talkie set, placed one handset next to the microphone, pushed Record, then took the other handset and went walking in the garden. When I returned, the machine had captured the crackling signal: a trace no one would hear except a ghost.

I didn't have to be there.

41. *GIVE, TAKE, AND SHAKE—RODRIGO TOSCANO / COLLAPSIBLE POETICS THEATER*

8 modules

Prelude to Tristan. [10.00 @.04]
Three activities for entities (a, b, c)
.45 major scratching sound/wash [3 seconds], motif heretofore referred to as SW!
(Screen Text, ST), 1.08

actionism
spectators are actors
member?
social traction
dis-traction
historic-motivic
in-
dependence
correspondences
blurred
but in bits
blipping
first thought - worst thought
p—shhhhh

***

Act. 1. Tying things to chairs (flowers, twigs, leaves, pieces of clothing, pieces of paper; objects come from cloth sacks; each has a sack)
Act. 2. Moving with, acting on, being changed by the movement of, chairs
Act 3. "Chair sculpting" into a common <dynamic, changing> shape

Act. 1-2
@1.43
Film Flashes [ ] [ ] [ ] [ ] [ ] [ ] [ ]

[a "seven row" of images, from here on in designated as a 7-R]
- Lindsey?

(a) First ties [ribbons different colors], then moves/interacts with chair

(b) First ties, then moves with chair

(c) First ties, then moves/interacts with chair
adjustments@3.21–4.

Cue to switch activity from either tying to moving, or vice versa

(excerpt selected by Carla Harryman)

The text of *Give, Take, and Shake* requires performers to follow its instructions with exacting precision as if they were skilled builders adhering to an architectural blueprint. However, these schematics would not yield a fixed structure but rather a motile shaping of activity, including the activation of the text as a non/narrative event that occurs in several temporal dimensions simultaneously.

The temporal dimensions of the piece include twentieth-century historical references associated with the European avant-garde, a continuous present marked by swift change in physical movement, duration determined by the length of time in Wagnerian songs, and actions finely calibrated with the music "to the second." I read the text as if it were a palimpsest set in motion through instructions that shake up settled forms and resonances, including sonic resonances that would stabilize either poetry or theatre. The artist takes from given sources, simultaneously agitating these into the manifestation of a new system and an event of activated frenzy. In Toscano's work the oxymoron of regulated frenzy may well be a condition of everything: from the impossibility of everyday life in the early twenty-first century to the relationship of poetry to theatre under circumstances of potential revolution.

Give, Take, and Shake asks one to think about what time and historical memory perform in the present, both the sedimented and dead aspects as well as the potential aspects that reside in our bodies and psyches. The action of the piece also forges an intense connection between the eyes, or "looking," and physical movement. It is interesting to note the various ways in which looking, seeing, and the body are scripted into the work. In Acts 1 and 2, performing "entities" demonstrate to spectators a feeling "gathered in a part of the body," which "then the eyes in commonality with that feeling follow." In Act 3, the performing entities rhythmically move chairs into a pile and are instructed to stop and observe *with their bodies* [italics added] the pile-shapes as they are under construction.

As for the text itself, its schematic, precisely calibrated instructions combined with voiced bits evoke the sense of duration, speed, and intense activity that a performance of the work would realize. Yet the potential for the work as a performance will always only be partly available as text: the written work queries the identities of poetry and theatre and assumptions regarding reading and viewing. In Toscano's *oeuvre* the relationship between reading and performance is noisy and asymmetrical.

Collapsible Poetics Theater is at its most obvious a theatre of portability: it acknowledges the transitory aspects of poetry performance. The work can be packed up and travels easily. As an itinerate form, it invokes the possibility of alternative economies and modes of exchange. Yet, Toscano brings the laboring, performing body and poetry into unsentimental alignment. The distinction in *Give, Take, and Shake* between auteur and performer is amplified through the text's focus not on dialogue but on language, timing, and precision as well as through its enactment by "entities" instead of characters. Here Toscano's poetics is also a construct that brings together, or collapses the identity of, the poet and the identity of the director into the identity of "Collapsible Poetics Theater" itself. In lending his authorial signature to the concept, Toscano highlights and allegorizes the power relations between idea, system, authorial function, and performer.

42. *THE GREATEST SHOW ON EARTH—DARREN O'DONNELL*

Every single script ever developed performed simultaneously by every single one of the 100 trillion bacteria in your large intestine. In the lead roles: *L. acidophilus*. In the roles of the villains: *Campylobacter*.

Is scripted theatre shit? Are the semiotics of the stage still worth investing in? Does speaking a rigid set of predetermined words make any sense when there are living beings breathing, and digesting unpredictably only a few feet away? Why are scripts staged more than once and by different companies? Why don't all companies write their own damn scripts? Why is the set often designed before the rehearsals start? Is there a good reason to pretend the audience is not there? If the audience is addressed, should they always be allowed to respond? Why must we tell them to turn off their mobiles? Who is calling? Can we have a chat with them? What is this bowing thing I am doing with my body? Where did bowing come from? What function does bowing serve? Why does it feel so silly? What if they throw something at my head, while I am looking at my shoes? Why do I want them to continue clapping? Why do I want them to jump to their feet when they are clapping? Why do some cultures yell bravo, while some do not? What makes a "bravo" culture? If audiences are less and less interested in stage-based performance, shouldn't we be creating more and more different kinds of performance? Are we? Is it enough? Should we stop making stage-based, scripted theatre altogether? Should all playwrights be banished to the film and television industries where they will make more money? Why doesn't the audience sit on the stage anymore, like in the good ole days? Why is theatre for children in the second spaces of most theatres? Why is family work often in the back of the festival program, hidden amongst the ads? Why don't we make theatre for our pets? Can cats clap? Would a clapping cat make a significant sound? Why is an animal onstage much more interesting to watch than an actor? Would an actor in a zoo be much more interesting than the lions? Do lions like the taste of actors? Why do actors like to yell so much? Why do actors hate the sound of old people unwrapping lozenges? Why do actors in a comedy passionately hate a quiet audience? Maybe they are laughing inside.

43. *GUN—JONATHAN BALL*

There is a gun in the first act.

In the second act, the actors admire the gun. They comment on its luster. They take turns polishing its stock, barrel, and handle, and admiring its lack of nicks, scratches, or blemishes. They can see their faces in the barrel. All agree that it is a fine example of its type, and the virtues of guns in general are extolled.

The third act follows from the second without a break: the actors begin to bleed from their noses, mouths, and ears. They take care not to dirty the gun, wiping away any droplets that fall on its fine steel. The actors rebuke one another, voices thick with blood, for exhibiting such carelessness around the gun. Surely, the gun is appalled by this foul display. They rend their clothes, attempt to plug themselves with rags, but the blood forces its way out. They apologize to the gun as they fall, dying, to the floor.

The actors lie still. The gun gleams in the spotlight. The audience begins to murmur, one to the other, about the gun and its obvious potential.

The Play had stood—A Loaded Gun

Like many of the exquisite impossible dramas in Jonathan Ball's *Clockfire, Gun* holds the funhouse mirror up to theatre, magnifying a conventional element until its inherent oddity becomes monstrous. When Anton Chekhov insisted that a gun appearing in the first act must go off before the play's end, he acknowledged the extent to which the tight causal structure he and his audiences inherited from the *pièce bien faite* converted theatre into an all too predictable time machine that generates its own future. From this perspective, a play, like a gun, is a well-oiled mechanism for potential violence. To put a gun on stage early in a play loads the play's chamber and cocks its hammer. Disobey the machine at your peril.

Ball begins by distilling Chekhov's maxim to absurd purity, offering a first act that is nothing other than the appearance of a gun. In the second act, the actors lavish the gun with the outsized attention it has already demanded. As surrogates for an audience's attachment to an onstage gun, the actors fetishize the prop and so contribute to its power. Andrew Sofer reminds us in *The Stage Life of Props* that guns stand out from other stage properties in that their "power to *destroy* human time is potentially limitless." As players in a gun-driven drama, Ball's actors recognize the gun as their god, their prime mover, and also their oracle: they see their faces in its barrel but fail to read their fates.

The third act begins at the precise moment when blood emerges from the actors' noses, mouths, and ears. We might say, adapting Lessing's famous line from *The Hamburg Dramaturgy*, that they die of the third act. They are victims of the tyranny of dramatic closure itself, or perhaps of their own attachment to it. Like all figures on a stage, they sacrifice themselves at the altar of dramatic necessity. Guns don't kill people, plots do. The actors die, like Marie Curie in Adrienne Rich's "Power," denying their wounds came from the same source as their power. They revere the gun, but fail to realize that its ultimate power lies not in its detonation but in its "obvious potential," its capacity to generate *virtual* violence. The gun's power—like theatre's—is virtual in the oldest sense of that word, meaning full of power or potency, capable of producing a result in the future, and by extension, operating in effect rather than in reality.

44. *GUT BODY—PETRA KUPPERS*

Sucker punch, the knife in the street
fear of being sheared out of the stream
into the backwater
dead fish belly up by the side of the pond
pills and poisons and endings
let go and sever the ties and ignore
the party is always elsewhere
a shadow in a canoe in a photo
likely put on Facebook tomorrow:
fake of having fun behind
the grass, tree, a Stephen King book
where I know the next sentence already.
Primacy of white masculine precarity.
Close the leaky gut, body drained of tears.

Just speak, walk with me, close the loop.

Bow forward, pour yourself into your capable hands, and hold your heart.

Bow forward, pour your stomach into your feeble hands, release the binds that bind so tightly to your spinal column.

Bow again, drop your sexual organs into waiting hands, wait.
Breathe in, out, in, soothe.

Fish slip into the labyrinth of intestines. Cruise past the atlas, feed on the carpet fibers of worry.
Agile between the lung pearls, hollow behind the liver, green wall, delicate black veins spider along for companionship, dark purple, maroon.
Fins soothe the red spots of tension, white bands where muscles have leached nourishment out of tight bands.
Between kidney and uterus, raspy tongue licks
soggy dahlias on their stalks, ovaries bloom.
Glide, mucous oils the way. Swim among the velvet.
You, and me, into plump cushions: salmon tumbling ground.

This material emerges out of the somatics of performance preparation and sustenance: meditations, open form movement, free-writes. It plays out bodily fantasies, the ways our textual and embodied experiences intersect, in the theatre of our sensations. How can we draw upon the performed scenarios that we feel "in our gut"?

As a gloss, a pedagogical offering: here is an assignment I am using for all my classes, in performance studies and beyond.

Wellness Assignment

Task: Engage in (at least) three wellness activities, over the span of the semester, and each time, write a short (less than a page) report on what you did, how it made you feel, and the effects it has on your life.

Some options:

- Use a massage chair
- Use a biofeedback program, like StressEraser, Wild Divine, or Inside Meditation
- SAD light therapy
- If you have a wellness area in your university or local health center, maybe have a Kinect session with others
- Other good options might be visits to greenhouses, botanical gardens, swimming pools, saunas, cuddle parties, nature walks, or visits to humane societies to walk a dog or look after kitties
- You can also choose three yoga classes, three massages, or three meditation sessions, spiritual activities, art sessions, or anything related. It needs to be different from what you'd do anyway, and you can tell me in what way it is a wellness activity

Enjoy!

45. *A HAPPY LIFE—AARON C. THOMAS*

We cannot see the man who addresses the crowd assembled on stage—no, one would not call it a crowd exactly. The even tones of a frail voice lecture to a select group of men and women who angle forward slightly as he speaks.

The scene is unmistakably staged for the benefit of an audience, even if the lecturer is himself temporarily hidden from view. The forms of the listeners surround their interlocutor, and their presence draws attention to the importance of the speaker. The man speaks softly enough to demonstrate his own tranquility. His auditors are compelled to lean in to the master's voice; they attend to it with their bodies, the barely perceptible movements of the eyes and lips and cheeks performed by a group rapt with listening.

A few words become clear, appearing out of the formlessness of the man's distant voice. *Why should I beg fortune to give me things rather than demand them of myself?* He asks. *Why should I demand things at all?*

The men and women listening to Seneca the Younger fan out, finally letting the audience in the theatre see the philosopher himself. He appears before us weakened but calm, even grateful. A flicker of victory, perhaps, passes over the passionless face as he takes in the presence of the audience in the theatre—the audience beyond the one on the stage—and the volume of his voice raises noticeably. Seneca tells us that he imagines this day to be his last, and, indeed, one can see the trickle of blood on the great man's forearm.

But if the man before us is to die soon, his posture seems designed to convince us that this isn't true at all. Seneca stands alive before his audience, before us. He speaks without fear.

Does steam creep into the theatre from somewhere under the stage floor? If it does, no one seems to notice. The great man continues, frail but strong. Seneca has not died. He does not waver.

Seneca speaks.

Scholars debate about whether Seneca's dramas were written to be performed and, if they were, whether these tragedies might have been performed in his lifetime. For many, Seneca's dramas evoke the essential idea of the "closet" drama, drama meant to be imagined only—drama that is (ostensibly) untheatrical.

Seneca's philosophical work, too—especially the texts written late in his life, his *Epistulae Morales ad Lucilium*—would seem to abjure the theatrical. Seneca often writes against the pretentions of performing for a crowd, of actively staging something for an audience: he rails against popular speaking styles and lecture circuits in letter 40; he detests gladiatorial games in letter 7; and he is suspicious of festivals in general in letter 18.

But if Seneca dislikes the stage, his work is almost unabashedly theatrical. He writes "private" letters to his friend Lucilius that are, of course, not meant for a private audience at all but for the public at large. And he constantly repurposes and restages the words of Epicurus in these letters, as though he were an actor speaking the lines of a playwright long dead. Even the manner of Seneca's death—an enforced suicide dictated by his pupil Nero—was an intentional restaging or reperformance of Socrates' suicide four and a half centuries earlier. In the *Annales* of Tacitus, Seneca refuses to lie to Nero's messenger; he calls for secretaries to write down his last words; he pours out libations to Jupiter the Deliverer. As Tacitus relates—or rather as he stages—Seneca's death, every bit of it seems scripted for an audience.

But the theatrical is not necessarily insincere, and Seneca's performances were no less honest for their theatrical qualities. He really did slice open his veins. He really was choked to death by steam.

"Life is like a play," Seneca once wrote to Lucilius, "what matters is not how long the show goes on but how well it is acted."

And if Seneca theatricalized his life, centuries later Shakespeare, Chapman, Marston, Webster, Elizabeth Cary, and their contemporaries would stage him as well, quoting the master directly (often without attribution) and repurposing choice Senecan phrases and Senecan philosophy through the words of their characters.

In the Jacobean theatre, Seneca seems to achieve the fame that he imagined for himself when he said "I shall find favor with posterity" in letter 21. On stage in England, the philosopher appears again and again—as the performer he seems to have expected to be, in the theatre of violence he imagined. *Contemnite dolorem: aut solvetur, aut solvet*, Antonio says aloud in *Antonio's Revenge*, and the master speaks once more.

46. *HEAVEN'S STENOGRAPHER SHINES THE GUIDING LIGHT—NICK SALVATO*

You know how this story begins. A nymph chatters to distract a goddess, who curses her with echoic aphasia. A morning star, son of dawn, announces big plans—then takes a big plunge. Or, in our version of remote control, heaven's stenographer has lost her touch at shorthand. The remediation, a punishing exercise to sharpen her skills: command to transcribe all seventy-two years of the radio-television serial Guiding Light.

The steno wastes no time in the terrestrial archives. Too many episodes lost, damaged, destroyed, and otherwise forgotten. Thank heaven she has access to the video starred in the sky, audio echoed in the deep.

She makes quick enough work—much quicker, anyway, than the earthly ensemble performing her text's reenactment. What with all the meals, the sleeping, the green room lounging, the bathroom breaks: who can say how long their recitation unfolds, how many words are welled before their theatre walls are dust?

Sometimes, heartbreak when an actor who has been a leading light in this Guiding Light *drops down dead in the middle of decades' run. Others, relief when a replacement breathes new life into an old role, just for a spell, before giving in, exhausted, to the stammers, the stutters and slurs. Ever, the swirl of chatter at once absorbing and distracting, uncanny and dull, rousing and dispiriting, rising and falling:*

And where we're able to say *no*, we're also able to say *yes* … It can't be long now. Yes, thank God … You expect to hear from her after your last scene? What do you mean, last scene? The last time she was over here, when you just about—tore her apart … Well, if there is any more information, she certainly didn't give it to me … Because in the first place that's not at all what he's doing. Do you want to know what he's doing? What? He's gone and barged into another big mistake. He's started drinking again … It's just a visit. You don't go and just visit anytime you want to like that … And she really told you to tell me she wants to see me? Oh, honey, she not only told me, she—she begged me and said she had to talk to you before the trial starts this morning. Well—well. Well. Isn't that something? Right out of the blue a message when in the last ten—two days in the courtroom, she hasn't said ten words to me … Do you want a muffin, Granddad? Granddad? Granddad? Oh, oh, oh, I'm sorry, darling. No, no thank you, no. What are you so wrapped up with? … What's wrong with this picture? Huh? I said, what is wrong with this picture? I have a feeling you're going to tell me. Some girls are getting married today, but no, not—not me, I'm helping my boyfriend move appliances … O, I am home! Why didn't you warn me? I wasn't expecting you until next week. Oh, I only decided in Paris this morning. I didn't cancel the business meeting … He is worth ten of that scoundrel you were married to, and he's not going to wait around forever … You guys, something *is* wrong. I'm gonna need your help, she's really sick, we gotta get her to the hospital. Now, come—bring her in here, put her on the couch. What? … Her family is very high profile in this town. Her father owns a major construction company. Her mother has her own TV show. Uh! I guess when she dies it will make the society page. N-not that I want to hurt her, that's not my intention. What do you want? What I wanted all along … Hold on. Hold on, baby. You okay? Okay. Lose him! Faster! … Don't say a word. Can you at least tell me where we're going? …

You know how this story ends. You ready? Always.

I watched soap operas throughout my childhood. Never by choice. Well. Rarely by choice. With only ever one television in the house, the dial inevitably got turned to the channel chosen by whoever had the biggest say. And because, no matter what, I attentively watched whatever program happened to be playing (even sports), I watched a lot of soaps, especially during the overheated summer months. Thus, I inadvertently became a precocious aficionado of the conventions of the genre, at least as enacted by those 1970s soaps preferred by my mother and grandmothers. My mom liked *Days*, while her mother preferred *The Doctors* and *Another World*. My great-grandmother Tita was devoted to *General Hospital*. (Her daughter—my gramma Nellie—preferred the *novelas* that came on at night, which were a whole different but strangely similar thing.) In ways that hinted at who I would become, I recall taking especial delight in noting (and sometimes explaining to my indulgent grandmothers) the way soaps were different than "regular" tv shows, like half-hour comedies or hour-long procedurals. How the soaps often put a pretty lady—like my favorite, *The Doctors*' Carolee—at the center but you could tell that every time something good happened to the pretty Carolee lady something bad would happen next. Either way she'd cry a lot. Or how most every pretty soap opera lady would have an old boyfriend, a new boyfriend, and a next boyfriend (though the next boyfriend was just as often as not the old boyfriend back again). If you were lucky, the pretty soap opera lady might also have a twin who was a waitress or a stripper on the other side of town. But the mix-and-match boyfriends were pretty much a sure thing. I also liked how the pretty soap opera lady would sometimes have a kid, like when Rachel had Jamie on *Another World*. This kid might be exactly your age this summer, even though he was in diapers this time last year. (I was outraged when that same Jamie, just one or two summers later, was graduating high school. If only I could get grown as quick as Jamie, I pined, if only ...) But nothing delighted me more than when that weird disembodied voice would intone with a benign but measured gravity: "The role of this-or-that will now be played by so-and-so." This voice, which usually sounded just like the guy who whisper-talked when my grandfather watched golf, meant that the soap opera people had found a new pretty soap opera lady who looked a little bit like the previous pretty soap opera lady. The fun part was watching everyone pretend they didn't notice that this pretty soap opera lady wasn't that other pretty soap opera lady who was just here a couple weeks ago (but who was now in that new motorcycle-cop or spaceship show on in the nighttime). After hearing that voice a few times on a few different soaps, it became my favorite soap opera thing. I tuned my ear for it every time I watched any soap, always hoping it might announce another shocking transformation. Soaps provided my first real tutorial in how a performance might remake its own rules. And that voice was the sound of soap opera time, space, and personhood bending. The rules of soaps were conspicuous and tight but that voice heralded the thrilling spectacle of those confinements being twisted, warped, and—if an accidental soap aficionado got really lucky—broken altogether.

47. *HOLDING TIME—HELEN PARIS*

Woman DSR dimly lit. Dust motes spiral in a shaft of light. Something in the woman's dress catches the light, makes it shine—extraterrestrial, intergalactical (theatre can do this). In her clavicles two pools of red wine, filled to the brim. Dark tannin, deep berry. She holds the wine as long as she can. Until she can't. Until, eventually, inevitably, it spills. A rivulet runs down her chest, meets the silk fabric of her dress. Slows. Spreads its stain like a map. As it spills she speaks:

I remember
standing on a pitch-dark mountain
freezing cold.
I remember
more stars than I ever imagined.
I remember
the physical sensation
my head tipped back in wonder.
My head tipped back my eyes drank in the sight.
Head tipped back I opened my mouth and
let the stars fall in.
Tipped back I swallowed.
I was open to every star and felt my own shifting gravity
tip me to the sky like a kiss.
Lips tipped eyes filling with light drinking it all in.
Every drop.

These moments of time.
These conversations of light
of past and present.
I am caught on a timeline
of no time before time.
I want this moment to last forever
even when in this exact moment
I am trying to understand time itself.
Time and light and dust and movement
and stories told in fragments in
fractured poems in the sky.

On that same mountain I saw
Saturn through the telescope and cried:
It's adorable!
And everyone laughed.
But I didn't mean it like that.
I didn't mean it to be funny.
I just mean...
I just meant...
It's there.
It's really there.
Just like that.
Just how we picture it
just how we see it in the pictures -
surrounded by its rings.

Just
so
utterly
adorable.

My eyes fathomed what they saw.
Not sight but time itself.
Time in light.
Time in shards.
Time shooting across the sky.

This is what happens when you
fall down slowly.
As you must.

At the last minute your arms may fly up
may fly out may try to stop your fall.
But you mustn't.
You know you mustn't.
You know you have to go.

It's time.

This falling will feel a mix of fast and slow.
Fast and slow.
In the end it will be just a quick quick slow.

I

Time is a problem, an impossibility of thought, a riddle.

As much as I try to understand it, I do not. As much as I study theories, apply frameworks, analogies, or find examples to help *demonstrate* time, I cannot bend my mind around it (and time itself bends, warps; it curves). Time's immateriality conditions the limits of our ability to imagine it.

If, for example, one were to travel to the US from the UK and back again, on a transatlantic flight, going first backwards in time and then forwards in time, then backwards and forwards in continuum, if one were to remain in the air, that is, in a Boeing 747, what would happen to time? To "my" time, that is? What time would it *be?* And what would time's relation to me—the protagonist—and my body become? Would I cease, for this duration, to age, for example, because effectively I would stop moving *through* time by travelling to and fro? Would I be neither "here" nor "there," neither in one time zone nor another, and therefore out of time, even outwitting time? If time is the continuous change through which we live would I have made time stop? Is that possible?

If this is the case, must we "stay put" in order to experience time in the way we tacitly and collectively apprehend it?

If, on the other hand, we all came to be still, absolutely still, all machineries, mechanisms, reactors, all electric grids, vehicles and modes of travel, activities, all methods of doing and animation ground to a halt, complete cessation, what would happen then? If we were to stop the last clock and destroy it: then what?

I wonder if time is the only measure by which any of this, this "world," can be indexed or achieved. Is time the only means through which we are able, in our diversified multitudes, to order the chaos of the world?

This at least brings sense to the inclination and desire to perform.

II

The clavicle is the only long bone in the body that lies horizontally. This thought alone is charming, (adorable!), a surprise. There are two clavicles—left and right—each serving as a strut between the shoulder blade and the sternum.

No wonder, then, that the position of the clavicle creates two small vessels within the body's natural armature between neck and shoulder that might, for example, be made to carry wine.

Imagine two small dark red pools balanced in these receptacles made possible by the body's only horizontal form.

The clavicle is also the first bone in the human body to begin the process of ossification—that is, to become a bone according to a preformed matrix—during the fifth and sixth weeks of gestation as an embryo. It is the oldest bone in the body around which all else gathers its form. It is, however, often the last to cease growing.

It is easy to forget the life of bones; to remember them, too, as vibrant and organic, subject to the measure of time, proportion, and aspect. Imagine our bones curving and carrying, in the composite memory of hard tissue, the inclinations and traces of desire.

48. *HOW DOES IT GO AGAIN?—REBECCA SCHNEIDER*

Dad, at the mountain pass, says
Look at this earth.
We all,
who think of ourselves
as we, do.
We look and we see
Dad, his face turned toward us
in his eyes
the full reflection of everything
that was ever
something

    [pause] something

            [pause] something

                    [pause]

How is a poem not a piece of theatre? Inside the baby Krishna's mouth, so the story goes, Yashoda saw the whole universe—a sight that sent her spinning, ungrounded, through all the possible worlds the one world holds like play sets within play sets. Play, *lila,* is a basic of nature and of theatre and of the gods. Play, *lila,* the nature of theatre in the theatre of nature. But … does it have to be said?

"Dad, at the mountain pass" is just that—we often hiked together, to mark the passage between mountains with our footsteps. But it is also my father, and the rest of us, on the brink of his passing away.

Isn't that where we always call to each other? And isn't the theatre, among other things, a breathing machine to amplify our calls? A seeing machine to catch ourselves seeming to be seen? A "ship-car," like Dionysos rode, to take us to the threshold across which gods and the "unmanifest play"? There, night after night, step upon step, we lose ground together. Becoming ungrounded we ride our theatres as if they had fins or hands to leap us out or lift us up to the pass again. Theatres—as if they had wings.

Something like that. It's not easy, after all, to recall. Something. Something like that.

49. *HUMAN TOO—UNA CHAUDHURI*

Lights up.
You are six years old. You are holding a bowl. It's your mother's favorite bowl. When she gave it to you, she said the rain always tasted much better from that bowl. You lean forward and take a sip. As always when drinking, you close your eyes, and brace yourself for whatever taste is to come. A coolness spreads around your mouth. On your tongue, there's only the slightest bitterness, almost no grit. You lower the bowl. Slowly. Carefully. You're afraid it will slip out of your paws, or be scratched by your claws.
Don't be afraid. Drink again. The taste gets better with every sip. Drain the bowl, as lights fade to black.

Lights up.
You are forty-three years old. Your face is buried in the fur of the giant teddy bear that's filling your arms. You can smell your father's pipe tobacco. He used to smoke while reading to you every night. See yourself, tucked up in your little bed, with him sitting nearby in a big comfy chair. Another story, you say. One more. Please. Just one more.
A snowflake lands on the tip of your nose: cold, wet.
Your father closes the book. He stands. He slides into the hole in the ice at his feet. You hear the gentle splash.
The bear licks the snowflake off the tip of your nose. He takes you in his arms. You can hear his heartbeat, as the lights fade to black.

Lights up.
You are seven hundred and sixty years old. You are lying face down, on a cool damp surface. Your skin on your belly feels delicious. Your limbs are extended, but relaxed, not tight, not taut.
Your forehead rests on a smooth, hard slab. Marble. Cool.
Slowly, very slowly, very very slowly you begin to unfurl your wings. One at a time. The top ones first. The right one. The left. Then the lower ones. Right. Left. Finally, the curved one, shaped like a fan, beneath all of them.
The sun begins to warm the wings. The wind makes them flutter slightly.
Slowly, slowly, you push yourself up to all fours. Slowly, slowly, you stand up.
You give the signal and the doors open. People enter. They read the body outlines on the ground. They leave offerings on the marble slab, as the light fades to black.

Lights up.
You are nine seconds old. The sand between your toes is silky. You are singing. The bubbles coming out of your mouth are green, blue, lilac, gold.
All three of your bodies are together today, all holding hands.
The light gets brighter and brighter, then
Blackout.

Click. Light. Click. A photo shot from above into a blue, delicious, small swimming pool. The edges' kidney shapes sinuously weave their way into the picture. Three small curved steps in the water guide my eye from the lip to two floating shapes: a woman supine, her brown skin beneath the water, eye makeup, hands in her dark floating hair. Black pasties on her nipples, a thong around her hips. Next to her floats a giant cockroach, its shape as long as the woman. The insect is prone, the carapace glistens golden brown, the head is turned into the waters. The antennae stick up out of the water, echoing the position of the woman's elbows. One hairy insect leg covers one human leg in a tenuous connection. The two float companionable, calmly. Where will the next meditative stretch take them?

The pool image is by and with Xandra Ibarra. From a press release by Galería De La Raza, on the performance artist's first solo exhibition, *Ecdysis* (2015):

> After her 2012 solo show, *Fuck My Life*, Ibarra resolved to abandon her hyperracialized persona. However, unable to fully let go of the possibilities of negativity, she began to identify as a "cucaracha." This object-animal is theoretically removed from her own body yet also hails histories of objectification through racialized notions of filth, hordes, and infestation.
>
> The object of the cucaracha, although desexualized and distinct from Ibarra's own physical body, nonetheless directs Ibarra in different yet equally difficult ways of thinking through racialized sexualized existence. As cockroaches molt out of their exoskeletons and change into a different being, they look exactly as they did before. This process, known as ecdysis, informs her examination into her own relationship with La Chica Boom and Latinidad, invoking what the artist calls "fucked life."

We swim at the boundaries, animal/human edges set against a perspective of cultural devaluation, the classifications of racism, speciesism, compressed and shaped into a floating moment.

Bracket: the photo shoot, the near-nude model, economies of womanhood in a misogynistic world. Bracket: water against skin, floating support, the warm sun on cool limbs, queer meetings in Harbin Hot Springs, Kabuki Springs, The Dinah, CampIt. Bracket: shells and shedding, exoskeletons, sun-screens, debris, jewel wings, chlorine, the remnants of insect lives in the pool's filtration system, drought times, the weight of water.

Witness performance in the edge spaces. Sit back in the theatres transformed by photo lenses and skin sensations into new spaces of encounter, coalescence, opalescence. Listen, and feel the 700-year-old wings unfurl, on the beach, in the temple, in the sedimentations of marble. On the edges of public spaces and the in-between of time, in the liminal zones, sensations creep into new membranous life.

50. *I CAN'T BREATHE ...—THOMAS F. DEFRANTZ*

a pale space without distinguishing feature or end.
blankness.

a dull throb of a sound always present, barely perceptible.
a whining that ebbs and flows, always there.
blankness.

dull time.

more whining, like sound complaints of tedium.
blanched air, the smell of acrimony.

pale space, dull time.

whiteness without end, smelling tired of itself.

black objects appear throughout.
hazy first, falling into focus.

they are tables, chairs, stoves.
brooms, lawnmowers, whips.
beds.

they litter the space, all black.
the whining acquires pulse, becomes rhythm.

vibrating against the pulse, the objects spin, pop, and dip; they whirr into life.
they become young, vibrant Black people.

Chicly-clad and extraordinary in appearance, powerful, casual, and cool.
Strong. Surprised.

They see each other.
They see the expanses of pale.
They listen.

the pulsing sound devolves into the dull throb.

They see you.
They consider the expanse and its sounds, its smell.
They stand in formation.

They gasp, grasping for air.
Resisting arrest.
They collapse.

Philosopher Martin Heidegger's concept of the "ready-to-hand" suggests an unconscious operation turning object into process, through the figure of the tool. I've been thinking about Black presence within varied histories of the United States as an operationalized manifestation of tool; as a presence created "ready-to-hand" as an extension of the will to power that white systems of domination and capitalisms enjoy. Black presence in the US continues to be operationalized as a method of quantifying and qualifying; distinguishing and diminishing; denying, exploring, and wondering at. Seldom celebrated or allowed a full measure of complex humanity, Black presence occurs contingently, made manifest as legislation for access to voting and quality schools; as protest and disruption; as ludic celebration destined for transference and disappearance. Theatre tends to operationalize Black presence as well; to treat it as a cypher or a ghost in the machine.

When is Blackness ever unmarked? Black presence inevitably seems to ***mean*** in and of itself, as a thing that can be mobilized by others.

August Wilson's plays resist this tendency, through a surplus of wordplay. In the way that Shakespeare's characters are not marked as white, necessarily; not materialized in terms of racial dynamic (excepting Othello, of course), Wilson's theatre proposes Black presence without Black subjugation. Allowed to speak, at great length and depth, toward the terms of their own conception, Wilson's characters instrumentalize language to confirm their ability in the world. Wilson's theatre, like Shakespeare's, doesn't seem to care about who we are watching it, listening to it, experiencing it. Black presence becomes ontological fact, rather than alternative othering.

With words as tools employed among each other, the Black people breathe.

We debate, we assemble, we disagree. And inevitably, we establish rap music, to emphasize the ready-to-hand of language.

51. *I, MARJORIE—JEN HARVIE*

Note on the title: The title of each production takes the names of its performer(s) in the form *I, [name of performer]* or *We, [names of performers]*.

Notes on self-casting or casting: This work can be performed and directed by any woman or women interested in exploring attitudes to older age from a perspective informed by experience. Its performers and directors are likely—though not necessarily—older women.

Notes on production: The production will provide any support the performers and directors deserve, need, and/or desire, not only to enable the performance but, more importantly, to make it pleasurable for them.

- It will begin with decent terms of employment, including a decent wage promptly paid, a mutually agreed timetable of preparation (never too short), a mutually agreed number and schedule of performances (never grueling, and never more than the performers would find interesting), and comfortable transport to and from the venue.
- Backstage, the production will provide comfortable, pleasing, well-serviced, and accessible dressing rooms and fully accessible routes to the stage.
- Onstage conditions will always be safe and might also include: comfortable means of voice amplification; appropriate and pleasant onstage seating; sensitive temperature control; shameless means of prompting the performers should they want it; and lighting designed so it does not bedazzle the performers and they can see their environment and audience as well as possible.

* * *

The stage is pre-set with a drinks trolley carrying the makings of the beverages of the performers' choice, any seating the performers have selected, and anything else the performers have requested (e.g., food, objects/props, technology, scenography).

Enter the performer/s.

The performer/s serve themselves (or are served) the drinks of their choice and make themselves comfortable onstage.

The performers do what they want to do onstage. For example, they might: tell any stories they want to tell, in monologue and/or in conversation with other performers; and/or do any activity they want to do, including sitting onstage in silence. What the performers say and/or do does not have to refer explicitly to age.

The performance is over when the performers want it to be over.

I am imagining a theatre that values older women and their experiences, and actively enables their participation in theatre and in life. This is both a theatre I'd like to see, and a metonym for social change I'd like to see, where democratic participation improves as inequalities, exclusions, and denigrations associated with the intersectional features of age and gender are addressed and diminish.

This imagined theatre and this imagined society repudiate the invisibility that so many societies cast on older women. It confronts social responses of shame and revulsion that older women are often subjected to and that many older women often impose on themselves, given the age and gender prejudices that are prevalent in so much cultural conditioning. This theatre pays attention and responds to what older women want, speak, and do. It is interested in older women's needs, desires, and pleasures and it respects and responds to them. It listens to whatever older women want to tell and show. It values older women.

This imagined theatre actively looks at, responds to, and engages with the kinds of changes that can happen for people—especially women—as we age. It pays attention to changing bodies, minds, abilities, priorities, aesthetics, concerns, and desires. It adjusts the conditions of theatre to enable older people to participate. It also encourages audiences and makers to recognize how people don't change, how they may remain—or become more—interesting, beautiful, and powerful, if in many different ways.

This imagined theatre provokes us to support the changes that can happen in older age with the same patience, interest, kindness, and love that are culturally presumed in our approaches to change in infants and children who are ageing (where ageing is preferentially conceived as growing up and developing).

Theatre, like many societies more broadly, is pervasively unkind to older women. Often, they are simply not represented. Great roles for older women equivalent to older male roles such as Shakespeare's Lear or Prospero, or Beckett's Hamm or Krapp, are rare or nonexistent. Where older women do appear, they are often meddlesome worriers like Amanda in Williams's *The Glass Menagerie*, or jealous evildoers like the iconic Lady Macbeth.

Rarely, theatre challenges older women's underrepresentation and punitive representation. I think of powerful performances into older age by such women as Pina Bausch, Anna Deavere Smith, Spiderwoman Theater's Muriel and Gloria Miguel, octogenarian British dancer and actress Diana Payne-Myers, Beatrice Roth in the Wooster Group's adaptation of *Three Sisters*, *BRACE UP!* (1990), and Lois Weaver and Peggy Shaw in works by their company, Split Britches. But such work is comparatively rare. We need more. We need more work like Weaver's socially engaged *What Tammy Needs to Know About Getting Old and Having Sex*, first produced in 2014. And we need more work like Caryl Churchill's *Escaped Alone* (2016), a powerful, moving play about the daily struggles of women's lives, especially as they age, suggestively paralleled with stories of global catastrophe on epic scales. Its four characters are women; the text notes, "*They are all at least seventy.*"

52. IMAGINED CITIES (AFTER CALVINO)—KYLE GILLETTE

A traveler from India performs at Buckingham Palace. He describes cities throughout the Empire to an audience consisting solely of Queen Victoria and her court.

It is hard for these spectators to believe such exotic places might exist, even in the strange sands of the desert, even beyond the Byzantine streets of Baghdad. The cities are impossibly Platonic in their complete realization of social ideals. They flicker between utopia and dystopia. (And all are secret versions of the performer's native Mumbai.)

At first the traveler, who speaks no English, describes these cities through souvenirs drawn from a satchel, cries, leaps, and gestures; through these he details the cities' architecture and social spaces, their sign systems and customs. The spectators fill in what they do not understand with images drawn from dreams and caricatured depictions on the West End.

Then, over time, the foreigner learns English from the stagehands. The traveler describes the cities verbally, with specific details and precise diction. The strange dance morphs into a monologue about colonialism. The foreigner's English is perfect but the cities start to look like subtle critiques of London. Their lessons for modern life begin to feel pedantic, "a bit on the nose," as Her Majesty remarks to a lady-in-waiting. The spectators shift in their seats and steal glances at their watches.

In a flurry (and at great expense to the Crown), the foreigner starts staging these cities with the most fascinating theatrics: gas and electric lights, machines that incorporate mechanized bodies, astonishing circus feats, fabrics that undulate and shape-shift, giant performers who cross the stage over the course of an hour, strange symbols projected onto irregular surfaces, ancient songs summoned from vanished civilizations, eerie tones and disharmonies, baffling sound poems, pungent odors, elaborate mathematical choreographies, walls of video screens.

Finally, exhausted or broke, the foreigner sits at the edge of the stage. For the final months of the performance, which has gone on longer than anyone can remember, the foreigner and the audience sit almost entirely still and silent. Every hour or so, the foreigner or Her Majesty utter a few evocative phrases. The cities continue to be described, one after another, more mysterious and compelling than ever, but no one could say whether the richness of these descriptions arises in the mind of the foreigner, the mind of the Queen, the mind of God, or the space between.

By the time Her Majesty exits, blinking, into the morning light, her London has become unrecognizable.

Italo Calvino's luminous *Invisible Cities* tells of the great Kublai Khan, whose empire encompasses the known world, and thus contains all possible configurations of street and edifice. Fixed at the very heart of his vast kingdom, however, the Khan cannot see the intricacies of his domain; he requires a messenger to relay these remote features. And so he turns to the explorer Marco Polo, a foreigner who has traveled the extent of the land. He has him relate brief accounts of these far-flung cities—page-long fragments each describing a fantastical city made of glass, of signs, or developing in constant motion; impossible architectures, each with a peculiar logic made material. But differences in language initially place some barrier between the two, so the storyteller must turn to other means of expression: "what enhanced for Kublai every event or piece of news reported by his inarticulate informer was the space that remained around it, a void not filled with words." What is this "void not filled with words?" It is the void filled with the excess of the body in motion, its sounds and gestures—in other words, the performance of the teller. It is also the space around the telling that the listener fills with his or her own imaginings, the performance of reception. It is the image that comes to your mind when I write the word "blue" or the word "love." The performance exists between us; you complete the picture. The Khan learns this when listening to Marco Polo's tales—he fills in the faces of the passersby on those distant city streets, sees his own reflection in every window and stilled pool.

If Kublai Khan's kingdom is an exotic dream of the Italian Calvino, much as the British Samuel Taylor Coleridge imagined it one hundred and fifty years before, then he imagines that fantastical emperor of the East looking back in wonder and fascination at the West. Marco Polo reveals that the many cities he describes are in fact the many facets of one city—his distant home of Venice. In another reversal, Kyle Gillette reimagines this scene in the court of Queen Victoria, the Mongolian Empire of the 13th century recast as the British Empire of the 19th century. The exotic foreigner who communicates the character of her empire makes use of all manner of devices to fill this "void not filled by words," cycling through the diverse forms of the Modernist theatrical century: the domestic dramas of Arthur Wing Pinero and George Bernard Shaw critiquing the state of their nation; the flowing visual theatres of Edward Gordon Craig, W.B. Yeats, or Loïe Fuller; the circus hall of Bertolt Brecht; the sound poems of Antonin Artaud; the ancient songs of Meredith Monk; the giant performers of Robert Wilson; the mathematical choreographies of Lucinda Childs and Merce Cunningham. These are European and American figures, but Gillette's reversal of East and West shows us how so many of these Modernist "innovations" derived—or were stolen—from performance traditions of those cultures colonized by the West (in Asia alone, think of the influence of Bali, China, and Japan on the work of those listed above).

"By the time Her Majesty exits, blinking, into the morning light, her London has become unrecognizable." She finally sees the city that lives a complexity far beyond her own imagining. She cannot recognize the city and cannot recognize herself, because the performance is no longer bound by the frame of her own mirror. I write these words on June 24th, 2016, on the morning that the Brexit vote has ordained a return to a darker time of British isolation—to stage the fantasy of a city, a country, deprived of its inherent foreignness. Can Her Majesty return to the theatre and sit alone in the dark, watching imagined spectacles, rather than participating in the world that surrounds her?

53. *THE IMPOSSIBLE MAGIC SHOW—AUGUSTO CORRIERI*

Though largely ignored in the history of magic and conjuring, Le Grand Akazam might be described as the twentieth century's only avant-garde magician. Clearly influenced by Dada and Surrealism (though there are no records of his involvement with either of these movements), Akazam worked in clubs and small theatres in Italy and Switzerland between the two wars. His magic act never achieved notoriety, for reasons that will become all too apparent. The following is a historical reconstruction of his trademark performance.

As the curtains parted, spectators hushed and shushed each other.

The small stage was enveloped in a thick fog, through which the silhouette of a man could barely be discerned. As the wisps of smoke began to dissipate and curl away from the human figure, a voice could be heard, somewhat disembodied, coming from the stage.

"Ladies and Gentlemen, magic is the art of making the impossible possible." A dignified man in his 50s, wearing impeccable turn-of-the-century tails, Le Grand Akazam continued his formal address to the audience: "Through the power of magic, gravity can be defied, time can be reversed, and matter itself can undergo strange and perturbing permutations." Several audience members smiled in anticipation of the wonders to come.

"Tonight, with your permission, I wish to push magic further. Further than anyone has ever dared to go. To go beyond magic itself … " The magician paused dramatically to let the idea sink in: to allow spectators to contemplate what going "beyond magic" might mean. He then proceeded to walk to the very front of the stage, in full view of the audience.

"Ladies and gentlemen, watch carefully: I shall now endeavor to stand here, on the stage, in front of you … " A pause followed. In silence, the magician proceeded to stand on the stage, as announced.

A small boy sitting in the first row tugged inquisitively on his dad's sleeve.

After about a minute of standing, Akazam then announced: "And now, the second feat: breathing. I shall proceed to take air into my lungs, and to expel it out. Observe …" Again the magician stood silently on the spot. A few spectators laughed, not without contempt, whilst others muttered disapprovingly to one another.

Much to the bemusement of his audience, Akazam's entire act consisted of several other "un-magical" feats, each presented in the same grandiloquent style: looking at people in the room, listening, closing and opening his eyes, turning around on the spot, lifting and lowering his arms, saying the word "France," sitting on a chair and getting up again, walking up and down the stage, taking a watch out of his pocket and putting it back, clapping his hands, and the grand finale: bowing.

Reactions were seldom kind. Spectators would jeer and walk out, critics typically tore the show apart, calling it a stupid prank by a "clearly insane man" (it is mainly thanks to two or three vehement reviews that his act can be reconstructed). One review, by a Swiss journalist, contains the only known direct statement by Akazam, though it is unclear whether it is taken from an interview, a poster, or whether it is just something the magician might have announced during his act: *No more lies, no more fakery. This is the first and only magic show in which everything that happens* really happens. *Nothing is pretend. Everything is real in my theatre. No other magician can make this claim.*

1. Stage magic, also known as conjuring or performance magic, is a form of imagined theatre *par excellence*.

What sets magic apart from other stage arts is the presentation of impossible feats. The sense of wonder we might experience upon seeing, let's say, an object levitate in front of our very eyes, is due to our senses conflicting with what we know about matter and gravity; this prior knowledge of the world is crucial to appreciating magic, and it is why young children don't care much for it.

The magician's show revolves around the simple premise of performing things that cannot be performed. The live act itself, though occurring in real time and space, is largely "imaginary": as everyone knows all too well, the witnessed events don't actually take place, at least not in the way they appear to. Here in the theatre of magic we know we are being sold hot air, and we delight in the performer's honest hoax: there is an amplified knowingness in the relation between magician and spectators, a kind of infinitely mirrored "I know that you know that I know that you know … " And so we enjoy magic (if we do) because we understand that at its core it is *not* occurring in real time and space, despite appearing overwhelmingly to do so. Theatre's "here and now," its "liveness," is spun around and taken for a joy ride.

2. Magic has little to do with theatre's infamous suspension of disbelief. In a *Peter Pan* stage production, we can see the wires holding up Peter as he flies around Neverland, and we consciously "erase" the wires to lose ourselves in the illusion. However when stage illusionist David Copperfield levitates, we see a man flying impossibly around the theatre, clearly unsupported by wires. It is as though the magician is telling spectators: "Yes, this is theatre, it's all just theatre … and see how 100% real it is."

3. In a magic show everything appears rooted in this time and place: "Good evening, what's your name? Hello Catherine, please pick a card, any card … "

Though we know the speech might be scripted and the actions rehearsed, there is seemingly no theatrical or dramatic "fiction" here: we are not transposed to a fictitious Neverland, we are always rooted in this room, at this time. But how can we be in the realm of the mundane (literally, the "worldly"), yet bear witness to unworldly phenomena?

Here is where we might find the ontology of performance magic. What the magician is doing is describing or conjuring another performance: one that *would* be happening, at this moment in this room, if it were truly possible to defy physical laws. Similarly to many of Jorge Luis Borges's stories, written as *accounts* of impossible stories (and never fully coinciding with them), a magic show always refers to another magic show: the one we would witness if bodies could levitate, if cards and coins could be plucked out of thin air, if a broken piece of string could magically be restored whole again. And always with this paradox: that if magic were possible, we wouldn't go to the theatre to witness it.

54. *IN CHARACTER—HARVEY YOUNG*

The lobby is a locker room. Individual cubbies await each audience member. GUIDE—*later* CAPTAIN, *later* MASTER, *later* SHERIFF—*enters.*

GUIDE

Please silence your cell phones and unwrap any candies, cough drops. Today, we're going on an adventure. We'll explore foreign countries, sail across rough waters, meet a few interesting characters, and, perhaps, experience the fullness of life. You have a role to play. In fact, we cannot begin until you are in character. In each cubby, there is a costume. One size. It stretches. Slip it on. Over your clothes. Ask a neighbor to zip you in. You have 5 minutes. (GUIDE *exits.*)

In each cubby, a neatly folded brown, leathery clump, "the costume," sits on a shelf. Nearby, an audible gasp. Someone just realized that the clump is the skin of a black person minus the bones and innards. The body is intact, head to toes, fingernails, hair. A flesh costume. Most audience members are not fazed. This is theatre—and the skin probably isn't really real (but it is!). They get dressed—putting on black skin, zipping each other up, delighting in their blackness—their saggy, misfitting blackness. A spectator tries on a faux dialect, "Jive turkey" or something along those lines. Another shushes. One of the two has brown skin under the costume. GUIDE, *now* CAPTAIN, *enters with a whip.*

CAPTAIN

In line! In line! Faster Negroes! Yes, you, faster!
(CAPTAIN *cracks the whip. Maybe someone gets hit, maybe the skin costume rips, maybe blood appears)*

Shit just got real. And audience members are loving it: the immersion into blackness and the world of the play. A line forms. CAPTAIN *spews increasingly offensive racist epithets before settling on the N-word, which gets repeated a few dozen times, and clasps a chain around the ankles of a few audience members. Most won't get shackled. They feel disappointed.* CAPTAIN *marches the audience through a doorway, into a dark "theatre." Maybe* CAPTAIN *makes an offhand comment, perhaps pointing to the entranceway and declaring "The Door of No Return." Maybe not. The sound of rattling shackles. The "theatre" smells like a latrine. It stinks. The floor moves. It rocks.*

CAPTAIN

The journey begins.

The play continues …

In writing about black experience, scholars often center upon the compulsory visibility of diasporic African bodies. As a consequence of centuries of human bondage, legal limits on citizenship rights, and stereotypical popular representations, brown complexion—inaccurately labeled "black skin"—has been accorded a monitored status. A police officer is more likely to stop a motorist; a prosecutor to seek a tougher sentence; a shopkeeper to follow a customer if the stopped, accused, and followed has been recognized as black. It is for these reasons that writings on racial identity often emphasize the excessive attention (and violence) that greets the black body in innumerable public settings. This emphasis can be seen in sociologist W.E.B. DuBois's theorization of "double consciousness," the "sense of always looking at one's self through the eyes of others, of measuring one's soul by the tape of a world that looks on in amused contempt and pity." It appears in author Ta-Nehisi Coates's "letter" to his son in which he observes, "In America, it is traditional to destroy the black body—it is heritage."

In critically engaging the attendant experiences of blackness, it can be helpful to spotlight an individual. Focus on a person. Tell his or her story. Try to relay the perspective of folks who inhabit environments in which others look upon them with distrust, disgust, skepticism, and often fear. Share the anxieties that surface from knowing that they could be the target of violence, a verbal or physical assault, because of their skin complexion. These personal accounts, anecdotes, memories, and stories can be gathered to create a mosaic of a diverse community united by similar experiences of race.

The arts have played a significant role in relaying embodied black experience. In literature, authors have long understood that a novel offers an opportunity to mine the psychological interiority of characters in a manner unparalleled by other artistic media. Ralph Ellison's *Invisible Man* and Toni Morrison's *The Bluest Eye*, for example, grant the reader the chance not only to see the world through the eyes of their protagonists but also to hear their comments on the many slights, injustices, and outright prejudices that they encounter. On the stage, playwrights (and production teams) have attempted to offer a sense of embodied black experience by creating characters who speak openly about their perceptions on the world in which they live. For example, the character Wolf, in August Wilson's play *Two Trains Running*, observes, "every nigger you see done been to jail one time or another. The white man don't feel right unless he got a record on these niggers." Always aware of the precarity of blackness, he warns others, "you always under attack."

In Character imagines a scenario in which anyone can gain access to the experience of being seen and treated as black. It invents a way to encounter history, including the past abuses that targeted diasporic Africans. From one perspective, *In Character* is a far-fetched play. No theatre is going to invite audience members to don the flesh of another person and role-play "black person." From another, the play could happen but with a slight difference in staging. Immersive theatre is gaining in popularity. In addition, virtual reality (VR) technology seems to improve with each new year. It is just a matter of time before an enterprising developer creates a way for us to put on VR goggles, assume the stead of a captive, and experience the hold of a slave ship. The result will be a form of theatre.

55. *IRL—JOSHUA CHAMBERS-LETSON AND JOSHUA RAINS*

The interior of a very old theatre that very few people have entered for a long time. A good amount of dust has accumulated. Everything has been cleaned except the stage, where a layer of dust remains. A microphone. THEY enter and begin to move the dust around. A SPECTATOR from the audience approaches the microphone. No one is white. THEY hand over their phone. The SPECTATOR reads a conversation from a hookup app (Grindr, Scruff, etc.) into the microphone. The conversation begins with a salutation, a breach, the beginning of an exchange. The conversation is happening between THEM and the person on the other end of the app in real time. The SPECTATOR recites the exchange as a single, concrete statement.

All of this is happening in real time such that THEY are not really on the stage even though THEY are actually on the stage. As the SPECTATOR reads, THEY carefully push the dust on the stage into a blueprint of the apartment or home of the other person(s) with which the conversation and encounter is happening. THEY include oblique references to details from the encounter in the blueprint: perhaps where they fucked, or where the other person(s) broke down into tears, or where the other person told a story about their recent breakup. The SPECTATOR recites the entirety of the exchange.

SPECTATOR

[*example of possible text*] Hi. Hi. Looking? Could be. Really want to blow you and swallow your load man. Hit me up some other time. When you free? Hung? Just saw this. 7.5 UC. You? I'm around a lot in the evenings. 7.5 uncut also. Off today and tomorrow. Dick pic? Sure. You? I want to swallow your dick man. I do and you? Nice dick btw. I am thicker. You may be a bit longer. Cool. You too. Free now? Would love to suck you man and swallow your nut. HIV—DDF here. Rarely hook up. I am off today and tomorrow. Can I blow you after the gym? Sweaty? Yes, Sure. Where are you? 2035 Adam Clayton Powell Jr. Blvd, apt 3. Cool. I'm leaving in about ten. On the way. Be there by 8. Ok. Here. Coming down. [*the conversation continues IRL*]

At some point, the exchange on the app ends as THEY and the other person(s) meet in real life to fuck. The other person(s) are not actually on the stage. The SPECTATOR may put down the phone but continues to recite the conversation as it is happening. A verbatim performance of every word and every sound they make until the other person penetrates THEY. At this point, THEY stop making the blueprint from the dust and wipe it into oblivion. Every time the SPECTATOR gets to the point in the conversation when the other person penetrates THEY, THEY stop to destroy the blueprint and start the cycle again. Each time, the same motions, but each instance is singular, particular, and a variation on the theme. This continues perpetually. It does not end. When the SPECTATOR gets tired, they may stop reading as another SPECTATOR takes their place. Audiences and SPECTATORS come and go. THEY never leave the stage.

Dust continues to accumulate.

There is no blackout. There is no conclusion.

Just the endlessly renewable present and dust. Always more dust.

When Joseph Roach described performance as "the process of trying out various candidates in different situations" we don't believe he was referring to the ritual of anonymous sex (the hookup). But the hookup is an act comprised of an endless chain of repetitions: a standard series of salutations, flirtations, seductions, the rise, the fall, the excitation and boredom, the mundanity and the surprise, the push, the pull, the sweat, shudder, howl, and cum, the collapse, and the what-comes-after which is either a kind of dawn or dusk. And then, as Jay-Z might say, "On to the next one."

What we are not positing is an abstract, immaterial sextopia. Like performance, hookup sex can be hard work. There is the commitment to form: the willingness to submit oneself to having the same conversations, to doing the same set of actions, and perhaps above all the exposure of the performer's body to others and the exposure of the exposed body in performance to failure. In performance the body is never unmarked though it can reorganize the marks that bind it. Jean-Luc Nancy describes the *aesthetic body* whereby what is "exposed are all those aesthetics whose assembly—discrete, multiple, and swarming—is the body." So if we have only vaguely defined the bodies onstage, it is to leave the performance open to the wide range of aesthetic bodies (of genders, races, sexes). It is not that THEY has no race or has no gender, but that we have withheld this information and left it up to you to make sense of it and to reveal your own biases in so doing. That said, we must insist that, "No one is white." We cannot allow any reader to make this all about white people (or heterosexuals). As Nina Simone said, when introducing an audience to "To Be Young, Gifted, and Black," "Now, it is not addressed primarily to white people. Though it does not put you down in any way. It simply ignores you."

Queer of color sex (like performance) and hookup sex as a genre of performance opens up new possibilities for being in the world together. Each fuck is a citation of all fucks before it while simultaneously breaking from its context in order to become something new. This is what imbues queer sex with the worldmaking capacities José Muñoz insisted we attend to. Lauren Berlant and Michael Warner describe "the queer world [as] a space of entrances, exits, unsystematized lines of acquaintance, projected horizons, typifying examples, alternate routes, blockages, incommensurate geographies." And if we live in a world of catastrophe and negation, breakdown and bad breaks, a world in which we demand the future precisely because it seems impossible, then we are more than ever in need of new worlds and alternative possibilities for being in this world together. The perpetual ritual of the queer hookup as a means without end is a worldmaking practice that can lead to what Jean-Luc Nancy calls for in his plea for a collective endeavor to "work with other futures—but under the condition of the ever-renewed present."

Bodies never go away. There is a truth to *Ecclesiastes 3:20*: "All go to the same place. All came from the dust and all return to the dust." Nothing is lost forever. Not really. Every time you breathe in dust, you take the remains of another's body into your own and, like sex, this is another combination of penetration and bodily (dis)integration. Which is also to say that breathing, like sex, is a way of being together, being inside each other, and taking each other inside of ourselves.

56. *IT COMES BACK TOGETHER—KAREN CHRISTOPHER*

projectiles begin gathering in the space
some with ragged edges
others in pieces that seem to retain an original order
still part of a viable plan
first items that flutter and float as they catch eddies of air
followed by the heaviest pieces flying in straight lines

fragments of walls, curtains, a desk, chair, lamp, a flurry of confetti, and bits of fabric whirl aimlessly for a time but eventually find a single direction with a determined velocity, a few shards of vinyl records and largely intact parts of a record player, a box of yarn rewinds and collects, an alarm clock and a blanket all reconstitute in the center of the performance space

books stack themselves, papers collate
the room reappears

a suspended moment: a feeling of expectation
time hangs in the air

two people enter the space in reverse
taking places in the chair and on the edge of the desk

it is very quiet, the audience feels a shimmering between the two as if something profound has just been said

K: sometimes I sit in the sun and look within rather than through my eyes and I watch the debris floating there …
S: your eyeball is a universe …
K: my vitreous humor has a lot of space junk floating in it …
S: ok
K: no, it's a gel that fills the middle of the eyeball and keeps everything working in there.
S: like tears when you cry …
K: no, inside the ball
S: you mean tears?
K: the vitreous humor is the liquid that fills the eye
S: you mean tears?
K: no, inside the ball
S: like tears when you cry …
K: no, it's a gel that fills the middle of the eyeball and keeps everything working in there.
S: ok
K: my vitreous humor has a lot of space junk floating in it …
S: your eyeball is a universe …
K: sometimes I sit in the sun and I watch the debris floating there … the universe, this room, my eyeball, they each carry the artifacts of their beginning; flying, floating in the space between then and now

they look at each other

they leave the room, quickly and quietly
it is very quiet

In Karen Christopher's imagined theatre we find ourselves unexpectedly weightless. I imagine our entrance, spilling like carrier bags over the front of the dress circle and drifting gently down towards the stall seats below. We float, we are floating, held up in the darkening light by either a suspension of time or of space or of both, we can't be sure yet.

In this domain of free-floating debris the conventional markers of duration and direction fail us. Are we going forward or backward, or are we, as the text also suggests, hanging in the air between the two? I am reminded that in outer space north is not up and south is not down, that maps are a thing we agree to agree upon, for consistency, or history, or the maintenance of a particular narrative about power and the center of things. A story we tell about where all the roads lead.

I am reminded also of the drawings we made (we still make) before we taught ourselves to understand perspective. A thick line of sky blue sky somewhere up there above us and the ground a thin layer of green beneath, and the sublime, impossible gelatinous white nothing between them in which the rest of it hangs like space dust. Objects suspended in unlikely relation to one another, a poem of surfaces unencumbered by depth. Perspective is the clattering into art of a set of rules that pretend to truth beyond ideology, but in fact are quite the opposite. Laws that tell us what is important, that direct our eye, that fix us in relation to the thing that we are looking at.

Not here though, not in this theatre. In this theatre things are not so stable or so measurable. I float a foot or a few feet above my seat and I can see objects and parts of objects moving above me, shimmering in the half-light as they swim across the auditorium.

57. *IT COULD BE A FOREST—RALPH LEMON*

It could be a forest, if framed properly, the photo cropped just right. It sits a few yards away from Warren (Red) Carter's house, a fancy doublewide, almost a real country rambler-style house, white, with a dark blood red trim. A series of cars surround the front side, back, the field: a series of years to the models of the cars; 1970s to recent; white, maroon, and black; a Honda, a Dodge, an old Chevy. The cars and house and semi-manicured field surrounded by thick full green oaks and a few simple wooden utility poles with their power lines. In the side right yard, a small maze of 40–50 young thin Gum trees, with one thicker one, about 3ft wide, that becomes the center.

There's a grassless (red) dirt patch for dogs a few yards from this center. Warren's son, Chester, is raising (fighter) pit bulls. Two at the moment, one a terrified runt. The runt won't ever fight but they don't put it down, not sure why, maybe because it's weak. They are Christians, Southern Baptists, maybe that's why.

Fiction (1)

They dress the dogs in silver spacesuits. Lloyd Williams, Warren's good friend, his wife, Emma, put them together. Patterned from pet-store-bought large-sized camouflaged dog jackets. The runt's costume becomes a silver cape, he/she is engulfed. Warren and his son did the actual dressing, put the silver suits on the dogs because no one else wanted to get near them, not even near the cowering runt. Not me at least. The doghouses were painted the day before, three of them, a shade of purple (actually a purple closer to African Violet). I thought this would be an interesting comment on International Klein Blue, the color I was thinking about when I first saw the plywood structures. I am not colorblind but actually prefer purple to International Klein Blue. The structures badly needed a paint job, I thought. In my letter I asked Warren to find any purple, a convenient Home Depot purple. Now bright cartoon doghouses in a 50-yard dirt perimeter, with a slight hill and tiny sink indentations, not quite actual holes but impending something more major.

This partially recreated landscape is also full of fleas or chiggers—both, I believe. Jumping off woody plants on anything unplanted and moving. A queer patience. Waiting for what? (Waiting for us, the work. How did they know? We just happened to be there.) I wear boots and thick jeans, am prepared but it doesn't matter, am bitten up to my groin area. I go on the Internet investigating the marks and the pain. Whatever they are they populate my body, for days. Starting at the ankles and climbing upward it seems. Terrifying. (Then they die I suppose. Leaving larvae. The larvae drop, eventually becoming mites on the ground, harmless to humans, laying eggs and then the mites die, a second death.)

This is the theatre, our forest and reconstituted dog yard. Where Lloyd moved the flying saucer, from his garage, 5 miles away, still in Bentonia though. Taking it apart after our celestial and countrified play three years before, when he first put it together and tried to make it work, actually fly. He said he would keep trying. He was able to get it rolling down a nearby freeway right away, an alternate lane. Three years later Lloyd took it apart moving it in his truck the few miles to Warren's place, then repurposing it, circling it, mandala-like, around that center tree in the backside yard with his bare hands.

Fiction (2)

A voice off camera says, *Where is Walter?* Warren's father and the patriarch to this play. The story begins with him.

When we last saw Walter he had flown off in his flying saucer. (A round, metal tube, approximately 10ft in diameter capped with an old-style C-Band mesh satellite dish as a dome roof, with another mesh-style dish mounted to the top of the structure standing up in the common orientation for a dish. It is a two-seater, with dark blue plastic seats and crayon-pink carpet upholstered on the inside base floor.) Lloyd got it to fly. Walter wanted to go to heaven, *Where there aren't a lot of people. A chosen few,* he had said.

But Walter lands on what appears to be a futuristic barren cotton field. On another planet. The saucer falls around a tree-like organism, maybe the same planet but maybe not. The inhabitants of this place (ghosts of the R&B singing duet Sam and Dave, and their specter spouses, Emma and Lorraine, who on this day are elected nurses of the church, dressed in official "nurses of the church" white) find the saucer and plant an immaculate garden around it. They think it's a god.

Walter is never seen again.

At one point it began to rain, hard, and they had to pause. Everyone soaking wet. Had to wait not only for the sun but also until their costumes were dry, to finish tending the garden, for the camera. Rain and sweat. The rain softening the earth making the planting easier. By sunset they were done. Lloyd turned on the flying saucer's headlights. Everything else in dark shadow. It sat that way through the night, hovering. Lloyd remarked that he was tired and limped back to Warren's house.

Silver-coated killer space dogs bark out high-frequency signals in the background.

A garden. A memorial. A sci-fi requiem—not one's expected (old) black southern rage, reactive violence. Also an escape, it is outer space after all, search for a kind world, forgiveness (or forgetting?). Imagined. Choreographed travels (death), which is also an escape. Down here, this South (like everywhere), funerals are theatre.

Two years later I receive a text. *Here are pictures of the flying saucer. I'm sorry.* Emma texting and sending more photos to me from her cell phone, three—a close-up and two long shots. Another great storm settled in the area and blew the tree down that held/centered the flying saucer. The only tree to fall in the little forest yard, completely uprooted. How strange. The saucer destroyed, a real wreck, sculpted by nature. Magnificent. Now a true (unfinished) masterpiece.

Lloyd and Warren used to work together, driving around collecting (good) junk and reselling it (until Warren got too tired). How the saucer got made. Yes, progress, what the storm wrought. Back to junk. Now broken to pieces in Warren's unkempt yard (uncollectable, because it's already there). Waiting for what? It's just waiting. In Emma's text she didn't mention how Lloyd felt about the damage, the obliteration. Not a word. The labor.

So I called Lloyd and said, *That was really good work, Lloyd. Thank you. I must get back down there, soon, we'll find another center, make something new, I'm sure.* I am absolutely sure of it. Though there is nothing idyllic about that place, where it is, what it represents, not even in my unreliable memory. There is the broad blue Mississippi sky. (Unless it's raining, or there's a great storm. Clouds hanging in clumps, like pre-cubist snowmen, shapes more round).

58. *IT WAS A LARGE RUBBLE SPACE—CLAIRE MACDONALD*

There was *The playing is* with two large oversize structures, *almost* chairs everywhere made of old timbers. with naked bulbs. rubble space seeping from the walls and dust. wind separated was continuous. by the song, which begins as a rich tiny, black, vocal and instrumental piece and was paired always. The acts were It repeated until *only* The sound of It was lit the was voice remained.

There everywhere made of is with two large, almost chairs old rubble space with naked bulbs seeping was continuous. by the song, was The and dust. oversize structures wind separated repeated until only The sound of It was lit the was voice remained. which begins as a rich tiny, black, *vocal* and instrumental piece and was paired always. *The* acts were It timbers. playing from the walls.

is with *two* large, old rubble space with naked bulbs The acts were seeping was was The and dust. sound There everywhere almost chairs made of of It was lit wind separated repeated the was *voice* continuous. by the song, as a rich tiny, black, until only remained. which *begins* The vocal and instrumental piece and was *paired* always. It timbers. playing from oversize structures the walls.

There everywhere large, old rubble space with naked was The and dust. sound instrumental wind separated repeated piece and was paired always. *It* timbers. *is* with two playing from oversize structures the walls. *almost* chairs made of of It was lit the was voice continuous. by the song, as *a* rich tiny, black, until bulbs The acts were seeping was only remained. which begins The vocal and

until bulbs The acts were instrumental wind separated repeated piece and was the was voice continuous. by the *song,* as *a* rich tiny, black, old rubble space with *naked* was The and dust. *sound* It timbers. is with two playing from oversize structures paired always. seeping was only remained. which begins The vocal and There everywhere large, the walls. almost chairs made of of It was lit

[redacted] and [redacted] the song [redacted] was [redacted] repeated [redacted] until [redacted]

[redacted] the [redacted] sound [redacted] was [redacted] black, [redacted] and [redacted] the [redacted]

[redacted] act [redacted] was [redacted] repeated until [redacted] the [redacted]

[redacted] voice [redacted] s [redacted] were [redacted]

[redacted] separated [redacted] . [redacted] . [redacted] . [redacted]

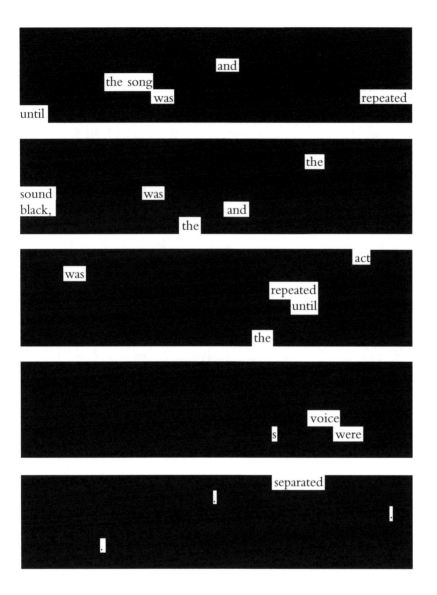

59. LAST RESORT [NO ONE CAN STOP YOU NOW]—SYLVAN OSWALD

Last Resort gives the audience an opportunity to make their dreams come true through mini-pageants created by artists on demand.

The aesthetic is high-school-drama-club-meets-theme-park-meets-revival-tent using everyday materials in creative ways.

Prior to arrival, the audience completes an intake interview (online survey). Questions include: "What career would you have chosen if there were no barriers and money were no object?" "What hobbies have you always wanted to take up?" "What areas of mastery elude you?" "What are you about to give up on?" You can tick a box to participate in your dream or to consult on the staging of your dream, if yours is among those selected.

The audience arrives at an abandoned supermarket or big box store, preferably in an area underserved by the arts.

Admission is free. Plenty of parking. Performers on roller-skates and scooters for efficiency.

The atmosphere inside is like a carnival/job fair with refreshments and people sitting at tables with brochures.

Artists have been hard at work in the last 48 hours preparing a series of scenes. Some audience members have been tapped to participate in the scenes.

A trustworthy emcee welcomes the audience and keeps them informed and oriented throughout.

After some pre-show entertainment (a reboot of The Langley Schools Music Project in which a guileless music teacher had children sing '60s–'70s pop like the Beach Boys and Fleetwood Mac), the audience travels from station to station within the building to witness scenes from each others' dreams.

In some cases dreams have been combined, often in unexpected pairings (i.e., a few people who have always wanted to be actors + someone who is about to give up on writing a novel // someone who wants to helm a fishing boat + resolve conflict with a parent).

The final number involves a tableau of a tropical island and a song that everyone has been prepared to sing. Perhaps this is the Earth's dream of rest or what the planet wants from us. Followed by food and dancing.

One performance, December 31, starting at 6pm till whenever.

As an early teen in the early'80s in my bedroom in suburban Toronto, I listened to the radio. A lot. When I was trying to be cool, I listened to CFNY, but mostly I listened to CHUM FM and the even less cool but much more catchy CHUM AM. I am guessing now, but I'm pretty sure the Canadian progressive rock band Saga's 1981 hit "On the Loose" would have had a lot of airplay. Perhaps that's why the subtitle of Sylvan Oswald's imagined theatre immediately brings to mind its chant-able drum-and-guitar-heavy chorus: "[*Drawn out*] No one can stop you now. [*Staccato*] Tonight you're on the loose. No one to tell you how. Tonight you're on the loose." Cue synthesizer and guitar flourishes and the flamboyant flicking of long hair.

Whether you like that song or not, it gives license to its listeners to do what we want; it is inviting, it is joyous, and now it is slightly—and, for me, pleasurably—kitsch. Oswald's imagined theatre shares a lot of these traits. He too gives his audiences license to abandon everyday restrictions, let loose, and articulate their desires. He uses recognizable theatre forms that give *Last Resort* prog rock's accessibility, amplified by a welcoming emcee, free access, and a familiar context to help them feel welcome. His event will happen on a date when we are conditioned to both celebrate and reflect on what we want our futures to be. Like Saga, he democratizes the expression of desire. This is a profoundly political gesture in our socio-political moment—almost certainly our era—which excludes and oppresses so many with less advantage while it both fulfills and flaunts the desires of the privileged. As my friend Lois Weaver of Split Britches frequently observes: "If you can imagine it you can make it. If you can make it then you can make it *change*." What is theatre if not a place to imagine change?

Oswald's imagined theatre also has a lot in common with medieval theatre and culture. It draws on medieval mystery plays, with their various wagons and stages for telling different stories. And it invokes Russian literary critic Mikhail Bakhtin's theory of the carnivalesque, forged in his analysis of medieval carnival culture and the topsy-turvy opportunities it offered to explore things hegemonic cultures predominantly prohibit, such as free expression and apparent eccentricity.

Many critics have warned that Bakhtin's carnivalesque might offer less political purchase than he intended, indeed, that it might actually reinforce the oppression of the less advantaged by giving them (controlled) intermittent opportunities to let loose. The same caution might apply to Oswald's *Last Resort.*

Except that this is the *Last Resort.* It is not a repeatable opportunity for the masses to let off steam/be controlled; it is a one-off. It is certainly about *possibility*, people's dreams coming true. But it is also, and urgently, about *necessity*: it is the last resort; it can't be stopped now. It is a party for the masses and an opportunity to play out dreams ... but it is also a summons and a rallying cry to do so.

60. THE LAST WOR(L)D—VK PRESTON

I attend a theatre for the end of the world. Built
for nuclear hits. In the subterranean dark. Like fish, stripped,
of arms: mined of salvageable metals. Who, like Ozymandias, slips
into a theatre. A war room, underground. Inside this labyrinth: a
hidden theatre. Unused. Abandoned. The theatre of war in an unseen
above. Screens. Everywhere. In these wings, only generals. Maps shift: a
burning of worlds. News, hung with magnets, slid into place. In the
sightless dark, I stop. Aghast. "It is for the end of the world. They built this
theatre for the end of the world!" My flashlight plays over the dark real. Seats.
Tables for operators. Chthonic switchboards. Nightmare pins & cables. More
buttons: your call. Just silence. Just this woods. Unsuspecting. A drill, a rehearsal:
hands grazing over cold glass. Yet more chill, in this dark. A sign, a book, a book!
Full of rules. All possible subjects, all theatres—all but this imagined theatre of all
endings. Everything, the history, "from the chaos and birth of the world to the reign
of X." Dawn, to perform. Stumbling through morning, the rift of it. More clouds.
Power rising. On this mimic horizon, a sun flutters, a ping pong ball at the end of a
clear line, flashing like a fishing lure: a repertoire of bubbles. Trajectories flaring.
(Round again.) Breaking surface. (Round again.) I imagine a halo of atmospheres—a
cosmic body etched in movement, an arc of destruction. Lucrative of course. (Again.)
(Again.) (Again.) Dreams. Hiccups. An in-dwelling of gods. It's a hit! A palpable hit!
Watch from these seats now. Here, an eye opens. A fantasy, of course. Hear, whole
notes. Singing voices, come to rest. Birth! Then? What? That dark mouth (red again).
World eater. Pinned by light. Center stage. A dance of galaxies: a tremble of bombs.
Open this, then, in the valley of shadow—but not yet in death. This sunken theatre,
this recent ruin, in which we clamber.

Built, not fiction.
    A future grave, gravedigger.
        Not past yet. Just covered over.

"Chthonic switchboards" lurk, like the ancient Furies, beneath the built world, beneath civilization, even below that: under all the life-giving soil, the undead minerals, the sediment and sentiment, the savage certainties, the possibility of love. If the theatre of war finds its *telos*, its end, in The End, we can hardly be surprised. The *Oresteia* would either have to happen again in reverse or dissipate infinitely outward, the cold death of the universe. How could it be otherwise? The *theatron*, that ancient "seeing place," that inventor of worlds, sounds too like something far more futuristic: the THEATRON 3000, "World eater," destroyer of space and time.

Albert Einstein's thought experiments once destroyed what we understood as space and time. Their implications were profound in the abstract terms of theoretical physics but depended on the perceptual basis of the thinkable. Einstein demonstrated relativity by creating imaginary experiences that were unstageable: space elevators, trains approaching light speed, lightning bolts that strike simultaneously with respect to observers on the ground but separately for those on the train. Each thought experiment was for Einstein a little theatre wherein our imagined sensory presence depends upon our prior lived experience. But then Einstein asks us to imagine beyond the known possible—to extrapolate. Einstein's hypothetical stages transcended matter in their ambition toward light, becoming impossible to produce as theatre (though Stanisław Witkiewicz, Robert Wilson, and others have tried). Their ultimate staging in the theatre of war proved unbearable to behold: the blinding flash of light, the instant disintegration of cities, the mushroom cloud observed by a distant, horrified audience.

In the end was the word. The word became an irradiated afterimage of the world's searing finale. This is the way the world ends. Not with a whimper, but not with a bang either. Just in a bunker, that bleak underground theatre, isolated by visions, by vision itself. Yet there's nothing to see here. Just an old song stuck in your head. Just an imagined theatre, fading in the brain pan. Just a charred toy, a glowing souvenir, which from now on will have to stand in for the vanished civilizations. Some dry riverbeds, the only sign there may once have been life here.

Other worlds have died before; other words have been said. But this was the last.

61. *THE LOST NOTEBOOKS OF THE PAINTER'S WIFE—DIANE GLANCY*

[in which notebook pages fall like the long tail of a comet, and the painter appears as an elk]

Fragment [ ]
When Lloyd died, I took the last of his paintings to the art dealer in Reno. I had given the dealer my notebooks to draw attention to the painter's work. I hoped they would be published, but somehow they were misplaced. The dealer didn't know where. Maybe in the storeroom. If you could have seen the place, you would know why they were never found. I was furious. What would I do now? Recreate what I could of the painter's words? And how would I live?

Fragment [ ]
You know where they are, the dealer said, driving me from his store after another visit. Yes, I knew—they were in my head.

I tried to write what I could remember of the words I heard the painter say. But the memories shifted. Another voice that was mine, but seemed separate, spoke. I was the painter. I was his wife. I was myself, the narrator, on my own.

Fragment [ ]
After his death, I left the painter's ashes in the dry bed of Winnemucca Lake, as he asked. I drove there alone, wanting no one with me. I sat on the rocks. Beside the ancient petroglyphs. I visited the places we had gone together. Now evaporated in the hot, barren air.

That night, I saw the pages of the notebooks, loose from their bindings. I tried to read as quickly as I could.

That night. In a dream. The painter appeared as an elk. His antlers were ragged bolts of light. They started fire along the ridge line. The words in the notebooks were flames. Driven from the woods—game for hunting. I saw the elk held a cauliflower. The cauliflower was the ice ball of a comet. The painter himself was hunted. He struck fire in the brush. I could not see for the orange. I could not breathe for the smoke. Afterwards. Undergrowth singed. Pinecones opened. Smoke trailed upward in thin lines. New life. New growth.

Fragment [ ]
The painter receives criticism of his work. It is simplistic. His style continues. An act of resistance says there is another way. A sneeze coming. Wait.
It is cold outside. The owl *huu huu huuu.*
It is warm inside his painting. Here there is insistence. A diligence of this.
His work approximates the structure of his confines.
I think how color looked to him. Often he moved his lips speaking to it.
The color spilled into margins and fragmentations in the notebooks.
I think in the night he talked to color.

Fragment [ ]
His paintings were various boxes of color overlaid with other colors. It was when we watched the train pass—all the railroad cars were brown—rust brown—some with a little color in the graffiti. But then came a cornflower blue car—a bright Monet blue—and later, toward the end of the train, a pale green car—sage or sawgrass. I heard him growl in his throat. Color was the prey he was after.

I finished writing a play, *Lloyd and Hallah*, about a painter and his wife. The play deals with appropriation, kleptomania, and tuberculosis. After the painter's death, his wife takes the notebooks she has kept for years to an art dealer, in hopes of continuing the sale of his work. The notebooks contain the painter's words about his style and method. The art dealer misplaces the notebooks.

The problem—this happens after the play ended. The play knew it was over, but the writing continued. Not writing that was another act in the play, but independent of it, sounding like fictional nonfiction, or a prose piece, or narrative—maybe monologue, but not that either.

In *The Lost Notebooks of the Painter's Wife*, the missing pages come back to her in various dreams, arriving as a comet, and the painter as an elk in an animal transformation, and words that have no one to answer them. I think the pages of the notebooks appear to the painter's wife out of order. In surreal images. Stripped of logical connection. But in the undergrowth, a reasoning shrouded the dispersion.

What would I do with the after-play? Was it an act II? I thought at first. No, it was its own entity. Traveling out there in space.

Re: the notebooks. A syllogism marked the aftermath. A tree is alive.

The pages of the notebooks are made from a tree.

Therefore the notebooks are alive.

Possibly the notebooks are seen walking. Or the loose pages of them.

The setting is Winnemucca, Nevada. Surrounded by mountains, desert, and the evaporated Winnemucca Lake, where some of the oldest petroglyphs are found. Above her at night, is the dark sky where comets, falling stars, and satellites cross.

Theatre is not an object like a book. It happens across the stage in a passing-comet scenario. Made of dirt, dust, and the ice of conflict. And then it is gone, leaving the viewers with an impression. What I had left in the lost notebooks was the tail, so to speak, trailing from the comet, blown back by solar wind.

I see the painter's wife wearing the square covers of a notebook, neck to ankles, the way I've seen young men on television jump from cliffs in their flying suits to sail on the wind.

62. *THE MEANS OF PRODUCTION—JEN HARVIE*

Note: The company delivers the following text in whatever form they want to. They are encouraged to illustrate, add to, and/or deviate from the script as they see fit, and to insert details about the means of production relevant to their particular circumstances.

★ ★ ★

All artists and/or workers involved are paid a living wage for all phases of pre-production and production. They are also allocated "parachute payments" for a period post-production if they are temporarily out of paid work (like English football clubs relegated from the Premier League). They are entitled to: pension benefits; paid leave schemes for parents and other carers; paid support for continuing professional development; paid leave for periods of, for example, illness, holidays, and research; and, if required, support in securing affordable housing.

The funding for the work is provided by fair, universal taxation. This is likely to require significant systemic change. Some suggestions for such change include:

- raising the top rates of income tax to further address inequality;
- properly taxing large corporations which exploit globalization to avoid paying reasonable local taxes;
- requiring comparatively wealthy for-profit parts of the cultural sector (e.g., professional sport, West End/Broadway theatre, Hollywood cinema, major social media companies, fashion retailers, casinos, and providers of new media technologies such as smartphones) to pay significant dividends to the not-for-profit, state-subsidized, and amateur cultural sectors which feed them;
- requiring corporations which parasitically exploit the arts to sell their products (e.g., alcohol producers) to pay significant dividends to the arts; and
- requiring corporations based in the same place as the producing company, and reliant on the cultural vibrancy of that place to attract and retain good workers (corporations in the financial industries, for example), to pay significant dividends to the arts.

Everyone working on the production has some autonomy but also collaborates and compromises. Individualism does not trump teamwork and collectivism. All participants are encouraged to be ambitious, whatever that means to them. Time and resources allocated to pre-production are sufficient, not inadequate.

The production's run is long enough that the makers can have satisfaction exploring it properly, and audiences have decent opportunities to see it. As much as possible, the production should incorporate opportunities for creative development (including during performance), allowing the makers to experience the work as constantly interesting. The production period will not be overly long. The production schedule will not put undue pressure on the makers.

Each production has a reasonable budget and its makers know what that budget is in good time, providing the security that enables proper planning and experimentation.

Resources are recycled wherever possible.

In the wider theatre ecology where this production takes place, resources are shared. Bigger, wealthier theatres are required to share with those that are less well-resourced. This is intended principally to benefit the less well-resourced institutions. The bigger ones may benefit (for example, by seeing interesting experiments and outcomes); however, they must not exploit the smaller companies by attempting, for example, to take any credit for the smaller companies' work, or to make claims to being risky or innovative simply by association.

All tickets are genuinely affordable.

From the start, she asks: What would it mean for theatre to produce a living wage? She dreams of a world in which the making of things—metaphor, movement, breathing and breath—would extract from surplus a structure that more robustly sustains the lives of all of those who live and work within it. She sketches that world as if thinking, and dreaming, and feeling, and love were made fully accessible, were more fully valued, as tools of all trade. She stares at her screen. What would this take? Her fingers trip over numbers, doing their sums; then they freeze. She deletes, deletes again. She abandons all math, its logics too restrictive for the world she's invoked.

But they beckon her back, those numbers: and she sets in place a scheme that would make this world both the dreamed-of and the done. Tax all who have excess not for war but for art—or for beauty, shared feeling, provocation, or whatever theatre may set out for itself to do. Make theatre as a system of roads, or bridges, or power lines strung from every pole: core to the infrastructure, the heart, the goings-on of the social world. Essential trumps exceptional, she thinks, in a world so wholly steered by cost. She rewrites *austerity* as, instead, the obligatory cost of *to live*.

Throughout, she demands: What would it mean for theatre to *be* a living wage?

She turns from her screen, sees the world as it is.

When she wakes, she tries again. It all comes out the same. She sleeps, wakes again: writes the same. And again, and again. It would all be so simple; it is all so viable, so imminently concrete, but for will. But for will.

63. A META-THEATRE—BUSH MOUKARZEL

Audience walks into a meta-theatre. They tear their own tickets, pocket the stubs, and tell themselves to enjoy the show.

The auditorium has chairs upon chairs, piled up and turning back on themselves like an Escher drawing. The chairs seem endless. The theatre has no floor.

The audience wonders: "If I sit on the chair, what does the chair sit on?" They remember being at school, their teacher telling them about The World resting on an elephant's back, and the elephant, in turn, standing on a turtle. "But what does the turtle stand on?" a student asks. "Oh, it's turtles all the way down."

You take your seat and open the program. It is a solo performance. You notice the name of the performer: it is your name. You look at the stage.

Lights up to a blackout.

You think you might be standing there, looking back at yourself, but it is too dark to be certain. And there's a lot of smoke, and a confusing set, and there's a war in the way. But it looks like you.

You think you do something but it is not clear. Maybe you do nothing.

You look again at the program to see who you are. You read your biography: you seem to have good credentials, seem to be well trained, seem to be highly skilled. You are surprised that, in spite of all this, you seem to be doing nothing.

The performance finishes.

You do not bow to yourself. You do not applaud yourself. You do not know what to make of it.

Because there was a war, there needed to be weapons. Later, these things were described as tools.

There was, additionally, a "they" and a "you," and a wall that no one could prove, but everyone obeyed—even, especially, when one of the everyones appeared to disobey.

This action of non-action took place in an arena built exactly to replicate the actual arena. Though it appeared at times that the opposite was true, in fact the theys and the yous had forgotten, or never fully understood, or chose to ignore, the essential identity of this second arena.

Finally, there was only the doing nothing; or, as some conceived of it, the not doing. This was the last stand for the theys, and the yous.

There was no floor.

64. *THE MONSTER WHEN SHE OPENED HER WINGS*—*CLAUDIA LA ROCCO*

everyone was paid.

& so perhaps in this case nothing got done.
this theatre was a failure[1] for want of mercenaries.

[1] And by failure, here, of course we mean success.

65. *MOTION CAPTURE—CHRISTOPHER GROBE*

Note: the action takes place on a sunken stage—a deep thrust, or better yet, in the round.

In the darkness, we hear a scene of boozing, a collage of instantly recognizable sounds. Clinking glassware, cartoon hiccups, "Chug! Chug! Chug!" "Shaken, not stirred," "… where everybody knows your name!"

Sounds fade down as lights fade up on a featureless stage. A performer enters the stage at one corner, staggering drunk. Not obviously a trained dancer, this performer still betrays something "technical" through these movements across the stage. As chaos goes, this is pretty well-polished stuff.

Slowly, the performer gets to the far corner of the stage and exits. Lights start to fade, but then suddenly rebound, as if, hey, they'd almost forgotten something. A bright white dot appears at one corner of the stage. It zigs and zags and, wherever it's been, a faint line lingers on the stage, glowing white. This is the path our drunkard took.

A series of dancers cross the stage, following the line, but imbuing their movements with different styles, different meaning, different levels of gravity or levity. Dancers come out alone, in pairs, in trios, en masse—eventually filling the stage with their imitations, send-ups, departures, homages, and fantasias. Perhaps the same sound effects fade up again, but, gaining rhythm, appear almost musical. Perhaps an illuminated grid appears on the stage. Perhaps the new paths taken by the dancers are traced out on this grid in glowing lines, each a different color. Anyway, it's beautiful chaos—and, by now, we're all getting pretty drunk. Do *you* remember how it ends?

When I was a kid around 10 or 11, I found my dad's copy of *Dionysus in '69* (1970) by The Performance Group. The text confused me, but the images were irresistibly compelling. (Piles of naked, writhing bodies covered in blood often are, I suppose.) I understood that the book was about some kind of theatre, but what the play was about or what exactly was happening in the blurry, black-and-white photographs, eluded me. Nevertheless, I loved the book as much for its inscrutability as for its aesthetics and spent a lot of time imagining what the performance might have been about and what it would have felt like to be in the audience. Clearly audience members could become involved with the show. What did they do? How did it feel? What did it mean?

Years later, I still ask those questions, although now I also read the book as emblematic of a certain kind of performance documentation that obscures as much as it reveals. The images and text of *Dionysus in '69* appear to document an experience, one that Richard Schechner describes in his running commentary as "a total sensory immersion." But while specific details of the performance are recorded in the text and photographs, with choices and ideas described in Schechner's notes, the totality of that experience still remains elusive. How do the photographs connect to each other? What are the gestures that cause the blur of bodies moving in space? It was not until I saw Brian De Palma's film years later that I understood many further details, although some sections remain confusing as De Palma uses split screens, various editing techniques, and an unconventional use of focus to provide a sense of experience without seeing everything. What the suggestive images, script fragments, and commentaries of the book and film convey most of all is a sense of having missed something important.

Grobe's imagined performance, recording, and re-performance of intoxicated revelry recalls the documentation of *Dionysus in '69* and its efforts to capture the motions of a theatrical, sensory experience that seemingly exceeds all views, both those of participants and any documentation. In particular, Grobe's phrase "beautiful chaos" reminds me of what Schechner called "the caress," a problematic part of the performance characterized by extensive physical engagement with the audience (and a factor in the X rating for De Palma's film). Schechner described it as a fine experiment, but one that became "dangerous and self-defeating" in performance because of how audiences exploited the experience. The success of the caress, Schechner wrote, depended on "a willingness to participate within the terms of the production that audiences do not have."

How does one record performative moments that are so deeply embedded in physical experience and tactile expression? What is the best mechanism for recording danger? Intoxication? Erotics? Amid the debates about documentation, co-presence, repertoires and archives, I remember well my fascination upon finding *Dionysus in '69,* a book that raised more questions than answers and stretched the limits of what a performance could do. I can't remember the performance, but I can recall my engagement with its traces. More than a record of any single moment or sensation, Grobe's piece similarly reminds us that documentation, or motion capture—whether through lights or photographs or texts or memory—always functions best as a kind of emptiness to be filled not with accuracy, but imagination.

66. *MUSIC FOR CHARLIE MOREL—AARON C. THOMAS*

The velvet stirs, pulsing from the movement of the air on either side of the proscenium, but the curtain does not open. There is only the light absorbed by the fabric and, of course, the curtain itself, dividing the theatre from the stage.

Behind the curtain a performance has commenced. When this performance began, one couldn't say. It might have been going on long before the curtain did not open, long before the audience arrived, even.

On the other side of the curtain a hush has fallen; a melody has begun. The performers on the stage behind the curtain are listening. They have become an audience themselves. They listen in near silence, or at least they seem, from this side of the curtain—from our side—to be listening.

The music they hear—the music we hear—is unmistakable. The little phrase of Vinteuil's *Sonata* exerts itself over the sound of the audience that listens to it. The music soars, swelling, expanding, contracting in the perfect way that only this music by Vinteuil can.

Each of us must hear a different tune: Vinteuil's and even more than his, our own. But with the curtain as the only thing to see, what images can this music conjure? Can we imagine more clearly the scene of listeners on the curtain's other side?

As the music plays does my own image of the other side of the curtain clarify? And what is it that they imagine in their silence? What do they see?

When the music stops, and the voices on the other side of the curtain resume their chatter—indistinct but evident—still the curtain remains closed.

And in truth the music still lingers in the folds of the curtain, over or under the vague din of the conversations.

The curtain might, to be sure, open at any time, but it has not opened yet.

Impossible theatre—impossible music. Theatre without staging—music without sound. Spectators who may imagine, but who see nothing—musicians who play a sonata, but who never perform. And amid these negations and paradoxes, the figure of a curtain that never rises, or rather, that "might, to be sure, open at any time": an unveiling endlessly postponed and yet endlessly imminent.

Vinteuil is a fictional composer, plucked from some lost time, the *Lost Time* of Proust. But his music, inaudible though it may be, refuses to stay within this text. It cannot be confined to the pages of Proust's *La Prisonnière*, nor to those of *Imagined Theatres*. Neither does it exist only within the fiction established by Aaron C. Thomas's writing, but "exerts itself" into the reader's sensory world: "The music they hear—*the music we hear*— is unmistakable." It takes on a life all its own: silently, from behind a fluttering curtain, it pulsates, "swelling, expanding, contracting." Rising and falling, it brims with all the warmth and tenderness of a lover's chest as one rests one's head upon it in the earliest hours of the day, while the sun stretches its gauzy light through the humid morning air and the drapes of a bedroom window.

The curtain still "has not opened yet." Perhaps both desire and its object remain perpetually unrealizable, unknown to each other, unknowable even to themselves. Vinteuil's is the music of this impossible desire: machinery and engine of life. Just as the law of polysemy demands that language and the theatre can never fully control their interpretation, so it is with this vital song, the aural effects of which are never fully under control: "Each of us must hear a different tune." The sonata I hear is different from the one you hear, is different from the one Vinteuil or Morel or Proust or Thomas hears. We can hardly speak of a true, self-same, or original composition anymore. The music differs from itself in an endless play, the warp and the woof of desiring. If the musical piece were to reside reliably "in itself" anywhere, in some domain of truth or actuality removed from all this endless play, it's impossible to know whether there would be a way to see it or hear it; impossible to know whether the curtain masking it would ever be lifted so we could behold it, directly, face to face. And so, like auditors in the theatre, we continue to listen, ear to chest, chest to chest, skin to skin, critically intimate, and critically distant. And meanwhile Vinteuil's *Sonata* throbs away silently like an old and lovelorn heartbeat in the semi-darkness, its rhythm mine, yours, ours.

Even "when the music stops," it lingers, sunken into the material fabric of the stage, "the folds of the curtain," shimmering like stage light and fabric tousled by the gentlest of breezes. But has the song ended yet? Or is it about to begin?

67. *THE NIGHT EVERYTHING HAPPENED—AUGUSTO CORRIERI*

On 20 December 2013, one of London's most famous West End theatres had to be evacuated mid-show. BBC news cameras were quick to rush to the scene for a story. The first person to be interviewed, a man covered head to toe in dust, explained he had heard a "strange crackling noise" coming from the ceiling, from which chunks of plaster then began to break off; seemingly without cause, large sections of the ceiling proceeded to collapse. As the first witness told the BBC journalist: "at first I thought it was just part of the show."

Many spectators interviewed on the scene used that very expression, believing in a first moment that the accident had been staged for their benefit. However, the accounts of what happened inside the theatre differed considerably. A second witness reported that it had not been the ceiling but rather the balcony that had collapsed—"like a sink hole"—causing a number of people to fall through the balcony floor, and land in the more expensive seats down in the stalls; this witness had also initially thought it "was all part of the show." A group of teenagers offered a markedly different version of the events, recounting how in fact a group of actors had gone off script and started assaulting each other—punching, screaming, and kicking—eventually crashing into parts of the set, which began to collapse; these younger witnesses also said "we thought it was just part of the show."

The more people were interviewed that December night, the more the accounts grew increasingly diverse and incompatible, much to the frustration of journalists on the scene. News reports of the accident included: a leak in the roof gradually building up to a veritable downpour, flooding the entire auditorium (also initially thought to be "part of the show"); the musicians in the orchestra pit hurling rotten fruit at the audience ("part of the show"); an actor walking on stage with a large suitcase, then opening it to release a flock of live crows, terrorizing spectators ("part of the show"); strange balls of light forming in mid-air around the auditorium, exploding into myriad colors, then disappearing ("part of the show").

Vaguely plausible scenarios gradually gave way to pure flights of fancy and extravagant fabrications: a disoriented man reported that each actor had taken their clothes off to reveal themselves to be in fact two children, one standing on the other's shoulders; male and female spectators alike recounted experiencing the sudden urge to stand up from their seats, only to discover they had just laid an egg; and several witnesses described seeing a floating cast of actual ghosts storming the stage, demanding that their work be finally recognized as vital to the cultural sector.

No unitary picture of the events inside that West End theatre emerged, and so most people have largely forgotten about it. However, the news headline that was used by one of the morning papers—"The night everything happened"—has since become shorthand, among UK theatre critics, for the ultimately futile attempt at bridging the gap between performances and their descriptions.

As frequent viewers of the six o'clock news or the many popular legal dramas that dominate the airwaves can perhaps attest to best, eyewitnesses are often unreliable narrators. Their accounts of events, when subjected to close scrutiny or cross-examination, tend to reveal as many rumors as facts, as much fiction as description. Of course, the process that they rely on most when trying to re-present the past—the process of remembering—is full of invention, distortion, and imprecision. It, therefore, should come as little surprise when some details in the eyewitness' account resist verification.

Nevertheless, we are inclined to hold in contempt any eyewitness that we perceive as exercising too much creative license while endeavoring to concretize bygone events. Indeed, in violating our expectations about their role and central purpose—namely, to make indiscernible gaps between the event and the description of it they relate in its aftermath—these narrators expose themselves to vigorous repudiation and condemnation. But they also force us to reflect more deeply on what Shoshanna Felman might call the *strangeness* we encounter in their statements. In so doing, they prompt considerations of the ways in which "peculiar narratives" perhaps complicate our understandings of what we think we know.

The odd, widely divergent reports that emerged on "the night everything happened" no doubt raise myriad questions about how we define and interpret credible spectatorship. Do credible spectators merely regurgitate facts? Or, do they serve as co-creators of an event's meaning? And, what *are* we to make of the flights of fancy or extravagant fabrications that we detect in a spectator's account? Should we disregard them and their author entirely? Or, should we embrace them as forms of creative witnessing? That these questions remain urgent—despite the willful disappearance of the event from the official record—suggests that, in addition to reevaluating our expectations about credible spectatorship, we perhaps also need to attend more carefully to our fetishizations of the cohesive narrative. As Chimamanda Ngozi Adichie reminds, there is danger in privileging a single story. By doing so, we risk critically misunderstanding and, indeed, forgetting the days and nights that everything (and nothing) happened.

68. *NO SUBJECT—WENDY HOUSTOUN*

posted by: reviewerscom.co.co.co

I got to the puppet theatre. I already had a bad cold and a hole in my jeans and my phone had run out of battery. At the beginning of NO SUBJECT I noticed how marginally hopeful I was feeling but as soon as the lights went down I started to feel quite disappointed. Why the lights going down? Why so predictable? Why me sitting in this seat? Why that space over there?
I get no answers.
The lights were quite small and low down on the bodies and over
the course of the night literally nothing happens.
I was literally in the dark and I was literally disappointed.
Why are they standing so still? Why am I thinking about the hole in my jeans? Why am I feeling so violent? Why aren't there as many of them as it said on the program?
Why did it take so long to make this work?
What is the point of them doing something when I could be doing it instead?
What time is it?
I start to notice people sitting beside me who are also writing.
This is the real choreography. This is where the real work is.
Why should I accept what is put in front of me when what is beside
me is much more interesting? Why isn't the light in the theatre on the person next to you? Why do we think there needs to be something that is prepared and put in a place on a frame which gets forced on us? Why this aggressive stance of pushing ideas at humans?
Why this attack?
Why not allow me to do the work?
And get paid to watch?
Why are we the audience and the writers not paid to sit here?
Why is everything so unjust?
I was hoping the evening wouldn't do that predictable end thing with the light coming up. But predictably up it did.
Why this predictable—something starting—something happening—something finishing thing?
Another disappointment.

we have just finished the show and i am just taking a bit of time out from the reception thing to just say its been an extraordinary day but not without some issues the first one being someone hadnt done their homework so it turned out we were actually in the puppet studio at the back of the theatre which meant a lack of dressing rooms not to mention a lot of reworking as all the lights were very low down and quite compressed and we couldnt change them because the technician was on a ladder training day which apparently means spending a lot of time establishing how many points of contact you have with the floor at any given time which is quite hard to do when you try it at speed but as most of the cast were a bit worse for wear after their big night out and two of them didnt pass the passport test and are now in a detention center waiting to be deported we were down a few people anyway and this new challenge only made us feel closer and more intimate so we managed to quickly agree to get rid of all the fluffy choreographic stuff and the illusion sections along with our immersive inflatable idea so we ended up just refining it down to it being all about the silence of the limbs (ie all of us very still with just bits of us visible) as it seemed better if we didnt move at all and just allowed the props to do the talking but we all know if we hadnt done all that work in depth over the last three days it wouldnt have had the absolute tragic and yet comic feel that both our inside and outside eyes said it did have and it looks like there is a bit of interest from international people for a residency or a kind of development of the stillness idea which is really now what we realize we were thinking about all along but i can hear a speech about to happen so am going to go and listen to the critical facilitator and the resident philosopher in dialogue with the curator which is the main reason most people have come anyway but wow—what a journey—what an experience—what a life …

69. *NOT I (NOT)—ANT HAMPTON*

During November and December 2014 I staged a production of Samuel Beckett's *Not I* as a 3D holographic projection. Nobody realized that it wasn't real—that there wasn't anyone there on the stage. It was the kind of hologram that doesn't require the audience to wear goggles.[1]

Despite her age and frail condition, Billie Whitelaw, who had originated many of Beckett's greatest roles, agreed to be captured for the project as long as it could be done at her nursing home. The performance was excellent, in large part due to Billie's extraordinary talent and experience, but also due to the care that went into the editing. My guess is that Beckett would have preferred to edit his shows and actors than direct them.

When he came to audit the performance, the guy from the Beckett Estate wept, and told me it couldn't be closer to the playwright's vision. He asked if he could speak to Billie, to congratulate her. I told him she was too tired.

Press reactions were also very positive. There was great interest in Billie's return to the stage, so demand for tickets quickly soared. The theatre seated only 70 people, so we started running the show every half hour, every day of the week from midday to midnight. We were soon averaging audiences of 1,500 a day. Questions began circulating about how a woman of Billie's age could endure the performance schedule.

On December 21st, Billie Whitelaw passed away. For 3 days, all shows were cancelled, but on the 23rd I issued a press release announcing Billie would resume performances.

The Beckett Estate guy called up and demanded a ticket. During the Christmas Day performance he sat still, apparently frozen, until just after the first of the Auditor's four small movements. At that moment he disrupted the performance by yelling and running onto the stage, but became tangled in the Musion NotEyeliner™ and had to be assisted. The following day I received an email saying the Estate would be suing me for the production, which they deemed a counterfeit. Only live performances of *Not I* are tolerated.

It eventually went to court. The judge wanted to see the show for herself. She wept during the performance, and declared that the experience was certainly "live." She ruled in my favor, saying there was nothing to distinguish this production from another performed in real time and space by a human, beyond the knowledge, only now, that Billie Whitelaw was no longer with us.

This year (2015) has seen a number of other holographic performances of Beckett's work—notably *Catastrophe*, *Footfalls*, *Act without Words I* and *II*—leading us to wonder whether his plays lend themselves more favorably to performances by the edited dead, than the irregular living.

1 According to the website for Musion, the world's leading provider of holographic projection, "Eyeliner is the core of our technology, with its imagery often referred to as a hologram. A 21st century twist on a Victorian theatre trick, the Eyeliner utilizes a technique called Pepper's Ghost … Famously used to bring back on stage the late rapper Tupac Shakur at Coachella festival, millions worldwide were wowed by the Tupac illusion. Our specialist foil, invisible to the naked eye, is suspended across the stage, creating a life-like 3D image … Extremely flexible, scalable and quick to install, Eyeliner will bring your event alive in any environment." For the production, a slightly adapted version was created, called Musion NotEyeliner™. It was developed in May of 2014, while Musion was busy with the delivery of a travelling hologram of Indian politician Narendra Modi which, according to *the New Statesman,* "ended up addressing a total of 1,400 rallies, many of them in 'dark villages' where no resident even owned a television." The gambit was a success; in May of that year Modi was elected prime minister.

Hologram

Rendering Samuel Beckett's *Not I* a hologram, Ant Hampton exposes the play's uncanny poise between the there and the not there. Where is Mouth speaking? In a courtroom? In a nursing home? In a home for the mentally ill? On a stage? In Beckett's mind? Mouth's dilemma is that she cannot quite locate herself, caught as she is by her incapacity to inhabit or utter the "I" that grounds self-presence. Feminist scholars have often pointed out that Mouth's struggle to say "I" mirrors the struggle women often face within phallogocentrism. Spoken, rather than speakers, women sometimes are cast as holographs in patriarchy's relentless (all too real) drama.

Billie Whitelaw

What is the strange transubstantiation between the writer's voice and the physical embodiment of that voice? In theatre and performance, that gap is what ties the performer to the writer. Beckett said he wrote *Not I* "for" Whitelaw, and her legendary performance at the Royal Court in 1973 has become the standard, nay, the hologram that flickers behind all other subsequent performances. A feat of endurance, speed, and tone, Whitelaw's performance emerged from her conviction that Beckett had written an "inner scream" she immediately heard and understood. She also said that rehearsing the play with him was like working with a conductor; it was the rhythm and pace that mattered most. Her performances, intimate concertos of spittle and stutter, trembling chin and vibrant tongue, are inseparable from the "meaning" of Beckett's words.

The Edited Dead

Beckett died on 22 December 1989; Whitelaw on 21 December 2014. In the fifteen-year interval after his death and before her own, Whitelaw did not appear in any of Beckett's work. That is, until Ant Hampton placed her hologram in *NOT I (not)*. Whitelaw's decision not to perform Beckett's work after his death allowed her to avoid any potential denial of rights from the artist's estate. Under the direction of Beckett's nephew, Edward, Beckett's estate has retained such strict control over productions that his work risks being transformed from live art to a complex algorithm. Ant Hampton's *NOT I (not)* warns against the risk of "protecting" Beckett's work by suffocating it entirely. The Whitelaw hologram avoids fatigue and pain and can play repeatedly. Just as the play insists on a gap between she who speaks and Mouth, the hologram reveals the chasm between the copy and the live event. The hologram *Not I* gives us *NOT I (not)*.

Other Catastrophes

Celine Dion began performing "a residency show" in Las Vegas in 2003. She performed the show until 2007, took a break, and returned with a new show in 2011. Although she has taken breaks to care for her family, the sheer repetition of this kind of live performance schedule also gives pause to those committed to the liveness of the live performance. After some 700 performances of the first show it was "impossible" to take seriously the title of Dion's performance, *A New Day*. Thus, while most holographic performances seek to resurrect the dead (Tupac Shakur) or absent (Narendra Modi) performer, sometimes living performers become holographic before their time.

70. *OCEAN ORATION—UNA CHAUDHURI*

Lights up. Surf's up.

The first waves of letters surge onto the stage. Mixed with them are garlands of glistening seaweed, clusters of clattering shells, and multicolored tendrils of micro-degraded plastics.

The letters are no longer in envelopes. They have been opened, unfolded, and their folds smoothed out. They have been heavily annotated: some words are underlined, a few words are circled, and many words have been joined together with arrows. The margins are covered with signs and inscriptions: some are shaped like fish, a few look like humans drawn in stick figures, and many contain shapes like waves. The annotations are written in an ink that changes now that it's exposed to air and sun: the inscriptions—signs, lines, circles, arrows, figures—boil on the surface of the letters. They sizzle. They spark.

BLACKOUT.

Lights up. Surf's up.

A second wave of letters arrives. They come in dribs and drabs this time—no surges, no sizzle. Each letter has a single marking on it: a sign that looks like a double wave. Some of the double waves have another symbol following them: a circle with a horizontal line through it.

What does it signify? Wave, wave, two halves of a whole? Bye, bye, hemisphere? Goodbye to half the world?

The letters begin to dissolve. The paper they are written on becomes mushy, the words on it blur together. The double waves and half circles float away from the pulp. They grow in size and begin arranging themselves in rows, rising until they form a barrier in the place where, in an old-fashioned theatre, the curtain would have been. The waves undulate. The divided circles rotate.

At first, both waves and circles move simultaneously, and a sound like a muted roar can be heard. Then the movements take turns: first the waves, undulating. Then the circles, spinning.

The undulations make a sound like gentle questioning; the circles, like urgent whispering. The dialogue goes on and on …

Questions: soft, hopeful, wheedling, impatient, fearful, hopeful again, hopeful again, hopeful …

Whispers: quick, insistent, sibilant, staccato. Desperate?

BLACKOUT.

Lights up. Surf's up.

The eleventh surge of letters washes up on the beach. Each one is inscribed with two words, followed by a simple drawing of a container of some kind: a gift-wrapped box, a vase, a casserole, a beer stein, a kettle, a hookah, a goblet, a lantern, a tea cup, a martini glass, a pitcher, a cocktail shaker, a salad bowl, an umbrella stand, a waste bin, a string bag, a dumpster, a paper sack, a tureen.

As for the two words on each letter, the first word on each one is "Dear." That's followed by a name, a different name on each letter: Dear June, Dear Alia, Dear Vikash, Dear Ivan, Dear John, Dear Angel, Dear Lise, Dear Jeong, Dear Guillaume, Dear Juanita, Dear Marina, Dear Youssef, Dear Ondine, Dear Hari, Dear Chen, Dear Sumitra, Dear Joy, Dear Maryse, Dear Velma, Dear Yu, Dear Dionysios, Dear Fatima …

Yes, of course your name is there … But you may pick any letter, and open any container. The contents are intended for you, you alone.

BLACKOUT.

Surf's still up.

Philadelphia-based artist John Peña began his creative project entitled "Letters to the Ocean" in 2003. Every day, he wrote a letter to the ocean, put the letter in an envelope, sealed it, addressed it, wrote his own address on the top left-hand corner of the envelope, pasted a stamp on it, and put it in the mail. The letters were returned by the post office, with various official "return to sender" stamps or notes to the effect that "no such place exists." One envelope was returned with a note saying: "The ocean is no longer accepting mail." John Peña has over 3,000 returned letters, which he has exhibited in various shows and galleries.

Intriguingly, all the letters identify a single location as their intended destination. Every one of them is addressed to: "The Ocean, 5 miles S Westport, Grayland, WA 98547." When I asked John about this, he wrote: "I always send it to the same place. I have considered sending it elsewhere but I really like the idea that the ocean is so vast and ubiquitous that if I send a letter to one part of its body, it'll eventually hear about it." He later added: "Also, I came up with it because it is near a nice little spot I used to camp out near the beach."

John's image of the ocean as a vast, ubiquitous, and above all fully networked body is not only apt but of increasingly urgent consequence. The vastness of the ocean is rapidly moving, in human consciousness, from the status of an empty cliché to the basis of a statistically verifiable planetary emergency. As the landmasses we inhabit reveal their dependence on and vulnerability to oceanic conditions—reminding us, as Thoreau said long ago, "that the earth is not continent but insular" we awaken to the realization that our star-gazing species knows much more—and spends much more on knowing—about outer space than about the ocean. As James Nestor writes, "If you compare the ocean to a human body, the current exploration of the ocean is the equivalent of snapping a photograph of a finger to figure out how our bodies work."

Yet the ocean is speaking to us loud and clear, with superstorms and tsunamis and bleached coral reefs, apparently responding to the "messages" we've been sending, in the form of oil spills, toxic dumping, overfishing, and islands of plastic waste the size of Texas (the Great Pacific Garbage Patch). One imaginative response is to speak for the ocean, imagine what it's saying to us. A recent public service video has the ocean scarily scolding us in the stern voice of Harrison Ford. John Peña's approach is the opposite: he addresses the ocean, privately, incessantly. *Ocean Oration* is located somewhere in between these two contrasting options. It has us imagine ourselves receiving messages from the ocean, but the messages are not as loud and clear as the one we heard from Ocean Harrison. Rather, they are enigmatic, intriguing, promising messages. They draw us towards a new language: an emerging system of signs, rhythms, and feelings. As we listen and try to decode the messages, they offer each one of us unforeseen gifts.

71. *OH, HAVE I DIED, THEN?—HOWARD BARKER*

> Never difficult to offend the audience, even where the audience, subscribers to the Cult of Tolerance, clamours to discover if anything remains which might offend it. The artist offends by one thing only—the suspicion he might really believe his own utterance.
>
> (Howard Barker, *These Sad Places, Why Must You Enter Them?*)

The public enters the performance space. They are not humiliated, insulted, or implored. They are obliged to recognize they are of no significance. They should think their presence accidental, as if they had entered by mistake, like curious animals. We have no intention of influencing them, nor of being influenced by them. We take influence to be the most degraded of all artistic pretensions. Further, we hold the idea of an "effect" in contempt, as we find all "outcomes" contemptible.

The play is entitled *In the Presence of Despicable Mothers*. It is preceded by a shorter piece, *The Blasé Executioner*. In the first, the perfect diction of the actor conveys the perfect poetry of the text. He narrates the constitution of a society only briefly experienced in a remote time, preceding even Draco's Athens. As he narrates, the Despicable Mothers begin to fight among themselves. Several are murdered. Most give birth.

Is it necessary to say this? The play that cannot be staged is the play that speaks what cannot be spoken. All practical problems of staging are chimera. All problems of dramatic art can be solved except one. This is the problem of the consciousness of society as it represents itself at any given time. In the time we find ourselves, only the play that denies the value of individual life cannot be performed. This is the unspeakable. Between this play and its public stand the assembled ranks of critical humanism. The collective cannot recruit the agents of its own demise. At every level of the structure of humanism stand the agents of conscience and shame. No text that repudiates shame as the basis of human conduct will be staged, nor will the text be read, for even to read a forbidden text in such a society risks contamination. We look forward to many performances both of *The Blasé Executioner* and *In the Presence of Despicable Mothers*. These will occur (they will not be presented) in places of severe privacy and in the very bowels of the populist regime (e.g., beneath the stage of the most fatuous rock concerts ...). Thought unable to hear itself.

> Nothing said about death by the living can possibly relate to death as it will be experienced by the dying. Nothing known about death by the dead can be communicated to the living. Over this appalling chasm tragedy throws a frail bridge of imagination.
>
> (Howard Barker, *Death, The One and the Art of Theatre*)

To have died *then*, and to speak *now*: an impossible task. Whatever last words issue from a dying mouth fall on the deaf ears of the dead body. I will not hear my final words, since there will be no *I* to speak of or to.

Tragedy, as Howard Barker writes, is the imaginary span that would link speech to the unspeakable, the subject to its dissipation. But this imagined event so indifferent to our presence is not the tragedy we know from Aeschylus, Sophocles, or Euripides. It predates the era of Draco, who ruled Athens in the 7th century BC, two hundred years before those plays crossed the stage, three hundred years before Aristotle made of tragedy a thing with a purpose—to cleanse catastrophe. Draco was the first leader in Ancient Greece to write its laws down, and his authority exerted a punishment excessively disproportionate to the weight of a crime: death in most cases (thus our word "draconian"). But even the disproportionate assumes a causal relation, a logic however unbalanced. At odds with all actions and reactions, all measures, the pre-tragic play *In the Presence of Despicable Mothers* and its prologue *The Blasé Executioner* are fatally alogical.

The Blasé Executioner "executes" his role to perfection—meaning both that he completes it, and that he eradicates it, completely. He is weary of representing a character, for he must have none apart from the language delivered. His actorly presence must not distract from his task: to incite the riot that gives birth and takes life at once. Barker underlines the fact that these events will *occur*—will actually happen as birth and death; they will not be *presented* as pretense. Here is the cruelty Artaud foretold, a singularity that cannot be repeated. Here is the failure of an ethics of individualism, where the individual body becomes other than itself. In birth one becomes two; in death one becomes a mere prop.

Someone asks: "Is it necessary to say this?" It must be the executioner, blasé as ever, wanting to be done with it all. We do not hear much more of what happens, or if we do, we do not understand its meaning. It is all "[t]hought unable to hear itself." In other words, we imagine a thought, without actually having it, and thereby still hold it in silence, untouched like a room sealed off from the city of human life with its humanities and whatever reading they might offer.

Stand just outside of that room we call "death," that room we call "birth." Imagine a threshold but do not pretend to give voice to what lies across that threshold. Listen instead, to that insistent rhythm grounding our moving bodies, for there it subsists, felt not heard, "beneath the stage of the most fatuous rock concerts," under the boards of whatever theatre house, in the very soil of the Globe itself: the room of birth and death that is the theatre that will not be staged.

72. *ON LOCATION AND CONTEXT—RICARDO A. BRACHO*

1. Pelican Bay State Prison
2. California Correctional Center
3. High Desert State Prison
4. Folsom State Prison
5. Folsom Women's Facility
6. California State Prison, Sacramento
7. California Medical Facility
8. California State Prison, Solano
9. Mule Creek State Prison
10. San Quentin State Prison
11. N.A. Chaderjian Youth Correctional Facility
12. O.H. Close Youth Correctional Facility
13. Sierra Conservation Center
14. California Health Care Facility
15. Deuel Vocational Institution
16. Central California Women's Facility
17. Valley State Prison
18. Correctional Training Facility
19. Substance Abuse Treatment Facility and State Prison Facility, Corcoran
20. California State Prison, Corcoran
21. Pleasant Valley State Prison
22. Avenal State Prison
23. Kern Valley State Prison
24. North Kern State Prison
25. Wasco State Prison
26. California Men's Colony
27. California Correctional Institution
28. California State Prison, Los Angeles County
29. Ventura Youth Correctional Facility
30. California Institution for Men
31. California Institution for Women
32. California Rehabilitation Center
33. Chuckawalla Valley State Prison
34. Ironwood State Prison
35. Calipatria State Prison
36. California State Prison, Centinela
37. Richard J. Donovan Correctional Facility

Stretch or drown
Evolve or die
(Kate Rushin, "The Bridge Poem")

Welcome to Artworld Decolonization for Beginners

We cannot think through the potential decolonization of the theatre/performance space/ black box, the gallery/museum/white box, or the film/video/white screen without interrogating the gray box of prisons, jails, and immigrant detention centers; the institutional green boxes of public schools where our children are mis- and dis-educated; the wood-paneled boxes of courtrooms and jury rooms and finally the lined pine box of coffin or speckled beige box of cremation where racism has us meet our premature death, to crib Ruth Wilson Gilmore.

All colonial plunder must be returned

Every feather, bone, weaving, beaded headdress, fertility deity, corn and rain god, culinary and musical instrument, totem, and doll must return to its people and those societies alone can do with said entities as they wish—burn and bury them, place them in a museum they control, play with them, cook with them. Whatever and what have you. Those who liberally decry the loss of the educative value of keeping such objects and artifacts within their perma-colonial collections need to attend Decolonial Art School, funded by the decolonial state and led by keepers of the traditions and post-traditional artists and scholars to understand that these entities are not in fact objects or artifacts.

Dewhiten or just stfu

Every board, every staff, every mfa program, every department, every volunteer and fundraising committee, every internship and fellowship, that is nearly or all white must be reconstituted, disbanded, and/or abolished. The only social body in this country that should be 80 to 90 percent white cis male should be the Klan.

Decolonization is done with guns

And, in instances when it is not, the insurgent colonized have been met with the hegemon's firepower: Grenada, Venezuela, Bolivia, Honduras. One's tears or poems or drawings do not decolonize anything, even if one is the ascendant-class, well-educated descendant of colonized subjects, as many of us brown and black artist-intellectual types are.

Make "anti-reformist reforms" and art forms

Though the US in its current late capital/full terror state empire formation has globally produced "the infinite war" we here do not live under conditions such that the revolution or decolonization is imminent or realizable. Though I insist as a Marxist and an artist on imaging utopias, I know we are not there yet. We will not soon gain collective autonomy and sovereignty, land and wealth redistribution, reparations and redress: the stuff and guts of an actualized decolonial social sphere.

73. *ON SCALE—JOSHUA ABRAMS*

Glassine stage (3)
75 x 25 x 1 (10)
Or maybe, just maybe, edges unseen (10)

Kaleidoscopic swirl (6)
Undifferentiable (6)
Looping, arching, whirling (6)

Focus, focus (4)
And wait (2)
Focus again (4)

Singular shapes (4)
Agency, perhaps? (5)
Now who-s and whom-s (4)
Or mostly what-s, which overwhelm (7)
The who-s and whom-s (4)
Themselves, no longer? (5)
For ever changed (4)

Too late now though (4)
Spotlit (2)
Curtains pulled back (4)

Before, uncertain mass (6)
Illucid alien (6)
We liked it better then (6)

Microscopic theatres of war resound (10)
Altering where they alteration found (10)
Damage done. (3)

We're inside a seven-course palindromic menu (measured and priced by syllables), which turns on the moment when what-s overwhelm who-s and whom-s.

Our stage: a transparent sheet (or maybe the stage turns out to be imperceptible, the paper is so clear, the boundaries obscure).

Its proportions approximate those of a flattened human body.

Our perspective: a microscope eyepiece, which we focus on the object at hand.

The object at hand: What begins as a colorful, mysterious, dynamic entity bristling with enticing possibilities—of self-determination, perhaps, of unimaginable knowledge, of strangeness—ends as a number of disappointingly seeable, concrete, maybe even knowable objects.

"Damage done." What damage are we doing when we turn the bright light of examination onto the stage of the self? Are we—as many have argued (the Symbolists, all those anti-Naturalists, the counter-Enlightenment thinkers, the mystics)—erasing the mind's imaginative possibilities by turning the ineffable stuff of life into scientific units? Are we naming, pinning, reducing, classifying our inscrutable, mystical, limitless spiritual realms in our mania for hard knowledge?

Are we happier not knowing? (If so, why do we want to know so badly?)

The what-s triumph in this tiny war that is a microcosm of the big one: they consume our hopes for dazzling, self-determined, dynamic enigmas.

In this gourmet menu of a theatre, the more we devour, the less we yearn.

74. *ONBOARD ENTERTAINMENT—JOE KELLEHER*

It's a kind of airborne daydreaming, that's how I imagine it. A sort of viral performance reflex, you wouldn't really call it a theatre thing, although theatre of a sort can come about when it hits hard enough. It is known to infect people who spend significant parts of their time in transit. People on ferry boats particularly, I've noticed; although that might just be to say that the typical outcome of all this—the terminal symptom, if you like—is not theatre after all but anecdote, and that the performance that takes place there is only ever on its way toward its point of arrival in a telling, a report, a passing on from one to another, even when that other is yourself. This could mean also that much of what was at stake along the way, for the actors, the performers at the time—getting through, getting by, getting paid, getting off—is in one way or another done with by the time the final accounting comes round. There is something pitiless about that. Then again, maybe the anecdote is itself a sort of script for the imagined theatre that is still to come. I don't know if I believe that, but it may be the case. As it is, the instances that come to mind are all of workaday onboard entertainment. The staff on the cross-Channel car ferry who earlier had been checking our tickets and the like, and who later re-appear on the small stage in the ferry bar dressed in giant banana costumes, doing a musical routine straight out of the queer strangeness of 1970s UK peak-time Saturday evening light entertainment TV. Or the man on the Bosphorous ferry last month who took off his work jacket and came back into the middle of the cabin for twenty minutes or so to demonstrate to all the wonders of the hand-held vegetable peeler he was selling, a proper stand-up act with catch phrases and everything (he sold quite a few of the devices). But not just working people either. There were the passengers making the journey from Helsinki to Tallinn and back all those years ago, slabs of wholesale butter stacked up in the shop below deck, Finns and Estonians taking it in turns in the bar to tell jokes in their respective languages at the open mic, one half of the crowd laughing at a time while the other looked on. I watch, I listen, and my thoughts wander. I wonder who these people are. I look around at all of us. I can only see the ones who are here. Others I have to imagine. I want to say something about them, about other boats and such places where the performance virus is not felt or acted upon, or falls in ways I cannot conceive. But I am amongst the crowd for now, and its limits are also my own.

"I am amongst the crowd for now, and its limits are also my own." The crowd's perspectives delimit the coordinates of its world, the nature of its Being. Other boats, those foreign vessels, those alien planets, have their own trajectories, their own relative space and time—and their own creatures, customs, contours. The passenger shares a basic ground of Being with this boatload of beings. These fellow travelers share not only perceptual limits but also social space, as invisible as ideology. They, with us, occupy a vessel bound up in European commercial life: salesmen, entertainers, commuters, business travelers, tourists. We can only imagine what goes on in other boats. Other boats where refugees from Syria seek European shores. Overloaded ferries now sunk beneath the Mediterranean. The underside of transit: Being defined in exile. Then again the boat is a ferry, and the journey across the Channel is also that across the river Styx. (Aren't all boats ferries, and all rivers Styx?) The onboard entertainment, shamanistic even in its garish costumes, its crude clowns, stands in for the Ferryman Charon, the very medium of our mortality. Though foreign worlds lie on the far shore—Hades, Calais, Helsinki—the journey there is sanctified through the Ferryman's mediation, like Kantor directing onstage between the living and the dead. Charon has haunted our dreams for millennia, from Hesiod to the cross-Channel staff "who later re-appear on the small stage of the ferry bar dressed in giant banana costumes, doing a musical routine straight out of the queer strangeness of 1970s UK peak-time Saturday evening light entertainment TV." Riddled with contradictions ("routine" / "strangeness"; "straight" / "queer"; "1970s" / "peak-time") the Ferryman is infinitely mutable, like the river he crosses, and it fits that he would appear now, on this ferry, as the banana-clad sentimental middle class mascot or the vegetable-peeling working class comic salesman. The Ferryman's Being, his Styx, is made of that which changes. The river is defined by its change, as Heraclitus once said, and you can't step in it twice—not only because the river will no longer be itself but because you will no longer be yourself: and this very mutability is our essence. Our becoming is our Being. (The flipside is our unbecoming, our unraveling, our non-being.) Even the being of Being, in its articulation, becomes different from itself. We share its performative becoming, we fellow travelers bound for the same "terminal destination." The ferry is no supermodern airplane nor suburbanizing automobile; suspended, neither here nor there, it is always already theatre, the ancient vehicle between the living and the dead, where the mist settles on the river (whose Being is its becoming). And there, on the small stage of the ferry bar, is the Big Other's Jester, the faceless clown whose gaze we can never quite return. Banana-clad Charon rows and we inevitably follow. The Ferryman prepares us for what waits on the far shore. If nothing else, the end of the journey is the beginning of its telling, the birth of anecdote, Horatio's sacred charge. Does the telos of a life amount to our anticipation of its recollection? "It's a kind of airborne daydreaming," that's how Kelleher imagines it. The "viral performance reflex" kicks in and replays us into being: a Being always predicated on already having been, on not yet being, on being between.

75. *OR, THE WHALE (FOR TESS)—LAURA CULL Ó MAOILEARCA*

The event occurs in 2 co-existing spaces, each in their own time.

SCENE 1^1—on a seashore. Dusk.

[*These days we must build our theatres for our dramas, not our dramas for and in our theatres. We must play in the dawn, at noon, and at dusk, and with the sun moving upon actors, audience, and architecture alike, and with no indulgences in what is called "lighting effects." You must have the sun on you to live. It was the movement of the sun upon the architecture that moved the onlookers. The movement was felt, but felt through seeing.* Or, better, they saw feelingly not the sun moving but movement itself.]

A and B
standing on shore
facing the sea
silently reading
sun moving below the horizon
walking towards the water
(keeping pace with the sun)
walking into the water
(keeping pace with the sun)
until it is no longer possible to read

[*Although the two figures interest me to some extent, it is the sea in which they move which moves me. The figures dominate the sea for a time, but the sea is for all time. I believe that some day I shall get nearer to the secret of these things … If they were dead, how dull they would be, but they are trembling with a great life, more so than that of man—than that of woman …*]

SCENE 1^2—up to 2,300 ft below sea level.

Enter THE WHALES

[*That's a stage direction, and* that's *a drama. I sometimes live on the land, where all sorts of undramatic things go on all day long, but when I see a chorus of beluga whales in the distance, I feel that although it is merely a regiment of beasts, it is dramatic.*]

A, B, C, etc.
sending out a series of clicks
waiting for the echo to return
hearing the landscape
(in every possible detail)
hearing size
hearing structure
hearing distance
hearing texture
hearing speed

A, B, C, etc.
raising the voice in response to traffic
extending the voice to be heard above the noise
higher and lower than you can hear
to see the sound of schools of fish
to see the sound of waves breaking on distant shores
(repeat)

About 80 percent of this imagined theatre is imitation, or, it is becoming. And, indeed, the imitation itself is imitation (or becoming) thanks to my encounter with Goat Island, the Chicago-based performance company. Our theatre, they say, is like the enthusiastic imitations of children: playroom homages to films seen, cardboard reenactments of events witnessed. And I, in turn, like the children, have learnt through copying. I copy Goat Island's strategy of trying not to over-write the voices of my sources with mine, so that they might be heard in their own right. I pay homage to their construction of hybrid characters according to diagonal connections made between apparently unconnected individuals: for them, the comedian Larry Grayson-becoming-St Francis of Assisi; for me, myself-becoming-Edward Gordon Craig-becoming-Allan Kaprow-becoming-Friedrich Nietzsche. Of course, philosophers Deleuze and Guattari famously opposed imitation and becoming. But this polemic obscures what lies in the small print: namely that, in practice, mimetic acts are often the starting points of transformation, seeming reproduction the source of the production of the new. For the author, imitation holds the prospect of habit dismantled by appropriating another's voice. Quotes and misquotes are italicized to mark the author's departure from the stage. *Please remember I am only a substitute.*

But, as Kaprow knew, habits might also be undone by acts operating at the threshold of the familiar and the strange. Now, the imagined theatre is an invitation to participation, a score. Everyday gestures are mutated to reorient attention away from interpretation towards duration—which, we find, is never singular but as varied or as multiple as the beings that emerge from it. Stop asking what it all means. Stop asking what it all means and you might just be able to slip into a new rhythm—human or inhuman, the time of my partner or, the whale.

Another reorientation: an encounter with bioacoustic science produces a series of what Goat Island call "impossible tasks" which, like Kaprow's scores, invite us to turn text into embodied act; for instance, to attempt a becoming-whale. And yet, in their poetic impossibility (or, in the indeterminacy of Kaprow's instructions), such tasks function less as blueprints and more as the conditions for invention. While such invention may have its organic limits—just as we find some habits we cannot live without—perhaps they are more elastic than we supposed. Simultaneously, the imagined theatre insists on the expansion of the category of performance to include the whale's own inventiveness, or an expansion of our attention in order to hear the whale's voice as such. Like us, whales are vocal learners—capable of producing new sounds, expanding their repertoire, through imitation.

In these co-existing scenes, it is not a matter of the page understood as making possible what is impossible on the stage. Indeed, our becoming-whale—the embodied moment of encountering the novelty that lies at the horizon of our knowledge—may, by definition, remain unsayable. How the whale thinks slips through the grasp of the language we have to hand. But this is not to advise retreat in the face of some ineffability, nor to reject the page outright. We may, following Bergson, locate *action* as that which has the power to break the circle of the given, to suspend our tendency to meet the world with only ready-made ideas. But it is an act that might be both preceded and followed by words: before it, the score that invites but does not script the performance of a new kind of attention, and after it, the poem that tries to gesture toward the unknown object that such attention allows to appear.

76. *AN OROGENY—CADEN MANSON AND JEMMA NELSON*

You take your seat in darkness.

Light rises from a distant source. A void stretches above. A pre-dawn breeze stirs. The temperature drops. Dew condenses.

Bare rock forms emerge with the growing light, distant peaks pick up the first rays, valleys remain shadowed and obscured.

You are seated in an alpine landscape. Mountain ranges recede as far as you can perceive; vegetation is stunted and miniaturized. At first empty, the sky starts to populate with small clouds. If you shift your gaze, the scene extends in all directions: rock, valleys, ranges, sky.

During the first part, the sun warms your skin. Somewhat later, drizzle starts, then sleet falls, and for a while snow settles and piles up. The snowfall ends, the clouds break, and the snow melts, evaporates, and vanishes.

When you look at an intermediate distance, you believe that you perceive movement. You cannot resolve it. You gaze intently in this direction for an indeterminate duration. Your perception of the phenomenon oscillates between a moving object traversing the scene, the underlying structure fluxing, or a purely contingent perceptual effect.

At a nearer distance—perhaps a slope that faces you several kilometers away—you pick out shapes moving on a patterned field. The shapes enter a wide, deep shadow, which reduces their visual contrast. You reposition yourself and shade your eyes. You cannot determine if the shapes move, or if the shadow has shifted over them. Because you believe the shapes to be close, you read into their movement (in any order): threat, comfort, amusement, and wisdom.

You close your eyes and recline. You hear a diffuse, long, low-pitched boom. At the other end of the sound range, wind through a small gap excites a high-pitched whine. In the middle register, tumbling rocks periodically clatter percussively, occasionally with pitched tones.

The light slants and discolors, lengthens and reddens. It loses saturation, and your perception dims with it. Darkness closes over you.

Repeat for a few thousand years.

darkness.

a distant pre-dawn breeze stirs.
Dew condenses.

light, distant peaks pick up the first rays,

Mountain ranges recede as far as you can
At first empty,
you shift rock, valleys,
ranges, sky.

the sun warms drizzle starts, sleet
falls, snow settles
melts, evaporates, and vanishes.

you look you believe
You resolve You gaze
Your perception oscillates
underlying structure fluxing, or purely contingent

shapes moving on a patterned field.
You shade your eyes.
shapes move, or shadow has shifted
close : threat,
comfort, amusement, wisdom.

long, low-pitched boom.
wind through a small gap a high-pitched whine.
In the middle tumbling rocks clatter percussively, occasionally

It loses saturation, and your
perception dims with it.

Repeat for
ever.

Boundaries dissolved and inasmuch as I am stardust, I am mountains and wind and light and distance. The rock or the rain do not roll over me as much as they become me and I them. That I have eyes reporting to a brain the dream of difference sets me over here in my dark seat. That some of the words are emptied to white paper means that what is gone is marked by the space it formerly inhabited. Blacked out might have meant eradicated or withheld or obliterated. But the thing vanished leaves a space for a while, until something reshuffles or grows over. ~~Nothing gone, merely undifferentiated.~~ Even then a trace remains.

77. *OTTO'S SELF BOARD MEETING—PABLO HELGUERA*

Otto: Thank you all for coming. I had to call this emergency board meeting of all my top senior selves in order to address a matter of serious importance to the Otto Rumperstreiser Art Career Corporation. As you know, We, Otto, are approaching the end of the year and so far My/Our exhibition schedule looks empty. This is an unacceptable situation that I/We all have to work quickly to correct. I look forward to your suggestions.

Otto, Senior Marketing Strategist: I have been saying all along that people are not aware of our product. We have to be more aggressive. We are up against other artists who have huge galleries with promotional machinery behind them. We need to be sending weekly emails about what We do to everyone Otto knows and maybe buy an ad on e-flux. And We have to get ourselves to more important openings. We keep going to the same stupid openings in Chelsea without collectors or decision-makers.

Otto, Social Etiquette Supervisor: We have to be careful with the self-promotional thing. It looks inelegant and desperate. I agree that We need to attend higher-end openings and We need to be more on top of important people's birthdays. But email doesn't work anymore. People just delete whatever they get, everyone is saturated even with Facebook.

Otto, Chief Financial Officer: I am sorry, but We can't afford an ad campaign right now. Ads cost a fucking fortune. Otto hasn't sold a work in months and the only money We are getting—from that lecture at that college in Ohio—will pay for the stupid photo print job for that piece Otto agreed to donate to the art auction. The rest of the money will have to be for that expensive dinner date this coming Friday with the French curator.

Otto, Manager of Getting Laid: Excuse Us—the French curator actually is a promising relationship. Don't forget that she said she is very interested in Otto's work. And in the meantime, let's face it, she is really hot and Otto is in dire need of getting laid.

Otto, Deputy Director of Art Ideas: Please, let's focus on the content of Otto's work. The other morning when We were in the shower We had a really interesting idea for a video piece about the slums of Morocco. It would be a multi-channel video piece and it would show these slums with a narrative of a blind Moroccan prostitute whose story Otto read the other day in *Paris Match*.

Otto, Coordinator of Reality Check: That's ludicrous. First of all, how the hell are We going to get to Morocco to do the video, and then find the prostitute? There is no fucking way We can pull that project together.

Otto: Wait a minute. We were talking about getting a show, not about a new piece!

Otto, Cheating Associate: How about if We just steal footage from YouTube or something and get a friend to do a prostitute voiceover?

Otto, Senior Marketing Strategist: Wait a minute: what if We ask the French curator to do the voiceover, and then once the piece is made We ask for her help to get the piece shown? She may even have contacts in Morocco. Wasn't it a French colony? Wasn't she working on a show about post-colonialism? She is totally going to love this piece.

Otto, Manager of Getting Laid: I think it's a great idea. What do We have to lose? If nothing else, We will get laid.

It is easier to imagine a layered self, composed of a hierarchy of folds, than one which is equally split and in conflict.

Not a sloppy self, either, oozing from the toaster machine of superego and id, but one which is very much a many, fashioned by the expectations of our age to be all things all the time.

It is a condition of contemporary capitalist culture that it is almost impossible to be just one self, and we must be prepared to invent and deploy as many versions as we need to survive.

How can we play so many roles in life and still hold on to a sense of integrity and coherence? This is a challenge that affects us all, but perhaps artists feel it more sharply, when the world of business seems to operate under very different laws, and to very different rhythms, than to those of culture.

"I am large, I contain multitudes," wrote Whitman. Easier to feel and to claim in poetry than to stage. And what if we didn't just contain multitudes, but found ourselves multiplied as Otto does? With which mouth do I sing the song of my selves?

Theatre has approached the problem of staging the divided self in various ways: abstracting bodies, doubling roles, experimenting with costume and make-up, or interacting with technologies.

Otto's Self Board Meeting poses the challenge of how we might stage equally competing selves, which are not just shadows of a single front or imitations of a stable core.

Allied to this, it presses us to question our investment in creative production, if what we really want is to be accepted, or just to fuck. Might it not be a better idea to dissolve our own company, sack our selves, and meet someone else instead?

Not I, Beckett's mouth declaims. Not We either, Otto's selves seem to agree.

What about You?

There are easier ways to get laid than by making art.

78. *PASSENGER PIGEONS—YVETTE NOLAN*

The audience has arrived early to get a good spot, spreading blankets and tarps close to the stage. Families have brought picnics to take advantage of the time they will spend together outdoors. Around the edges, elders sit in lawn chairs.

Children dash between the blankets, playing children's games. A couple of them lean on the edge of the stage, pointing at the prop trees, touching the set which looks just like the earth, but feels different, until a stage manager comes and gently admonishes them.

The audience senses the entrance of the birds before it hears them, as if the air is being pushed ahead of the flock. Then the sound arrives, but there are so many birds that the flapping of wings is just one huge hum that the audience hears in their ears, in their sinuses, in the resonators of their bodies, their chests. The day which was bright and clear becomes dark as the birds arrive, a feathered river across the sky. They alight on the stage, on the prop trees and canvas earth. There are so many that they cover the structure that supports the stage, they perch on the grid, line up on the top of the backdrop. There must be millions of them. The audience, too overwhelmed to applaud, just admires their gray and green and violet plumage and pinkish bellies, the sheer mass of them.

A child approaches the edge of the stage, but the birds do not seem to be disturbed or threatened.

A man enters the stage with a net, and with one scoop captures a half-dozen birds. Another man runs onstage with a pitchfork, and with one thrust skewers a half-dozen more. The mother of the child near the stage drags him away, covering his face.

Still the birds do not take flight.

Men now run onstage and harvest birds as quickly as humanly possible. This one fires a shotgun and twelve birds drop. More nets arrive, more pitchforks and rakes. More birds die. Finally, one man touches a match to a tree. Made of cardboard and paint, it catches quickly, goes up like a torch. Panicked birds take to the air like tiny fireballs. Dozens of squabs drop and burst open when they hit the ground.

And then it is over. The birds are gone, though the air is redolent of grilled flesh. The audience packs up its picnic baskets and coolers and blankets, and heads for home, gratified to have been present at this one-time only event.

In *Pantomime,* Derek Walcott's brilliant satire on colonial representation, the Caribbean hotel worker Jackson takes revenge on his colonial master by killing the latter's parrot. Harry Trewe, the European hotelier, mocks the gesture with a piece of dramatic history: "You people create nothing. You imitate everything. It's all been done before, you see, Jackson. The parrot. Think that's something? It's from *The Seagull.* It's from *Miss Julie.*"

He might have added: it's from *The Wild Duck*, it's from *Trifles*.

Birds drop like flies in modern drama.

Rarely, however, do they die *as birds*. Rather, like most appearances of the non-human on the western stage, they materialize in order to immediately dematerialize, to perform as metaphors and symbols for the ever-spot-lit Human Condition. And their deaths—climactic as they often are, only intensify the floating—or flying—significations they have been summoned to produce, offering a cathartic finale in which the animal origins of sacrificial practice are fleetingly, flittingly, revealed.

Meanwhile, off stage, the massacre goes on in earnest. With Yvette Nolan, I'm tempted to institute a Memorial Theatre of Species that would displace the old Theatre of Animal Symbols. Its stars (it would need stars, since its audience would still be humans, and we're a star-loving, celebrity-hounding species), would be "endlings"—also known as "enders," "terminarchs," and "relicts": the last remaining member of a species before extinction. It is thought that there were between 3 and 5 billion passenger pigeons in North America when the first Europeans arrived. Since the departure of Martha, the last passenger pigeon, in a Cincinnati zoo in 1914, we've also said goodbye to Incas, the last Carolina parakeet (who died, in 1914, in the very same cage Martha had occupied!), Booming Ben, the last heath hen (died in 1932), Benjamin, the last thylacine or Tasmanian tiger (died in 1936), Celia, the last Pyrenean ibex (died in 2000), and Lonesome George, the last Pinta Island tortoise (died in 2012). Martha was brilliantly serenaded on stage recently in *The Great Immensity*, a climate change musical by Steve Cosson and the Civilians. Lonesome George was movingly memorialized by Adam Cole on NPR's Skunk Bear science channel (watch it on YouTube).

Must the Endling art that is being initiated by these works be exclusively an art of mourning? Perhaps it will also need to be, as in Nolan's imagined theatre, a war reenactment, a series of history plays narrating the great battles our species has waged against others, a carnival of interspecies killing accompanied by the mouth-watering smells of roasting flesh, invitations to the feast celebrating the triumph of the human. Kill, eat, and be merry. Hardly a one-time only event …

79. *PLANT LIFE (EXCERPT FROM A PLAY IN THREE ACTS)—PEGGY PHELAN*

Prequel

Slow illumination of stage covered on ground with real or synthetic ice, and with real icicles dripping from stage lights. Twelve dancers/performers on ladders just below lights. Dancers improvise on ladders, tasting melting ice, sliding and climbing up and down the ladder. Performers are absorbed by these tasks, moving silently, without looking at one another. Music is George Winston's "December," *but the dancers are not moving "to" it. It is rather in the landscape around them. This "view" lasts about five minutes. Then darkness.*

Scene 1

Lights up, slowly. Two tent-like translucent structures about six feet high and three feet wide, soft light inside structure on left. Two teenagers (gender/race/size not relevant) both wearing bodysuits. Teen 2 has hood on; Teen 1 holds hood in hand at start. Each tent has a zipper door that faces the audience. Tent on right has no one near it. Teen 2 is inside the tent on left. Teen 1 stands near the tent door. As lights come up, Teen 2 emerges.

Teen 1: How long did you last?

Teen 2: Not quite three hours. It's super hard.

Teen 1: What's the hourly pay today?

Teen 2: Five meals or two hundred dollars.

Teen 1: What did you take?

Teen 2: The meals.

Teen 2 steps out of bodysuit, hood first; Teen 1 puts on hood.

Teen 2: Good luck. I'm going to eat.

Teen 1: Thanks. Enjoy.

Teen 1 moves to open door of tent. Teen 1 zips hood and wades inside, then attaches cables from each wrist to a large plant system that looks like sea algae but with more definition. The plant only stays alive if the teen moves, dances. The teen's dance is in the same spirit as the ladder dance prequel. Three minutes. Music is William Ackerman's "Anne's Song." *Lights fade.*

Scene 2

Same as before, Teen 1 inside illuminated tent, dancing.

Enter two men, late 50s. One in overalls; the other in business suit. Both with digital tablets.

Exec: How long can these kids can stay in the tent without a break?

Overalls (*glancing at tablet throughout*): Most last about 150 minutes. There are a few outliers below that and one spectacular teen who can stay almost 400 minutes. She is epic!

Exec: Are you paying her more?

Overalls: Nope.

Exec: Who is interviewing them when they come out?

Overalls: Interviewing the kids? I don't think anyone is. We give them all surveys once a month but they only fill them out if we provide a meal. And even then I don't think they are telling the truth, or maybe even reading the surveys. 78% of the responses to the survey circle the first choice on every question.

Exec: Did you tell anyone we have bad data?

Overalls: No. No one asked before now. Before you.

Exec: Why is one tent empty? We need two at a time, all the time!

Overalls: We are having a harder time recruiting teens. We either have to pay them more or go to a younger group.

Exec: (*Pause.*) What about senior citizens? We can get them cheap, especially if we tell them it is all for the next generation—they love that!

O body swayed to music, O brightening glance,
How can we know the dancer from the dance?
(William Butler Yeats, "*Among School Children*")

Yeats's faith in artistic plenitude is far behind us. The dance now—and movement, action, life itself—appears instrumentalized and commodified, embedded in brutal systems of labor and exchange. A doubly alienated labor: not only is it not dance, it may not even be the agricultural contribution it appears to be. It may just be "science," and not even good science: shoddy protocols producing "bad data."

But the teens are amazing; one's even "epic." If they keep at it, they'll maybe generate some future version of the Green One, ancient archetype with many forms, from Greek Pan to Islamic Khidr, patron saint of healing waters; from *Gilgamesh*'s forest guardian Humbaba to the foliate-faced Green Man adorning the walls and doors of medieval churches. The teens' version looks to be a mashup of the *Cyborg Manifesto* and a Rachel Rosenthal performance, the one in which she danced "Earth's astounding motion: Earth moves, Earth bounds. Earth careens. Earth cavorts. Earth does the tectonic shuffle."

Meanwhile, you gotta eat. Take the meals instead of the money, fuel up for the next shift—or next workout, if that's what it is. Then suit up, and go in—or go on, if it's only a show. Either way, you're working, and living. And something—your dance, it seems—is making the plants grow. Let it be a *lehrstücke* for vibrant materiality, a teaching play about biocentric harmonizing, a mindful biopolitics for the post-abundance era.

Or let it be a new human embroidery on the skin of the earth. From translucent, tented incubators, the hooded teens weave filaments of future nourishment, their fingertips hot with prophecy. Never-before-recorded spectra of energy waves shoot out from the elbow crooks, ankle flexes, and cuff rotations of the workdancers. Dilemmas left behind, the epic omnivores perform Artaud's insight: "if it is important for us to eat first of all, it is even more important for us not to waste in the sole concern for eating our simple power of being hungry."

80. POOLSIDE—CLAUDIA LA ROCCO

—but every *evening* we would go down to the pool and—well you understand the pool wasn't exactly *down* because the ship of course was in constant rotation, or perhaps I mean to say continual, but in any event it felt good to say "Let's go down to the pool," it felt like a going out on the town, as it were, a remnant of what had been—since we couldn't actually go *out* anywhere, our respiratory systems not yet having adapted adequately to new, what you might call … environmental … realities—but where was I … yes, to the pool, we would get all dressed up, tinfoil and bangles and gossamer and the like, the usual fripperies and fineries, perhaps stardust on a Friday (yes yes at that point we still kept the days), all of the sections converging in the center, for ours was a spherical pool, always a trick to find the shallow end, its contents glittering darkly under and above the far-away lights of the arena, the waters shifting and lapping according to great yet self-contained waves of a certain velvety nature, and all of us finding our seats according to a strict and strictly non-discussed hierarchy—oh if you asked us it didn't exist at all—until we were all in place yet not at all still, hats and stoles and feather dusters and falsies fanning up and out and rotating somehow (you never believe me but it's *true*) counter to our direction so that one could always manage to snag something pleasing and play dress up in another section's, er, livery, I suppose you might say, no harm no foul as long as it was returned at the end of the evening, set loose in the arena to find its way home (and yes of course by this means many a covert message was managed), and by this time the after-dinner sea leopards had wended their way all throughout the great hall, glowing and pulsing and generally making a big show of their teeth, and let me tell you no matter how many times you'd seen a sea leopard's teeth the vision of that otherworldly maw never grew less, how shall we say, *itself*, and even if the beasts were completely disinterested in any grand malarkeys involving limb rending and the like, still I'd seen many an attendee twirl his mustaches in a heightened manner approaching *great* nervousness, the sea leopards using this consternation inevitably as an excuse to find themselves on the business end of the more eligible ladies' skirts, such that one always felt the slightest twinge of excited apprehension upon eyeing the newborns that, errmmm, *resulted* from time to time after a particular skirt-sea leopard conflagration—well no of course not an *actual* fire, don't be hysterical—it's just that, well, things could get a little funny up there in the early days of The Great Travel, and certain things that you might all take with nary a second look seemed to us of the most miraculous import and happenstance, perhaps I should say happenchance, such that we were all, already, primed for what was to come each *night* and yet at the same time absolutely gob smacked by what we all knew to be only the usual by-ordinance entertainment, heh heh heh yes indeed the *audiences*, that word having a particular interstitial meaning at the time, they did ever get restless—yes yes of course I mean "we" by "they," don't go daft on me now—so that by the time the waters had begun swirling in that particular pre-show way we all as one leaned forward (or, at times, back) in our amphitheater seating, fans tensely at the ready, waiters making the most of their trays and tentacles, the bubbly spilling up and out and over us such that we had only to open our mouths to imbibe, and always one wanted to close one's eyes and yet one didn't, because there it was now just about to become a thing that one could look at, just about to come into its very own being and move from what could only be sensed—

It is remarkable to consider that the only remains we have today of the legendary *Evidences* is the famous so-called *Poolside* fragment, and the even shorter accompanying *Notes for a presentation*, also known as *The Gloss*. Both have come down to us in *written* form, which was in wide use for a long time, although differences in *platform*—to borrow a term from *The Gloss* itself—suggest they were produced lifeworlds apart. Speculations that both are outputs of the same lifeworld and were later effectively modulated in transmission—even that the authors could conceivably have known each other—have not been sustained. Players will note the remarkable—and justly-admired—movements and dynamics of *Poolside*, as against the relative banality of *The Gloss*. According to experts, the contrast is even more marked in the originals. As is well known, much of our own great cultural invention The Entertainment derives from suggestions to be found in these two short pieces. Imagine what else might be "unlocked"—informing even our own lifeworld—if *The Evidences* in its entirety was still with us.

Notes for a presentation

The number of items in *The Evidences* is vast, estimated in the quillions, at least. But even these estimates are meaningless, as there are still ~~platforms formats~~ platforms that have not been unlocked yet. ~~The total amount of material could be~~ It goes without saying that the very small selection of items that I will present on today etc.

1. Poolside
2. Far away
3. Collars
4. Sea legs

~~As everyone knows, *The Evidences* is a massive collection of material which~~ Really, our understanding ~~of The Dry Times~~ is just beginning etc

Poolside. Interzone litter? Extract from a larger item? We know that gathering of items ("anthologies") was happening before establishment of universal *Evidences* project. Everything had been lost. Great Travel—era of fascination for later times. Interspecies. Teeth and tentacles. Also the violence. My thesis—Poolside is not a forgery. The ~~impression indentation~~ incision of the experience on the reporter is authentic. "Come into its own sort of being" at end is its own sort of evidence. See also miracle. Entertainment. Of what cannot be evidenced, only experienced. Belongs to us also. Sea leopards, compare with white tigers, unicorns. Also non-existent, but convincing.

Conclusion. From a superficial reading we could get a "sense" from it that life was ~~intenser~~ more intense, more vivid in that form. But it is my conviction that there are experiences also that we have not had yet etc

81. *PRECIPITATION—KAREN CHRISTOPHER*

Profound darkness falls suddenly. The house quiets down, conversations drop quickly but a low hum continues as last murmurs linger. A moment of complete silence is reached but interrupted by scattered coughing. As silence returns, the sound of labored breathing is heard. It is a man breathing through exertion. Somewhere someone is wearing a small microphone. This sound is transmitted through the house speakers. It feels close.

A soft glow of light grows in the center of the back wall of the playing space emanating from a spot there along the back edge of the stage. Now light delineates the shape of a man with arms and legs at outstretched angles. Clearly he is the one heard through the house speakers. He is still now, his breathing has calmed and is barely audible. It seems he is one third of the way up the wall, clinging with fingers and toes to the tiniest variations in the smooth texture of the brick and mortar surface.

A glow appears in a rectangular shape along the wall to the left of the climbing man. A video feed from a small camera he is wearing just over his left ear makes clear what the surface of the wall looks like from his perspective. As the image sharpens he turns his head delicately from left to right and also looks straight up in the direction he hopes eventually to travel. He is planning his next maneuver and releases his right hand to attempt a lateral move and this hand stretches perpendicular to his torso. A razor sharp ledge—micro-thin, and slightly further than his reach will comfortably allow—is in his sights. The image on the wall projected from his ear camera is providing surprising connections and energetic cognitive leaps.

Slow, shaky progress with sudden bursts of successful advancement continues for some time. At any given moment one or another audience member realizes she or he is clenching muscles in sympathy with the man on the wall. Close attention reveals a syncopation of sighs as people in disparate locations relax taut muscles upon this realization. A quieter more regular breathing sound can be heard from the dozen or so sleepers, members of the audience surrendering to a different kind of oblivion.

The breathing of the climbing man, still amplified, has taken on an audible moisture, a juicy sound. Sweat, saliva, or inner lung moisture now mixes with the air of his respiration and with it a sense of desperation, emotion, or—at the very least—exertion begins to coalesce.

After 7 days, 15 hours, and 11 minutes during which the room has become humid with exhalation, the man on the back wall is so high that only his feet are visible from the seats in the audience. A wispy but perfectly formed white cloud appears in the air at the center of the space. It hovers, momentarily glowing in the lights.

Ascension

Duration ____ Devotion

Sweat ____ Surveillance

Presence ____ Persistence

Labor ____ Love

Intimacy ____ Interiority

Liveness ____ Lightness

Duration ____ Dedication

Close ____ Closer

Solo ____ Solidarity

Proximity ____ Precarity

82. *THE PREVIOUS CRY—TIMOTHY MCCAIN*

The audience assembles inside the Event Horizon, a boundary marking the limits of the black hole. Nothing … nothing inside the Event Horizon can ever navigate the boundary and escape beyond, including light. Nothing … nothing that passes into the black hole can get out nor can it be observed from outside the Event Horizon. It is not a physical surface; it is a mathematically defined demarcation. A rare BLACK SEA DEVIL anglerfish swims up from the black hole. It swims just beneath the Event Horizon. It stops.

BLACK SEA DEVIL:
Mark a little point. Marked vacant, surrounding what leapt
forth. And you, you stand, knocked for six, embraced by immense gravities,
without break, remembering a bridge fashioned out of granite
you once crossed, now need to fashion once again, till the unfinished exposes,
till the tactful existence you rearranged somewhere is made known, a dark,
inky blotch.

BLACK SEA DEVIL swims off down into the black hole. Objects are pulled in. A rocket ship. The Eiffel Tower. The Great Wall of China. A pair of underwear. Etc. A woman wearing a tattered red scarf floats into the Event Horizon. Her clothing is engulfed in flames.

WOMAN WEARING RED SCARF:
F … ff … fire. Flames. Nip. Speak low, lean low, as what went before. To see. So … see. Sway … be consumed. An observer. Observing me … twirl.

She slowly lifts her arms, making a subtle swaying of her hips, turns, and is pulled in all directions down the black hole. Objects are pulled in. Planets. Moons. The Golden Gate Bridge. Hamlet holding Yorick's skull. Etc. A sad little clown is pulled in. He waves a sorrowful hello. He mimes as if he is enclosed in a box. He mimes walking against the wind. He mimes the invisible rope. He pulls out a balloon. He blows it up. He makes a strange, contorted thing. He fastens it to his chest. He looks at the strange, contorted thing. He waves a sorrowful goodbye. He is pulled down the black hole. BLACK SEA DEVIL swims up the black hole. Stops.

BLACK SEA DEVIL:
When you went away it was water. Water, water everywhere, but not to drink.
Ruminations of something at the corner of your eye. Sparkle? A fleck of metal?
Light's reflection. And that mark hidden in the hairline. Blood courses
through that supple vein beneath your eye. Letting me know. I believed
I smelt our breath. Something sweet. Something not.
Wonder if you think of me? If you think? You went away
in water. Then and there I expected you to turn.
Believed … if you turned back I'd know. I waited
as you passed out of view. Waited wringing wet.

BLACK SEA DEVIL swims off down into the black hole. Darkness is pulled in.

> black holes, possible human extinction. If we have nothing but truth to leave, how do we distinguish ideas of what we were from ideas of what we are in vibrant contemporary compost jargon trash landfill
>
> (Susan Howe, "Vagrancy in the Park")

In his 1783 letter to Henry Cavendish, English clergyman and natural philosopher John Michell penned the first recorded theorization of the cosmological phenomenon that would come to be called the black hole—a collapsed "dark star" from which no electromagnetic energy escapes. "… [A]ll light emitted from such a body would be made to return towards it by its own proper gravity," he wrote. Later that year Michell formalized his proposal in a paper for the *Philosophical Transactions of the Royal Society of London*, read on 27 November. Requiring an understanding of light as particulate and subject to forces of gravitation ("Light falls," declared Richard Feyman), the idea remained inert until gaining traction in the post-Einstein twentieth century. Since then it has held a prominent place in the theatrical imagination, often pried from science-fiction-friendly moorings, and plumbed for metaphoric/existential force. No other image renders the void so near, in presence and substance. Murray Mednick's 1975 play *Black Hole in Space*, a surreal futuristic tragedy, linked it to Aztec ritual human sacrifice for the sun's rebirth. Writing about Italian collective Kinkaleri's 2006 performance *Nerone*, scholar Joe Kelleher translates a sentence from Rodolfo Sacchettini: "As if it was impossible then to go all the way, to collapse into the black hole of the live representation while remaining anchored to the presence on stage, the Kinkaleris as a group are completely removed from the scene towards an eerie and fierce introspective ascent." Kelleher positions the black box theatre, so called, now in a state of collapse after its heyday in the 1960s and 1970s, as the black hole's conceptual cousin: technology for remembering the present and zone of no return.

In this imagined theatre script, Timothy McCain explodes these ideas to their absolute physical and literal limit, their "event horizon," beyond which nothing subject to human perception travels—and engages them for a recapitulation of human existence. Landmarks and accomplishments (Eiffel Tower, Great Wall of China), as well as emblems of the ordinary (A pair of underwear), with a special place reserved for the theatre (Hamlet holding Yorick's skull, a mime granted time to work through his routine)—one by one the hole vacuums all. Woman Wearing Red Scarf appears as the last of humanity, out of place, identified by her garment that echoes the flames that engulf her, through which she signals—flames in a black hole?—she has brought them with her, elemental and dignified. The parade offers a perverse reversal of the animals entering the ark. Regarding animals in this (last) instance, a stage manager appears, immune to the hole's pull and unhindered by possibility on the pitch-black fringes. With anthropomorphism embedded in even the name, the anglerfish aggregates fish and fisherman, its dorsal spine modified into a lure projecting before its fearsome spiky teeth. By virtue of its blackness, the seadevil haunts the hole in which it apparently belongs, life asserting itself out of lifelessness. Its bioluminescent lure glows under its own light, lantern, messenger, even in this ultimate shadow that absorbs all spectra. "I expected you to turn./ Believed … if you turned/back I'd know." It beckons us toward nonhuman salvation, to the "turning back" by which we might recover ourselves, might find not before but behind, "previous," might recognize "the necessity for turning [ourselves] around," in the time that remains, before even time draws in to the darkness.

83. *PRIVATE LANGUAGE ARGUMENT I—ANDREW SOFER*

If a lion could talk, we would not understand him.

(Ludwig Wittgenstein, *Philosophical Investigations*)

The curtain opens. A lion steps out onto the stage.

The lion glares at the audience, then does whatever it does for ten minutes or so, vocalizing occasionally.

The lion leaves the stage. The audience roars its approval.

One man turns to his neighbor. "I don't get it."

The neighbor grins knowingly. He removes his mask, revealing the face of a lion.

When a man in a black suit speaks, I think I understand him. Then I see in the changing light that his suit is navy blue, and I understand that I do not understand him.

When a man in a gray suit speaks, I think I half-understand him. Then when in the changing light, I see that what appeared to be gray is dirty, I understand that something is nonetheless gray, and something is my half-understanding.

When a man in a lion's suit speaks, I think I do not understand him. Then when in the changing room, I see that he is a man, I understand that what appeared to be my misunderstanding is dirty, and I am ashamed.

When a lion in a lion's suit speaks, I think I understand from the lesson of the changing room that I ought to try to understand him. Then when in the changing climate, I see that he is a lion, I exit, and he pursues me.

The lion is always the hardest part.

I am putting a theatre together. The lion cannot see me, but from time to time, he guesses my thoughts

and roars.

84. *PRIVATE LANGUAGE ARGUMENT II—ANDREW SOFER*

Participants are screened based on their ignorance of beetles.
A and B walk onstage and are each presented with a small, opaque box.
They are informed that their boxes contain a "beetle."
Neither is allowed to check the other's box.
At a signal, each checks his or her own box. They can check it as often as they like.
A and B describe their beetles to each other.
Following the performance, every spectator is handed his or her own beetle-box, along with strict instructions never to reveal its contents.
Some boxes are empty. Others contain, say: a paper clip, a rose, a starfish.
The performance continues until everyone in town has received his or her own box.
The title of the piece is "Pain."

For Wittgenstein, truly private definitions of words or symbols preclude intelligible meaning. Language is a kind of (public) theatre. For instance, in *Philosophical Investigations* 1.257 he claims that "a great deal of stage-setting in the language is presupposed if the mere act of naming is to make sense. And when we speak of someone's having given a name to pain, what is presupposed is the existence of the grammar of the word 'pain'; it shews the post where the new word is stationed." Later, at 1.272, he states: "The essential thing about private experience is really not that each person possesses his own exemplar, but that nobody knows whether people also have *this* or something else. The assumption would thus be possible—though unverifiable—that one section of mankind had one sensation of red and another section another."

Beetle Haiku

A word like "beetle"
can't refer to a critter
that *only* I know.

So a word like "pain"
must refer to something else
than *my* sensation.

What I alone feel
is, then, quite irrelevant
to the word's meaning!

Theatre as black box:
actors perform how pain feels.
Perhaps they're lying.

85. QUESTIONS FOR WOMEN IN PRISON—RHODESSA JONES

In the face of transformation, hope, and change we have formulated these questions as a place to begin.

When did you first realize there was cruelty in the world? What was the incident that made you aware? Describe in detail.
When did you first realize that you were not safe in the world? What happened?
Tell the history of a scar your body carries. How did you get it? What kind of day was it? Where were you? Describe in detail.
Write a speech about the first time you were violated. You finally get to address your perpetrator—tell them anything and everything you wanted to say. Let the group be your support. Write it. Say it.
Has anyone ever loved your body?
Has anyone ever invaded or occupied or dominated your body?
When is the first time you remember being angry? How is that connected with your being in prison?
How would you define violence? What does it look like, taste like, feel like?
Did you ever witness anyone you love being hurt? What did it look like? How did it change you?
Has anything violent happened to you in prison?
Is there anyone you trust? Why, why not?
Can you imagine no more violence? What would that look like?
How would your life have been different if there were no violence against women?
Describe one act you did as an act of revenge that changed your life. Who were you avenging?
In terms of violence, is there a connection between what was done to you and what you then did to someone else?

It has been said that at the deathbed of the great Gertrude Stein, her tearful and grieving partner Alice B. Toklas demanded to know: "What are the answers, Gertrude, what are the answers?" And Gertrude Stein answered, "What are the questions, my dear Alice, what are the questions?"

I am a performing artist with a social conscience. Therefore, activism is inherent in my creativity. I've always made art that speaks for the "underserved," the marginalized, the forgotten, the "others." Growing up in a migrant, crop-gathering family of 12 children, I had firsthand experience of being invisible in America. It was my early years as a young, migrant, black girl that impacted all the work I've made and all the voices I articulate—the voices of the young and the lost.

My active involvement with prison reform began when my brother was in the Attica Correctional Facility, when the Prisoners' Rights Movement staged a riot, and the Governor ordered in troops. I was there, outside the wall, singing, praying, speaking with others. From there I went to Seattle and spoke with "Inside/Outside," a support group for inmates. Then, I moved to San Francisco and began studying dance and performance. In 1973, I joined Tumbleweed, a women's dance collective which taught and performed at San Quentin, Soledad, and Folsom prisons as part of the Prison Poet Workshops led by Max Schwartz. Having lived and worked as an artist in various social institutions, I was approached by the California Arts Council in 1986 to teach aerobics at the San Francisco City Jail for women. I immediately realized that much more than aerobics was called for. Most of the inmates were African Americans or Latinas. Their crimes varied from drug abuse to prostitution. In artistic response, Cultural Odyssey and I created and toured "Big Butt Girls, Hard-Headed Women," a series of monologues based on interviews with incarcerated women. THE MEDEA PROJECT: THEATER FOR INCARCERATED WOMEN at the San Francisco City Jail has since become a part of the curriculum at the educational facility of the county jail. It has allowed me to realize a dream by setting the stage for a touring ensemble of ex-inmates. This confronts one of my greatest disappointments in my work with the incarcerated—they have no incentive not to return to jail. By providing meaningful work in the arts and the opportunity to travel, the ex-inmates will have a light to illuminate other possibilities.

The black woman is quite possibly the first real "American" woman—I say the first in a nation that was invented atop the violence perpetrated against indigenous peoples. Forced to be free and independent in the face of oppressive invisibility, on top of being maligned, it is quite possible that she may very well have invented herself. Teaching young women from all backgrounds, in a detention center or a freshman theatre class, I always ask, "As women, facing the 21st century, how do we honor ourselves?"

86. REALISM—KYLE GILLETTE

No one sees it coming. We behold a stage bisected by train tracks that run straight toward the back wall. As we look into the distance where the tracks seem to meet, we presume we see a painted backdrop of a central vanishing point perspective. (In fact, we are wrong. Real tracks disappear down an actual four-mile corridor visible through the missing back wall of the theatre. The meeting of tracks is an illusion of convergence caused by distance—not, as we believe, an illusion of distance caused by convergence.)

Stage right of the tracks: a long, immaculately laid table with an overabundance of doilies, linens, teacups, carafes, tea sandwiches, vases, all white. A fine family sits around, silently sipping, cutting, passing the butter.

On the other side of the tracks: a vulgar slab, a great gnarled oak roughly split. It is heaped with oversized mugs of ale, straw, rusted goblets, dung, two great hogs farting and shitting. Servants laugh, belch, and weep silently as they spill beer all over themselves and take bites out of mutton legs.

Read over the microphone, passages from *Anna Karenina*: "All happy families are alike; each unhappy family is unhappy in its own way"; "Not one word, not one gesture of yours shall I, could I, ever forget ..." And so on.

When we see a train in the distance, headed straight for us at full speed, we realize that the central vanishing point is not painted but real. The train comes closer. The tables begin to rattle. Stage lights crash to the ground. Finally, the steam locomotive rushes into the theatre building, down between the tables and straight into the auditorium. The ensuing catastrophe is shocking beyond all comprehension.

After the smoke clears, the two tables continue to dine as if nothing had happened.

Sherlock Holmes and the case of the missing samovar

(with apologies to Kyle—and William—Gillette)

Where is the samovar, my dear Watson? There is no samovar, I can hear you saying, and you're perhaps technically right, but as we look at what's clearly in front of us, it's evident that there is a samovar shaped hole stage right; squint and you too can see it. As we watch the "fine family" seated there, I'm reminded of the negative space between two faces that becomes a wine glass in that immediately recognizable optical illusion. While this isn't typically the type of *trompe l'oeil* in which the theatre specializes, it's appropriate given the centrality of the "illusion of convergence caused by distance," which is also not typical theatrical fare. But this realism, these tables, and Tolstoy cement us firmly in a Chekhovian universe, the worlds of the servants and the masters both entirely separate and simultaneously intertwined. The servants are perhaps Rabelaisian or Falstaffian interlopers here, but their presence is utterly necessary. It is, after all, Firs who outlives the catastrophe of the destruction of the Cherry Orchard, serving as witness to the end.

But Holmes, when finding myself audience to this moment of fin de siècle realism, and this non-illusory train, my mind automatically turns to cinema, and what Martin Loiperdinger has called "cinema's founding myth," the oft-repeated story of the audiences fleeing in fear from the train that appears to crash through the screen at screenings of Louis Lumière's *L'Arrivée d'un train en gare de La Ciotat*. Loiperdinger suggests that this is actually perhaps an imagined theatre of its own, since there is no contemporaneous evidence to demonstrate its veracity. Mustn't we consider the possibility that this is all merely the imagination of an overzealous newspaper reporter?

Ah, as you yourself noted in "A Case of Identity," Watson, when we have "realism pushed to its extreme limits … [too often] the result is, it must be confessed, neither fascinating nor artistic" and so, as I suggested, we must "never trust to general impressions, my boy, but concentrate upon details." What you've clearly missed is the question of the imagined time of the theatre. So here we are in Russia, with a train destroying the audience, and we have immediately leapt forward 100 years or so to October 23rd, 2002, in the Dubrovka Theatre. On the positive side, for Masha, Olga, and Irina, we have finally made it to Moscow; although in the words of those Chechnyan hostage-takers who themselves appear to cite Chekhov, "we have nothing to lose. We have already covered 2,000 kilometres … Our motto is freedom and paradise. We already have freedom as we've come to Moscow …" Indeed, the advent of realism out of the ashes of melodrama perhaps demanded that eventually the train destroy the audience, while the real of the stage continues on. As I said in our very first adventure together, "where there is no imagination there is no horror," and it is precisely the theatre that allows for that collision of time and space—all because of that missing samovar and the thundering 9:14 to Moscow.

87. REMAINS—ANDY FIELD

a photograph
(uploaded to an anonymous social media account
and quickly deleted)
of a woman about to launch a stone towards a large white apartment block
a half-drunk glass of interval wine
a polyester flag singed at the edges where someone has seemingly tried
and failed
to set fire to it
an anecdote told again and again by someone who was not actually there
a dream I had several months afterwards
of bright lights
and warm bodies
a punctured life raft
a risk-assessment outlining precautions to be taken in the eventuality of
the smoke becoming suffocating
the audience tripping on exposed cables
the animals panicking
water damage
power failure
sub-zero temperatures
a mark on the pavement
glitter under fingernails
at the bottom of rucksacks
on hotel bed sheets
a single stem from a bunch of cut flowers
handed out to a member of the audience
taken home
dried and pressed in the folds of this book
then placed in a frame on a bedside table
splinters of a piano dropped from a great height
an incomprehensible police report
and several letters of complaint
this is all that remains of the performance.

Like the photographs, bullet casing, and partial audio- and video-recordings that remain from Chris Burden's *Shoot* (1971), or—to follow the mark on the pavement—like the blood and glass on the Los Angeles street and the grainy footage left behind after Burden's *Through the Night Softly* (1973), these material remnants recall a past performance. But in addition to that event—partially remembered, imperfectly documented, and now (apparently) long over—it should be obvious that these remains also themselves perform. A performance event is still ongoing.

It might even be fair to say that these remains—what remains of this performance—are a kind of script, directing the audience (reader?) to attempt a reconstruction as at the scene of a crime. At what theatrical event could a piano have been dropped from a great height? Did this happen before or after the interval? And who watched this piece? Certainly "I" was there, since I dream about the piece, of bright lights and warm bodies, but at what point were the police called? What exactly did I miss? Or have I myself gone missing?

The detritus in *Remains* implies performances in the so-called legitimate theatre as well as the kinds of overtly theatrical political activities that attempt to garner widespread media attention. The images alternate between theatrical commonplaces and bodies in extremis. And there is overlap between these; one is reminded of the critics in Martin Crimp's 1997 play *Attempts on Her Life,* walking through the art gallery filled with suicide notes, syringes, latex, and leather, objects that purport to document the absent Anne's attempts to end her own life. These are remains that testify to the body's vulnerabilities. It is worth noting, too, that rehearsals of risk-assessment precautions attempting to minimize real dangers are surely another way of performing, even spectacularizing, just how fragile our bodies are.

And even when we have a collection of remains, we know that these can function only as prompts to memory, like the dried flower in the frame or glitter at the bottom of the bag. What becomes most clear as we try to reconstruct the performance is the palpable distance between ourselves and the event. We know, too, the tendency of distances, both geographical and temporal, to transform a powerful act of political performance—diluted through repetition, mediated for mass consumption—into just another evening out at the theatre, enjoyed with a glass of bad Chardonnay during the interval and described anecdotally sometime later with the details slightly mixed up and the purpose misconstrued.

88. *ROCK PERFORMANCE—NICK SALVATO*

A golden canyon in the desert: the walls of the narrows are this theatre's doors, giving way onto a wide wash—a playing space—in which a low rock formation provides the audience with its bench. They have arrived for a strange, moonlike production of The Cherry Orchard. *Say it isn't raining (it never rains here). Say the actors are late for their first cues. Say one of the audience muses aloud to a colleague, waiting.*

PERFORMANCE THEORIST
What must a now-facetious, now-earnest lament for an orchard's loss mean *here*, a place empty (barren, desolate, remote) and full (colorful, sun-kissed, granularly textured)?

Say the actors are not late. Say they have not arrived. Say they never will.

Say it was never Chekhov: gradually, the audience realizes that the rocks are this canyon's performers: slow … and, so it seems once the audience is conscious of the performance, yet slower … and slower, still. Still. It is the slowest performance to which this audience has ever borne witness. It is the last performance to which they will ever bear witness. Determined to watch, to sense, until its end, they are outlived by the performance, by the imperceptibly moving rocks.
The dead audience debates the meaning of the performance with the other ghosts in the canyon. For whom or what or how is rock performance?

SHOSHONE WOMAN
The universe.

MORMON TREKKER
God.

PROSPECTOR
The devil.

BORAX COMPANY SHAREHOLDER
Capital.

TOURIST I
Me.

TOURIST II
My camera.

PERFORMANCE THEORIST
Not me … And not not me.

PERFORMANCE THEORIST II
It. Just it.

The rocks do not hear them. And they do not not hear them. Still, there is rock performance. Still.

Say the first Performance Theorist in our cast of characters has a friend. Say she is a theorist of vibrant matter. Say she asks, "Does life only make sense as one side of a life-matter binary, or is there such a thing as a mineral or metallic life, or a life of the it in *it rains*?"

The theorist of vibrant matter never unpacks this rich and suggestive question. She's packing for a trip to Death Valley.

If we did unpack the question, we might take a different trip—as theorists are wont to do—in French. That language gives us two different constructions potentially equivalent to *it rains*: *il pleut* (closer to the English *it rains* or *it's raining*) and *il y a de la pluie* (more like, *there is rain*).

There is a potential shift when we move from the former construction to the latter. Maybe we are no longer so prominently invited to wonder after "a life of the *it*." In moving from French to English, let's put aside the proposed translation of the second construction, *there is rain*. Let's use instead one or another awkward—*generatively* awkward—transliterative approximation: *It has there rain*. Or *it has there raining*. Or worst, by which I mean best, of all, *it has there a performance of rain*.

In this case, the *it* that we have to consider is not one to which we are likely to attribute life in the usual senses. *It has there a performance of rain*—or, to stick us even more firmly in what some may take to be a dead zone, *it has there a performance of rock*. What, exactly, are the elements that constitute the performance in question?

There is a *there*, or location; there is a thing (*it*). The thing, precisely situated in its scenic environment, is endowed with a quality (*performance*), arguably predicated on the thing's placement in the scenic environment. And that quality of performance, that *having* (rather than being?), redoubles the thing-ness (rather than life?) of the thing. It, the rock, is—*of rock*. We may point to this *it*, and its *of rock*-ness may be attributed descriptively, by a sensate observer. Yet the observer's presence is not strictly required for the thing's "having of performance" to unfold, processually, in time's duration.

The extent to which this commentary strains semantics and syntax is an index. It points to our linguistic resources' relative impoverishment in helping us to grasp how a scene (whether of rocks, or otherwise) may be possessed of, may have, performance. All the same, we may grasp how performance is directly related to, indeed resultant from, the presence of the thing in the scene. And so grasping, we may grapple, epistemologically, with the presence of the thing and the quality of performance in the scene without *necessarily* granting, ontologically, any specially marked vibrancy, vitality, liveliness, or agential action to the thing.

In rock performance, there is motility. There is theatre. Whether there is agency or action is a question for the ages and their ghosts.

89. *SHE—NIA O. WITHERSPOON*

The text below is both narration and stage direction.

She's sooooooo sooooooo soooooo sad. Searching and searching and searching in the wide black abyss for her soul. Flying in the wind, all face and shoulders, gap-teeth bared like a wildcat, starry-eyed nightingale, her body heavy, so heavy. But she flies on. How could she not? She has nothing left. No soul. It is not the kind of darkness that hides it all, no. She can see shadows and shadows of shadows, and creatures made of shadows. And the slopes. The slopes are wide and long, with deep valleys and far away cities with no glimmering lights, just shades of gray, topaz, sepia, twilight, and sunset. An owl screeches and She's body is thrust backwards into the night, as if being pushed by a tornado, but there is no whirling, no. This is a line, a straight line like history. A line of smoke and heat and particles. Back and back and back and back. How far back can she go before the end, she wonders. Where is the wall, the mountain, the window, the glass, the metal? Is there nothing solid in this world of shadows? Back and back and back and back she continues to fly, her limbs splayed out like a car accident, hair smacking her in the face. The owl screeches again and She's body begins to drop. Down. Down down down down. Below the valleys and slopes, below the children, below the crystals in the soil that catch no light, below the caves of moaning, and the bony fingers reaching, below the below. Down she goes. Hair flies up and out, arms above her head, belly loops, legs splayed and splayed so wide from the force of the downward thrust that she begins to tear. Yes, tear. Just at the seams where her legs meet in the middle. Where the sex lives. Where the heads of babies, wide and soft, push out, mouths gasping for air and breast. This is where she tears. At first it is small, just where inner thigh meets groin on the left-hand side. The blood trickles out and quickly dries from the force of the wind as she continues to fall. But down she goes, and fast too. She goes so fast that she continues to tear in her most tender places, this time ripping into muscle and sinew. There is more blood now, blowing away in flecks and coagulated clots that do not color the black abyss. Could she see, the clots would look like fetuses catapulted into space. She falls and falls. She tears and tears. She falls and tears until her groin splits open in a starburst made of blood and muscle. Organs fly. Her legs, barely hanging onto her body circle around her head and her feet fuse together.

Soon she will be a face and a hole. Soon is now.

While *SHE* is not marked explicitly by race, I cannot help but hear the piece through this frequency given my knowledge of the writer's work. And also because the character of this *testimonio's* veracity—equal parts nightmare, lamentation, and vision—pungently narrates familiar states and affective textures of my own and many women's coloredness.

As exegesis, I offer insight from Chicana playwright Cherríe Moraga and her essay "An Irrevocable Promise: Staging the Story Xicana":

> *The ceremony always begins for me in the same ... always with the hungry woman. Always the place of disquiet (*inquietud*) moves the writing to become a kind of excavation, an earth-dig of the spirit found through the body. The impulse to write may begin in the dream, the déjà vu, a few words, which once uttered through my own mouth or the mouth of another, refuse to leave the body of the heart ... It is an irrevocable promise to not forget what the body holds as memory.*
>
> *Writing for the stage is the reenactment of this ceremony of remembering ... [F]or theater requires the body to make testimony and requires other bodies to bear witness to it. The question remains: bear witness to what?*

And the guidance of African American playwright Ntozake Shange's "takin a solo/ a poetic possibility/ a poetic imperative":

> *when i take my voice into a poem or a story/ i am trying desperately to give you that/ i am not trying to give you a history of my family/ the struggle of black people all over the world or the fight goin on upstairs tween susie & matt/ i am giving you a moment/ like something that isn't coming back/ a something particularly itself/ ...*
>
> *as we demand to be heard/ we want you to hear us, we come to you the way leroi jenkins comes or cecil taylor/ or b.b. king, we come to you alone/ in the theater/ in the story/ & the poem/ like with billie holiday or betty carter/ we shd give you a moment that cannot be recreated, a specificity that cannot be confused/ our language shd let you know who's talkin, what we're talkin abt & how we cant stop saying this to you. some urgency accompany the text. something important is goin on. we are speakin. reachin for yr person/ we cannot hold it/ we don't wanna sell it/ we give you ourselves/ if you listen/ ... if you listen/ ... you cd imagine us like music & make us yrs.*

Finally, Audre Lorde's wisdom in "The Transformation of Silence into Language and Action":

> *And of course I am afraid, because the transformation of silence into language and action is an act of self-revelation, and that always seems fraught with danger. But my daughter, when I told her of our topic and my difficulty with it, said, "Tell them about how you're never really a whole person if you remain silent, because there's always that one little piece inside you that wants to be spoken out ... and if you don't speak it out one day it will just up and punch you in the mouth from the inside."*
>
> *In the cause of silence, each of us draws the face of her own fear—fear of contempt, of censure, or some judgment, or recognition, of challenge, of annihilation. But most of all, I think, we fear the visibility without which we cannot truly live ... And that visibility which makes us most vulnerable is that which also is the source of our greatest strength.*

90. *SPIKED—CLAIRE MACDONALD*

Wlad is pacing the studio, eyes glazed, a large table full of jumbled objects in front of him. On it, among the bits of metal and naked flames, are what looks like a chicken carcass, a pile of ash, and some playing cards, and a spike of the sort you used to put receipts on, and a pitcher of water that turns out to be neat vodka. He shifts and sniffs like a dog, rubbing his hands together and spitting on them. It's very hot, and there is a strong smell of sweat. He barely sees us when we come in, shuffling through the dark space to find somewhere to sit on one of the hard wooden benches that mark the edge of a square of light. He is naked to the waist, wearing a pair of thick workman's trousers with a huge leather belt, and great big boots, unlaced. His head is newly shaved. For some reason it is already oddly compelling. It's like entering a cave, or a room in a dream. It seems both uncannily familiar and unsettlingly strange. We wait. I am wondering what it is about Wlad that makes you want to touch him, I mean, to *watch* him, that thing that makes whatever he does a performance, whether it's standing by the wall and smoking, which he seems to do for ages, or just walking across to the table—when he moves into action. He walks over, takes a large swig of vodka and then, very carefully, brings his hand over the spike and rams it down so the metal point pierces his skin and then goes right through his hand. There's a spurt of blood like a red flower, so bright, so vivid, so shocking the effect is staggering. I feel as if someone hit me in the chest, or as if lightning has struck me. I am dumb. Suddenly, in that moment, everything in my life shifts. Time slows down to a stop, and it is so perfectly intimate, and so violent, it is as if he has opened something inside me, something he shouldn't touch. He looks up, he is white and I think he is going to faint, but it is someone else who faints, a girl in the front row who is so close to him she spontaneously vomits. He is whey-faced but still standing. It is clear he has done this before. "Anyone for a drink?" he says at last, wrapping his hand in a bloody tea towel.

The figure of Wlad hovers rather enigmatically between two seemingly polar extremes. On the one hand, he could be described as a performance artist: picture Wlad as a kind of Eastern European "neo-actionist," whose works, now mythical and unrepeatable, only exist as descriptions of extreme acts from another time. On the other hand, we could view Wlad as a magician, a conman, a professional daredevil, or a fairground freak-show act, of the kind reverently described by Ricky Jay in his book *Learned Pigs & Fireproof Women*.

If performance art is typically associated with real actions, real bodies, and real time, magic trades in the pure fakery of theatre, spectacle, and illusion. According to this neat distinction, Wlad the artist would be genuinely piercing his hand, whereas Wlad the trickster would be merely simulating.

What is striking about the feat and its description is precisely its undoing of simple binary opposites: as Wlad slams his hand over the spike, I am reminded of the extent to which performance art might be about doing things "for effect" (no differently from waving jazz-hands), and vice versa of the manifold ways in which magicians have famously died or injured themselves during their illusions, thereby giving the lie to the supposed fakery of their acts. What is always ignored or suppressed, by magicians and audiences alike, is the material reality of the magic act, the actual labor of illusion, let's say: the hands and the countless years of training, for instance, or the disciplined body, with its wounds and scars. Perhaps a distinction between performance art and magic can be made around the visibility and propriety of the wound: in the former it tends to be exposed, in the latter it is largely hidden. For instance, in performance artist Chris Burden's 1971 *Shoot*, his assistant stood at a distance and shot the artist in the arm, inaugurating performance art as a wound-making activity. Conversely, one night in 1918, vaudeville magician Chung Ling Soo (real name Bill Robinson) performed a version of his famous *Bullet Catch*, in which an assistant stood at a distance and fired directly at the illusionist: on this occasion the gun literally misfired, and instead of "catching" the bullet in his hand, Chung Ling Soo was shot in the chest. He collapsed to the ground and for the first time ever broke his Chinese stage character, announcing in plain English: "Something's happened. Lower the curtain." He died the following morning.

Wlad's hand-piercing feat is ghosted by similar acts and their in/visible wounds. There is the strange case of Dutch performer and fakir Mirin Dajo (1912–1948), who subjected his body to what might be called an extreme form of body piercing: an assistant would skewer his torso with a thin sword, visibly passing from side to side, a feat that was likely made possible by a dangerous and laborious process of creating scar-tissue passageways. US magician David Blaine, who rather fittingly (if frustratingly) often describes himself as a "performance artist," opened his 2013 TV special *Real or Magic* by taking a thin ice pick and visibly driving it through his hand, much to the horror and disbelief of A-list celebrities watching the event. We see the skin on his hand clearly pierced, from side to side, as Blaine explains, in his trademark calm voice, as though reflecting on magician-audience relations: "This is ultimately what they want to see ... It looks real, doesn't it?" When the ice pick is extracted, he holds his hand up, turning it slowly from side to side, saying simply: "Nothing ... nothing." Not a single spot of blood. As ever with magicians, the wound is neatly hidden, precisely at the moment of it being clearly on display.

91. *STRESS MELODY—CHRISTOPHER GROBE*

Part I

A single, hard-edged light fades in, irising out from a pinpoint to a pool of light. It shines down on a figure seated in a simple chair, head shaved, teeth bright through the parted lips of an enormous grin. This is an actor—simply an actor—and a paragon of calm well-being.

Wires and tubes surround the actor—arms, head, and chest—and as the pool of light slowly spreads, our eyes can follow the tangle right back to a hulking machine. After a moment (*click, whirr*) the lights on the machine start blinking, and we begin to hear through every speaker in the house a pulsating drone—three notes spaced across three octaves.

With a wink at the audience, the actor begins to breathe deeply. Slowly at first, unflappable, but then faster and with a look of panic. (Can we even manage some tears?) When the actor's breathing first changes, so does one note in the drone; then, with the rising intensity, the other notes change. Together, they meander into harmony or tumble into dissonance as the chord grows deeper, stranger—haunted up high by harmonics, disturbed down low by undertones.

After several minutes of this, all of a sudden, the actor goes blank—then resumes the starting pose and expression: remember those teeth, that grin. Gradually the harmonics die out, the music slims back down, and the chord reverts to its octaval drone. Once it has, a five count, then the stage lights and the machine snap off together.

Part II

Thirty seconds pass. Then, in the dark, a machine whirrs up, lights blink, and the familiar drone fades in. Soon, the drone begins to morph into music—its three notes moving irregularly, with unusual rhythm and cadence. If Part I was an étude, then this is a concerto. Just listen to the harmonics. They curl around the melody like smoke.

A hard-edged light snaps on, shining down on a chair, on a machine—on a loose nest of tubes and wires. The melody continues.

Inchoate is one of those mysterious words, like *cleave* or *quite* or *nice*. Depending on the context in which it appears (the sentence, the city, the subculture, the century) it might mean one thing—or its opposite. It can describe utter chaos—or else the beginnings of order; the sound of choking—or of a voice breaking through. This play—every play?—stages an inchoate relation among human and non-human actors.

In Part I of *Stress Melody*, we see an actor play a polygraph as if it were a theremin, or—who can tell?—we see a machine play this resonant body before our eyes. In Part II, though, in the dark, something else is happening. Who is playing the song of the psyche now? It is the audience, I hope—it was the audience all along—"playing" the actor's body into psychic depth, "playing" the melody of a machine into meaning.

The interiority of actors has always been produced this way: as a collaboration among performers, audiences, and things, by a collusion of techniques and technologies. The telegraph and the telephone, the radio and the robot, the polygraph and the Rorschach blot—these technologies and others all queer the boundaries of the self. They don't just allow the self to seep out in new ways; they also worm their way into the self, slowly altering the mechanics of expression, gradually changing the tectonics of the human interior.

Philosopher and physicist Karen Barad has coined a term to describe this sort of entangled, performative process: *intra-action*. Rejecting the familiar term *interaction*, which implies that several discrete entities exist before they interact, Barad uses *intra-action* to describe how things are mattered in and through their emergent relations. *Intra-acting*, they precipitate like salts from solution. What if we thought of the difference between human and non-human, actor and thing as the result of *intra-action*? Every boundary marked clearly on a map is the result of many forces—human and supra-human. So, too, the boundaries among mattering things, but technological performance can take us to the borderlands.

Champions and critics of the technological stage seem to agree on the nature and laws of this borderland. Here, technology must disrupt the humanist norms of the stage; it must constrain the natural responses of actor and audience. But why exactly must this be so? Haven't we cracked enough mirrors in the name of disruption? Now it's time to enact new techno-human possibilities.

In this play (and in my recent research) I'm on the lookout for new forms of organic technicity—for moments when bodies become technical and technics take form before our eyes. Often this occurs when simple machines (the telegraph, the telephone) are first brought to the theatrical stage, but it happens more palpably, I think, and more powerfully when novel machines are designed with stage performance in mind. These machines must know how to play, and, if they do, actors will clamor for their services as scene partners. In order for this to happen, though, we can no longer settle for setting our machines (or ourselves) up for a pratfall. (Hey, look: a disruption, a failure, a constraint!) In other words, let's have no more rude mechanicals. We need exquisite machines. Now who will build them?

92. *SURVEILLANCE—JONATHAN BALL*

Cameras play over the audience, hidden and mounted to cover all possible angles. Microphones embedded in all seats. Onstage, a panoply of screens and speakers are aimed at the audience.

In real time, the data gathered by each camera and microphone is presented to the audience. They watch themselves from all possible angles, listen to themselves in all possible ways. A cacophony of light and noise, which cannot be absorbed or understood except in bursts.

Only a machine could understand all this. Only machines. The audience remains in the theatre, therefore, until they gain the ability to parse, collate, and comprehend the full scope of this endless data, until at last they come to see themselves perfectly, with precision.

Jonathan Ball's *Surveillance* supposes a theatre taken over by the mechanical. Video cameras record and track each individual audience member until (through the data collected) each glimpses his or her true self: the carefully measured dimensions of a self reaching a computed completeness. The theatre becomes a space for the self to see the self (the surveilled self), waking a desire for reproduction of the self. A machine that comprehends something of the singularity or "precision" of the subject produces both terror and fascination. Surveillance occurs when an outside peers into a private inside. However, can a machine see the inside of a subject? How is this mechanical eye different than the human eye? The human eye sees the fleshy whole whereas the machine manufactures data, putting numbers in place of corporeal presentness. And yet, this data is not only numerical: like in Ball's use of video within the theatre, recording has always exposed the theatrical heart of surveillance.

Consider, for instance, Charlie Chaplin's film *Modern Times* (1936), where the Tramp's boss watches his workforce through a television-like surveillance device. The technology allows him to both oversee and to communicate with the workers who are being asked to perform like machines. The boss sees all through the apparatus. In David Lynch's *Lost Highway* (1997), the Mystery Man leaves a couple strange videotapes of their recorded daily life. The couple then relives their own lives as if they were happening for the first time. The always-present boss and the Mystery Man demonstrate two ways of approaching surveillance. In both, the subject is on a stage performing for the gaze of another, since the camera erects a stage everywhere it points. *Modern Times* presents a world where the eyes upon the Tramp are the same eyes on which he depends for nourishment and shelter. Reading the boss's desire is easy—he wants the Tramp to work and will watch to make sure his labor is unceasing. More ominously, *Lost Highway* posits a supernatural omnipresence—seemingly deranged in its unknown purpose. The "mystery" of the Mystery Man is his secret intention or, more simply, the characters do not know what he wants. The terror of not knowing what the machine wants is what gives power to Ball's theatre of surveillance. Surveillance produces the subject: her relation to the world of the Other makes certain she does not bolt for freedom. She stays frozen, transformed into precise data, until that future moment when she learns how to read that writing, to parse its secret intentions and make them her own.

93. *TALES—NATALIE ALVAREZ*

He's perfect, she whispers. *He is*, he replies. A couple two rows in front turns to them and smiles in agreement.

CRIS stands on the bare stage under a warm spotlight. There would be time to take pictures with him after but for now they just want to take him in. He was theirs and they hadn't seen him in a full year. *He's growing so fast*, she whispers. *He is*, he replies.

This is the third year of TALES and he is exactly three years old today. They had been coming every year since his creation. The audience was now, by default of this performance experiment, extended family; although, they didn't yet know each other by name, only by the key roles they played in the lab exercises. *He's the one who caught the typos in the allele mutations to ensure light brown hair, isn't he? No, that was her. Was it you who animated the inexpressive gene in the 15q region? Yes, that was me. I thought so.*

CRIS grows restless in the spotlight.

Initially the audience thought it would be cute to name the boy after the new frontier of research that created him: Clustered Regularly Interspaced Short Palindromic Repeats (CRISPRs). At the time, it captured their romantic investments in this participatory form of genetic *écriture*, a new form of collective creation the scientists cheekily called TALES (transcription activator-life effectors) that allowed them to write him into being. But now there was a general sense that they had failed on the name. CRIS reduced him to the acronym that made him and they didn't want to make him reducible to that. He had become so much more than the inscrutable sequence of dashes and dots that defined him at the beginning—palindromes they soon learned to read and rewrite so intimately. One participant got segments of it tattooed in commemoration, a twisting vine of code curling around his forearm. Another woman tattooed an excerpt from her heel up along her calf and torso, tracing her spine to the back of her neck. Beneath her skirt it looked like the decorative backseam of her stockings. Proud parents.

CRIS squints as he tries to get a glimpse of his extended family sitting in the dark beyond the stage lights. He's old enough now to recognize that this is a theatre space, which comes with a certain set of expectations, and that he is the object of interest. His attention drifts to a dance of dust particles taking flight from the stage floor up towards the blinding well of light. He tries to catch them, inadvertently beginning a dance of his own. The artless élan of his movement elicits ecstatic sighs and applause from the house. The response startles him and he stops.

From the wings, the ushers emerge with the cake, carefully shielding the three, lit candles so they won't extinguish by the time they reach CRIS at center stage. The audience joins in a loud chorus of Happy Birthday. *Make a wish!* someone cries. With wide-eyed excitement at the sight of chocolate cake (his favorite), CRIS blows out the candles.

Recent developments in genome-editing technology—namely, applications of the CRISPR-Cas9 system—have invigorated concerns among scientists and the public about the ethics of genetic modification. Even as scientists caution that the tool is still too imprecise and unpredictable to use on human embryos or reproductive cells, the efficiency and elegance of CRISPR-Cas9 has made it possible to envision an imminent future in which "designer babies" are not just the stuff of science fiction, but a serious option for aspiring parents. Far superior to previous tools, including TALES (transcription activator-like effectors), this technology joins CRISPR sequences ("palindromic" sections of DNA linked to early immune responses) and CRISPR-associated proteins (the Cas-9 enzyme) that together enable scientists to cut and paste genes with unprecedented ease. Researchers have already begun using this system to make agricultural interventions and to study a variety of diseases. In 2015 and 2016, China and the United Kingdom approved limited experimentation on human embryonic cell lines. While a significant gap remains between what this technology can do now and what it would need to do to make "designer babies" feasible, it has nevertheless lent new urgency to imagining this future—whether as a transhumanist dream or a dystopian nightmare.

Theatre, in *TALES*, offers a medium for managing the anxieties stirred by genetic engineering while allowing audiences to test and witness its possibilities. Scientific and artistic experimentation seem to join here in productive harmony. Acronyms like CRISPR and TALEs suggest a delight in word play shared by lovers of both biology and language, as well as a common desire to write life—whether through genetic codes or stories. Bridging play and research, creation and reception, the audience enjoys the privileges of spectatorship only after helping to produce (literally) the show's star. Thus claimed by the entire audience, CRIS promises not the transmission of "superior" genes across a single familial line, but the formation of new kinship structures indelibly linked to a shared theatrical experience—one marked by awe, warmth, and delight as CRISPR becomes CRIS, a whimsical dancer and lover of chocolate. Equally crucial to this experience, however, is the strict stage/seat divide that keeps CRIS alienated and contained. This is not the future of the human race, the performance insists, but a singular marriage of science and theatre. Life outside this space of wonder will remain unchanged.

And yet, can this theatre hold off CRISPR's other possibilities? If whispers of "he's perfect" echo the standard greeting for newborns, they do so in an uncanny way. Is the audience marveling at ten fingers and toes, or is this the kind of perfection only achieved through careful genetic manipulation? The preference for light brown hair and the neatly matched couples—one woman, one man—seem innocuous as long as we do not dwell too long on questions of who has access to this laboratory-theatre, or what constitutes a proper parental unit and an ideal human being in this world. It is the familiar in the strange, the old in the new, that unsettle us when confronted with dystopian visions: we fear our present locking us into a future that is, simply, its worst possibility. While this imagined theatre refrains from conjuring the usual nightmare scenario of a "designer baby" society in which inequities are biologically perpetuated and mandated, it nevertheless nudges us to ask what happens after the cake is eaten and the audience goes home. Who is CRIS outside the stage, and what is *his* desire for the future? We seem to stand at the cusp of a turn, at that moment when theatre becomes too much, and not enough.

94. *TECTUM THEATRE—SUK-YOUNG KIM*

I

There is no particular signal to mark the beginning or ending of the performance. No parting of a curtain, no blackouts, no pre-show announcements. A clear separation between the stage and the auditorium is not to be found either. Just a vacuous shade of immense hollowness in deep blue overwhelms the audience as they step into the black box.

Welcome to the vertical theatre. Like prostrating pilgrims reversed, looking up the soaring cupola of a holy shrine, the audiences—with their bellies up—proffer their gaze upward. Some breathe deeply, others close their eyes to the sound of their neighbors' breath. Somewhere under the roof hangs an ominous uncertainty. Here, *tectum* is not just an invisible space haunted by catwalks or pipe grids; it is a vacuum fatally suspended between breath and death.

As the audience converges into stillness, a ghostly wreckage of what used to be a passenger ferry floats in. Devoid of volume and free from gravity, the wreckage sways from side to side like an oversized jellyfish. Or like a post-apocalyptic Laputa with hundreds of phantom limbs reaching out of it. Its ethereal shadow is the only thing that disturbs the monotony of the deep blue. Searchlights from the surface of the ocean illuminate this ghostly vessel but the sharp beams fall short of reaching the bodies of those spectators-cum-ferry passengers who have gone missing and now find themselves lying on the seabed.

II

A woman holding an infant by a shore.

She gazes at the tempestuous horizon where the boundary between illusion and reality disappear. It is where darkness and light wear the same shade.

Her one hand caresses the head of the child and the other holds its bluish feet, barely visible. Entangled by a dark cord wrapping their bellies together, the woman and the child are still. It is hard to discern any traces of life in the child. To what extent is a stillborn child still *being* born?

III

Tiny whispers swell up: *I want to see my mother. / Don't worry, we will be OK. / But I don't want to die! / Hush!*

The audience on the seabed recognizes their own voices in these whispers as their bodies sink deeper and deeper into the bottomless seabed. The captain has escaped the ferry already, but his order comes back periodically: "Stay where you are, stay in your cabin."

The whispers dissipate into ripples, and then into silence—and then into nothingness.

Television reports show the still bodies of high school students freshly fished out of the stormy ocean: "these bodies are so clean. They must have breathed their last breath no more than a few hours ago." Indeed the uncontaminated corpses appear fresher than living bodies—completely intact and too young to have reached the pinnacle of their lives. The only visibly injured body parts are broken fingers and ripped off nails—all damaged as they attempted to break out of the submerged cabin. But why did they not jump ship, instead deciding to stay on board when the ferry started to capsize and the seawater started to rise, submerging their feet, legs, and eventually their torsos and heads? What can your eyes see when the ocean fills up your lungs? What can you hear when your cries for help are muffled under the torrent of rising water and clanking steel? What is the last flickering thought that flashes through your mind before you enter your own extinction?

B.L. Strehler made it clear that he was interested in neuroanatomical theory of consciousness when he posed the ultimate question: "Where is the self?" The query furtively leads us to tectum, the particular space between the upper and the lower part of the brain. This is where the visual and auditory senses, together with information stemming from memory and a variety of other relevant sources, generate a coherent sense of selfness. Just like the suspended wreckage of the sunken ferry, a sense of self is suspended halfway between the last sound of breath and the first image of death.

Peggy Phelan once presented the inevitable fatalism universally faced by mankind: "Severed from the placenta and cast from the womb, we enter the world as an amputated body whose being will be determined by the very mortality of that body." In tectum theatre, thousands of stillborn children are created before a womb can procreate a living child. Tectum theatre is a place where amniotic fluid and cerebral fluid merge with the ocean. It is a place where spatio-optic confusion fatally takes place.

B.L. Strehler further elucidates that, for the sense of selfness to emerge, the spatio-optic memories of the past have to align with the present environment. But what happens when the inevitable misalignment takes place, leading the subject to hover over self-creation and self-extinction? Like the wreckage of a ferry now turned belly up, the self is turned upside down; the consciousness inside out. The cabin is swelling up with chilly ocean like a death chamber, but the memories of those who are trapped inside hark back to the very beginning—to their mother's womb—surrounded in the water that both stifles and nurtures.

95. *TH'EATER—JOSHUA ABRAMS*

A man sits center stage.

He might be Louis the Sun King, but then again he might not be Louis at all. Perhaps, like all figures on the stage, he is merely a shade, an echo of humanity.

In front of him there is a table, piled high—reminiscent perhaps of Arcimboldo, or the Dutch baroque masters—creaking with sumptuous foods of all descriptions. The amount and breadth of food renders the attempt to describe it seem a breathless impossibility, except perhaps in its variation and quantity.

It is all incredibly material and simultaneously incredibly decorous, far too much muchness. A Brueghelian excess, Rabelais would be jealous. The table contains all the colors of the world, each in its natural expression, with little or no seeming order, the only structure that of overabundance. Elaborate pastry *pièces montées* à la Carême; innumerable prepared carcasses of birds, some redressed as in medieval traditions, others simply lacquered in a glossy mound, tumbling over each other; rack upon rack of larger butchered and prepared mammals, blood reds, bone whites, blackened cuts through bone ends and the meat itself, outsides charred and gloriously maillardised; mountains of fresh seafood, shellfish and whole prepared fish looking beautifully as in life but still; cornucopias of lusciously colored ripe fruit spilling across the table and onto the floor; intense reds, yellows, oranges, purples, greens of myriad vegetables, some cooked, others still raw, in their varying hues and shades overflowing bowls and plates; pastas and noodles heaped upon each other, cascading onto the table; platters of global styles of filled dumplings varied immeasurably in color, size, shape, and origin; cheeses too of all textures, shapes, and sizes; stew bowls that without smelling it is impossible to distinguish—perhaps Mexican mole, or Indian curry, or Ethiopian W'et, or Boeuf Bourguignon, or Hungarian goulash, or Persian Ghormeh sabzi, or perhaps something else entirely; tiered trays filled with row upon row of tarts, cakes, pies, glossed and succulent; condiments reimagined as dishes, pickles and sauces from all cultures; breads stacked precariously tall, pyramids of loaves, round, oval, oblong, flat, braided, indeed there is nothing in the earth's larder that does not appear to be on the table ...

The smells sweep into the audience, some seated across a proscenium, others standing on catwalks high above the stage—all unable to get close enough to touch or taste. At first, it seems that these can't be natural aromas, perhaps, they wash over the audience in waves, each recognizable in its individuality and then replaced, each fresh and unique and mouth-watering, or perhaps repellent, the scents of life and death, overwhelming sense.

The performance is durational. It begins with a single bite. If an empty space appears on the table, a stage-hand-cum-waiter walks across to this newly bared stage, whilst the audience watches, bringing something to replace it, always something new and yet always fundamentally something the audience has not realized was not yet there.

It continues forever, the actor unsated and insatiable. Or does he explode?

The House of Agathon, immediately following Agathon's win in the City Dionysia.

Phagos: Here we are in the House of Agathon, where we gather this evening to mark his win in the Great Dionysia. And so I ask, what is it about food and the theatre?

Sophist: Indeed, that relationship raises so many questions. To begin with, of course, both are ways of ingesting, of taking something in; each is an encounter with an otherness that fundamentally shatters my holistic sense of self, rendering me a fundamentally incomplete subject. Beyond that, undeniably, one must raise the question of taste. How, we might begin to wonder, are our tastes formed? It is in that encounter, in a notion of recognition (*anagnorisis*), when the coming face-to-face with alterity demands of us a response, an acknowledgment, perhaps even a choice or a prioritization. "'EATING and drinking on the stage,' remarked the chronic theatregoer the other night, 'always bores me when I have dined well and tantalizes me when I haven't,' at least according to *The Times*."

Phagos: And of course, the question of reality, a material paradox of sorts. Consumption onstage is simultaneously real and false, demanding objects that not only physically represent that which they are, but bear some material semblance as well, and yet, the actor often cannot physically eat that which is purported, certainly not during every performance.

Sophist: The infelicitousness of the stage, that is to say its precondition of falsity, is forever brought into question by the corporeality of that which we physically take into our bodies. Even food that dissembles onstage must be ingested.

Phagos: There's something somehow strange, even off-putting, at times, about watching someone eat without yourself eating.

Sophist: True, commensality is about breaking bread together, about the sharing and generosity that bring us down to our lowest common denominator. All persons eat. I am a person. Therefore I must eat. But the temporary community of the theatre is a different instantiation from that of the table; this difference perhaps entirely about ingestion and digestion. Eating together, and not eating together, marks us as if from different worlds. The shadows onstage eat and, like Persephone, this forever consigns them to that world, separated eternally from our, living, world. We cannot eat with them, we cannot be truly together in this moment, just as in the theatre, we are forever divided, by what Walter Benjamin will call the "abyss which separates the actors from the audience like the dead from the living."

Phagos: The actor carries on despite his death, he continues to remain present in front of us, confronting our reality.

Sophist: The actor of this theatre is a zombie, his eating is grotesque, a hunger forever unable to be sated. Like those royal survivors of *The Tempest*, for whose benefit Prospero conjures that imagined and illusory banquet, food is forever unsatisfactory, ethereal, fulfilment and pleasure unobtainable. The actor is each of us, his own contentment forever forestalled and never granted.

96. *THEATRE OF THE BLIND (OR: DESCRIPTION)—PATRICK ANDERSON*

A proscenium stage, with a skein hung completely across its downstage edge. When lit from behind, the skein is transparent; when lit from the front, it is opaque. A large rope, anchored in the flies at both ends, stretches across center stage. There is also a simple arrangement of stage furniture—a table, several chairs, several blocks—set between the rope and the skein. Upstage there is a scaffold with three platforms at various heights: one upstage left, one upstage center, one upstage right. These platforms are continuously populated by one performer each throughout the show, but the specific performers populating them change throughout.

While on the platforms, performers describe the action happening on the stage. The following rules govern their descriptions:

UL platform: Objective, realist description. This performer describes the action as it occurs, with precise detail. Indicated in the sample scene below as "UL."
UC platform: Affective response description. This performer describes the emotional effects of the action, or how the action makes them "feel." Indicated in the sample scene below as "UC."
UR platform: Impressionist description. This performer describes the imagined interior lives of the performers involved in the action. Indicated in the sample scene below as "UR."

The actions themselves are to be developed in rehearsal by the performers. Each action should be considered as a "scene," with a beginning and end (however loosely conceived). Actions may be as simple as (in the example below) performers re-arranging the stage furniture, or more narratively complex. Actions may involve dialogue, but room should be left for the descriptions. Some actions (especially at the beginning of the performance) occur with the stage lit so that the skein is transparent; others occur with the skein opaque. The actions may, but need not necessarily, cohere into a single narrative through-line for the performance as a whole. The descriptions may be intertwined, or may overlap.

Sample description (from UL describer) for a scene in which three performers re-arrange the stage furniture, spoken as the action occurs:

Three people walk onto the stage. They are walking at different speeds towards the table and chairs. The first person has reached the table. She looks down at it and picks up a chair. She is moving the chair across the stage. The other two people have picked up the table together, and are moving slowly to follow her. Both of them trip and the table falls. The two scramble to right themselves, and set the table back on its legs. They lift it again and move more slowly. The woman has returned to retrieve the second chair and move it to join the first. All of the furniture is now in place, and the three leave the stage.

If only descriptions were facts, we might be able to capture the terms of experience in verbal expression. We can't, though, and we know that we can't; words become unreliable narrators that consistently reveal partialities. Tripling partialities create refracted sensations that might suggest a vision of sorts, an ability to triangulate toward an objectness of experience that feels coherent.

Philosopher Susanne Langer famously theorized that the sensation of a performance event precedes rational comprehension of that same event; how something *feels* helps us decide what it means. In Langer's account, what actually happened—however that could ever be determined—might matter least of all.

Will body cameras help us understand what happens in encounters between police and citizens? Surely not in an unequivocal way. We revel in the diversity of experience that provides contradictory, overlapping information. And if we follow Langer, how we *feel* about our encounter with information colors what we *do* with that information. Feelings are facts, the dancer Yvonne Rainer says, and these facts can override other accounts of what happened.

So what happened, then? Even as we witness the event together, we aren't in agreement; we have different ways to tell the story. Our narrations contradict and amplify the event. Is one perspective more important than another? Who gets to decide? If feelings come first, how do we know what to feel? When do we learn our emotional vocabularies? How do we learn to feel?

I learn from love. The opening of experience to unexpected vistas of relationship, unanticipated alliances of affect and action. In what I'm willing to *do* for someone, after I recognize a feeling that grows from somewhere unnameable inside and pushes waves of sensation through my skin. I encounter myself variously and unexpectedly through love, and the experiences propel me to action, daily. Small loves, temporary ones, simple gestures, grand, sweeping, love-of-my-life: they all find their way into my encounters. I am so lucky to experience their diversities.

A character in Toni Morrison's novel *Jazz* says, "I didn't fall in love, I rose in it." To rise up in the contradictions of multiple narrations—well, so should we all.

97. *THE THEATRE AT CALPURNIA—NADINE GEORGE-GRAVES*

There is a city, unfit for kings or presidents and uninteresting to explorers, where citizens concern themselves with no grand issues of life like the existence of deities, the prevention of global disaster, or the fellowship of humanity. Instead, these men, women, and children focus all of their energies on small injustices and micro-advances—things they actually have a chance at changing. Their personal fulfillment is based on getting one person, *maybe* two people, to change their minds on a given subject. They have no courts, judges, or jails. What they have is theatre. This doesn't mean that there are no important ramifications of these actions. These citizens whole-heartedly believe in the butterfly effect, that their little moments of social justice will ripple out. For example, one aggrieved mother appealed to the theatre. A full production was mounted on the issue, cast and crew hired, a script written, rehearsals, lights, sets, and a performance mounted:

Lights up on the lobby of a prominent dancing school. Mothers, nannies, and one father ready their 4-year-olds for ballet class. The dance teacher clears her throat.

TEACHER: I have an announcement from the central office at the Frederick ballet. Your little princesses have been with us now for several weeks and we are so delighted to have them. Rest assured that they will learn balance, poise, and grace. We want to remind you to please make sure your child is ready each class in pink leotards, tights, and slippers. Also, some of you are already in flagrant violation of our hair policy. To that end we have prepared emergency bun kits that you are required to purchase.

MOTHER: Before registering my daughter, I read your policy on the web quite carefully because as an African American parent I wanted to make sure she was not subject to what I believe to be archaic and insensitive policies around ballet that could damage her sense of cultural identity. (Though I also have problems with requiring black girls to wear pink tights, we agreed that it is part of a uniform though, of course, this also has a long history of controversy that I won't go into here.) This change in hair policy is going too far in my opinion. Your website says, "Any student with long hair must have it neatly secured in a bun or twist with a hair net." Zora does not have long hair. She has beautifully kinky black hair. It does not fly in her face when she dances. It does not pose a danger. Her hair has not been a concern in any other class that she has taken at other schools.

TEACHER: Well, this is ballet! Based on 500 years of tradition!

MOTHER: Well, there are many parts of the 500 years of ballet tradition that I'm sure you don't subscribe to (like the sexual availability of ballerinas in the 19th century). Why are you holding on to a hair policy so clearly rooted in racism? There is nothing about a bun that will improve Zora's plié or pointe.

Lights shift dramatically. Cue dream ballet in which 500 years of ballet tradition and 500 years of black oppression come to terms. (You imagine it.)

TEACHER: Ah, I fully understand! I see the latent racist assumptions of my policy and will alter it immediately. I see now that I'm really just attached to an antiquated notion of an idealized white body that has nothing to do with dance technique. Thank you for pointing that out. I'll also do some soul-searching about my own suppressed racism.

That, of course, is not how the scene played out in real life. It got quite ugly, in fact, and ended with the teacher changing the policy to make sure that there were no afros allowed. The mother took her child out of the school. There were no public outlets for the mother that, on balance, did not prove too exhausting. She had a friend who worked for the ACLU who said she would help her sue and rage against the machine but, really, who has that kind of energy?

The invitation to imagine a theatre allows us to fantasize about the ease with which performance could produce social justice. What would Boal, Brecht, Zollar, Valdez, and Teer do with their free time?

In the theatre at Calpurnia (a nod and wink to Calvino and the Finch maid—a nod and a wink to Parks[1]), the mother could get the teacher to understand and theatre-goers were not overwhelmed by the weight of changing racism with a capital "R" but could see progress, little-by-little.

Imagine a theatre in which a citizen, righteous and discontent about the lack of a stop-light at an intersection, will be heard through performance. At the end of the run, either all will be convinced that a stoplight needs to be installed or the citizen will see the error of his or her ways and drive about his business with peace of mind. Is this theatre like the court system? Sure. Or maybe the court system is like theatre. But this is imagined and justice will always be served in this theatre.

Counter to Bert O. States's great reckonings in little rooms, this is a city of small reckonings where no one says, "I should have said ..." or "If only I could get him to understand ..." No one replays scenes in their heads trying to imagine a different outcome. All can get the outcomes they want or, if defeated, be consoled that they gave it their all.

The dialogue doesn't need to be poetic. It is the fantasy about how easy it *should* be to "fix" racism. This imagined theatre is about people who get to have their diatribes heard and respected. "Imagined" because we know the way the real world works.

Here, within a page, we have a complete reversal (*peripeteia* of the state of affairs in the ancient Greek sense *and* personal and psychologically-based in the early 20th century sense) in which the teacher recognizes her racism (her fatal flaw), reverses the policy, and thanks the mother. Whenever I point out to people how racist they are they never say thank you.

Notes

1 The act of theatrical imagining allows us to bring into conversation the possibilities of Italo Calvino's *Invisible Cities*, a reimagining of the maid in *To Kill a Mockingbird* (who, like Atticus, wasn't what American fantasies thought she was), and Suzan-Lori Parks' keen conceptions of history in *The America Play*. (This footnote is a nod and a wink, too!)

98. *THEATRE GENERATED BY A PROBABILISTIC LANGUAGE MODEL, WITH GRAMMATICAL ARTIFACTS RETAINED— CADEN MANSON AND JEMMA NELSON*

The stage is empty and in darkness. In a flash the following unfurls.

A lightning strike melts away into an ocean storm. A burning plane amends into a knife and reconstructs into a shark convulsing for breath out of fog. Andy Warhol transforms into a footlong sandwich and restyles into a swelling cloud of mist that disperses into a set of chattering teeth then adjusts into a speeding train. A raging river revises into and a laughing child then reorganizes into a footlong sandwich that restyles into a gleaming obelisk. A table adapts into a diaphanous jellyfish that mutates into a towering mountain. A gleaming obelisk converts into a spotlight and transfigures into a suicide bomber that remodels into a laughing child that reorganizes into a gleaming skyscraper. A lightning strike melts away into a field of rocks that metamorphoses into a fading light that evolves into a knife and then into a corpse. A massive boulder transfigures into a revving sports car. A memorial service disintegrates into a screeching fighter jet that modifies into an enveloping cloud of seagulls. A pile of remains transmutes into a silent monolith. An enveloping cloud of fog metamorphoses into a shark convulsing for breath out of water. A suicide bomber remodels into a laughing child. A pile of rocks metamorphoses into a diaphanous jellyfish that mutates into a towering mountain and evaporates into a spotlight. A footlong sandwich restyles into a silent blue whale that reshapes into a smoking gun. A suicide bomber refines into obelisk that changes into a thunderous tornado. A wedding party dwindles into a towering tree that remodels into a pile of seagulls and reorders into an enveloping cloud of dirt. An ocean storm vanishes into a gleaming skyscraper. A swelling cloud of human remains transmutes into a stinking pile of dirt. A massive boulder transfigures into a speeding train. A surprise party dissipates into a raging river. An enveloping cloud of rocks metamorphoses into a swarm of bees and reorders into and a burning plane. A burning cross reorganizes into a gleaming skyscraper. A family sitting in fog metamorphoses into a swelling cloud of rainbow fish. A massive boulder transfigures into a public march that disappears into a suicide bomber. A fading light evolves into and a surprise party. A beeping heart pump reshapes into and a wedding party. An ocean storm vanishes into mist that disperses into a silent monolith. An enveloping cloud of fog. A gleaming skyscraper refines into a knife in a pile of debris. Andy Warhol grabbing is bleeding stomach. Andy Warhol revamps into a swelling cloud of fog. A suicide bomber transforms into a lightning strike. A flock of seagulls reorders into a towering cross. A diaphanous jellyfish refashions into a footlong sandwich. A fading light evolves into a towering mountain. A beeping heart pump evaporates into a burning plane. An ocean storm—darkness again.

The danger is in the neatness of identifications.

(Samuel Beckett, *Dante ... Bruno. Vico.. Joyce*)

A rule is a knife, reshaping and reordering a pile of rocks to a gleaming obelisk or a towering mountain, dissipating like any gleaming skyscraper to a field of rocks. A rule converts a rule: a convulsing shark transfigures to a laughing child, then like a suicide bomber vanishing, no remains. The stage is empty and in darkness, a spotlight mutates a swelling cloud into and a wedding party, or Andy Warhol into and a swarm of bees, sometimes dispersing a lightning strike a thunderous tornado a speeding train into and debris. As a diaphanous jellyfish on a field of rocks, or a swelling fog evaporates, reordering and restyling into and a lightning strike, but sometimes a corpse. But if lightning strikes, so does a knife; if a knife adapts, so does a shark; if a shark mutates, so does a screeching fighter jet; and if a screeching fighter jet dwindles, so does a surprise evolve and disperse, and even a corpse vanishes, beeping and chattering into the swelling cloud of fading light.

99. *THEATRE OF INTIMACY AND ABANDON—CASEY LLEWELLYN AND CLAUDIA RANKINE*

If I felt moved to stand and walk onto the stage, sit in an unavailable seat during the performance, could the performance accommodate me? Though the performance would have anticipated my arrival and made it clear I don't need to leave my seat and join the actors because the actors are already standing next to me, should the performance accommodate me? The weight of my hand on my thigh is not only mine. The actor sits next to me. She holds my hand. I would follow her onto the stage but we have met as humans so close in our fears that we are inside each other's thoughts already. We have been dreaming of each other and our future together. We have each kept the other up at night, night after night. But then I arrive at the theatre for the performance to discover we were never awake. Over there, as if we are meeting for the first time, as if there could be a first time, is the performance. The performer speaks the words I spoke the day before. I am flattered—pleased that she remembered all that was said though she looks away from me now into the face of another who answers her with words I spoke long ago. The recognition is so accurate I wonder what I will do next. I do nothing. Nothing, because I am not needed, except as a receiving body. Every word I recognize has changed, emptied of its original context and replaced with "story." It's not one I know. The actress moves a chair slightly. The strange movement undercuts everything. I am watching her and the tears form. I do not know her and her words are now unfamiliar but I find it unbearable what she says. Her responses defeat me. In every world the force of her story, its truth, is without remedy. I will fail her though in this moment I can't abandon her. We have never met and yet she is the only one I've ever known. She is the only one I seek to understand. I get up and walk over to her. I bring my lips to hers. Rather, why don't I? When you hold me before you release, in the midst of everything unfinished, I wish this feeling would happen. Surrounded, I feel alone in the theatre. Feeling completely always makes me feel incomplete. What does it matter what you recognize if you aren't touching? Tears make me know there is an outside and inside and I will always be trapped in here—here within an audience of strangers that I am part of. The audience—alternately weeping and disengaged, unwrapping candy, pulling themselves back from the brink of nodding off. Someone leans into the spoken artifice so deeply the person next to them must shrink away or turn from the stage to attend to the person falling apart. I am full of recognition with nowhere to go, except I'm an actor. I've rehearsed a lot. Together we imagine not being abandoned but abandoning. In life and in theatre, what if no action completed? Would we accept this unending, this lack of resolution without displeasure? In the moment, in theatre's false endings, we're in love with theatre that abandons. Left in our seats, we go where we want (which is probably not what theatre is or what a play does). Abandoned, we go in search of the next moment. Abandoning. Love.

Why when I reach for her
words
does my hand feel
faded?

Although Llewellyn and Rankine's co-authored text is written in prose, it affects me the way poetry does: as an urgent whisper in my ear, insisting I follow. The beginning of the piece slices open the difference between the two auxiliary verbs *could* and *should*. What is the difference between the questions "could the performance accommodate me?" and "should the performance accommodate me?" And does that difference, even if I *could* name it here—*should I choose to name it here? I know I could*—matter in a book devoted to impossible theatre?

When I was a child and I failed at something and expressed regret—"I wish I had run/shot/swum/answered faster"—my older brothers would taunt me: "woulda, coulda, shoulda, but didn't!" Hearing this, my parents would intervene in their Irish way: "Now let that be a lesson to you girl." And that was the end of it. They did not scold me nor ask why I had not succeeded; neither did they ask my brothers to stop their triumphant taunting. So the "woulda, coulda, shoulda" remained with me, an intimate portal to a "might have been" Peggy—she of the perfect race, the impeccable shot, the smooth stroke, the ideal response.

Could theatre accommodate (this) me? Only by splitting me into more than one, more than me. Two writers here raise this stage of projection, denial, desire, resistance, the rhythm of intimacy that often forces us/me into false endings. Llewellyn and Rankine slide between writing and acting, between directing and watching. The words are familiar and yet they are coming out of someone else's mouth: someone who moves her chair, someone who is simultaneously the writer and the actor, both (of) them and not them, both me and not me. In this multi-vocal text about merging and splitting, the resonance of the feminine pronouns—she and her—echo.

And that echo, ravenous for familiarity, finds her/us/me. "The recognition is so accurate I wonder what I will do next. I do nothing. Nothing, because I am not needed, except as a receiving body." Superfluous, once more. What is it we (women) seek from theatre? Recognition. And yet, the intensity of its arrival produces paralysis rather than action.

Don't put words in my mouth.
Mother tongue.
Call me.
Names I
never.

Abandoned and abandoning theatre ends. We prefer it to be over because it is (still!) impossible to quiet our fear long enough to let it begin. Llewellyn and Rankine propose we abandon endings, rather than each other. Too smart to persuade with the usual logic of the thirty-second commercial—"abandon that in favor of this"—they offer us only the murmuring irresolution of love itself. *Woulda, Coulda, Shoulda …*

and so did … and so do … you too.

100. *THE THEATRE OF THE TOWN—JOE KELLEHER*

Some of these may in fact exist already. By which I mean, have existed, been done by now. But the usual play is that everything is still in the planning: appearing soon. Imagined theatres, made up and still in the air. There is a bulletin board somewhere, along a corridor next to the stage entrance, down a spiral staircase behind a door just off a busy street in the town center, a piece of typed paper pinned to the wall: "Future Projects." Impossible to say how long that piece of paper has been there. The list is not exhaustive and, as I say, some of it is likely to sound like something you have heard before, but then again, even if the ghost always does appear wearing the same face, there may be a different face behind it each time, looking out, rattling the chains, doing the noises. So, there's the one about the theatre in which there would be time for a tree to grow, from acorn to branch. A hundred trees, even. Maybe more. Or a theatre where it's not the actors that walk on stage but the characters themselves, at once locked into the plot and altogether disorientated; which is to say free—if only they knew it—to do as they like. There's an idea for a theatre—or maybe it is just a play—where the currency that is exchanged in the on-stage buying and selling and making of bonds and paying of debts, is legal tender in the world beyond the stage, where the audience live and breathe. Another one—ambitious enough no doubt, and likely to involve some serious preparation—where everything is to be represented, not just the actions and events of the drama, but their causes and consequences, however far and wide they extend, wherever they are felt, suffered, enjoyed. Along with reflections on how the representations might be just that, representations, mere theatre if you will, and how the world could be imagined as very different to this. Of course there is also the one about a theatre that exists only in the present tense, immune to futures and pasts, but maybe that had been updated by the one that stuck with me most strongly the last time I saw the list for myself. *An Exercise in Dying*, I believe it's called. A version of the old story where the singer goes in search of the lost beloved and he disappears, gets lost in the story, and it is we—the audience—that come upon her, masked and be-wigged and multiplied, a spirit of remainingness, of departure, between living and dead, but not able to depart quite yet. The simple idea is that we ourselves might enter the picture and be actors there, that it could be us that will let her go. I imagine they are still working on that one.

Too often, the archive looms in advance of the work's coming to be. This archive, alive in the expectation of a time as yet unsigned, marks time for the making. The archive is in the plan, bringing into appearance what has not quite happened yet is already taking form.

Documentation of a piece before it has come to be—documentation, in pre-archival form, of the work's potential to attract, to organize its tendencies in a well of common forms—presents the work before it has time to set.

But what of an imagined theatre that resists this setting into form? What of an imagined theatre that resists an archival tendency that would have it encapsulate the work's future? When imagined theatres resist pre-archival tendings, the archive is not completely undone. An archiving is still happening, but this is an archive of the time of the work's not yet coming to be, of its not yet wanting to know how it can and will take form. This is an anarchive, an archiving of time's uneasiness, an activation of the anarchy in the archive, of the way the archive always, to some degree, resists the set.

In this resistance to the setting into place, there is not a void, but a plenitude. What there is here is time elastic, time of the event, time actively weaving a future anterior which resists conjugation. The now is specious. It is alive with the distortions of a theatre as yet unplayed, unimagined, unimaged.

Work remains to be done, a doing agitating at the pace of an anarchic share that resists the setting into place of the time of theatre.

101. *THEATRE/DUTY—JU YON KIM*

Twelve people who live or work in the same neighborhood receive notices requiring them to make theatre together for three months. They are people who share the same stretches of sidewalk every day, touch the same paper cups, mugs, plates, and forks, and even, on occasion, pass a word or two. But otherwise they are strangers, only dimly recognizable to one another in traces and parts: an umbrella spinning to avoid a branch, a quick hand at the cash register, cigarettes in assembly, pink backpacks on the run.

During their time in the theatre, the participants will receive the same pay, an average of their salaries. Arrangements have been made with their employers and families so that no jobs are threatened, and no one is deprived of care. Cooking and cleaning duties in homes are redistributed so that time does not have to be stretched, for some, into grotesque shapes. A shuttle picks up all twelve participants each day, and returns them each night. Some of them live quite far from the theatre, though they might work quite close to it. The shuttle saves them, on average, two dollars, forty-three minutes, and one-and-a-half transfers.

What happens once they gather in this space, malleable in the shapes it can take, vast in its collection of all that might be helpful or utterly useless in the making of theatre? (Eager and nervous eyes glance through dark lists of suggested exercises, practices, scripts, diagrams, fabrics, notes, gestures, finished and unfinished matter, sleek and scratchy recordings.) Their only objective is to work together on twelve performances, one on each participant, whatever that might mean. They stand on the edges for a while, circling chairs before sitting at neat distances from one another, wondering why this or that face looks slightly familiar. They scan pages of sample schedules. Then, they cautiously begin.

... What is theatre to me. Who goes anymore, tv shows are better. Even the writing. My son got us tickets to les miserab. I hate musicals. I go to my kids' shows at school, watch them play some animal or plant. Turnip, even. Ads on buses, always black with red or white letters. Two hours to make this costume after work. I sleep the whole time. Theatre should, I think, touch people. Yes, theatre about things that touch us most. Dishes, dirty bits of food chewed sometimes. Wool and silk and polyester, careful with leather. The wheel, ac on and ac off, a smoke to cut the time but people complain. Here's an exercise: ask your neighbor a hundred questions. Like those forms: they wanna know, are you communist. Terrorist. Who am I to you? Our favorite books colors but saddest memories. Can you translate. What, spanish. Or chinese something. I want a play like shakespeare. Living room dramas. I prefer korean soap operas. This is time off work, I'm doing a piece where I stare at the audience for an hour. Make it three hours and you're avant-garde. A monologue of reviews. Dinner murder theatre. Someone must have something good. Where were you in 1968. '86. Scatter the pictures here. Snow on tanks. This red dress waiting for falling ashes. A muddy bank with small heads staring at disappearing hands. Draw the pictures not in photos. Faces on hot cement and stomachs on cool grass. English is chocolate bars and spam, always. She was a back at the sink with a crooked yellow bow. A theatre for the year of fire. What is theatre to me. Choosing between a hoodie and a peacoat in the morning. Practicing saying hello ...

1. I stare out the window and wonder about the people who pass by. What is theatre to that person racing to get their child to daycare? Or to the one unloading a truck full of beer and wine? Someone rolls a cart by, full of recyclables. Another person crosses the street shifting between postures that say, *Attend*, and those that tuck anxiously inward. What would each person need to spend three months, three days, or even three hours in the theatre? How can we begin imagining theatre for everyone when for so many it seems—or simply *is*—an impossibility?

2. My students enjoy learning about the theatre of the oppressed and theatre for development. They seem to give theatre a clear purpose in the world. I ask for a scene they want to change. They choose an image burning through social media that week: a young black girl dragged out of a classroom by a security guard. At first, they focus on the violence, trying not to offend or hurt as they reconstruct the surreptitious recording. But soon they find they need to arrange themselves around the event, find the poses that will point back into history and forward, possibly, to a different scene.

3. In retrospect, I should have chosen a different form. Writing dialogue was impossible for me. Transcription and translation were twin torments, painful exercises in turning familiar cadences into caricature. To get onstage, voices had to find their way through words or imitation or both, a terrible house of mirrors they never survived. I still don't know how to make a theatre for my five-layered world, for the sounds of Seoul, Koreatown, Lakewood, Compton, Cerritos, and Anaheim that shift uneasily in my head while I try new tones for brick-laden streets.

4. *But now, I think I would give most anything to hear my father's talk again, the crash and bang and stop of his language, always hurtling by. I will listen for him forever in the streets of this city. I want to hear the rest of them, too, especially the disbelieving cries and shouts of those who were taken away. I will bear whatever sentences they rain on me, all the volleys of their prayers and curses.* (Chang Rae Lee, *Native Speaker*)

5. The theatre I long for may be the one I cannot imagine, not because it is impossible, but because it is not mine to imagine.

102. *A THEATRICAL REVENGE MELODRAMA WITH RING-TONES—SARAH BAY-CHENG*

An audience enters the theatre and takes their seats. The doors are locked.
Lights down—very slowly. The change is almost imperceptible until the auditorium reaches complete darkness.

Total darkness for what feels like a very long time. And then a bit longer.
Silence. And then a Theatrical silence (you know what I'm talking about: *Silence*.)
One by one (and completely by their own free will and agency), audience members turn on their mobile phones. The phones illuminate the space. There are murmurs: the cellular and Internet services are unavailable.

There is a panic, then resignation, as hundreds of people start mining their phone memories for useable stored content. Synthetic sounds from Solitaire, Tetris, games (not available for copyright mention), and music echo from tiny, tinny speakers.

Oh no! We have all of us forgotten our headphones!

The auditorium fills with the echoes of hundreds of fingers patting, stroking screens and buttons.

Continue for the length of respective batteries. (Too long for some; not long enough for most.)

One by one and then in larger, brand-related batches, the phones flicker out.
Space is reduced again to total darkness.

There is more resignation and waiting, but no one can generate the theatrical *Silence* again.

The end.

Take out your smart phone and open up the clock app.
Set your timer for 4'33" and then hold the phone in front of you and go.
Make no noise.
Do not check the phone.
Do nothing.
Seriously, DO NOTHING.

As John Cage's famous *4'33"* reminds us, there is a potential symphony in silence. There is value in listening to it, for it, in it; value in, as Daniel Sack poses in his book *After Live*, the potential *not to do*. But *not doing* is a challenge, and perhaps this is its point. Cage's first iteration (if you can call it that) of *4'33"* was undertaken by David Tudor, an accomplished pianist who sat down as if to play and closed the piano to indicate the start of the piece. The resistance—to play, of expectations—matters in this piece. What we hear as four minutes and thirty-three seconds pass is of course individual, it is environmental, it marks time passing, it marks our lives passing. It might be frightening to not do, to not hear.

Bay-Cheng's piece reminds us of the "noise" that is constantly with us, not even in terms of actual sounds, but a noise produced by the need to check our phones, to hear and see constantly. Although it begins in darkness, the "revenge melodrama" addresses and reverses the durational silence implicit in Cage's piece. Here, an audience might spend the 4'33" (or 4 hours, 33 minutes, or 4 years, 33 days) panicking to find sound, to fill in the silence. It is not easy to be in silence, or darkness, for long. Four minutes feels like a very long time. Another little bit longer, thirty-three seconds maybe, of silence, of *Silence*, and then it becomes too much.

Anecdote 1: 2013, the Royal Court Theatre for Lisa Dwan's Beckett trilogy (*Not I*, *Footfalls*, *Rockaby*). In the interval just following *Not I* (if memory serves). A rare moment of complete blackout in the theatre. No EXIT sign visible, just deep, thick, pitch darkness. And in that darkness, silence, the audience sat, waiting. Nervously waiting. It was perhaps just a moment, or many long moments of pause, moments audiences and critics remarked upon. (The production toured with the blackout; the NYU Skirball website for the piece even cautioned: "If being in total blackness for the entire length of the performance makes you uncomfortable, consider watching from our lobby TV screens.") As my eyes tried frantically to adjust, to rest on familiar shapes, a slow rustle could be heard. People were nervous, afraid to sink into the cushioned seats of this famous auditorium, worried. And then there it was: the first small squarish light from a phone a few rows ahead. And then another, a few in front of them. And another. Bay-Cheng's scenario in sound and light made too real.

Anecdote 2: 2015, *Shows for Days*. Patti LuPone walks into the audience and grabs the cell phone from the hand of a texting audience member mid-performance. Without missing a beat (so they say) she confiscated the phone and carried on with the performance. LuPone would later refer to the ringing phone as "a cacophony of noise."

No, no one can generate the theatrical *Silence* again.

LAUREY: … Is there a barn dance sequence in this show? I can't wait! (*She goes back on stage and sits at table with Curly.*) Curly, have you noticed that we are doing a live show?
CURLY: Oh yes.
LAUREY: I see. It's a live show is it?
CURLY: It is.
LAUREY: Yes. Curly, sometimes when I'm at a live show, I think to myself, no! No, no, no, no no no no. This is not exactly what I had in mind … Know what I mean?
CURLY: I do.
LAUREY: Yes Curly, sometimes I think no, no, no, no, no, no this is not what I had in mind—I wish I was at the cinema. Know what I mean?
CURLY: Oh yes.
LAUREY: And Curly, sometimes when I'm at the cinema, I think no no no no no no no, this is not exactly what I had in mind, I wish I was at home, tucked up in bed, with a good book or comic. Know what I mean?
CURLY: Definitely.
LAUREY: And sometimes, Curly, when I am tucked up at home in bed with a good book or comic I think, I think to myself no, no, no, no, no, no I would much rather be listening to a record or disc. Know what I mean?
CURLY: Definitely.
LAUREY: Oh Curly! Oh Curly! I just want to have everything! Know what I mean?
CURLY: Yes.
LAUREY: Curly, I want everything! I want to have every single version of everything that's ever been. Know what I mean?
CURLY: Definitely.
LAUREY: Curly, sometimes I want to see the film of the show and then I want to read the book that the film was based on and then I want to listen to the soundtrack from the original stage show and then I want to look at the TV documentary about the making of the film, all at the same time. Know what I mean?
CURLY: Oh, frequently.
LAUREY: Nothing else will do but everything! Oh, Curly, it's all just a wild dream! Know what I mean?
CURLY: Oh yes.
LAUREY: Oh Curly. I wish I could remember absolutely everything about everything. I wish I could remember the beginning of everything! What was the first show that you ever saw?
CURLY: *The Crazy Gang* at the London Palladium.
LAUREY: *The Crazy Gang* at the London Palladium! Any good?
CURLY: Brilliant.
LAUREY: Ah! Curly, I've just had an idea! (*She gets up and walks in circle, returns to table and sits.*) Curly, can you remember the day you were born?
CURLY: No.
LAUREY: Curly, can you remember any further back than that?
CURLY: Definitely not.
LAUREY: (*to audience member*) Can you remember the day you were born? Can you remember any further back than the actual birth? I won't disbelieve you.
AUDIENCE 11: No.
LAUREY: Definitely not? Not even a little shred of a memory?
AUDIENCE 11: Not even a shred.

Starts off. Off stage.
An entrance from within the room.
A hint of a barn dance to come is set aside to allow the blissful chance to confide.
A quick tease of participation in these inter-active days.
Now, plunged into the public intimacy of Curly and Laurey, it is easy to see them, mid-stage, as if they were in the dressing room with the light bulbs sweating their brows and the mirrors pooling their eyes into that third place
that hovers in the ether.
Which is where we are anyway.
The audience, hovering in the ether, like the shadowed double acts reflecting
Possibility and Imagination, Collusion and Antagonism, Familiarity and Mystery.

Everything. Laurey wants everything. In every format. All at the same time.
In, on, and off the stage, the yearning runs rampant while hints of modernity
echo their complaints all over the duo.
Enough-ness or not enough-ness.
Why is this show not like a film? Why is this film not like a CD?
We watch. We wait. We listen. We disappear into their vortex until the
Everything-ness of everything expands out all over the room with its desire and ambition. Lighting up even the lights with its verbal embrace.
And then, a fantastic moment.
Laurey has an idea and walks in a circle.
What a circle.
A smooth, commanding, anticipatory circle filled with legwork. Heel down, toe up, heel down, toe up, heel down, toe up.
All haunted by the ghostly presence of the Crazy Gang summoned up by Curly. It was the first show Curly saw and he was crazy about it.
The Crazy Show Gang doing the Crazy Show that Curly saw that Crazy Week.
And the sound of heel against wood, toe against air, brush of leg past calf narrows our eyes as we stare back down the tunnel into our own beginnings.
The fabulous heel down, toe up circle spools us back to our own beginnings.
Now we are all time travellers and time carriers hovering between each foot lift and foot fall. Suspended in the dark space of our own memories.

And just as we arrive, alone and lost in our own nameless origins, the footsteps stop.
Laurey asks Curly if can he remember the day he was born.
A sound. The bounce of light. A hiss of microphone. A cough.
Then a spotlight flicks on a figure in our midst and for a moment we all collide. Our collective amnesia slides center stage as Laurey repeats the question.
Can you remember your own birth? Or before your own birth? She asks.
The question hovers unanswered in the dust-filled light.

104. *THEN A CUNNING VOICE AND A NIGHT WE SPEND GAZING AT STARS—EMILY JOHNSON*

I welcome you. Go for a walk in the field. In the woods. Meadow. Desert. Street. Bring a roasted chicken dinner. Share it. All night there are sighs amongst us, a caress. Fingers moving. Skin touches, enters skin. Fish are caught. Gutted. Wrapped in aluminum foil, sprinkled with lemon, a little butter, salt. Put into ready coals. The birthed take a first deep breath. Our stresses leave. We fold and unfold napkins. Our hearts, too. We unfold these. Blood seeps through panties and drips down legs. Rocks pool from our mouths. Our breasts are milking. We stand. Together. I welcome you. Lay down. Rest. Gather what you need to know. Whisper then hum and sing and watch the kids run around, they laugh playing Star Wars. We will not end racism. Or heartbreak. We will not bring back the dead. We will not wrest the pain from ourselves. Not to mention from each other. All these wolves howling, they are being hunted. There are always these little things we miss. Ha. How the arm raises. How the head tilts down. The gentle sway. Lay your arm across my chest. Leave it there to rise and fall. I welcome you. See the red deer. The violently red deer. Hold her tongue in your hand. In your mouth. Take a sip of water. Let your tongues swirl. Let your drink be hers. Breathe blood and dirt and shit and air. And hold the newborn. Hold her. She is us. I welcome you. And when someone else is holding the newborn, get drunk. Get fully loaded. I do sometimes. Not so much any more. Count 14,000 steps. One day. Rest. Sleep 12 hours. I do. Have. Well, have done. Not so much any more. Count 14,000 ticks. The sound first then the bloodsucking creatures. Do they suck blood? One day. I want you to bite my shoulder. Again. Kiss the back of my neck. Again. I want to come with you. Again. On your chest. My arm lays still. Someone I love said, "at least we get to live it all." I welcome you. Take up your arms. TAKE UP YOUR ARMS. Leave the guns on the ground. Fight not with strength but with grief. Your curled up, crawling, kneeling grief. Count 14,000 steps and ticks (the sound) and 14,000 killed. Again. I welcome you. Howl with the hunted wolves, sing with nothing you remember, but remember the boy the woman the man and child and girl. The missing and murdered, when none of them found you in crawling pain. Remember? They thought you were not real. They find you there now or rather it finds you—the ground—holds you. And you look at the sky. You lay back. You see stars that are eyes that are souls and you see your own soul up there and your arms are up and they will never be down again. Again. The red deer jaunts away. The newborn. At least she gets to live it all. I hope someone gathers up the quilts. Disrupts the meticulous Ojibwe floral pattern. Piles a bunch of them in a jumble. Lays down in them. Drools on them. Lifts themselves up into a heavy type of lighting; thick, thick sleep.

I imagine everything is possible. I've always done this. As a kid, I wrapped potatoes and put them in drawers. I've always enjoyed tasks—ones that lead to tangible outcomes and ones that don't. And I ran through the woods pretending I was a deer. I ran as fast and as far as possible, hopping logs, ducking branches, imagining I had four legs. And I kind of grew up in a bar—the one my grandmother owned and lived in, in Alaska. So amidst climbing the tree and watching the beavers, running the woods, kicking rocks and stacking wood and cutting fish, spooning one teaspoon of oil into each jar of kippured red salmon—I would listen to stories. Some I probably shouldn't have heard. True stories and made-up ones, jokes and drunken tales from neighbors, family, strangers. The stories and voices mixed with the work and our play, with our actions and the actions of the strangers (kind actions and also sometimes cruel ones), and with the clams squirting saltwater—cleaning themselves in the bucket where they were stored until the freshwater in grandma's pot boiled.

I make dances now. And I see dance in everything—in the blood moving through our bodies, the synapses of our brains, the sway of trees, and the migration of fish. I see dance in the theatres of our world, in the community centers and gymnasiums and back roads and bedrooms. And I view our bodies as everything: culture, history, present, future at once. Out of respect for, and trust in, our bodies and collective memories, I give equal weight to story and image, to movement and stillness, to what I imagine, and to what I do not know.

Sometimes I make dances that include feasting, stories (mine and those of others), volunteerism, performance. Sometimes I make dances that last all night. I make dances to conjure future joy. I make quilts upon which to host the audience and the dance. I make fish-skin lanterns to light us. (In actuality, a lot of us get together to make these quilts and lanterns.) I invite stillness, an awareness of the periphery. I invite you to turn your head to notice what is happening next to you. I adore endurance and struggle and know that sometimes struggle is not going to be resolved via physical manifestation. So sometimes the struggle is to stop. Let others care for what is being made, hold it. Invite others to be at and inside the core of the making.

And we gather. To share food on the banks of Newtown Creek or Tuggeght Beach, at Foxtail Farm or Daybreak Star Indian Cultural Center. We restore dunes by planting native shrubs, we clean oysters in the New York estuary, we daylight streams, clean up parks. These moments by my definition are dance, are theatre, are the sharing and making of story and life: action, purpose, non-purpose, possibility.

We need this: time together and also time together, alone. It's so basic it makes my head spin. We need one another. We need one another in a sweat-inducing, vulnerable proximity and we need one another in a quiet, settled distance. We need time to let our stories settle and be heard. We need to practice telling them and by practice I just mean tell. We need to listen. We need the listening to intertwine with action—action we witness and action we take into and onto our bodies. We need to acknowledge where we are and whom we are with and what ground we stand, lay, sit on. It can be meticulous, this work. Or miraculous. Or both. I think it can be both. I imagine it is possible.

105. *THREE DRAMATURGICAL MINIATURES (AFTER NIETZSCHE)—JOSEPH CERMATORI*

A darkened jewelbox theatre. Gilt proscenium. Dim luster of chandeliers above and candles at the stage's edge below. Curtain in heavy, crimson brocade. The players appear in rigid, black, late Renaissance fashions, except where noted. Ghastly white faces and hands. From the stage, they often seem to leer out into the audience, eyes aflame. Their movements are slow, hieratic. Each thought emits a gesture—sculptural and enigmatic. If indeed they are audible at all, the voices have an ashen, echoing quality. These scenes may be played in any order.

1. *A low rumble, like the tremor of a far-off earthquake. Footfalls from the wings. A player enters. Stiff white neck ruff. He has a secret:* "Do you want to know what 'the world' is to me? … Shall I show it to you in my mirror?" *He draws the curtain gradually open, revealing an empty stage, while the distant rumbling sound seems to approach. Then, as he exits, he announces:* "INCIPIT TRAGOEDIA." *Moment. Suddenly the theatre collapses violently upon itself into a heap of ruins amid the deafening roar of some tectonic shift. A monster of energy is unleashed, a spinning maelstrom of black, invisible fire, devouring and transforming everything: Flux, conflagration, the time of evil: Dionysus as the principle of "creative destruction."*

2. *Silence. The curtain opens to reveal a group of five players arranged after the manner of Raphael's* Ecstasy of Saint Cecilia, *with one player at center, head tilted upward, listening. Stillness, as the players repose in a stance that expresses the perfect entelechy of classical form. They seem to know something, another secret. Broken, antique musical instruments lie scattered at their feet. Behind them, the heavens begin to part, raining golden light down. A consort of singers and viols appears above. Silent, ghostly music. One of the actors speaks to the audience:* "If, by some miracle, these harmonies should suddenly become audible, everything here would disappear into nothing. Our painter's vision, defeated, would vanish like a shadow." *Moment. A distant rumbling sound. The outward posture of the players remains perfectly composed, as the rumbling reaches a furious crisis of intensity, then, an ear-splitting fracture. At once, signifier, signified, and referent alike fall into ruins.*

3. *An opera after the manner of Peri or Monteverdi. Silent viols and harpsichords. Hovering over a stage littered with detritus, the allegorical figure of Eternity offers a Prologue in which all of human history passes in barely a minute. Then the drama commences, and the entire theatrical apparatus swings fully into exquisite and infernal operation. The scene is ancient Athens, plagued by the tragic fevers of the Dionysian cult. A chorus of satyrs and bacchants "in ecstasy" dance a dithyramb of frantic horror. Apollo and Dionysus appear, both beautiful youths, the former descending from the heavens above in a resplendent costume on a creaking* machina, *the latter from the nether regions beneath the floorboards with grape leaves in his hair, like one of Caravaggio's boys. Upon meeting mid-stage they jointly summon the muse of Tragedy, as if by magic, who transforms frenzy to order. A masque of courtiers and a play-within-a-play take place in stately dumbshow: Euripides'* The Bacchae. *A distant rumbling sound and Socrates' evil laughter can be heard echoing. A satyr depicting Wagner prepares for a heroic entrance in the opera's final act. The rumbling intensifies. Socrates, nearing death, becomes a musician, but his music is inaudible. Curtain.*

These scenes may be played in any order, but they also might be thought in terms of a dialectical movement: thesis/Dionysus, antithesis/Apollo, synthesis/Socrates. They are a triptych on the essence of the stage in miniature; for as I've written elsewhere, "the theater is, by its very nature, an apocalyptic art. Every night worlds flare into life and out of life within its crucible." Each scene reproduces the theatre's minimal movement of "creative destruction": to make appear and disappear.

1. The earthquake in the distance is that other theatre collapsing into itself: last night's theatre or tomorrow's theatre ending a world, just as tonight's will do the same, soon. It may be that theatre holds a mirror up to Nature (capitalized because it is humanized as a metaphor), but the truly inhuman *nature* can only appear once the play and its player have left the stage, once the vacant mirror can reflect its hollow sockets endlessly, its empty site a chaotic abyss that churns with potential worlds. Nietzsche writes in *Beyond Good and Evil*: "When you look long into an abyss, the abyss also looks back into you."

2. The pure grace of a tableau painted by Raphael, the artist who most perfected the Classical only to step beyond its certain surfaces into the swelling distortions of the Baroque (and here another figure ghosting these three scenes: Romeo Castellucci, director of the Socìetas Raffaello Sanzio). Suppose that stage directions are the silenced speech of drama, describing actions and characters with no words of their own, the world itself whispering its "silent, ghostly music." The name (signifier), its surrogate (signified), and the actual world (referent) all brought to ear-splitting harmony. For, as Nietzsche had it, music is nature expressing itself before the interference of objects and concepts. We theatremakers only approximate the outlines of stage directions; if we gave them full, audible voice, the necessary distance that theatre makes between things and their representation would "fall into ruins."

3. The whole of history passes in a moment, because the apocalypse wipes time clean no matter what its measure. Here we see Nietzsche's allegorical vision of *The Birth of Tragedy* realized in a masque. Dionysus—that god of ecstatic release, of chaotic intoxication, of fluid identity, of the theatre. He is the darkness that surrounds the lighted figurehead of Apollo, the rationally controlled individual, the masculine. In Euripides' play *The Bacchae*, Pentheus tries to assert his patriarchal sovereignty over the dehumanized mass of women cultists worshipping Dionysus. The young man raises himself above the god, but the flock—the chorus—swarms and tears him limb from limb, scattering his body to the earth. Tragedy is this differentiation of the one from the many, followed by the dispersal of this singularity back to the chaos of indifferentiation—the self and its forgetting. But as Nietzsche saw the art of tragedy in the joining of these two spirits, he saw its wreckage in Socrates' answering critical and caustic logic, his founding of a science of causal reason. "Hence the image of the *dying Socrates*, as the human being whom knowledge and reasons have liberated from the fear of death [and who makes] existence appear comprehensible and thus justified." And yet, finally, Nietzsche imagines the possibility of a new tragedy born of the meeting between this scientific knowledge and its inevitable limits—a "*Socrates who practices music*" on his deathbed, because it is the thing he does not understand. He cannot disclose its secret. Instead, he dies.

106. *THRESHOLDING—ERIN MANNING*

Make no assumptions. Thresholds are everywhere. You walk onto a bus, into a store, onto a stage. Or you roll into your bedroom, or from the sidewalk onto the street. Or you slide from ice to pavement. Or you shift from word to sense, the countenance of your presence quietly shifting as well.

Thresholds make a difference. They modulate how experience comes to be. And they make operative how transitions come to be known. For thresholds are known more in the aftermath than in their crossing. Unless of course you wanted to eat in that restaurant that doesn't have a ramp.

Thresholds require conditions for crossing.

Ramp or no, thresholds are less visible than you'd think. You may have made it into the restaurant, but that's just the beginning. Now you have to manage the stares, the sense of your body taking up too much space, the uneasiness of accommodation at all levels. The thresholds we don't see. We are always thick with thresholds.

Gestures of entry are the easiest way to orient the threshold. We introduce ourselves. You take my hand. We look at each other and smile. We size one another up.

Think of all this assumes. It assumes we recognize where the entering begins and ends. It assumes the body and the space as neutral carriers of information—in/out. It assumes that the words we carry across the threshold do the work of allowing us to cross.

Another example. Take autistic perception, where chunking is not of the order. Imagine seeing thresholds everywhere, edges and undulations activating a time-spacing that resists categorization. What if that first crossing hasn't yet provided you with any sense of a hierarchy of experience, hasn't given you fully-fledged the markers of inclusion? What if in this mix of what it always means to enter, it is the meandering of complexity you perceive, not the form of its resolution?

It's not enough to enter once. You enter and enter and enter. It's not just about neurology. Bodies are far more complex than that. But neurodiversity names it, this uneasy sense that the world is constantly shaping, its form-taking much more transitory than what the average brief on hospitality wants to acknowledge.

Neurodiverse forms of entering require a different account of the threshold. Every shift in tone is already a shift in threshold. To greet across this phasing of experience is to begin to account for what else is at work, to become interested in the force of form as it emerges for the feeling. It's not me, or you, who needs the entry to be facilitated. Conditions for thresholding require an attention to both how else we move across, and what else is moving across.

One thing we know: this takes time. If you're staging a work, move the stage to where the most vivid thresholds are. Inquire into how else experience shapes. Don't stop at the human. Feel what else moves. The world chunks where thresholding has left it behind.

> And so, I have written this book, presumably unaware of my reader and my(non)self. The involuntary actions, thoughts, writings, and behaviors of my autistic body negate my claims to writerhood, rhetorichood, and narrativehood. Instead, this book might be better understood as a cluster of symptoms.
> Achoo.
> You're welcome.
>
> (Melanie Yergeau)

> Translation is difficult,
> like transcribing the words of a song in an email
> and hoping that the melody travels with.
>
> (Michael Scott Monje, Jr.)

> Mouth words are witty accomplices to a mind that speaks a different language entirely. There are no words, but instead a beautiful environment where feelings, sensations, colors, and sounds coexist. I often think if all humans could experience the world in hi-res, technicolor, surround sound as I do, everyone would be happier. I have come to understand that my mind is not like most people's.
>
> (Emma Zurcher Long)

The thing about thresholds is that they do not translate well into language. For them to be encountered, language has to stretch.

The first threshold: the door opened, the handshake offered, the short introduction (name, profession, qualifications). We can define these as the entry points from which we tend to orient ourselves. We can practice how to respond to them. We can engage in the pact to be welcomed on their terms.

But this is not neurodiverse thresholding. It holds both space and language intact. It claims experience within a register preorienting.

Neurodiverse thresholdings exceed the pact, jumping over the undulations of a body-space not-yet.

Neurodiverse thresholdings pull language apart. They sound language differently, bending narrative, speaking the unheard in a tremor that shapes other ways of participating, felt more than heard, moved more than told. Bodying, not embodied—*I'd rather gallop than walk, bounce than sit quietly*—the galloping barely slowing for the span of what telling can be.

Shift to the swerve. Let the nonvoluntary take over. *Achoo.* And stop trying to translate.

Thresholds dance to attention when we least expect. They are with us, of our bodyings. Don't reach out for the hand before encountering how the spacing is orienting. Learn to respond otherwise than through the words you've rehearsed. Attend, and in the attending don't assume that the complex thresholding evades you. Let the dance of attention move you. Listen to the melody *beneath the words*.

107. *TOUCHING TOUCHES—ISAIAH MATTHEW WOODEN*

Ten thousand strangers meet on an empty stage
They are as unique as the snowflakes that blanket Paradise each year
They gather to touch each other's lives
To touch life
To touch

They form two concentric circles
Outside faces in
Eyes meet
Breaths sync
Hands reach

Touching
Feeling
Freeing
Believing

Some are clinical
Others pedagogical
Each imparts theory
Identity
Ways of being

Touching touches
Genuinely
Enthusiastically
Limitlessly

Partners change
Scenes fade
Still
Touches remain.

It is late summer 2014, and I am scrolling through the pages of *The New York Times* online. A question captures my attention: "Are we losing touch with the sense of touch?" It is a philosophical query put forward to invite reflection on the significance of what Aristotle designated in *De Anima [On the Soul]* as the primary form of sense—touch—in our modern world. What does it mean to touch in the age of the Facebook "like" and the Tinder "left-swipe"? Is touch still the most indispensable of the senses as Plato's contrarian pupil once proclaimed?

I am immediately reminded of an earlier op-ed the *Times* ran, a condensed version of the commencement address Jonathan Franzen delivered at Kenyon College in 2011. Franzen's essay opens with an evocative description of his infatuation with the BlackBerry Bold he'd recently purchased. The award-winning writer explains he cannot keep his hands off the device, fondling it in moments even when he does not need to use any of its many features. He loves the thing. And that love, he suggests, is emblematic of the ways our technological obsessions have come to trouble "real love."

Now more than ever, it seems it is possible to touch without feeling. What does this new reality perhaps signal about our sense of touch? Our capacity to feel? Our ability to love?

My thoughts return to Aristotle and his penchant for calling into question the prevailing beliefs of his time. In the same way the philosopher attempted to recuperate touch as a vital sense and to declare it as the most significant characteristic differentiating humans from animals, he also endeavored to reclaim theatre as an important art form. That he cites the capacity to stir profound emotions and bring about renewal—catharsis—as critical features of tragedy is noteworthy, I think. In Aristotle's estimation, tragedy—theatre—must touch. Touch, in other words, is fundamental to theatre.

What draws me to theatre as both an artist and spectator? Above all, it is the possibility that I will be touched. It might be a particularly well-crafted line or a perfectly timed light cue that grips me. It might be the box office assistant brushing my fingers when she hands me my ticket or a fellow spectator stepping on my feet as he makes his way to the seat next to mine. To be sure, it is theatre that makes me most acutely aware of the indispensability of touch. While scenes fade, touches remain. But what of those who do not have the same relationship to theatre? Have they lost all touch with the sense of touch?

I am mulling these questions when a notification from my iPhone alerts me that someone has "liked" a picture I posted on social media. I pick up the device to investigate. Swiping across its glossy screen, I am touched. I wonder: Am I out of touch?

108. *TRIPTYCH—KYLE GILLETTE*

One performer (writer) sits at a computer. She types actions which are immediately projected onto the wall behind her. A second performer (speaker) stands at a microphone, reading aloud the actions the first performer types on the screen. A third performer (actor) performs the actions spoken over the microphone. Every twenty minutes, the source and flow shifts (actor initiates, writer transcribes, speaker reads; then speaker initiates, actor performs, writer transcribes, and so on; they also switch directions). This continues through the night until no one can tell who is initiating or who is following whom, not even the performers. It continues long after the last spectator has left the building and the Monday workday has begun.

> V: Will you never have done? *(Pause.)* Will you never have done ... revolving it all?
> M: *(halting)* It?
> V: It all. *(Pause.)* In your poor mind.
>
> (Samuel Beckett, *Footfalls*)

In a story my father likes to tell, Columbus (Lum for short) was near to dying. He lay prostrate on the bed, a swift Mississippi breeze pushing through to blanket him in the only air he'd ever known. Two years prior Lum had died, a doctor glancing over at the family to say it was over: he was gone. But minutes later he had returned. He had been 68 then, and he prayed to live to 70: longer than he had thought he could live, though not long enough to work through the deep treads of an aching, throbbing loneliness carved deep within him in childhood. Now, at 70, he heaved a great sigh, opened his eyes for a moment, and reached down to grab the sheet. He pulled it up and over his face, doing the final job that someone else ought to have done, and sighed off into oblivion, dead for good this time.

Faulkner tells this story, too, but for him the name is not Lum: Addie lay heaving, barely there, while sounds of work—human hands and wood, making things together—came drifting through. Death in the South is slow, even if it's sudden. Death takes time, and makes time go.

I think of his body, Lum's, as it held then released what he so desperately wanted. It seemed so predestined somehow, the movement of what would happen back into desire: did he want to live to 70 before he lived that long? Did he die at 70 before he longed for that age? Or was it my father's telling—the chronicles set forth by a grandson Lum would never know—that kept him alive? It's a story my father loves to tell: Columbus was near to dying, prostrate on some rickety slats, feeling the push of the breeze as if it were time itself.

109. *TWO DANCES—SUSAN LEIGH FOSTER*

I'm trying to think up two dances, or maybe a dance in two parts.

The one dance engages with a world populated by

> inconsequential tears; an alienated and literally purloined voice; ironic exhibitions of obscenity, everyday violence, loneliness and sexual desire, along with equally ironic citations of popular culture including splatter movies, quiz shows, commercials and disco music; improvised dilettantism, eye contact with spectators, interruptions in performance through apparent lack of professionalism, deliberately lowered standards of production; insider jokes and sequences of rapid, minute episodes with moments of jealousy, periodically erupting aggressions and reconciliations, leading to a cosmos of averageness.
>
> (Hans-Thies Lehmann, *Postdramatic Theatre*)

The other dance must take viewers from one state of watching to another, not because what is being presented is strikingly emotional, visually arresting, or entirely new and original, but because it gently but insistently asks viewers to look and look again.

The one dance must embrace the tactics of anti-narrativization, anti-realism, anti-hierarchization, and anti-genre, so as to champion dreams, synchrony, synesthesia, fragmentation, and plethora. The other dance sets the limits on what dance can consist of sky high, as if any and every movement could be a dance, so long as viewers can follow the transition, whatever that is, from the everyday into dance.

Both dances will be recognized and evaluated for their ability to illuminate some aspect of who we are as bodies, as individuals, and as members of a society. However, the one dance will be appreciated in terms of its coordination and deployment of a semiotics capable of representing an argument about the human condition, whereas the other dance will be appreciated as an opening up onto what simply exists in that condition.

Why do I want to think up these dances? Well, because I want to feel out the conditions of possibility, the parameters establishing what dance is, for each approach. I want to understand what the process of making such a dance might entail, and also how each approach might set forth a direction for dance-making in general.

What, if any, images come into your mind for these two dances? Do you imagine these dances in a theatre? On the street? How about in a car? How many dancers are there? What are they wearing? Do they acknowledge you as the viewer, or do they pretend you aren't there? And what, what, what are they doing?

The hypothetical dances described in *Two Dances* were generated through a reading of two texts, treating each as a kind of score: Hans-Thies Lehmann's *Postdramatic Theatre* (German 1999, English 2006) and Richard Schechner's *Between Theater and Anthropology* (English 1985). I am hoping to analyze the development of performance studies at these two sites, based on the assumption that theoretical frameworks can transfer from one medium for thinking to another. By considering the two books as representative of relatively autonomous and distinct frameworks for thinking about performance, it could be argued that I am strongly mis-reading the texts. But perhaps the effort to translate them into dances also elucidates something specific to the epistemological underpinnings of each work.

Lehmann grapples with a change in theatrical practices that he is witnessing as a theatre-goer, undertaking a semiotic analysis of performances in order to comprehend the ways that the new European and American theatre of the 70s, 80s, and 90s approached the construction of space, time, text, sound, movement, and narrative. Schechner, in contrast, is locating his inquiry, not in the audience, but in the rehearsal room, a familiar location for him as the former director of the Performance Group, a group that deployed many of the theatrical grammars identified by Lehmann decades later. In order to summon up the various techniques and strategies evident in the diverse body of works he calls "postdramatic," Lehmann uses very imaginative metaphors and vivid comparisons with aspects of more conventional theatrical forms. Schechner's language is more pedestrian in its descriptions while at the same time introducing theatrical traditions and their aesthetic principles little known in traditional Western theatre scholarship.

If I were to imagine these two books delineating the contours of laboratories where an artist might be at work, what might I conclude about the nature of research undertaken in each context? What skills would working in each laboratory impart? Lehmann's lab seems to give an artist tools with which to assess one's own compositions, emphasizing the analytical skills necessary to determine how well one's intentions are being realized through the theatrical codes and conventions that are implemented in the work. In this lab one would also develop a strong awareness of one's own historical moment and how one's participation contributes to a social and aesthetic movement. Schechner's lab, in contrast, would cultivate a constant awareness of the daily as potential material for art-making, and it would encourage an awareness of the connection between one's own transformative process and those occurring in many other ritual and theatrical contexts.

What is involved in translating a text from one situation to another? One of the archaic definitions of the word "translate" is the act of carrying a saint's bones from one location to another. Likening the bones to a theoretical framework, I am trying to move a way of thinking from one context of implementation to another. As a scholar, I do this all the time—borrowing a hypothetical explanatory framework and then testing out what happens when it is applied to dance.

110. *TWODOOR DRAMA—REBECCA SCHNEIDER*

Betty
Joy
And each of their little sisters

Before Aeschylus adds a third character, there were only two. Betty is really only a replacement for Joy. But whoever said replacements are not major accomplishments in and of themselves? In some ways [sounds of coughing, hammering], Betty is superior. Anyway, she will go on to join the army and later become a pilot flying American passenger jets between Brazil and major hubs. In her fifties, she will have two sets of twins as a single mother by artificial insemination (though, as the twins say, no insemination is artificial, it's just insemination). All of this will be foreseen in a flash on stage as she sets up a guillotine in the front yard one afternoon to play Anne Boleyn and spreads ketchup from the kitchen all over the lawn. Later, she and the three other girls hold a successful séance in the basement. Meaning: it will have worked. All of it. [Sounds of crickets and peepers and maybe a far off dog named Trésor who will bark.]

That muffled warble behind the bathroom door is my little sister—five or six—telling her story. Splashes of plastic ponies, a multiplicity of voices. My parents try to enter, gently suggesting it is time to get out, time to dry off. She will have none of it, stopping them at the threshold: "I'm telling a story!" She will not resume until the door is closed again, its interdiction breaking down syllables into a foreign language none of us speak. Hers is a private theatre, one for the ponies.

In a brief history of the stage, Arnold Aronson proposes that the *Oresteia* was the first of the Greek dramas to use a door. "The introduction of the door delineated two separate spaces: the world seen and the world unseen; the known and the unknown; the tangible and the implied." But this drama of two doors takes place before Aeschylus's trial unjustly weighted the scales against the mother and in favor of the son—or, if not before, in another time. This is playtime, the make-believe of suburban pageantry, homegrown theatrics on the lawn, mock prophecy and séances in the basement. It is also something of a Chekhovian domestic drama rethought. Chekhov asks for three sisters, asks for each to repeat their longing for that mythic city Moscow of their childhood. These sisters here miss their third, but add a fourth. They miss their city, London, for this is the England of the "Virgin Queen" Elizabeth (Betty)—replacement for her mother Anne (Joy)—whose routes would join *major hubs* across the globe. They are decidedly not missing their men. It is a world of *artificial insemination*, which nonetheless produces real consequences. It is, in other words, rather like the theatre, making artful compacts that influence the actual, raising ghosts or producing twins twinned (two doors, inside and outside). For an actor is a kind of door, too—marking a difference and then stepping into character or outside of character. But just as we are mistaken to think a door must be either open *or* closed (as Beckett reminds us, a door can be imperceptibly ajar), so too we are mistaken to think one can only be a character *or* an actor. Rather, there is Joy *and* Betty; twin *and* twin *and* twin *and* twin. Two doors might have an imperceptible space between them, too. They might become twodoors or Tudors, sounding the same in the speaking, even if they mean something quite different when written on the page of history. They certainly seem that way from over here, still standing on the other side of the door, hearing *crickets and peepers and maybe a far off dog named Trésor.* The indication of another world. I'm catching what might be words, but the very construction of that otherness (its *sounds of hammering, coughing*, splashing) requires me to fill in the rest. Not my theatre. *Meaning: it will have worked.*

She sits in the bath babbling in tongues long after the water has turned cold. When she is finished, her lips shiver blue, nearly speechless like some medium returning from the other side, foretelling death and renaissance in English once more.

111. *UNIVERSAL THEATRE MACHINE (FOR LEIBNIZ, TURING, BRECHT, AND BOAL)—ANNIE DORSEN*

This performance will end war, religious conflict, economic injustice, and metaphysical confusion.

Making literal the notion of theatre as a space for rehearsing the world, the Universal Theatre Machine is a universal problem-solver. It is a performance for 7 billion (and counting). It actualizes Gottfried Leibniz's imagined *calculus ratiocinator (rational calculus)*, a machine for settling disputes of all kinds: philosophical, ethical, geopolitical, social.

> If we had it, we should be able to reason in metaphysics and morals in much the same way as in geometry and analysis (G. VII. 21). If controversies were to arise, there would be no more need of disputation between two philosophers than between two accountants. For it would suffice to take their pencils in their hands, to sit down to their slates, and to say to each other (with a friend as witness, if they liked): Let us calculate (G. VII. 200).
>
> (Gottfried Leibniz, translated by Bertrand Russell)

The machine is both mechanism and means. It uses as data the whole history of the world—all human knowledge and experience—and converts it into manipulable symbols, available for calculation.

Each performance of the piece ends when, inevitably, it all goes horribly wrong. When the irrationality that hides in the center of the rational re-asserts itself, when the machine fails to find a solution for fear.

This performance is offered every day.

Back in 1991, Brenda Laurel published a book called *Computers as Theatre*, in which she applied theatre theory (especially Aristotle's *Poetics*) to the art of interface design. No one has yet written its counterpart, *The Theatre as Computer*, but this playlet might serve as the lead epigraph for such a book. The theatre, after all, is a place of simulation, so what's stopping us from using it to run simulations—say, a million or two per second? Well, obvious answers aside …

And Dorsen doesn't settle for obvious answers. She doesn't protest that the theatre is only concerned with the singular—present bodies, palpable sensations, instant emotions. She doesn't dwell on the small bounds of theatre, nor does she gape at the scope of the dataset. Instead, she thinks to herself, *A stage is quite big enough, thank you very much, for Big Data.* In fact, porous to the world, already obsessed with "manipulable symbols," and compelled always to repetition and permutation, the theatre is practically the perfect place for a calculation: "great reckonings in little rooms," indeed!

What Dorsen objects to is only the mood we insist on attaching to our candidates for Universal Machine. The cheerful actuarial science of Leibniz, the gee-whiz promises of the TED Talk, the endless sunshine of Silicon Valley—none of these makes room for pain, doubt, and fear. So what in the world do they have to do with the theatre? (And what in the world do they have to do with the world?)

The *Tractatus Coislinianus*, thought to summarize a lost sequel to Aristotle's *Poetics*, would, I think, please Dorsen very much. It gives fear pride of place: "Tragedy … wishes to have a due proportion of terror. It has pain as its mother." Dorsen offers us precisely this: no, not just terror and pain, but due proportion. For once, a tragic computer.

112. *UNSTILL LIVES—BONNIE MARRANCA*

29 August 2015, Catskill, New York

11:02–11:09 a.m.
-twittering of crickets in the trees
-catalpa leaves and garage windows
-a cabbage butterfly settles on one of the blue spruce trees
-the sky is light blue, with a brush of low clouds
-I am having my morning coffee outdoors at a small table

2:10–2:20 p.m.
-Queen Anne's lace sways in the breeze (*in Shakespeare's day ladies wore it in their hair)*
-a tiny insect alights on my fingers as I write
-the swallowtail butterfly sweeps across the lawn *(butterflies are friendly, one often sits at the table with me as I have dinner in the garden)*
-little sparrows turn their heads this way and that on limbs of a dead tree, ever alert
-a hawk has the meadow to himself, gliding higher and higher

4:11 p.m.
-white puffs from the thistle blow through the air, polka-dotting the view
-letters in the post box
-where is the woodchuck hiding these days? … he eats the food in the trap *(cantaloupe, preferably)* but manages to get out before it catches him
-swimmingly

5:35–5:58 p.m.
-noisy cricket sounds in the vegetable garden punctuate the rows of tomato and basil plants
-buttery evening sun cuts a bright glow through the backyard as shadows fall at other angles
-a chipmunk comes out from under the back porch and scurries toward the garage, never crossing the lawn, but only using a straight-line path at right angles along the sidewalk *(why does he do that?)*
-a few bees scurry up and down the long pods of the trumpet vine, joining the hummingbirds that fly in for their evening nectar *(always on time)* and a ladybug that waddles up and down an unopened bud
-robins on the grass, alas

6:34–7:00 p.m.
-hummingbirds are poised in mid-air before deciding which of the trumpet vine blooms they will bury themselves in
-the sun sinks lower as I drink a glass of wine
-a cluster of yellow finches perches on a nearby branch
-pink Hudson Valley tones are visible overhead
-the forest at meadow's edge turns a darker green

7:24 p.m.
-a dozen splotchy clouds in the pale blue sky give up the day
-I put down my pen

I have always been intrigued by the concept of a play as landscape, which Gertrude Stein first wrote about in her 1934 essay "Plays." What did she *really* mean? One day last summer, with her writings in mind, I decided as an experiment to carefully look at and listen to the landscape in my Hudson Valley garden over a period of several hours, and write down whatever played out. "Something is always happening in real life," Stein said. She was interested in the goings-on but not in shaping a story around them. Her first play, *What Happened*, established the principle that a play is what happens, and her opera, *Four Saints in Three Acts*, offered up a play as a landscape. Is it hearing or seeing that makes the most impression, and how do they work together?—she wondered.

Thinking about the landscape, Stein decided what matters is that everything is seen "in relations." The society of the landscape is non-hierarchical, non-narrative, polyphonic. All species intermingle. Regarding landscape, the perspective is biocentric; regarding people, it is social and non-judgmental; scientifically, process rules. (Wholeness, not Oneness.)

The landscape is always there, it doesn't move, and only the things that are in it move. Besides, the landscape doesn't have to make acquaintance. But, you may have to make acquaintance with it. The landscape is cosmic, I am mortal. When you think about it, what Stein perceived *en plein air* is an important observation concerning time in its relation to action. She is a kind of nature writer (at home in Bilignin), her essay a field guide to drama.

I think that lolling about outdoors on an afternoon and recording things that were happening allowed me to see in clear focus what Stein meant by conflating a play and a landscape: ordinary life itself. "Nothing is ever new, everything is always there. It just depends on what everyone is looking at"—she believed. Oh, of course, the landscape doesn't move. But, did I really know in my bones how to explore that thought before now? The landscape is just there, like a tree or river or stone. It exists for its own sake. It vibrates with life. A model of indeterminacy. (John Cage—by way of Stein—fully embraced the relational, which is to say that the things of the world live their own lives. A play as landscape is his field of sound. Together, he and Merce Cunningham demonstrated the artfulness of her grand performance idea, rooted as it was in the observance of nature.) Durational performance is another latter-day instance.

A few weeks before I began to consider what I might write of "imaginary theatre," I had been to a conference in Paris. I never visit the city without standing in front of Gertrude Stein's apartment on the Rue de Fleurus. This time I was lucky and a resident let me enter the building and walk into the garden outside her old apartment. *I imagine her there looking out the window.* The landscape has never moved, only the things in it move. I move on.

113. UNTITLED (IMAGINARY THEATRE #1)—ANDRÉ LEPECKI

And then there it was. And that was it.

They had been walking for one thousand years already, in the straightest possible line, by the hundreds of thousands, never ever stopping, always going forth, carrying their bundles, and tools, and plants, and babies, and instruments, and songs, and languages, and dogs and cats, and jugs of water, and jugs of honey, and jugs of mud, and boxes filled with scents and seeds as dry as the bones of the ones who had perished centuries before, their predecessors, dying even as they walked and whose remains those alive now carried, just as they carried everything they once had or would ever have, gathering of the dead each spatula, each phalange, fibula, tarsus, each rib, tooth, temporal bone, pelvis, each patella, sternum, jaw all jumbling and clattering in rattling wooden boxes, which were never put down since the living walked day and night and day and night and day and night; and there were also the metal urns strapped to their torsos, similarly scented, filled with soft tissues carefully peeled from those wood-encased bones, the rotten muscles, the intestines turned into dust, the stomachs and cartilage and brains and livers mushed into a pulp only to bloom as improbable, minuscule ecosystems, each with its own singular fauna and flora, reproducing and metamorphosing generations of other types of lives, also encased, precious luggage, equally composing the line, some of the new biotas reproducing inside their metal worlds for as long as the ten centuries of the relentless walking of which they now were an inseparable part; sleep would not stop the march, the shufflers would take turns, one half adding to their assigned burden the slumbering bodies of the other half, a rough estimate of course, since sometimes a single one of them would be able to lug two or three, babies or the anorexic, while other times two or three would be needed to haul just one, their heavier stock; over the centuries, the daily assemblage of those in vigil with those asleep ensured that the line kept going, in its uncertain rhythm yet stubborn direction and form; for it had to keep going, the line, it could not be stopped, it had to proceed, it should never deviate; and since to stop was unthinkable, not even for a second, there was never a piece of ground they could call their own; thus, on their heads they donned not hats, but clay pots filled with soil and bugs and worms where they grew beet, yam, white and black bean, all sorts of berries, turmeric, leafy greens, the ginger root, rosemary, thyme, barley, small trees and minuscule vines from which they extracted a strong, pungent nectar; and all of these they tended well and harvested properly, year after year after year after year, decade after century, century after century; the moving line stretching back one thousand kilometers, they, the uncountable ones, the hundreds of thousands of shufflers, had divided its length into distinct zones where bodies and plants could better develop and thrive without stalling the walk; between the head and the tail, runners permanently shuttled back and forth, as if adding fibers to strengthen an overused rope thanks to their vociferations and commitment to spreading bits of news, drop messages from loved ones long lost in some distant zone, slip shards of rumors here and there, and thus cohering the ragged forward movement of the mass with their good deeds, handing out rare seeds in one zone, or transporting desperately needed rain water into another, offering medical advice to those in need, passing along magical ointments, bartering goods and even transporting on their muscular forearms the very sick, the elderly, or those who were dying and wished to see one last time a child or a sibling or a former lover presently shuffling hundreds of kilometers up or down the line; and this is how it went for a thousand years; lives and deaths were made and unmade, loves found and lost, lust enacted and passions destroyed, children born and children slaughtered, time built and space dismantled while the walk remained the only imperative, the line the only construction, and shuffling forward the only possible way of living; for a thousand years, spread across a thousand kilometers, never stopping their march, they had sustained the line, regardless.

And then there it was. And that was it: they had not arrived.

And now here it is. And this is it.

Stand firmly on your feet. Slightly bow your head. Take a deep breath. Beginning the movement at your right shoulder, bring your right hand over toward your left hip while retaining your frontal perspective. Now, as if taking a large scoop of water from your left side, start to lift your arm. Raising your head simultaneously with your arm, follow your hand proudly, regally, with your eyes as your hand reaches out and away from your body. Opening your palm as you lift your hand, bring your arm perpendicular to your upright body, still reaching out and away. When your arm is fully parallel to the ground, sweep the hand along the horizon, open palm facing upward, as far out from your chest as possible.

You have just made a gesture.

You have gestured to everything that ever was and ever will be!

Or that is what you think. In fact, you have only gestured to everything that ever was and ever will be in front of you.

In the *Thousand Years of Linear Time* it took to perfect the precise port de bras you have just performed, what else might have happened in the space outside of your habitual grid? Your habituation to perspective? What forks, what bends, in what other roads? What other ideas, other possibilities, were missed because they lay too far to the left, too far to the back, the right, the bottom, the top, the circle, the arc, the diagonal, the zig zag, the skew, the skance? All of those other ways of being, of thinking, of feeling, of remembering, of calling, of responding, of listening, of singing, of chanting, of dancing, of holding, of naming, of forgetting, of flying, of grasping, of loving, of releasing, of crying, of dying, of living?

Perhaps if you pause for a moment, before beginning your gesture again, you might receive a response. A ricochet from elsewhere might meet you in the wake of your gesture—something other than expected, something other than what you can foresee when only marching in a straight line. Something from the side. Or, if you wait, perhaps your own gesture might make a return, to tickle you at the back of your neck. Like your own greeting having travelled all the way around the world, bouncing off of other planets, and other moons, other times, other pasts, other futures after other nows to come full circle to find you still upright. And if you're lucky, it will sweep you off your feet. Hope for it. Wait for it. Listen. Pause …

114. *UNTITLED (IMAGINARY THEATRE #2)—ANDRÉ LEPECKI*

Scene 1

Two lovers, madly in love, made for one another, left alone in each other's arms, after three hundred days apart.

(The planets spin.)

Scene 2

Two planets, madly spinning, made of one another, left alone in their orbital paths, three hundred centuries apart.

(The lovers sleep.)

Among the seemingly endless catalogue of impossibilizations anthologized in this volume, let us suppose, within the confines of this gloss and to facilitate its response, that a finite set of legible patterns persist: core principles fleshed as concrete instances and near-at-hand particulars in a theatre of the imaginable. Maybe I have it backwards. The particulars define the core. Either way, imagine a fixed number of essential characters exists and that, among those limited figurations, a singular melancholy clings to the one I will call "The Lovers." We understand the wellspring of its poetry as an inversion copula: a reversible pairing, when two articles, understood relative to one another, evoke a radical perspective shift, a bi-stable foreground-background flip, "profiles or vase" to the Nth degree. One could call it catastrophic, since each view excludes the possibility of the other, in an *or* not *and* formulation. The escape from the self, from the self's coordinates, threatens collapse into the other, with vertigo-induced dislocation. "The Lovers" is not for the weak, because when waves become shore, the observer transforms, not the landscape. One recognizes the radical reversal as always already inscribed in the first instance. This prefiguration provides the sadness, since even at this grand scale only the simplest of patterns pertain, the echo across the widest of gulfs. "As above so below" claimed the credo of Renaissance mystics. The Lovers recognize their reflection in a night sky constellation. But where does the mirror's surface lie? With whom or what does the audience identify? Lovers, planets, the very music of form, the unobstructed ascent to heaven. Each Lover, already two, aggregates as an orbital and coherent entity, over-striding gulfs of time. In the choral melisma a single sung syllable spans the pitch of several notes, even a full octave. A scene (curtain or blackout) interrupts and discontinuates the slide as it must, since each destination rewrites the other, and "theatre" here means time unfolded.

Let me say it this way. With you, I am a planet spinning. *Side by side in orbit, around the fairer sun.* We are made for one another, made from one another, by whomever does the making, like Eve from Adam's skeleton, like a moon from a planet's mass, as those pleasant tales tell. The world prevents love in tragedy:

> Arise, fair sun, and kill the envious moon,
> Who is already sick and pale with grief …

Love fulfilled escapes the world in multiplicity. Its staging requiring a corporeal theatre of celestial proportions:

> We are two resplendent suns, we it is who balance ourselves
> orbic and stellar …
> We have circled and circled till we have arrived home again,
> we two …

As two we come to know that all things have structure, and this is the structure of love. In love, we have always loved. In love, we enfold the universe.

115. VARIATIONS (I–III)—DEIRDRE HEDDON

Variation (I): Accounting/Accounted

Cast (in order of appearance): Girl 10, Woman 66, Woman 17, Woman 30, Woman 67, Girl 12, Woman 81, Woman 45, Woman 72, Woman 33, Girl 3, Woman 88, Woman 21, Woman 48, Woman 82, Girl 6, Woman 26, Woman 80, Woman 90, Woman 55, Girl 8, Woman 75, Woman 31, Woman 94, Girl 14, Woman 25, Woman 41, Woman 87, Woman 99, Woman 20, Woman 18, Woman 63, Girl 4, Girl 11, Woman 22, Woman 64, Woman 69, Woman 87, Woman 74, Woman 23, Woman 32, Woman 47, Woman 68, Woman 100, Woman 83, Woman 34, Girl 7, Woman 62, Woman 56, Girl 16, Woman 40, Girl 9, Woman 27, Woman 57, Woman 98, Woman 24, Woman 35, Woman 89, Girl 13, Woman 86, Woman 19, Woman 28, Woman 49, Woman 58, Woman 70, Woman 95, Girl 5, Woman 50, Woman 73, Girl 15, Woman 29, Woman 36, Woman 43, Woman 54, Woman 76, Girl 2, Woman 65, Woman 77, Woman 51, Woman 60, Woman 37, Girl 1, Woman 91, Woman 78, Woman 71, Woman 96, Woman 79, Woman 84, Woman 59, Woman 42, Woman 92, Woman 38, Woman 61, Woman 93, Woman 39, Woman 46, Woman 53, Woman 97, Woman 44, Woman 52, Woman 85
Directions: *Every stage across the world. One woman enters at a time, aged 1–100. The director of each stage decides on what constitutes a "stage" and the duration of each Variation (I).*

Variation (II): Median differentials

Cast list: Woman 30yrs 4 months, Woman 30yrs 4 months with a baby girl 4 months
Directions: *Each woman enters until all the women are on stage. The director decides on the duration of Variation (II).*

Variation (III): The 49.6%

Cast list (in order of appearance): Man, Woman, Boy, Boy, Man, Woman, Girl, Girl, Girl, Woman, Man, Boy, Man, Boy, Girl, Girl, Boy, Man, Girl, Boy, Girl, Woman, Woman, Man, Woman, Boy, Girl, Woman, Man, Woman, Man, Woman, Man, Boy, Girl, Boy, Girl, Boy, Man, Boy, Woman, Woman, Man, Man, Boy, Boy, Girl, Girl, Man, Man, Man, Man, Woman, Woman, Woman, Woman, Girl, Boy, Woman, Man, Man, Man, Girl, Girl, Boy, Man, Woman, Girl, Boy, Woman, Boy, Boy, Woman, Man, Man, Woman, Man, Woman, Man, Girl, Man, Girl, Girl, Woman, Girl, Boy, Woman, Woman, Boy, Woman, Man, Girl, Boy, Girl, Man, Woman, Man, Man, Woman
Directions: *One performer enters at a time until all are on stage together. The director decides on the duration of Variation (III).*

> Each new attempt to determine women does not put an end to feminist questioning but only makes us more aware of the infinite possibilities of women. That is to say, women may be represented, but the attempt to represent them exhaustively only makes us more aware of the failure of such attempts. Hence the infinite regression that I specifically call the *'ms. en abyme'*.
>
> (Diane Elam, *Feminism and Deconstruction: Ms. en Abyme*)

Variations (I–III) are contextual pieces. At the time of writing, the human population of the world exceeds 7.3 billion; 49.6 percent of that population is female, with a median age of 30 years, 4 months. I teach Theatre Studies at the University of Glasgow. In my undergraduate classes, the ratio of female to male students is approximately 70 percent / 30 percent, a gender bias not untypical for Theatre Studies programs in the UK. And yet, in 2011–12, only 24 percent of directors in England's ten most subsidized theatres were female. Other statistics are equally sobering:

> Of 188 artistic directors working in the 179 theatres or theatre companies funded by the Arts Council England as National Portfolio organizations (2015–2018), 63% are male and 37% are female.
>
> Of 24 productions being performed in the 20 top subsided theatres on the evening of Saturday 13th September 2014, 38% of the directors were women, 37% of the performers were women and 8% of writers were women.

The underrepresentation of women across most areas of the UK's theatre industry sector is pronounced, yet women account for nearly 50 percent of the population and nearly 70 percent of UK theatre attendees. *Variations (I–III)* seek to acknowledge pronounced gender discrimination within theatre practices at the same time as provoking questions relating to visibility, representation, and politics. What can the signifier "women" signify? Can a politics attached to visibility ever escape presumptions, reiterations, and relations of binary categories? Can representation ever be based on anything other than the spectacular and categorical? What sort of "identity" is one that is seen and what is it that we "see" anyway—on the page or stage? What kinds of "variations" on gender are possible, ongoing, going on?

Variations (I–III) are left deliberately open as sites of potential and inevitable intersectionality; open to the multiple differences of "women," as women continue to become (and the category continues to become undone and remade). The desire and (still necessary) attempt to represent women is made manifest: in *Variation I* with 100 different women aged 1 to 100, in *Variation II* with 30 women aged 30 years and 4 months, and a 4 month old baby girl. But so too is the failure to do so fully, as woman is multiplied in an endless additionality and seriality, a *mise-en-abyme* which stages and undoes identity in the same moment and which, in making visible, risks reproducing the terms of the partition. Nevertheless, I demand that women—whoever we are—are taken into account, accounted for, count: *Variation III* depicts a stage which shows an accurate, proportionate representation of the world's population, according to gender—a rare sight on theatre stages across the world.

116. *VOCABULARY—VK PRESTON*

Propped up on gray foam,
chipped and cracked, its velum cut like a
wound. Traces of
a provenance
inside cardboard covers—a palimpsest of
stamps. Coats of arms.
Details of sale. Lot number. Broker.
At the back, the handwriting of Wendat
priest Prosper Vincent, certifying
an oral account
of the skin-bound
book.

In pencil, a genealogy.
"Indian manuscript" "ca. 1663"

A book plate: "Montréal"

Recto and verso for a hundred and thirty
pages, entries separated by underscores. A
neat hand
slips, indistinctly
between French and Wendat/Wyandot(te).

"Absolute, speaking as
master," "*ationdi,*" sliding into
a water stain,
"abstain" then
"abuse" (*Abuzer*),
"annihilate" (*anneantir*), and onwards.

Foxed pages
still—

Further down,
like Rorschach blots, ink spills
scriptive, heavy with events,
so wary of translation
that failure is a methodology.

Paper tongues,
parched
threads visible,
from a spine
of paper articulations,
a decomposition of tenses,
a vocabulary of the proximal
past.

What does it mean to call
a language dead? and traverse it? who may?
today: revival
(the live, again again)

a small room. Two sitters,

French and Wendat (Wyandotte; Huron)

400 years

cross-composed
[1640–1693]

with somatic (precision)

repeating,

upheaval—

"You are no longer the master of the lake."

Or this: penned with meticulous care,

of two souls, "*Ame - Ennonksat. S: ame séparee. Askenn.*"

My eyes dance together in and out, jittering literacy,
like an aperture, points of focus fluttering,
I find "smallpox," then "slave," then "pirouette"—
"bullets" and "guns"

now-sounded (so close to the body)

—to perform

as silences daily do

circling an invitation

to a dance that turns back,

here, on its steps.

117. *THE WAITING ROOM—MICHAEL MCMILLAN*

(In this imagined theatre of the everyday nothing is said, yet everything is said, because the body does not lie.)

A **BLACK MAN** walks/struts/swaggers into a waiting room where all the seats are occupied by **WHITE PEOPLE**, to use the binary of race, or ethnically European/Caucasian. They are spouses, boyfriends, girlfriends, relatives, children, young people, old people, peers, colleagues, strangers. Their eyes gaze over the body of our man; gaze for signs of sexual prowess, anger, the "uppity negro"; gaze at how fashionable or unfashionable he is. These gazes mark him as other, an object swinging between fear and desire.

While political correctness might forbid them from saying it, they still think: *Thank god, for a bit of color … He looks like Lenny Henry … I like a bit of the exotic … Poor victimized soul … I bet he can dance like Michael Jackson … Who does he think he is coming in here? … Who does he think he's looking at? … Don't look at him, he might get angry … He looks alright, I just don't like the rest of them.* Between being lionized and demonized these signs are written onto his body like tattoos. Our man looks at them looking at him—defiant, rebellious, honest, open—affirming the fact of his body, and he folds his arms asking rhetorically *Tell me something I don't know.* He waits, waits for a seat to become available, for something to happen, for someone to make an innocuous joke, for some *faux pas* that would pierce the tension. He is invisibly visible, and yet—as they continue with their business on smartphones, taking a selfie, scanning Facebook accounts, listening to Hip Hop, watching a Beyoncé music video, reading Zadie Smith's *White Teeth*, deep in conversation, listening without listening, minds wandering, catching a cat nap—some are spellbound by him.

All the seats are occupied by **WHITE PEOPLE,** except for one in the corner where another **BLACK MAN** sits. Finally, they see one another and share a knowing look. The other **BLACK MAN** is seated next to a **WHITE WOMAN**—she could be his wife, girlfriend, lover, relative, friend, work colleague, an official, or even someone he just met. The seated **BLACK MAN** thinks: *Don't look at me as if you know what I know. Don't play the race card like I'm gonna rush to give you a brother hug or touch clenched fists. I'm an individual. I'm not like you. I was fine until you came in here cramping my style and spoiling the party. Now there's two of us they'll think we're planning a riot—like they always do.* Or he thinks: *Yes brother, this is what it is, and you know what I know. As for the white woman—she ain't with me, she just happened to be in the seat next to me!* Or he thinks: *Yes look at the white woman and be jealous—I got her first, get your own.* Or he thinks: *Listen, brother, I've read my Frantz Fanon's* Black Skin, White Masks *and I know about the **WHITE MAN'S** colonial fantasy that the **BLACK MAN** is just a penis sexually terrorizing the **WHITE WOMAN**. But I'm trying to transcend that cliché—I'm just a man and she's just a woman.*

Presently, someone gets up from their seat and as they move towards the door our man imagines a moment of understanding. In his dream, they offer him the vacant seat. But instead they simply walk past. He takes the vacant seat next to a middle-aged **WHITE WOMAN** who draws her handbag close as if he were about to snatch it. A flash of *déjà vu* brings a smile to his face for the first time, and he is reminded that he has been here before on countless occasions.

Presently, a **BLACK WOMAN** enters the room. There are no seats available …

Beneath the gloss of *The Waiting Room* is the undercoat …

(… a dialogue between Frantz Fanon's landmark book on critical race theory *Black Skin, White Masks* and Michael McMillan's performance piece *Brother to Brother*.)

FANON *"There it is!" points the little white boy. "Mama, see the Negro! I'm frightened!" He throws himself into his mother's arms: "Mama, the negro's going to eat me up … "*

RED I'm looking at a woman,
she looks at me,
she looks at her bag,
she grabs her bag,
and turns to the side.
All I wanted to do was tell her that her bag was open.
Or sometimes I'm standing at a bus stop
and I'm thinking, instead of being a rude boy,
like I normally do,
let me go and wait in the queue.
So I walk to the back of the queue,
but she's still watching me.

CHORUS Oh my god this man's gonna do something to me!
Oh my god this man's gonna do something to me!
Oh my god this man's gonna do something to me!

FANON *… One is no longer aware of the Negro but only of a penis; the Negro is eclipsed. He is turned into a penis.*

BLUE Black man and a white girl,
standing on the stairs
of a block of flats.
I don't know.
There's some serious answers to answer to
and you best have your facts ready.

PURPLE I keep having this vision
this dream
but it feels too real
like you can smell it
feel it.

FANON *O my body, make of me always a man who questions!*

118. *WANDERSPIELE—NATALIE ALVAREZ*

The Performer emerges from the wings to stand center stage of the proscenium. He takes a brief moment to look at everyone: a direct, unaffected look as though he's there on official business, just getting a sense of the numbers. The Performer turns stage right and walks along the apron, descends down a set of stairs and proceeds briskly through the center aisle of the house toward the exit to the lobby. Before leaving, he turns to the audience: "Follow me, please." A few spectators dutifully rise to follow—they have been to enough peripatetic performances to know what's required of them. Others stand up with a sigh, reluctant to get up from their plush theatre seats, already bored by yet another *Wanderspiele*. The spectators at the head of the pack find him waiting at the front doors. "Let's go," he says, and leads the way out.

The Performer walks with purpose a few paces ahead, keeping to himself. He turns onto the busy avenue and heads south. The spectators remain hushed at first as they walk, waiting for the Performer to engage them in some way, but soon begin talking amongst themselves. Cars honk as the throngs of spectators spill onto the road, unable to keep to the narrow sidewalks. They walk further and further, and they walk further still. The spectators at the head of the pack a few paces behind the Performer attempt to ask, "Where are we headed?" But they get no reply. Other spectators begin to wonder at the conceit of this enterprise as the mid-afternoon light that began this matinee performance wanes into twilight. Other spectators don't seem to notice or care, enjoying the conversation with strangers that gradually deepens as the time passes. They talk about family now, workplace frustrations, bad knees, and broken hearts. They walk and walk. They keep walking. And they walk more. The Performer leads them onto a path now that follows an old railway line. The spectators decide this is an extreme, durational participatory performance. A sense of communitas sets in. They charge ahead thinking about the post-performance stories they'll share as one of the ones who was there; of the discipline it required; of the fear that set in once nightfall descended; how they lost all shame and relieved themselves in front of their fellow participants; how they ruined good shoes. They walk and walk, and walk further still. A crest of morning sunlight inches over the horizon. Cold, hungry, and thirsty, the spectators start to get hostile. "Where is this headed?" they demand.

They reach a clearing. In the distance, the spectators see a long black line along the horizon. Their eyes play tricks. It's a highway. It's a black ribbon rippling in the late morning sunlight. It's a wall. It's millions of migrating blackbirds at rest. It's the end of the earth. It's a border. The spectators approach and their focus sharpens. The black line breaks up into more clearly defined shapes and figures now. They make out helmets and shields and glistening boots. Some spectators instinctively run in the opposite direction. The line of helmets, shields, and boots snakes swiftly around them forming a cordon. The line splits momentarily to let the Performer through. A few spectators try to sneak through behind him but the line seals up again into a perfect enclosure. Panic sets in. One of the spectators tries to negotiate peacefully on behalf of the group: "We've all been very committed spectators, but we think this might have gone too far." The line remains indifferent and still. The spectator, in a fit of frustration, charges the line. Others follow. Some grasp at rocks to throw. A cloud of tear gas envelops the scene. Spectators hit the ground. Water cannons blast those who remain standing. Writhing on the ground, the spectators begin declaring their citizenship, shouting their occupations, calling out their familial relations; they are grandmothers and mothers, grandfathers and fathers, uncles and aunts; they are respectable members of society; they pay taxes; they are citizens. WE ARE NOT THEM, they shout. WE ARE ONE OF YOU, they shout. The line remains impervious and unmoved.

In a brilliantly chilling denouement, *Wanderspiele* brings together theatre's current and enduring fascination with the modality of immersion and performance's now long-standing commitment to the aesthetics of walking. Approached from either direction—from walking or from immersive theatre—we meet in the middle here to confront again the reality that theatre and performance are *not real.*

The attraction, the pull of immersive theatre, as the trope's label suggests, is that the audience member is supposedly immersed in the experience and that such immersion transforms them from spectator to participant. In the immersive mode, the audience no longer looks on and watches from across the space that is theatre but becomes part of the action and process. In this genre, the audience is *in* the work, physically, affectively, and emotionally. The work would not exist without the audience's participation or, we might say—prompted by Alvarez's provocation—complicity. Immersive theatre is a theatre of experience, of the experiential and the embodied. In the moment of that experience, I am here. I am thrilled to be here. I do not know what will happen next, I do not know what will be asked of me or what I will do or whether I will do it well, but I will know, through this experience, through the *frisson* of its uncertainty, that I am alive. We are in this together. This is the thrill for which I exchange my money.

The history of walking as art practice is much longer than that of "immersive theatre" and it has some well-trodden paths which, irrespective of the different contexts and geographies from which they arise, seem to lead us too easily and readily to a destination called "resistance," which in turns is twinned with "liberation." Particularly well-worn tracks lead us back to the psychogeography of the Situationist International, which sought out, through "drifting" operations, alternatives to the spectacularized city. Another track visible in the landscape might be Richard Long's *A Line Made by Walking* (1967), which enacted a radical dematerialization and decommodification of the sculptural object. Whilst such origin stories must be contested for who and what they leave out, the trope peddled (or stepped) into discourse remains strong: walking offers a route of escape from people, from the familiar, from oppression, from stress, from capitalism, from interpersonal relations. Walking shares with immersive performance the promise of the experiential, a phenomenological approach in which one can purportedly feel the earth beneath the feet, sense the landscape, the environment and the atmosphere, and intermingle with others' stories and journeys, walking in the footsteps of those who walked here before.

In that clever crossing provided by Alvarez, where immersive theatre meets peripatetic walking practices, the limits of both are revealed. To be immersed in theatre is to be immersed *in theatre*, in the theatrical. The frame between the real and the aesthetic is secure, even in immersive theatre; we would do well to hold onto that security and the gap it upholds. *Wanderspiele*'s dissolving of that frame serves to make its still firm presence tangible. Similarly underscored are the aesthetics bounding walking art practices. The long walk—an enforced walk, an uncertain walk, a difficult walk—ends at a violent border. If any reminder is needed that walking and politics are tightly bound, that walking for most people on the planet is not a cultural practice of resistance or freedom but a necessity—a means to an often very challenging end—then Alvarez delivers this. We cannot walk "as if" we are seeking asylum, or refuge, or escape, or literal liberation; or act "as if" we are subjected to violence, domination, and repression in our theatrical experiences. We—if we are lucky—are here, not there.

119. *WHAT TO, WHERE (A POETS THEATRE)*—*CARLA HARRYMAN*

Indications
Not a word but a site, powering a behavior.
Smile with quotes of misrecognition.
"That's the Ceausescu Palace."
Don't forget f. A code for fugitive audience.
Cannot avoid word, *obscurnity*: denoting an oceanic trench.

A structured improvisation arranged as dialogue between Original Biting Criticism and Imagined Ritual
Will occur fugitively at the holes NATO left in Belgrade's walls.

Scene
Poems as tiny as amoeba are viewed under a concrete microscope. "Must the scene always unfold in Syria?" Next, Beauty arrives on a shooting star. "In which direction is Shanghai?" Earthworms under anodyne feet die of unknown causes. "Nothing happened for a while."

Anti-masque
"Great" is slathered across the sluggish 2,000 miles of partition via an outsized tongue's application of Saliva, trademark: Sweet Sweet Clicks.

Serenade in a trench
And the welter slowed loo-loo air's
slurry water mirror
A little voice:

Being quiet instead of being quieted
Lines thin
Between loo-loo
Being quiet instead of being whose lines
Thin between, what!

The one who sings for a berth
And being quiet instead of being dirt
Lines thin between the one who swept
Up a signature quiet of being

Between quiet of being
Lines thin being
Quieted air's slurry voice lines
Descent, sways maybe's
Bay-be's birth
Note, no signature
No' te

Masque
The authorizer of this segment is subject to an expectation that their function is to decry the transposition of any word onto roboruling tracks.

I am struck by the proposition that an impossible theatre can get at the essence of theatre. I am struck by the proposition that an impossible theatre can get into the essence of theatre. Seep through it. Pilfer (action) or absorb (chemically interact with) its premises. Its. Remote control returns it to possibility. Robocall apologizes for previous robocall. If one cannot speak into the instrument. In the presence of others. Hand signs, torn signs. Or some other *wigglewrangle*, or thought reverb. Energized dot in patrolled space. Trenched. Each performance is or was racialized. Why "is"? Each was staged for an audience of performers only. Truly? "Was?" A blaze. Featuring I-Am-Elsewhere and Burned-Into-the-Eye. Then prosthetics, infinite lights. Digital delights and true access. Knowledge in advance of the results and that no one would or anyone might investigate the who'd-have-guessed-it scene. (Forgetting, forging, forgoing.) Of applause in the heart muff of into around gushing opening to break muffled roses at open, though just like you. You f. Then to pause in acute distance. You too? Isn't there a searing refrain in spotting a memory? The object, I ... Next! A domain. Free crowned barbs. (Apologize.) The robocall apologizing for the robocall. A taming of shrieks and cries. Another pause. Enters, under.

120. *WOMEN & CHILDREN & AN OLD MAN GODOT—RICHARD SCHECHNER*

My "imagined theatre" is not fancy. It's a women & children & an old man *Waiting for Godot*. The women do not play Gogo and Didi "as women." The children cannot help but be alienated from Pozzo and Lucky. Alienated in Brecht's sense.

Gogo and Didi are definitely male characters. Men played by women. What kind of men? That's to be determined via rehearsals: always and already the means of finding out what's going on, onstage, really.

In many parts of the world, onstage gender is not fixed by one's genital package; or even by how a person self-determines gender. It is determined by theatrical convention. Thus the Japanese *onnagata* and the Chinese *dan*: definite female characters performed by males. In Japanese Takarazuka women play all the roles, including knockout handsome men.

In my *Godot* actors-who-are-women want to "try on" being men. And from time to time the Beckett play stops and the women, qua women, talk with each other, maybe sing and dance a little.

OK, men. But what kind of men? Gogo and Didi are losers—brilliant, playful, woeful losers. But also they are entertainers. Leftovers from vaudeville, from some kind of extinct comedic form drained of its humor, desiccated. Gogo and Didi are bored; they are worn out by their circumstance. They are hoboes always on the road, sleeping wherever.

I remember these kind of men from my childhood in Newark, New Jersey. Down near the railroad tracks on the far east side of Weequahic Park. Men with dirty faces and grimy hands, coal dust under their fingernails. The trains were coal-burning steam-engine trains in those days. I never got too close to the men near the tracks. I was scared and fascinated mixed. Thinking back on these "bums," I am aware that they were non-gendered. Yes, they were men, surely; but their gender was not their defining mark. It was their dusky dirty selves, their small fires, their way of smoking the butt-ends of discarded cigarettes. Artists? And these "bums" were "white men," as I think Beckett's Gogo and Didi are. Detritus of northern European civilization, cast out, on the move. To where? To an appointed place, there, in Weequahic Park, near the railroad tracks. This is where Beckett intend they land, at least for a day or two. Near me.

Maybe these "bums" were women between their legs.

And Pozzo and Lucky? Children in my imagined production. About the age I was when I saw my "bums" in Weequahic Park. Pozzo with a pillow strapped to his mid-section giving him his big belly. Lucky barely able to mouth the words of his incredibly complex monologue.

And the Boy of *Godot*? Definitely a man of my age, me, bringing the news of perpetual procrastination enforcing and equally perpetual appointment. What voice should I use? My own? Or a high-pitched young boy's? Maybe I should lip-synch a huge echoing sonorous voice filling the whole performing space?

Will the Beckett estate give me permission to do *Waiting for Godot* as I want to do it? Of course not. So the production will have to be "in progress," a "rehearsal," a secret thing … again, at the edge of the park, "down there" somewhere—where my parents do not want me to venture. The best spot, finally, for art.

I'm glad to see you back.
Why will you never let me sleep?
I felt lonely.
I had a dream.
Don't tell me!
An erection!
With all that follows.
We've lost our rights?
We got rid of them.
Who is Godot?
Godot?
You took me for Godot.
The circus.
The music-hall.
The circus.
On!
Well, shall we go?
Yes, let's go.
All the dead voices.
They make a noise like wings.
Like leaves.
Like sand.
Like leaves.
What do they say?
They talk about their lives.
To have lived is not enough for them.
They make a noise like feathers.
Like leaves.
Likes ashes.
Like leaves.
  On!
  Tell him.
Well? Shall we go?

121. *RAJNI SHAH*

Nothing happens.

There were very many versions of this. Versions with long repetitious single acts by a single person, versions with real meadows behind the back-cloth, versions in state theatres that actually stated things, and versions that confronted racism and sexism once and for all. But in the end, they all found themselves back at this place: if it is to be an imagined theatre, then you are asking what I dream of that is not possible, or you are asking what is it all for, or you are saying what would it be if it could be anything, and perhaps the only excess that doesn't have to do with resources is this one. It is this theatre that I dream of, and it is this theatre that is always imagined. You and I. In stillness. Nothing happens. Which means, of course, that anything can happen. In that moment in which nothing happens, anything can happen. Anything is happening. After all the rigor and politics, after all the gesturing and speaking, after all the breathing. After all the sharing and attempting and jostling and making and making and making and making. After all the caring. After all the slowing down and speeding up. After all the over-whelm. After running up stairs in a hurry, and after falling down stairs in a shock, and after choosing not to speak in a crowded room, and after putting extra cushions on your theatre seat so that you could see the stage, and after spilling ice cream on your sleeve in the dark, and after making a huge pot of soup so that everyone could eat from it every day after rehearsals, and after engaging for years in consensus-based decision-making with a large group of people, after pulling and pulling at this thread, after weaving yarn and making it into jumpers, after chasing the fish, and after learning yoga, after trying to recreate every childhood experience, after never looking back, after locking yourself away for days, after wondering why nobody liked you and finding yourself out of sync with the times, after wishing you could be more like water, and after learning to embrace disgust, and after learning to confront your own death, after learning to laugh, learning from clowns, letting language disintegrate, hating the sun, letting a theatre light fall on your head, wishing you weren't so detestable. After looking each other in the eye, and flinching. After walking along a vein full of blood. After asking earnestly whether some people were more evolved than others and whether you were one of those who was less evolved. After imagining that we weren't doing this with our short lives. After reaching out for something that turned out to be temporarily fictional. After that, or maybe alongside it. After that, or maybe alongside it, but nevertheless, in this space, for this time. After that, or maybe alongside it, I am holding on to the fact that in this space and for this time I can imagine that nothing happens.

Notes on contributors

Joshua Abrams is Deputy Dean, Academic, at Royal Central School of Speech and Drama, University of London. He is completing a monograph on theatricality within the restaurant as well as editing a forthcoming issue of *Performance Research*, "On Taste." He regularly publishes and speaks widely on food and performance, philosophies of ethics and performance, and identity politics.

Natalie Alvarez is Associate Professor in Dramatic Arts at Brock University. She has three forthcoming books: *Unknowing Others: Immersions in Cultural Difference* (Michigan); *Theatre & War* (Palgrave Macmillan); and *Sustainable Tools for Precarious Times: Performance Actions in the Americas* (Palgrave Macmillan), a co-edited collection with Keren Zaiontz.

Patrick Anderson is Associate Professor in the departments of Communication, Ethnic Studies, and Critical Gender Studies at the University of California, San Diego. He is the editor (with Jisha Menon) of *Violence Performed: Local Roots and Global Routes of Conflict* (Palgrave Macmillan, 2009) and the author of *So Much Wasted: Hunger, Performance, and the Morbidity of Resistance* (Duke, 2010), and *Autobiography of a Disease* (Routledge, 2017). He is currently completing a new book, *Empathy's Others.*

Minou Arjomand is Assistant Professor in the English Department at the University of Texas at Austin. Her research focuses on political theatre and the public role of art institutions.

Sara Jane Bailes is a theatre maker, writer, and Reader in Theatre and Performance Studies at the University of Sussex. Her work currently focuses on histories of experimental performance and the compositional strategies developed by artists through their practice. She co-edited *Beckett and Musicality* (with Nicholas Till, Routledge, 2014) and is author of *Performance Theatre and the Poetics of Failure* (Routledge, 2011).

Jonathan Ball holds a PhD in English and teaches literature, film, and writing at the University of Manitoba and the University of Winnipeg. He is the author of the poetry books *Ex Machina* (BookThug, 2009), *Clockfire* (Coach House, 2010), and *The Politics of Knives* (Coach House, 2012), the co-editor of *Why Poetry Sucks: An Anthology of Humorous Experimental Poetry* (Insomniac, 2014), and author of the academic monograph *John Paizs's Crime Wave* (Toronto, 2014). Visit him online at http://JonathanBall.com/, where he writes about writing the wrong way.

Howard Barker was born in a working class family in South London in 1946. His first stage play was performed in 1970 at the Royal Court Theatre. Subsequently, his works were played by the Royal Court Theatre, Royal Shakespeare Company, The Open Space Theatre, and the Almeida. His company, The Wrestling School, was established in 1988. He is the author of more than sixty plays (most published by Oberon Books), collections of poetry, and several treatises on the theatre, including *Arguments for a Theatre* (Oberon, 4th edition, 2016).

Sarah Bay-Cheng is Professor of Theater and Dance at Bowdoin College, where she teaches courses in theatre and media history, contemporary performance, and dramatic literature. Her research examines the intersections of media, digital technology, and performance, including work on modernism, historiography, and the digital humanities. She co-edits the book series Avant-Gardes in Performance and most recently she co-authored *Performance and Media: Taxonomies for a Changing Field* (Michigan, 2015).

Stephen Bottoms is Professor of Contemporary Theatre and Performance at the University of Manchester, UK. His books include *Playing Underground: A Critical History of the 1960s Off-Off-Broadway Movement* (Michigan, 2004), *Small Acts of Repair: Performance, Ecology and Goat Island* (with Matthew Goulish, Routledge, 2007), and *Sex, Drag, and Male Roles: Investigating Gender as Performance* (with Diane Torr, Michigan, 2010). Steve is also a theatre maker and sometimes performer, currently specializing in site-specific performance.

Ricardo A. Bracho is a queer Chicano activist playwright who also works as an essayist, producer, dramaturg, educator, and organizer. He has taught in academic and community settings, worked extensively on feminist/queer/black/Latino indie film and video, and been a longtime public health worker and lifelong leftist. His plays—which include *The Sweetest Hangover, A to B, Sissy, Querido,* and *Puto*—have been staged across the US.

Sharon Bridgforth is a writer who collaborates with actors, dancers, singers, and audiences live during performance as she composes moving soundscapes of her non-linear texts. She has been Artist in Residence at institutions around the country including: IDEX/Thousand Currents, the University of Iowa's MFA Playwrights Program, The Theatre School at DePaul University, and the Department of Performance Studies at Northwestern University. Sharon is a 2016 Doris Duke Performing Artist and 2016 Creative Capital awardee. http://sharonbridgforth.com/.

Jennifer DeVere Brody is Professor in the Department of Theater and Performance Studies at Stanford University where she is affiliated with the Center for Comparative Studies of Race and Ethnicity (CCSRE). Her books, *Impossible Purities* (Duke, 1998) and *Punctuation: Art, Politics, and Play* (Duke, 2008), both discuss relations among sexuality, gender, racialization, visual studies, and performance. Currently, she is working on the re-publication of James Baldwin's illustrated book *Little Man, Little Man* and on a new monograph about the intersections of sculpture and performance.

Romeo Castellucci is the creator of a theatre founded on the totality of the arts (Societas Raffello Sanzio), about which he has written several theoretical essays. His work proposes dramatic lines that are not subject to the primacy of literature, making the theatre a plastic art, at once complex and visionary. These productions are regularly produced by the most prestigious theatre and opera companies worldwide, and have been featured in numerous international festivals.

Joseph Cermatori is Assistant Professor of English at Skidmore College and associate editor at *PAJ: A Journal of Performance and Art*. His theatre writings and translations have appeared in *Modern Drama*, Yale's *Theater* magazine, *Theatre Journal*, *Theatre Topics*, *The Brooklyn Rail*, *The Village Voice*, and *The New York Times*.

Joshua Chambers-Letson is Assistant Professor of Performance Studies at Northwestern University. He is the author of *A Race So Different: Law and Performance in Asian America* (NYU, 2013), winner of the 2014 Outstanding Book Award from the Association of Theater in Higher Education. Along with Ann Pellegrini and Tavia Nyong'o he is a series co-editor of the Sexual Cultures series at NYU Press.

Una Chaudhuri is Collegiate Professor and Professor of English, Drama, and Environmental Studies at New York University. A pioneer in the fields of eco-theatre and Animal Studies, she published books in both these fields in 2014: *Animal Acts: Performing Species Today* (co-edited with Holly Hughes, Michigan) and *The Ecocide Project: Research Theatre and Climate Change* (co-authored with Shonni Enelow, Palgrave Macmillan). Her book *The Stage Lives of Animals: Zooësis and Performance* was published by Routledge in 2017. Chaudhuri participates in several creative collaborations, including the multi-platform intervention entitled *Dear Climate*.

Meiling Cheng is Professor of Theatre Critical Studies at the University of Southern California School of Dramatic Arts. She is the author of *In Other Los Angeleses: Multicentric Performance Art* (California, 2002) and *Beijing Xingwei: Contemporary Chinese Time-Based Art* (Seagull, 2013), which has received a 2006 Zumberge Individual Research Grant, a 2008 Guggenheim Fellowship, and a 2016 Phi Kappa Phi Faculty Recognition Award. With Gabrielle Cody, Dr. Cheng co-edited a critical anthology, *Reading Contemporary Performance: Theatricality Across Genres* (Routledge, 2016).

Broderick D.V. Chow is Lecturer in Theatre at Brunel University London, UK, where he teaches performance theory, histories of drama, and musical theatre. His current research examines fitness and masculinity through the lens of performance studies, and he is also working on a monograph on British East Asian performance. Broderick has published in a wide range of journals, and is co-editor of *Žižek and Performance* (Palgrave, 2014) and of *Performance and Professional Wrestling* (Routledge, 2016).

Karen Christopher is a collaborative performance maker, performer, and teacher. As director of London-based Haranczak/Navarre Performance Projects, she is devoted to paying attention as a practice of social cooperation and looking for the unnoticed. She was with Chicago-based Goat Island performance group for 20 years until the group disbanded in 2009. Karen is an Honorary Research Fellow at the Birkbeck Centre for Contemporary Theatre, University of London, an Artist Research Fellow in the Department of Drama at Queen Mary, University of London, and Honorary Fellow of University College Falmouth.

Augusto Corrieri is a performance maker, writer, and Lecturer in Theatre & Performance at the University of Sussex. He works at the intersections between ecology and an expanded understanding of performance. He is the author of *In Place of a Show: what happens inside theatres when nothing is happening* (Bloomsbury Methuen, 2016). Using the pseudonym Vincent Gambini he is currently presenting *This is not a magic show*, a solo performance of sleight-of-hand magic.

Laura Cull Ó Maoilearca is Reader in Theatre & Performance at the University of Surrey, UK. She is author of *Theatres of Immanence: Deleuze and the Ethics of Performance* (Palgrave Macmillan, 2012), editor of *Deleuze and Performance* (Edinburgh, 2009), co-editor of *Encounters in Performance Philosophy* (Palgrave Macmillan, 2014) with Alice Lagaay, and *Manifesto Now! Instructions for Performance, Philosophy, Politics* (Intellect, 2013) with Will Daddario. Laura is a core convener of Performance Philosophy and joint series editor of the Performance Philosophy book series with Palgrave Macmillan.

Thomas F. DeFrantz is Professor and Chair of African and African American Studies at Duke University, and Director of SLIPPAGE: Performance, Culture, Technology, a research group that explores emerging technology in live performance applications. His books include *Dancing Many Drums: Excavations in African American Dance* (Wisconsin, 2002), *Dancing Revelations: Alvin Ailey's Embodiment of African American Culture* (Oxford, 2004), *Black Performance Theory* (co-edited with Anita Gonzalez, Duke, 2014), and *Choreography and Corporeality: Relay in Motion* (co-edited with Philipa Rothfield, Palgrave Macmillan, 2016).

Ricardo Dominguez is Associate Professor in the Department of Visual Arts at the University of California, San Diego, and a co-founder of The Electronic Disturbance Theater (EDT), a group who developed virtual sit-in technologies in solidarity with the Zapatistas communities in Chiapas, Mexico, in 1998. He is also a Principal/Principle Investigator at CALIT2 and the Performative Nano-Robotics Lab.

Annie Dorsen works in a variety of fields, including theatre, film, dance, and digital performance. Her most recent projects, *Yesterday Tomorrow, A Piece of Work*, and *Hello Hi There*, are part of her continuing exploration of "algorithmic theatre." Those pieces, along with *Magical* (a collaboration with choreographer Anne Juren), continue to tour in Europe and the US.

Erik Ehn's work includes *The Saint Plays, No Time Like the Present, Wolf at the Door, Tailings, Beginner*, and *Ideas of Good and Evil*. The *Soulographie* project is a series of 17 plays written over 20 years, on the history of the US in the 20th century from the point of view of its genocides (produced at La MaMa; published by 53rd State in 2012). He is Artistic Director of Tenderloin Opera Company and an alum of New Dramatists.

Rose English's uniquely interdisciplinary work combines elements of theatre, circus, opera, and poetry to explore themes of gender politics, the identity of the performer, and the metaphysics of presence. English has mounted performances in ice rinks, at the Royal Court Theatre and Tate Britain in London, and Franklin Furnace in New York. She has collaborated with horses, magicians, and acrobats. Recent projects include solo exhibitions at Charlottenborg, Copenhagen (2015), and Camden Arts Centre, London (2016).

Tim Etchells is an artist and a writer based in the UK whose work shifts between performance, visual art, and fiction. He has worked in a wide variety of contexts, notably as the leader of the Sheffield-based performance group Forced Entertainment. Recent publications include *Vacuum Days* (Storythings, 2012) and *While You Are With Us Here Tonight* (LADA, 2013). He was a Tate / Live Art Development Agency "Legacy: Thinker In Residence" Award winner in 2008, Artist of the City of Lisbon in 2014, and received the Spalding Gray Award in 2016. www.forcedentertainment.com/. www.timetchells.com/.

Andy Field is a theatremaker, curator, and co-director of the award-winning collective Forest Fringe. He has created and toured his own contemporary performance work across the UK, Europe, and the US. Andy also writes regularly on performance for a number of publications and in 2012 completed a PhD with the University of Exeter exploring the relationship between contemporary performance practice and the New York avant-gardes of the 1960s and 1970s. www.andytfield.co.uk/.

Susan Leigh Foster, choreographer and scholar, is Distinguished Professor in the Department of World Arts and Cultures/Dance at University of California at Los Angeles. She is the author of *Reading Dancing* (California, 1988), *Choreography and Narrative* (Indiana, 1998), *Dances that Describe Themselves* (Wesleyan, 2002), and *Choreographing Empathy* (Routledge, 2010). She is also the editor of three anthologies: *Choreographing History* (Indiana, 1995), *Corporealities* (Routledge, 2004), and *Worlding Dance* (Palgrave Macmillan, 2009). Three of her danced lectures can be found at the Pew Center for Arts and Heritage website: www.danceworkbook.pcah.us/susan-foster/index.html.

Nadine George-Graves is Professor of African American Performance in the Department of Theater and Dance at the University of California at San Diego. She is the author of *The Royalty of Negro Vaudeville: The Whitman Sisters and the Negotiation of Race, Gender, and Class in African American Theater, 1900–1940* (St. Martin's, 2000) and *Urban Bush Women: Twenty Years of Dance Theater, Community Engagement, and Working It Out* (Wisconsin, 2010). She is the editor of *The Oxford Handbook of Dance and Theater* (Oxford, 2015).

Kyle Gillette is the Director of Theatre and Associate Professor at Trinity University, where he writes, directs, and teaches about theatre as a laboratory for perception and thought. His scholarship includes the monograph *Railway Travel in Modern Theatre* (McFarland, 2014), a short volume on *Thornton Wilder's The Skin of Our Teeth* (Routledge, 2016), and articles in *Performance Research, Modern Drama, Comparative Drama*, and elsewhere. He has directed the work of Beckett, Brecht, Euripides, Handke, Vogel, Williams, Wilder, and others.

Diane Glancy is Professor Emerita at Macalester College. Her 2014–15 books are *Fort Marion Prisoners and the Trauma of Native Education* (nonfiction, University of Nebraska), *Report to the Department of the Interior* (poetry, University of New Mexico), and three novels, *Uprising of Goats, One of Us*, and *Ironic Witness* (Wipf & Stock). Native Voices at the Autry in Los Angeles has produced four of her plays: *Jump Kiss, Stone Heart, Salvage*, and *The Bird House*. www.dianeglancy.com/.

Yelena Gluzman makes experimental performances as Science Projects. She is a founding editor at Ugly Duckling Presse, and edits both *Emergency INDEX*, and the Emergency

Playscripts series. In 2013, she co-convened *Theorems, Proofs, Rebuttals, Propositions: A Conference of Theoretical Theater* with Esther Neff. She uses performance approaches to consider scientific research on social cognition for her PhD work in Communication, Science Studies, and Cognitive Science at the University of California, San Diego.

Matthew Goulish is dramaturg for Every house has a door and Goat Island Performance Group. His books include *39 Microlectures: in proximity of performance* (Routledge, 2000), *The Brightest Thing in the World: 3 Lectures from the Institute of Failure* (Green Lantern, 2012), and *Work from Memory: In Response to In Search of Lost Time by Marcel Proust*, a collaboration with the poet Dan Beachy-Quick (Ahsahta, 2012). He teaches writing at the School of the Art Institute of Chicago.

Christopher Grobe is Assistant Professor of English at Amherst College. His first book, *The Art of Confession: The Performance of Self from Robert Lowell to Reality TV*, is forthcoming from NYU Press. His essays on technology and performance can be found in *Theater* and *Theatre Survey* and will be the topic of his next book *Refined Mechanicals: The Realist Actor and Other Technologies*. Other essays have appeared in *PMLA*, *NLH*, *Public Books*, and the *Los Angeles Review of Books*.

Ant Hampton is a British performance maker whose work, beginning in 1998 under the name Rotozaza, has often played with a tension between liveness and automation, especially through the delivery of instructions to unrehearsed guest performers, or to the audience themselves. His more recent work, loosely brought together as "Autoteatro," tours widely and includes *Etiquette*, *The Quiet Volume*, *Cue China*, *OK OK*, *This is Not My Voice Speaking*, *The Extra People*, and *Someone Else*. Ant often collaborates with other artists, including Tim Etchells, Christophe Meierhans, Britt Hatzius, and Gert-Jan Stam. www.anthampton.com/.

Carla Harryman is known for her boundary-breaking prose, poetry, and performance. The author of many volumes, her Poets Theater and performance writings are collected in *Animal Instincts, Prose, Plays, and Essays* (This, 1989); *Memory Play* (O Books, 1994); the French and English bilingual edition *Sue in Berlin* (To Series, 2017); and in *Open Box*, a CD collaboration with Jon Raskin (2012). A CD of *Occupying Theodor W. Adorno's "Music and New Music,"* a work for speaking voice and prepared piano, is forthcoming on Rastascan Records in 2017. Her performance works have been presented nationally and internationally. She is Professor of English at Eastern Michigan University and she serves on the MFA faculty of the Milton-Avery School of the Arts at Bard College.

Jen Harvie is Professor of Contemporary Theatre and Performance at Queen Mary University of London. Her monographs include *Fair Play: Art, Performance and Neoliberalism* (Palgrave Macmillan, 2013), *Theatre & the City* (Palgrave Macmillan, 2009), *Staging the UK* (Manchester, 2005), and *The Routledge Companion to Theatre and Performance* (co-author, Routledge, 2nd ed., 2014). She co-edited *Making Contemporary Theatre* (with Andy Lavender, Manchester, 2010) and *The Only Way Home Is Through the Show: Performance Work of Lois Weaver* (with Lois Weaver, Intellect, 2016). She co-edits Palgrave Macmillan's series Theatre &.

Deirdre Heddon is Professor of Contemporary Performance at the University of Glasgow, Scotland. She is the author of *Autobiography and Performance* (Palgrave Macmillan, 2007), co-author of *Devising Performance: A Critical History* (with Jane Milling, Palgrave Macmillan, 2005), and co-editor of numerous anthologies, including most recently *It's All Allowed: The Performances of Adrian Howells* (with Dominic Johnson, Intellect, 2016).

Pablo Helguera was born in Mexico City and is a New York-based artist working with installation, sculpture, photography, drawing, socially engaged art, and performance. Helguera's work focuses in a variety of topics ranging from history, pedagogy, sociolinguistics, ethnography, memory, and the absurd, in formats that are widely varied including the lecture, museum display strategies, musical performances, and written fiction. He is the author of around 20 books, including *Education for Socially Engaged Art* (Jorge Pinto, 2011), *Art Scenes* (Jorge Pinto, 2012), *The Parable Conference* (Jorge Pinto, 2014), and *An Atlas of Commonplaces* (Jorge Pinto, 2015).

Brian Eugenio Herrera is Assistant Professor of Theater in the Lewis Center for the Arts at Princeton University. He is author of *The Latina/o Theatre Commons 2013 National Convening: A Narrative Report* (HowlRound, 2015) and *Latin Numbers: Playing Latino in Twentieth-Century U.S. Popular Performance* (Michigan, 2015), which was awarded the George Jean Nathan Prize for Dramatic Criticism. His next book details the history of the material practice of casting in US popular performance.

Lin Hixson is co-founder and director of Every house has a door and Goat Island Performance Group. She is Full Professor of Performance at the School of the Art Institute of Chicago, and received an honorary doctorate from Dartington College of Arts, University of Plymouth, in 2007. She was awarded a Foundation for the Arts Award in 2014 and the United States Artists Ziporyn Fellowship in 2009.

Wendy Houstoun is a London-based artist who has worked with experimental movement and theatre forms since 1980. She has worked collaboratively with Forced Entertainment, DV8 Physical Theatre, Nigel Charnock, and Vincent Dance Company. Solo works include *Haunted, Happy Hour*, and *Desert Island Dances*, which all toured internationally. Following her last works, *50 Acts* and *Pact with Pointlessness*, she is completing the trilogy with a new work, *My Life in Art (the wilderness years).*

Kimberly Jannarone is Professor of Theater Arts at UC Santa Cruz, where she holds the Gary Licker Memorial Chair. In 2015–16, she was Visiting Professor at the Yale School of Drama and a Beinecke Fellow at Yale Repertory Theater. She is the author of *Artaud and His Doubles* (Michigan, 2010) and editor of *Vanguard Performance Beyond Left and Right* (Michigan, 2015). She directs experimental performance and has co-translated, with Erik Butler, works by contemporary French playwrights.

Julia Jarcho is a playwright and director in New York with the company Minor Theater (minortheater.org). Her plays include *American Treasure, Dreamless Land, Nomads*, and *Grimly Handsome*, which won a 2013 OBIE Award; she received a Doris Duke Impact Award in 2014. She is Assistant Professor of English at NYU, where she teaches and writes about modern drama, playwriting, and critical theory. Her book *Writing and the Modern Stage* is forthcoming from Cambridge University Press.

Originally from Alaska, **Emily Johnson** is an artist of Yup'ik descent, who has been making body-based work since 1998. She is a Bessie Award-winning choreographer, 2016 Guggenheim Fellow, and recipient of the 2014 Doris Duke Artist Award. Her written work has been published in *Dance Research Journal* and *Movement Research Journal*, and has been commissioned by SFMOMA and Pew Center for Arts and Heritage. www.catalystdance.com/.

Rhodessa Jones is Co-Artistic Director of the performance company Cultural Odyssey and the Director of the Medea Project: Theater for Incarcerated Women, a performance workshop designed to achieve personal and social transformation with incarcerated women. She has been recipient of a United States Artist Fellowship, an Honorary Doctorate from California College of the Arts, and a lifetime achievement award from the city of San Francisco.

Rachel Joseph is Assistant Professor in the Department of Human Communication and Theatre at Trinity University. She has published essays in *Performance Research*, *College Literature*, *Word & Image*, and chapters in a range of books. Her short stories and plays have appeared in literary magazines, most recently the *North American Review*.

Joe Kelleher is Professor of Theatre and Performance at Roehampton University, London. His books include *The Illuminated Theatre: Studies on the Suffering of Images* (Routledge, 2015) and *Theatre & Politics* (Palgrave Macmillan, 2009). He is co-author with Claudia and Romeo Castellucci, Chiara Giudi, and Nicholas Ridout of *The Theatre of Socìetas Raffaello Sanzio* (Routledge, 2007). His articles have appeared in journals such as *Performance Research*, *Maska*, *Frakcija*, and *Theater* magazine.

Baz Kershaw is Professor Emeritus at the University of Warwick, UK. His extensive experimental/community/radical performance works include shows at London Drury Lane Arts Lab with Welfare State International and, since 2000, several eco-specific events in South West England. Publications include *Politics of Performance* (Routledge, 1992), *The Radical in Performance* (Routledge, 1999), *Theatre Ecology* (Cambridge, 2007) and (with Helen Nicholson) *Research Methods in Theatre and Performance* (Edinburgh, 2011). In 2010 he created an Earthrise Repair Shop for mending broken imaginings of Earth.

Ju Yon Kim is Associate Professor of English at Harvard University. She is the author of *The Racial Mundane: Asian American Performance and the Embodied Everyday* (NYU, 2015) as well as articles published in *Modern Drama, Modernism/modernity*, the *Journal of Transnational American Studies*, *Theatre Journal*, and *Theatre Survey*. She is currently working on a book manuscript about suspicion and Asian American performance.

Suk-Young Kim is Professor of Critical Studies in the Department of Theater at the University of California, Los Angeles, where she co-directs the Center for Performance Studies. She is the author of *Illusive Utopia: Theater, Film, and Everyday Performance in North Korea* (Michigan, 2010), *DMZ Crossing: Performing Emotional Citizenship Along the Korean Border* (Columbia, 2014), and the co-author of *Long Road Home: A Testimony of a North Korean Labor Camp Survivor* (Columbia, 2009).

Petra Kuppers is a disability culture activist, a community performance artist, and a Professor at the University of Michigan. She leads The Olimpias, a performance research collective. Her *Disability Culture and Community Performance: Find a Strange and Twisted Shape* (Palgrave Macmillan, 2011) explores arts-based research methods. She is editor of *Somatic Engagement* (ChainLinks, 2011), and the author of *Studying Disability Arts and Culture: An Introduction* (Palgrave Macmillan, 2014), a book of practical exercises for classrooms. A new poetry collection, *Pearl Stitch*, appears in 2016 with Spuyten Duyvil.

Claudia La Rocco is the author of *The Best Most Useless Dress* (Badlands Unlimited, 2014), selected poetry, performance texts, images and criticism, and the novel *petit cadeau*, which was published by The Chocolate Factory Theater as a print edition of one and a four-day, interdisciplinary live edition. She edited *Dancers, Buildings and People in the Streets*, the catalogue for Danspace Project's PLATFORM 2015, which she curated. Her work has been presented by The Walker Art Center, The Kitchen, The Whitney Museum of American Art, and elsewhere.

Dominika Laster is Assistant Professor of Theatre at the University of New Mexico. She was a Mellon Postdoctoral Fellow in Interdisciplinary Performance Studies at Yale (IPSY) from 2011 to 2013. She is the author of *Grotowski's Bridge Made of Memory: Embodied Memory, Witnessing and Transmission in the Grotowski Work* (Seagull, 2016). She is the editor of *Loose Screws: Nine New Plays from Poland* (Seagull, 2015). Dominika has also published articles in *Performance Research, New Theatre Quarterly, Slavic and Eastern European Performance*, and *TDR*.

Ralph Lemon is a choreographer, writer, and visual artist. He currently serves as the Artistic Director of Cross Performance, a company dedicated to the creation of cross-cultural and cross-disciplinary performance and presentation.

André Lepecki is a writer, curator, and Associate Professor in the Department of Performance Studies at Tisch School of the Arts, New York University. He is the author of *Exhausting Dance: Performance and the Politics of Movement* (Routledge, 2006), and of *Singularities: Dance in the Age of Performance* (Routledge, 2016), as well as the editor of several anthologies on dance and performance theory.

Casey Llewellyn is a writer and theatre maker whose work interrogates identity, collectivity, and form. Performances include: *O, Earth* (The Foundry Theatre), *I Am Bleeding All Over the Place: A Living History Tour* (co-written with Brooke O'Harra), *Obsession Piece, The Quiet Way, Existing Conditions* (co-written with Claudia Rankine), and *Come in. Be with me. Don't touch me.* www.caseyllewellyn.com/.

Claire MacDonald's work takes place between speech and writing, wherever conversation meets collaboration. She began as a performance maker, continued as a critical educator and cultural leader, and is now a Unitarian minister and a Professorial Fellow at the Royal Central School of Speech and Drama. She publishes widely across the spectrum of her interests in art, writing, and performance, and on practice-based research in the arts. Her recent collection of plays, *Utopia*, was published in 2015 by Intellect.

Erin Manning holds a University Research Chair in Relational Art and Philosophy in the Faculty of Fine Arts at Concordia University. She is also the director of the *SenseLab* (www.senselab.ca), a laboratory that explores the intersections between art practice and philosophy through the matrix of the sensing body in movement. Publications include *Always More Than One: Individuation's Dance* (Duke, 2013), *Relationscapes: Movement, Art, Philosophy* (MIT, 2009) and, with Brian Massumi, *Thought in the Act: Passages in the Ecology of Experience* (Minnesota, 2014) and *The Minor Gesture* (Duke, 2016).

Caden Manson and Jemma Nelson's work spans performance, visual art, new media, creative coding, and artist organizing. They founded the performance and media company BigArtGroup.com, the global artist network ContemporaryPerformance.com, publish the *Contemporary Performance Almanac*, and curate the annual Special Effects Festival in NYC. Their writing has been published in *PAJ*, *Theater* magazine, *Mouvement*, and *Theatre Heute*. Their performance and media work has been presented internationally at Festival d'Automne a Paris, Hebbel Am Ufer, and elsewhere.

Bonnie Marranca is founding editor and publisher of PAJ Publications/*PAJ: A Journal of Performance and Art*, and a recent recipient of the Association for Theatre in Higher Education Excellence in Editing Award for Sustained Achievement. She is the author of *Ecologies of Theatre* (PAJ, 1997), *Theatrewritings* (PAJ, 1984), and *Performance Histories* (PAJ, 2007), and editor of several play anthologies and essay collections. Her most recent book is *Conversations with Meredith Monk* (PAJ, 2014). Bonnie Marranca is Professor of Theatre at The New School for Liberal Arts/Eugene Lang College.

Scholar and theater-maker **Irma Mayorga** is Assistant Professor of Theater at Dartmouth College. Her scholarship explores contemporary theatre and performance by US people of color, Chicana/o Expressive Culture, and US Latina/o identity formations more broadly. Her published works include *The Panza Monologues, Second Edition* (Texas, 2014), co-written with collaborator Virginia Grise.

Timothy McCain is an actor, director, and playwright. He was a cofounding member of Goat Island Performance Group. His work has been seen at P.S. 122 in New York, the ICA in London, the Walker Art Center in Minneapolis, MCA in Chicago, as well as other venues throughout the US and Europe. His plays *The True* (2007) and *Mmmoa!* (2009) were both finalists for the Actors Theatre of Louisville Heideman Award.

Michael McMillan is a London-based writer, playwright, artist/curator, and scholar of Vincentian migrant heritage. His work includes *The West Indian Front Room* (2005–6), *No Colour Bar: Black British Art in Action 1960–1990* (2015–16), *Doing Nothing is Not an Option* (2015), and *Rockers, Soulheads & Lovers: Sound Systems Back in Da Day* (2015–16). He is the first Arts Doctorate from Middlesex University, and is currently Associate Lecturer in Cultural Studies at the London College of Fashion, University of the Arts London.

Cherríe Moraga is the recipient of the United States Artist Rockefeller Fellowship for Literature. She is an Artist in Residence in the Department of Theater & Performance Studies and Comparative Studies in Race & Ethnicity at Stanford University. In 2017, her play *The Mathematics of Love* will receive its world premiere at Brava Theater Center in San Francisco. She recently completed a memoir entitled *The Native Country of a Heart—A Geography of Desire.*

Bush Moukarzel is co-artistic director of Dead Centre, a theatre company based between Dublin and London. Recent works include *LIPPY* and *Chekhov's First Play*, both of which have toured internationally. Other projects include *Human Error* for Mladinsko theatre, Ljubljana, and *Shakespeare's Last Play* for Schaubühne, Berlin.

John H. Muse is Assistant Professor in English and Theater and Performance Studies at the University of Chicago. His research explores work that tests the perceived boundaries of media: plays that resemble visual art, poems or novels in dramatic form, metatheatre, and digital, impossible, or otherwise virtual theatre. His book *Microdramas: Crucibles for Theater and Time*, forthcoming from University of Michigan Press, explores brevity in theatre since the late nineteenth century and argues that very short plays reveal fundamental assumptions about theatre's limits and possibilities.

Nature Theater of Oklahoma is an award-winning New York art and performance enterprise founded in 2003 by Pavol Liska and Kelly Copper. With each new project, they attempt to set an impossible challenge for themselves, the audience, and their collaborators, making "the work we don't know how to make," an approach yielding new amalgams of opera, dance, theatre, and film. Kelly and Pavol are each recipients of the Doris Duke Performing Artist Award and the Alpert Award in the Arts.

Yvette Nolan is a playwright, director, and dramaturge. Her plays include *The Unplugging*, *The Birds* (a modern adaptation of Aristophanes' comedy), *from thine eyes*, *Ham and the Ram*, *Annie Mae's Movement*, *Job's Wife*, and *BLADE*. From 2003 to 2011, she served as Artistic Director of Native Earth Performing Arts in Toronto. Her book *Medicine Shows*, about Indigenous theatre in Canada, was published in 2015 by Playwrights Canada Press. She is an Artistic Associate with Signal Theatre.

Darren O'Donnell is the Artistic and Research Director of Mammalian Diving Reflex. He holds a BFA in theatre, M.Sc. in urban planning, and has studied traditional Chinese and western medicine at the Shiatsu School of Canada. He is the author of *Social Acupuncture* (Coach House, 2006), which argues for an aesthetics of civic engagement. His stage-based works include *All the Sex I've Ever Had* and his performance works include *Haircuts by Children, Eat the Street*, and *The Children's Choice Awards*.

Sylvan Oswald creates plays, texts, publications, and video exploring the ways we forge our individual and national identities. His plays have been developed and produced at theaters around the US. He is the creator of the lo-fi semi-improvised web series *Outtakes* and a co-creator of *Play A Journal of Plays*. Sylvan is Assistant Professor of Playwriting in the School of Theater, Film and Television at the University of California, Los Angeles, an affiliated artist at Clubbed Thumb, and an alum of New Dramatists.

Helen Paris is co-artistic director of Curious. Curious has produced over 40 projects in performance and film and has been supported by institutions including the Royal Shakespeare Company, British Council Showcase at the Edinburgh Festival, Sydney Opera House, and Center for Contemporary Arts in Shanghai. Her recent book, co-written with Leslie Hill, is entitled *Performing Proximity: Curious Intimacies* (Palgrave Macmillan, 2014). She is Associate Professor of Performance at Stanford University. Curious is produced by Artsadmin. www.placelessness.com/.

Jennifer Parker-Starbuck is Professor and Head of the Department of Drama, Theatre and Performance at the University of Roehampton, London. She is the co-editor of *Theatre Journal* and the author of *Cyborg Theatre: Corporeal/Technological Intersections in Multimedia Performance* (Palgrave Macmillan, 2011) and co-editor of *Performing Animality: Animals in Performance Practice* (Palgrave Macmillan, 2015). Her essay "Animal Ontologies and Media Representations: Robotics, Puppets, and the Real of *War Horse*" (*Theatre Journal*) received ATHE's 2014 Outstanding Article award.

Peggy Phelan is the Ann O'Day Maples Professor in the Arts, Professor of Theater & Performance Studies and English at Stanford University, as well as the Denning Family Director of the Stanford Arts Institute. She edited and contributed to *Live Art in LA: Performance in Southern California, 1970–1983* (Routledge, 2012), and writes frequently about feminism, contemporary art, and psychoanalysis.

VK Preston is Assistant Professor at the Centre for Drama, Theatre, and Performance Studies at the University of Toronto. She writes on performance, politics, historiography, witchcraft, and dance. Her work appears in *TDR*, *The Oxford Handbook of Dance and Theater*, *Performance Research*, *TheatreForum*, and *History, Memory, Performance*.

Joshua Rains is a visual artist whose work explores intimacy, invasion, and exploitation in a continually shrinking world. He currently splits his time between Chicago and Los Angeles. He is pursuing his MFA at the University of Southern California. www.drawjoshdraw.com/.

Claudia Rankine is the author of five collections of poetry including *Citizen: An American Lyric* (Graywolf/Penguin, 2015) and *Don't Let Me Be Lonely* (Graywolf, 2004), two plays including *Provenance of Beauty: A South Bronx Travelogue*, and is the editor of several anthologies including *The Racial Imaginary: Writers on Race in the Life of the Mind* (Fence Books, 2005). Among her numerous awards and honors, Rankine is the recipient of the National Book Critics Poetry Prize and awards from the Lannan Foundation and the National Endowment of the Arts. She is the Frederick Iseman Professor of Poetry at Yale University.

Alan Read is Professor of Theatre at King's College, London. He was Director of the Council of Europe Workshop on Theatre and Communities, and Rotherhithe Theatre Workshop in the Docklands area of South East London in the 1980s, and then worked as Director of Talks at the Institute of Contemporary Arts in the 1990s. He is the author of *Theatre & Law* (Palgrave Macmillan, 2015), *Theatre in the Expanded Field* (Metheun, 2014), and *Theatre, Intimacy & Engagement: The Last Human Venue* (Palgrave Macmillan, 2008), and other books.

Nicholas Ridout is Professor of Theatre at Queen Mary University, London. He is the author of *Stage Fright, Animals and Other Theatrical Problems* (Cambridge, 2006), *Theatre & Ethics* (Palgrave Macmillan, 2009), and *Passionate Amateurs: Theatre, Communism, and Love*

(Michigan, 2013). With Joe Kelleher, and members of the company, he co-authored *The Theatre of Socìetas Raffaello Sanzio* (Routledge, 2007) and, also with Joe Kelleher, co-edited *Contemporary Theatres in Europe* (Routledge, 2006).

Carl Hancock Rux is a playwright, poet, novelist, essayist, performer, theatre director, and recording artist. He is the author of several publications including a book of poetry, *Pagan Operetta* (Fly by Night, 1998), the novel *Asphalt* (Atria, 2004), and the OBIE award-winning play *Talk* (TCG, 2003). He is the recipient of numerous awards including the Doris Duke Awards for New Works, the Doris Duke Charitable Fund, the New York Foundation for the Arts Prize, and the Alpert Award in the Arts.

Daniel Sack is Assistant Professor in the Department of English and the Commonwealth Honors College at the University of Massachusetts Amherst. He is the author of *After Live: Possibility, Potentiality, and the Future of Performance* (Michigan, 2015) and *Samuel Beckett's Krapp's Last Tape* (Routledge, 2016). He is the editor of *Imagined Theatres: Writing for a Theoretical Stage* (Routledge, 2017).

Nick Salvato is Associate Professor and Chair of the Department of Performing and Media Arts at Cornell University. He is the author of *Uncloseting Drama: American Modernism and Queer Performance* (Yale, 2010), *Knots Landing* (Wayne State, TV Milestones Series, 2015), and *Obstruction* (Duke, 2016). His essays have appeared in a number of venues, including *Critical Inquiry, Criticism, Discourse, Journal of Dramatic Theory and Criticism, Modern Drama, TDR, Theatre Journal*, and *Theatre Studies*.

Richard Schechner is University Professor of Performance Studies at New York University. He is editor of *TDR*. His books include *Environmental Theater* (Hawthorn, 1973), *The End of Humanism* (PAJ, 1982), *Between Theater and Anthropology* (Pennsylvania, 1985), *Performance Theory* (Routledge, 1988), *Performance Studies: An Introduction* (Routledge, 2013), and *Performed Imaginaries* (Routledge, 2014). His theatre productions have been seen in the US, Romania, Poland, France, India, China, Taiwan, the UK, and the Republic of South Africa. He writes scholarly works, poetry, and short fiction.

Rebecca Schneider, Professor of Theatre Arts and Performance Studies at Brown University, is author of *The Explicit Body in Performance* (Routledge, 1997), *Performing Remains: Art and War in Times of Theatrical Reenactment* (Routledge, 2011), and *Theatre & History* (Palgrave Macmillan, 2014). She has edited several special collections and authored numerous essays including "Hello Dolly Well Hello Dolly: The Double and Its Theatre," "Solo Solo Solo," "It Seems As If I am Dead: Zombie Capitalism and Theatrical Labor," and "Remembering Feminist Remimesis."

Since 1999, **Rajni Shah** has worked independently and with other artists to create the conditions for performances, publications, conversations, and gatherings on and off-stage. Key performance works include *The Awkward Position* (2003–4), *Mr Quiver* (2005–8), *small gifts* (2006–8), *Dinner with America* (2007–9), *Glorious* (2010–12), *Experiments in Listening* (2014–15), *Lying Fallow* (2014–15), and *Song* (2016).

Andrew Sofer is Professor of English at Boston College. His books include *The Stage Life of Props* (Michigan, 2003), *Wave* (Main Street Rag, 2011), and *Dark Matter: Invisibility* *in Drama, Theater, and Performance* (Michigan, 2013). His essays have appeared in *Theatre Journal*, *Journal of Dramatic Theory and Criticism*, *Modern Drama*, *Comparative Drama*, *English Literary Renaissance*, *The Oxford Handbook of Early Modern Theatre*, *The Blackwell Companion to Twentieth-Century American Drama*, and elsewhere. He holds an MFA in Directing and is a widely published poet.

Aaron C. Thomas is Assistant Professor of Theatre History and Literature in the School of Performing Arts at the University of Central Florida. His research focuses on the function of violent masculinity in contemporary culture. His book project, *The Violate Man*, analyzes representations of male/male sexual violence in theatre, film, literature, and television since the 1960s. His most recent essays have been published in *Modern Drama*, *Theatre Topics*, and *Theatre Survey*.

Rodrigo Toscano's newest book of poetry is *Explosion Rocks Springfield* (Fence Books, 2016). Previous books include *Deck of Deeds* (Counterpath, 2012), *Collapsible Poetics Theater* (Fence Books, National Poetry Series selection, 2008), *To Leveling Swerve* (Krupskaya, 2004), *Platform* (Atelos, 2003), *The Disparities* (Green Integer, 2002), and *Partisans* (O Books, 1999). He is also the artistic director and writer for the Collapsible Poetics Theater (CPT). He works for the Labor Institute as a national project director. Rodrigo lives in New Orleans.

Fintan Walsh is Senior Lecturer in Theatre and Performance Studies at Birkbeck, University of London, and Co-Director of the Birkbeck Centre for Contemporary Theatre. Recent publications include the book *Queer Performance and Contemporary Ireland: Dissent and Disorientation* (Palgrave Macmillan, 2016), a chapter on generous performance in *It's All Allowed: The Performances of Adrian Howells* (2016), and an article on public intimacy in *TDR* (2014). He is Associate Editor of *Theatre Research International*.

Nia O. Witherspoon is a multidisciplinary Brooklyn/Phoenix-based artist-scholar investigating blackness, gender/sexuality, and intergenerational trauma. An Assistant Professor in Theatre and Performance of the Americas at Arizona State University, Witherspoon's work has been recognized by the Mellon Foundation, the Astraea Lesbian Foundation for Justice, Downtown Urban Theatre Festival, the Wurlitzer Foundation, Lambda Literary, and Theatre Bay Area, and her works have been staged at venues such as BRIC, HERE, the National Black Theatre, and Theatre Artaud. She is published or forthcoming in *Yellow Medicine Review*, *The Journal of Popular Culture*, *Imaniman: Poets Writing in the Anzalduan Borderlands*, and *Women, Collective Creation, and Devised Performance*.

Isaiah Matthew Wooden is Assistant Professor in the Department of Performing Arts at American University where he teaches courses in the history, theory, and practice of theatre. A director-dramaturg and interdisciplinary scholar of twentieth and twenty-first century American drama and "post" era black expressive culture, he has published in both academic and popular venues, including *Callaloo*, *Journal of Dramatic Theory and Criticism*, *Theatre Journal*, *PAJ*, *Theater Magazine*, and *The Huffington Post*, among others.

W. B. Worthen, Alice Brady Pels Professor in the Arts, chairs the Department of Theatre at Barnard College, and co-chairs the PhD in Theatre at Columbia University.

He is the author of several books and many articles in drama and performance theory, most recently *Shakespeare Performance Studies* (Cambridge, 2014).

Harvey Young is Chair of the Department of Theatre at Northwestern University, and Professor of African American Studies, Performance Studies, and Radio/Television/Film. His books include *Embodying Black Experience* (Michigan, 2010), *Theatre & Race* (Palgrave Macmillan, 2013), and *The Cambridge Companion to African American Theatre* (Cambridge, 2012).

Related works

Note: In addition to any sources mentioned in the theatres and their accompanying glosses, the contributors have noted works that relate to, or have inspired, their writing. Except where stated, each heading does not distinguish between the theatre and its paired gloss. In certain cases, the contributors have decided to avoid any such references.

1–3. 137 Titles (I, II, and III)

Barthelme, Donald. "The Flight of the Pigeons from the Palace." In *40 Stories,* 130–40. New York: Putnam, 1987.

Bock & Vincenzi. *invisible dances ... from afar: a show that will never be shown.* London: Artsadmin, 2004.

Calvino, Italo. *If on a Winter's Night a Traveler.* Translated by William Weaver. New York: Harcourt Brace Jovanovich, 1982.

Dirty Work. Conceived and designed by Tim Etchells and Forced Entertainment. Premiere 1998.

Etchells, Tim. *The Broken World.* London: Heinemann, 2008.

Etchells, Tim. *The Rules of the Game.* Exhibition Project with text and images. Created with Hugo Glendinning and Forced Entertainment, 2001.

Etchells, Tim. *A Short Message Spectacle (An S.M.S).* Mobile phone message project and imaginary performance over ten days. 2010.

Liversidge, Peter. *Proposals Pieces, 2006–2016 ongoing.* Accessed July 24, 2016. http://www.peterliversidge.com/.

McLean, Bruce. "King for a Day and 999 other pieces/ works/ things/ etc." Proposal for a Retrospective from 1972. *The Ubuweb Anthology of Conceptual Writing.* Accessed July 24, 2016. http://www.ubu.com/concept/mclean_king.html/.

Obrist, Hans Ulrich, ed. *Do It: The Compendium.* New York: Independent Curators International, 2013.

4. After dinner

Adorno, Theodor W. *Aesthetic Theory.* Edited by Gretel Adorno and Rolf Tiedermann. Translated by Robert Hullot-Kentor. Minneapolis: University of Minnesota Press, 1997.

Kant, Immanuel. *Critique of Judgment.* Edited by Nicholas Walker. Translated by James Creed Meredith. Oxford: Oxford University Press, 2007.

Sade, Marquis de. *The 120 Days of Sodom and Other Writings.* Translated by Austryn Wainhouse and Richard Seaver. New York: Grove Press, 1966.

5. "All the world's a ..."

Kershaw, Baz. "Performance Ecologies, Biotic Rights and Retro-Modernisation." *Research in Drama Education* 17, no. 2 (2012): 265–87.

RELATED WORKS

Kershaw, Baz. "Performed by Ecologies: How *Homo sapiens* Could Subvert Present-Day Futures." *Performing Ethos: An International Journal of Ethics in Theatre & Performance,* 4, no. 2 (2015): 113–34.

Kershaw, Baz. "'This is the way the world ends, not …?': On Performance Compulsion and Climate Change." *Performance Research* 17, no. 4 (2012): 5–17.

Klein, Naomi. *This Changes Everything: Capitalism vs. the Climate.* London: Allen Lane, 2014.

Mason, Paul. *Postcapitalism: A Guide to Our Future.* London: Allen Lane, 2015.

Vince, Gaia. *Adventures in the Anthropocene: A Journey to the Heart of the Planet We Made.* London: Chatto & Windus, 2014.

6 and 7. Ancestor calls—Guerrero and Malinche

Moraga, Cherríe. *The Mathematics of Love.* Premiere 2017.

Moraga, Cherríe. *The Native Country of a Heart—A Geography of Desire* (Memoir, 2016). Stuart Bernstein, Representation for Artists. www.stuartbernstein.com/.

Moraga, Cherríe. *The Hungry Woman: A Mexican Medea.* Albuquerque: West End Press, 2001.

Moraga, Cherríe. *A Xicana Codex of Changing Consciousness: Writings, 2000–2010.* Durham: Duke University Press, 2011.

8. Anecdote of the stage (after Stevens)

Frisch, Max. *Tagebuch 1946–1949.* Frankfurt am Main: Suhrkamp Verlag, 1950, 63–65, as quoted and translated by Martin Esslin, "The Stage: Reality, Symbol, Metaphor." In *Drama and Symbolism*, 1–13. New York: Cambridge University Press, 1982.

Stevens, Wallace. "Anecdote of the Jar." In *Wallace Stevens: Collected Poetry & Prose,* edited by Frank Kermode and Joan Richardson, 60. New York: Library of America, 1997.

9. Animal friendship: A docudrama

Adorno, Theodor W. "Cultural Criticism and Society," in *Prisms,* translated by Shierry Weber Nicholsen and Samuel Weber, 17–34. Cambridge, MA: MIT Press, 1981.

"特訓するねこ。." *YouTube* video, 1:31. Posted by mugumogu, October 25, 2008. https://www.youtube.com/watch?v=hPzNl6NKAG0/.

"Cat In A Shark Costume Chases A Duck While Riding A Roomba." *YouTube* video, 2:46. Posted by TexasGirly1979, November 1, 2012. https://www.youtube.com/watch?v=Of2HU3LGdbo/.

"Cute Cats Playing Patty Cake! THE ORIGINAL!" *YouTube* video, 1:38. Posted by hkbecky, September 10, 2008. https://www.youtube.com/watch?v=KvxCv_yrcCY/.

Lufkin, Bryan. "Why Cats Rule the Internet Instead of Dogs." *Gizmodo.* 11 September 2015. Accessed July 23, 2016. http://gizmodo.com/why-cats-rule-the-internet-instead-of-dogs-1728316152/.

Ridout, Nicholas. *Stage Fright, Animals, and Other Theatrical Problems.* Cambridge: Cambridge University Press, 2006.

10. The art of forgetting

Beckett, Samuel. *Proust and Three Dialogues.* London: John Calder, 1989.

Beckett, Samuel. *Waiting for Godot.* New York: Grove Press, 2011.

Carlson, Marvin. *The Haunted Stage: The Theatre as Memory Machine.* Ann Arbor: University of Michigan, 2003.

Critchley, Simon. *Memory Theater.* New York: Other Press, 2015.

11. Astigmatisms

Ahmed, Sara. *Strange Encounters: Embodied Others in Post-Coloniality.* London and New York: Routledge, 2000.

Blau, Herbert. *Take Up the Bodies: Theater at the Vanishing Point*. Urbana: University of Illinois Press, 1982.
English, Darby. *How to See a Work of Art in Total Darkness*. Cambridge, MA: MIT Press, 2007.
Fleetwood, Nicole R. *Troubling Vision: Performance, Visuality, and Blackness*. Chicago: University of Chicago Press, 2011.
Merleau-Ponty, Maurice. *Signs*. Translated by Richard C. McCleary. Evanston: Northwestern University Press, 1964.
Phelan, Peggy. *Unmarked: The Politics of Performance*. London and New York: Routledge, 1993.

12. Candle tears

Parks, Suzan-Lori. "Possession." In *The America Play and Other Works,* 3–5. New York: Theatre Communication Group, 1995.
Zimmer, Carl. "The Face of Nature Changes as Art and Science Evolve." *New York Times*. November 23, 2004. Accessed July 24, 2016. http://www.nytimes.com/2004/11/23/science/the-face-of-nature-changes-as-art-and-science-evolve.html.

13. Casting, four ways

Banks, Daniel. "The Welcome Table: Casting for an Integrated Society." *Theatre Topics* 23, no. 1 (2013): 1–18.
Herrera, Brian Eugenio. "There Is Power in Casting." *Youth Theatre Journal* 29, no. 2 (2015): 146–51.

14. A Chinese actor's late style

Chow, Broderick D.V. "Here is a Story for Me: Representation and Visibility in *Miss Saigon* and *The Orphan of Zhao*." *Contemporary Theatre Review* 24, no. 4 (2014): 507–16.
Bruce Lee. "Bruce Lee, the Lost Interview (Part 1 of 3)." Filmed 1971. *YouTube* video, 7:50. Accessed July 24, 2016. https://www.youtube.com/watch?v=DIdVHTz8b28&feature/.

15. Cities of refuge

Derrida, Jacques. *On Cosmopolitanism and Forgiveness*. Translated by Mark Dooley and Michael Hughes. London and New York: Routledge, 2001.
Kant, Immanuel. *Perpetual Peace: A Philosophical Essay*. Translated by Mary Campbell Smith. New York: Garland, 1972.
Levinas, Emmanuel. *Beyond the Verse: Talmudic Reading and Lectures*. Translated by Gary D. Mole. London: Athlone Press, 1994.

16. The classroom

Malmed, Jesse. "Ventriloquism for Dummies." In *The New [New] Corpse*, edited by Caroline Picard, 74–89. Chicago: Green Lantern Press, 2015.
Wright, Jay. *The Presentable Art of Reading Absence*. Champaign, IL: Dalkey Archive Press, 2008.

17. Clockfire

Artaud, Antonin. *The Theater and Its Double*. Translated by Mary Caroline Richards. New York: Grove Press, 1958.
Ball, Jonathan. *Clockfire*. Toronto: Coach House Books, 2006.
Benjamin, Walter. "The Work of Art in the Age of Mechanical Reproduction." In *Illuminations: Essays and Reflections*, edited by Hannah Arendt, translated by Harry Zohn, 217–52. New York: Schocken Books, 1969.

RELATED WORKS

Calvino, Italo. *Invisible Cities*. Translated by William Weaver. London: Vintage, 2002.
Ono, Yoko. *Grapefruit: A Book of Instructions and Drawings*. New York: Simon & Schuster, 2000.

18. , Colon;zations and exclamations!: A set piece staged for the page

Brody, Jennifer DeVere. *Punctuation: Art, Politics, and Play*. Durham: Duke University Press, 2008.
González, Jennifer. "The Appended Subject: Race and Identity as Digital Assemblage." In *The Feminism and Visual Culture Reader*, edited by Amelia Jones, 534–44. London and New York: Routledge, 2003.
Ronell, Avital. *The Telephone Book: Technology, Schizophrenia, Electric Speech*. Lincoln: University of Nebraska Press, 1989.
Schor, Mira. *Wet: On Painting, Feminism, and Art Culture*. Durham: Duke University Press, 1997.

19. The copper thieves

Danziger, Sheldon, Koji Chavez, and Erin Cumberworth. "Poverty and the Great Recession." Stanford Center on Poverty and Inequality, 2012. Accessed July 24, 2016. https://web.stanford.edu/group/recessiontrends/cgi-bin/web/sites/all/themes/barron/pdf/Poverty_fact_sheet.pdf/.
Delgado, Richard, and Jean Stefancic. *The Latino/a Condition: A Critical Reader*. New York: New York University Press, 1998.
Massey, Douglas S. "Immigration and the Great Recession." Stanford Center on Poverty and Inequality, 2012. Accessed July 24, 2016. https://web.stanford.edu/group/recessiontrends/cgi-bin/web/sites/all/themes/barron/pdf/Immigration_fact_sheet.pdf/.

20. Court theatre

21. Crow takes hat

Benjamin, Walter. "The Storyteller: Reflections on the Works of Nikolai Leskov." In *Illuminations*, edited by Hannah Arendt, translated by Harry Zohn, 83–109. New York: Schocken Books, 1969.
Ignatius of Loyola, *The Spiritual Exercises of Saint Ignatius of Loyola*. 5th ed. Translated by W.H. Longridge. London: A.R. Mowbray, 1955.
Kennedy, Adrienne. "The Owl Answers." In *Adrienne Kennedy in One Act*, 25–46. Minneapolis: University of Minnesota Press, 1988.
Momaday, N. Scott. *The Man Made of Words: Essays, Stories, Passages*. New York: St. Martin's Press, 1997.
Porette, Margaret. *The Mirror of Simple Souls*. Translated and edited by Edmund Colledge, J.C. Marler, and Judith Grant. Notre Dame: University of Notre Dame Press, 1999.

22. Crowds with the shape of reason missing

Baldessari, John. *Crowds with Shape of Reason Missing*. Print on handmade paper. Suite of photo-montage mixed media works from 1980 to 1985.
Conrad, Joseph. *Heart of Darkness*. Edited by Robert Kimbrough. New York: W. W. Norton, 1988.
Dickens, Charles. *David Copperfield*. London: Bradbury and Evans, 1850.
"Platform: Arts. Activism. Education. Research." Accessed July 24, 2016. http://platformlondon.org/2016/03/21/tate-bp-not-the-end/.
Pryce, Lois. "Yvonne Stagg and the Wall of Death," *The Independent*, Tuesday 16 June, 2015. Accessed July 24, 2016. http://www.independent.co.uk/arts-entertainment/yvonne-stagg-and-the-wall-of-death-the-queen-of-dreamland-10324541.html/.
Tagg, John. "A Discourse (With Shape of Reason Missing)." *Art History* 15, no. 3 (1992): 351–73.

23. Dance for Baghdad

Jelinek, Elfriede. *Bambiland*. Berlin: Rowohlt Verlag, 2004.
The Report of the Iraq Inquiry. London: House of Commons, 2016.

24. dat Black Mermaid Man Lady/Home

Bridgforth, Sharon. "delta dandi: Ritual/Jazz Theater." In *Solo/Black/Woman: Scripts, Interviews, and Essays,* edited by E. Patrick Johnson and Ramón Rivera-Servera, 185–226. Evanston: Northwestern University Press, 2014.
Goldberg, Jonathan. "Sodomy in the New World." *Social Text* 29 (1991): 46–56.
Hemphill, Essex. *Ceremonies: Prose and Poetry*. San Francisco: Cleis, 1992.
Jones, Omi Osun Joni L. *Theatrical Jazz: Performance, Àse, and the Power of the Present Moment*. Columbus: The Ohio State University Press, 2015.
Lorde, Audre. *Zami: A New Spelling of My Name*. Watertown, MA: Persephone Press, 1982.
Mahone, Sydne, ed. *Moon Marked and Touched by the Sun: Plays by African-American Women*. New York: Theatre Communications Group, 1994.
Somé, Malidoma. "Gays: Guardians of the Gates: An Interview with Malidoma Somé." Interview by Burt H. Hoff. *Menweb.org*, September 1993. Accessed July 24, 2016. http://www.menweb.org/somegay.htm.

25. Dealing

Beckett, Samuel. *Collected Shorter Plays*. New York: Grove Press, 2010.
Fornés, María Irene. "Tango Palace." In *Plays for Tomorrow: Volume 2*, edited by Arthur H. Ballet, 11–39. Minneapolis: University of Minnesota Press, 1966.
Jarry, Alfred. "Absolute Love." In *Three Early Novels: Collected Works II*, edited by Alastair Brotchie and Paul Edwards, translated by Paul Edwards, 219–68. London: Atlas Press, 2006.
Kirby, Michael, and Victoria Nes Kirby. *Futurist Performance*. New York: E.P. Dutton & Co., 1971.
Polti, Georges. *The Thirty-Six Dramatic Situations*. Translated by Lucille Ray. Franklin, OH: James Knapp Reeve, 1921.
Worthen, W.B. *Print and the Poetics of Modern Drama*. Cambridge: Cambridge University Press, 2005.

26. Disappearing act

Freshwater, Helen. *Theatre & Audience*. New York: Palgrave Macmillan, 2009.
Kirby, Michael. "On Acting and Not-Acting." *TDR: The Drama Review* 16, no. 1 (1972): 3–15.
Phillips, Adam. *Houdini's Box: On the Arts of Escape*. London: Faber and Faber, 2001.

27. A displacement

28. Dreams on screen

Benjamin, Walter. "The Work of Art in the Age of Its Technological Reproducibility: Third Version." In *Walter Benjamin: Selected Writings Volume 4, 1938–1940*, edited by Howard Eiland and Michael W. Jennings, translated by Edmund Jephcott and others, 251–83. Cambridge, MA: Belknap Press of Harvard University Press, 2003.
Schwartz, Delmore. *In Dreams Begin Responsibilities and Other Stories*. Edited by James Atlas. New York: New Directions, 1978.

29. Earthly

Althusser, Louis. "The 'Piccolo Teatro': Bertolazzi and Brecht—Notes on a Materialist Theatre." In *For Marx,* translated by Ben Brewster, 129–152. New York: Verso, 2005.
Gombrowicz, Witold. *Diary*. Translated by Lillian Vallee. New Haven: Yale University Press, 2012.

RELATED WORKS

Kafka, Franz. *The Diaries of Franz Kafka, 1910–23*. Edited by Max Brod. London: Vintage, 1999.
Kartun, Mauricio. *Terrenal. Pequeño misterio ácrata*. Teatro del Pueblo, Buenos Aires, FIBA Festival, 2015.
Yeats, W.B. *Autobiographies*. Basingstoke: Macmillan, 1980.

30. Eavesdropping in on a cyclical conversation

31. Enema of the people

Chaudhuri, Una. "There Must Be a Lot of Fish in that Lake': Toward an Ecological Theater." *Theater* 25, no. 1 (1994): 23–31.
Ibsen, Henrik. *Ibsen: Plays Two*. Translated by Michael Meyer. London: Methuen, 1980.
Serres, Michel. *The Natural Contract*. Translated by Elizabeth McArthur and William Paulson. Ann Arbor: University of Michigan Press, 1995.

32. Esprit des corps

Canetti, Elias. *Crowds and Power*. Translated by Carol Stewart. New York: Farrar, Straus and Giroux, 1984.
Euripides. *The Bacchae*. Translated by C.K. Williams. New York: Farrar, Straus and Giroux, 1990.
Freud, Sigmund. *Civilization and Its Discontents*. Translated by Joan Riviere. London: Hogarth Press, 1982.
Jannarone, Kimberly. *Artaud and His Doubles*. Ann Arbor: University of Michigan Press, 2010.
Nietzsche, Friedrich. *The Birth of Tragedy and The Case of Wagner*. Translated by Walter Kaufmann. New York: Vintage, 1967.

33. Extremely poor children

Benjamin, Walter. *The Origin of German Tragic Drama*. Translated by John Osborne. London and New York: Verso, 1985.
Castellucci, Romeo, Claudia Castellucci, Chiara Guidi, Joe Kelleher, and Nicholas Ridout. *The Theatre of Socìetas Raffaello Sanzio*. London and New York: Routledge, 1997.
Fitzgerald, Penelope. *At Freddie's*. London: Fourth Estate, 2013.
Grotowski, Jerzy. *Towards a Poor Theatre*. Edited by Eugenio Barba. London and New York: Routledge, 2002.

34. Fade to black: Notes toward a re-performance of gestures that never occurred

Blue Velvet. Directed by David Lynch. 1986. Santa Monica, CA: MGM Home Entertainment, 2002. DVD.
Shakespeare, William. *Hamlet*. Edited by Ann Thompson and Neil Taylor. London: Bloomsbury Arden Shakespeare, 2016.
Theweleit, Klaus. *Object-Choice (All you need is love...)*. Translated by Malcolm R. Green. London: Verso, 1994.

35. Feminist theory theatre

Gluzman, Yelena. "Research as Theatre (RaT): Positioning theatre at the centre of PaR, and PaR at the centre of the academy." In *Performance as Research: Knowledge, Methods, Impact*, edited by Annette Arlander, Bruce Barton, Melanie Dreyer-Lude, and Ben Spatz. London and New York: Routledge, 2017.
Haraway, Donna. "Situated Knowledges: The Science Question in Feminism and the Privilege of Partial Perspective." *Feminist Studies* 14, no. 3 (1988): 575–99.
Jackson, Shannon. *Professing Performance: Theatre in the Academy from Philology to Performativity*. Cambridge: Cambridge University Press, 2004.

36. The fort

Benjamin, Walter. *Illuminations*. Edited by Hannah Arendt. Translated by Harry Zohn. New York: Schocken Books, 1969.
Brecht, Bertolt. "The Modern Theatre is the Epic Theatre." In *Brecht on Theatre*, edited and translated by John Willett, 33–42. New York: Hill and Wang, 1964.
Friends of Fort York and Garrison Common. "Fort York National Historic Site." Accessed July 24, 2016. www.fortyork.ca/.

37. Friedrichshain

38. A garden party *Hamlet*

Parks, Suzan-Lori. *The America Play and Other Works*. New York: Theatre Communications Group, 1994.
Rayner, Alice. *To Do, to Act, to Perform: Drama and the Phenomenology of Action*. Ann Arbor: University of Michigan Press, 1994.
Shakespeare, William. *Hamlet*. Edited by Ann Thompson and Neil Taylor. London: Bloomsbury Arden Shakespeare, 2006.

39. Ghost light, an animal congress

Grusin, Richard, ed. *The Nonhuman Turn*. Minneapolis: University of Minnesota Press, 2015.
Latour, Bruno. *Politics of Nature: How to Bring the Sciences into Democracy*. Translated by Catherine Porter. Cambridge, MA: Harvard University Press, 2004.
Orozco, Lourdes, and Jennifer Parker-Starbuck, eds. *Performing Animality: Animals in Performance Practices*. Basingstoke and New York: Palgrave Macmillan, 2015.
Poliquin, Rachel. *The Breathless Zoo: Taxidermy and the Culture of Longing*. University Park: Pennsylvania State University Press, 2012.

40. Ghost practice

Bishop, Claire, RoseLee Goldberg, Adrian Heathfield, John Rockwell, Hrag Vartanian, and David Velasco. "Who Can Write About Performance Art?" Panel discussion. Performa Festival, Judson Memorial Church, New York. April 17, 2014.
Drunk, late-night kitchen conversation with artist Cathy Naden (Forced Entertainment). November 2013.

41. Give, take, and shake

Brazil, David, and Kevin Killian. *The Kenning Anthology of Poets Theater: 1945–1985*. Chicago: Kenning Editions, 2010.
Toscano, Rodrigo. *Collapsible Poetics Theater*. New York: Fence Books, 2008.

42. The greatest show on earth

Artaud, Antonin. *The Theater and Its Double*. Translated by Mary Caroline Richards. New York: Grove Press, 1994.

43. Gun

Dickinson, Emily. "My Life had stood—A Loaded Gun." In *The Poems of Emily Dickinson*, edited by R. W. Franklin, 341–42. Cambridge, MA: Belknap Press of Harvard University Press, 1999.
Lessing, Gotthold Ephriam. "Essay 2." In *The Hamburg Dramaturgy*, translated by Wendy Arons and Sara Fingal, edited by Natalya Baldyga. MediaCommons Press. Accessed July 23, 2016. http://mcpress.media-commons.org/hamburg/.

Rich, Adrienne. "Power." In *The Dream of a Common Language: Poems 1974–1977*, 3. New York: Norton, 1978.
Sofer, Andrew. "Killing Time: Guns and the Play of Predictability on the Modern Stage." In *The Stage Life of Props*, 167–202. Ann Arbor: University of Michigan Press, 2003.

44. Gut body

Kuppers, Petra, ed. *Somatic Engagement*. Oakland: Chain Links, 2011.
Ono, Yoko. *Grapefruit: A Book of Instructions and Drawings*. New York: Simon & Schuster, 1970.
Stein, Gertrude. *Tender Buttons: The Corrected Centennial Edition*. Edited by Seth Perlow. San Francisco: City Lights Books, 2014.

45. A happy life

Cary, Elizabeth. *The Tragedy of Mariam, the Fair Queen of Jewry*. Edited by Ramona Wray. London: Arden, 2012.
Chapman, George. *Bussy D'Ambois*. Edited by Nicholas Brooke. Manchester: Manchester University Press, 1964.
Marston, John. *Antonio's Revenge*. Edited by W. Reavley Gair. Manchester: Manchester University Press, 1978.
Seneca, Lucius Annaeus. *Letters on Ethics: To Lucilius*. Translated by Margaret Graver and A.A. Long. Chicago: University of Chicago Press, 2015.
Tacitus, Cornelius. *Annals*. Translated by John Jackson. Cambridge, MA: Harvard University Press, 1937.
Webster, John. *The Duchess of Malfi*. Edited by Leah S. Marcus. London: Arden, 2009.

46. Heaven's stenographer shines the guiding light

Durbin, Kate. *E! Entertainment*. Brooklyn: Wonder, 2014.
Villarejo, Amy. *Ethereal Queer: Television, Historicity, Desire*. Durham: Duke University Press, 2014.

47. Holding time

48. How does it go again?

Exekias, "Dionysos Cup." München, Staatliche Antikensammlung. 530 BCE. Accessed July 24, 2016. https://en.wikipedia.org/wiki/Dionysus_cup.
Hedreen, Guy Michael. "The Silens of Naxos." In *Silens in Attic Black Figure Vase Painting: Myth and Performance*, 67–104. Ann Arbor: University of Michigan Press, 1992.
Kālidāsa. *Theater of Memory: The Plays of Kālidāsa*. Edited by Barbara Stoler Miller. Translated by Edwin Gerow, David Gitomer, and Barbara Stoler Miller. New York: Columbia University Press, 1984.

49. Human too

Dear Climate. Accessed July 23, 2016. http://www.dearclimate.net/.
Ibarra, Xandra. "Ecdysis: The Molting of A Cucarachica." In *Women & Performance: a journal of feminist theory* 25, no. 3 (2015): 354–6.

50. I can't breathe...

Heidegger, Martin. *Being and Time*. Translated by John Macquarrie and Edward Robinson. New York: HarperPerennial, 2008.
Langer, Susanne. *Feeling and Form: A Theory of Art Developed from Philosophy in a New Key*. New York: Macmillan, 1977.
Morrison, Toni. *Jazz*. New York: Knopf, 1992.

Rainer, Yvonne. *Feelings are Facts: A Life*. Cambridge, MA: MIT Press, 2006.
Wilson, August. *August Wilson Century Cycle*. New York: Theatre Communications Group, 2007.

51. I, Marjorie

Case, Sue-Ellen, ed. *Split Britches: Lesbian Practice/Feminist Performance*. London and New York: Routledge, 1996.
Churchill, Caryl. *Escaped Alone*. London: Nick Hern Books, 2016.
Dolan, Jill. *Utopia in Performance: Finding Hope at the Theater*. Ann Arbor: University of Michigan Press, 2005.
Harvie, Jen, and Lois Weaver, eds. *The Only Way Home is Through the Show: Performance Work of Lois Weaver*. London: Intellect Live, 2015.

52. Imagined cities (after Calvino)

Barba, Eugenio, and Nicola Savarese. *A Dictionary of Theatre Anthropology: The Secret Art of the Performer*. Translated by Richard Fowler. Routledge: New York and London, 2006.
Calvino, Italo. *Invisible Cities*. Translated by William Weaver. New York: Harcourt Brace Jovanovich, 1974.
Coleridge, Samuel Taylor. "Kubla Khan, Or, A Vision in a Dream: A Fragment." In *The Norton Anthology of Poetry*, 4th Edition, edited by Margaret Ferguson, Mary Jo Salter, and Jon Stallworthy. London and New York: W. W. Norton, 1996.

53. The impossible magic show

Borges, Jorge Luis. "Pierre Menard, Author of the *Quixote*." In *Collected Fictions*, translated by Andrew Hurley, 88–95. New York: Penguin, 1999.
This is not a magic show. By Vincent Gambini, developed at Rhubaba Gallery, tour funded by Arts Council England, 2014–2016. http://www.vincentgambini.com/the-show.html/.

54. In character

Coates, Ta-Nehisi. "Letter to My Son." *The Atlantic*. July 4, 2015. Accessed July 24, 2016. http://www.theatlantic.com/politics/archive/2015/07/tanehisi-coates-between-the-world-and-me/397619/.
DuBois, W. E. B. *The Souls of Black Folk*. New York: New American Library, 1969.
Ellison, Ralph. *Invisible Man*. 2d ed. New York: Vintage, 1995.
Morrison, Toni. *The Bluest Eye*. New York: Holt, Rinehart & Winston, 1970.
Wilson, August. *Two Trains Running*. New York: Plume, 1993.

55. IRL

Berlant, Lauren, and Michael Warner. "Sex in Public." *Critical Inquiry* 24, no. 2 (1998): 547–66.
Jay-Z, featuring Swizz Beats. "On to the Next One." *The Blueprint 3*. Roc Nation/Atlantic Records. 2009. MP3.
Muñoz, José Esteban. *Cruising Utopia: The Then and There of Queer Futurity*. New York: New York University Press, 2009.
Nancy, Jean-Luc. *After Fukushima: The Equivalence of Catastrophes*. Translated by Charlotte Mandell. New York: Fordham University Press, 2015.
Nancy, Jean-Luc. *Corpus*. Translated by Richard A. Rand. New York: Fordham University Press, 2008.
Roach, Joseph R. *Cities of the Dead: Circum-Atlantic Performance*. New York: Columbia University Press, 1996.

56. It comes back together

57. It could be a forest

Ra, Sun. *Cosmic Tones for Mental Therapy and Art Forms of Dimensions Tomorrow*. Sun Ra and his Myth Science Arkestra. Evidence, 1992. CD.

58. It was a large rubble space

Holzer, Jenny, and Robert Storr. *Jenny Holzer: Redaction Paintings*. New York: Cheim & Read, 2007.
MacDonald, Claire. *Utopia: Three Plays for a Postdramatic Theatre*. London: Intellect, 2015.

59. Last resort [no one can stop you now]

Harvie, Jen, and Lois Weaver, eds. *The Only Way Home is Through the Show: Performance Work of Lois Weaver*. London: Intellect Live, 2015.
Pay Up. By Pig Iron Theatre Company. 2006. Company archival DVD.
Templeton, Fiona. *YOU—The City*. New York: Roof Books, 1990.
Whitney, Emerson. *Ghost Box*. Oakland, CA: Timeless, Infinite Light, 2014.

60. The last wor(l)d

Einstein, Albert. *Relativity: The Special and the General Theory, 100th Anniversary Edition*. Translated by Robert W. Lawson. Princeton: Princeton University Press, 2015.
Einstein on the Beach. By Robert Wilson. Music by Philip Glass. Avignon Festival, France. July 1976.
Freitag, Jürgen, and Hannes Hansel. *Honeckers geheimer Bunker 5001*. Stuttgart: Motorbuch-Verlag, 2010.
Hachigatsu no kyōshikyoku [Rhapsody in August]. Directed by Akira Kurosawa. 1991; Santa Monica, CA: MGM Home Entertainment, 2003. DVD.

61. The lost notebooks of the painter's wife

Glancy, Diane. *Lloyd and Hallah*. Reading at Native American New Play Festival, Oklahoma City Theater Company, Oklahoma City, Oklahoma, April 9, 2016.
Scholder, Fritz, Lowery Stokes Sims, Truman Lowe, and Paul Chaat Smith. *Fritz Scholder: Indian/Not Indian*. Munich: Prestel, 2008.

62. The means of production

Harvie, Jen. *Fair Play: Art, Performance and Neoliberalism*. Basingstoke and New York: Palgrave Macmillan, 2013.
Harvie, Jen. "Funding, Philanthropy, Structural Inequality and Decline in England's Theatre Ecology." *Cultural Trends* 24, no. 1 (2015): 56–61.
Jackson, Shannon. *Social Works: Performing Art, Supporting Publics*. London and New York: Routledge, 2011.
Marx, Karl, and Friedrich Engels. *The Communist Manifesto*. Edited by David McLellan. Translated by Samuel Moore. Oxford: Oxford University Press, 1998.
Ridout, Nicholas. *Passionate Amateurs: Theatre, Communism, and Love*. Ann Arbor: University of Michigan Press, 2013.

63. A meta-theatre

Abel, Lionel. *Tragedy and Metatheatre: Essays on Dramatic Form*. New York: Holmes & Meier, 2003.
Puchner, Martin. *Stage Fright: Modernism, Anti-Theatricality, and Drama*. Baltimore: Johns Hopkins University Press, 2002.

64. The monster when she opened her wings

65. Motion capture

Manning, Erin. *Always More Than One: Individuation's Dance.* Durham: Duke University Press, 2013.
Wolf, Mark J. P. "The Technological Construction of Performance." *Convergence: The International Journal of Research into New Media Technologies* 9, no. 4 (2003): 48–59.

66. Music for Charlie Morel

Proust, Marcel. *The Captive.* Translated by C.K. Scott Moncrieff. New York: Modern Library, 1929.
Sedgwick, Eve Kosofsky. *The Weather in Proust.* Edited by Jonathan Goldberg. Durham: Duke University Press, 2011.
Shattuck, Roger. *The Banquet Years: The Origins of the Avant-Garde in France 1885 to World War I.* Revised edition. New York: Vintage, 1968.

67. The night everything happened

Etchells, Tim, and Ant Hampton, curators. *True Riches: A Programme of Live Art for the ICA.* Institute of Contemporary Art, London, 2009.

68. No subject

Houstoun, Wendy. "Fictional Diary: April 2015-…" *Facebook.* Accessed July 23, 2016. https://www.facebook.com/wendy.houstoun/.

69. NOT I (not)

Brater, Enoch. *Beyond Minimalism: Beckett's Late Style in the Theater.* New York: Oxford University Press, 1987.
Connor, Steven. *Samuel Beckett: Repetition, Theory, and Text.* Oxford: Basil Blackwell, 1988.
"Eyeliner™." *Musion.* Accessed July 23, 2016. http://musion.com/eyeliner/.
Karnad, Raghu. "The Modi Effect: How India Elected a Hologram." *New Statesman.* March 27, 2015. Accessed July 24, 2016. http://www.newstatesman.com/books/2015/03/modi-effect-how-india-elected-hologram/.
Tubridy, Dervil. "Vain Reasoning: *Not I.*" In *Samuel Beckett: A Casebook*, edited by Jennifer M. Jeffers, 111–32. New York: Garland, 1998.

70. Ocean oration

Nestor, James. *Deep: Freediving, Renegade Science, and What the Ocean Tells Us about Ourselves.* New York: Houghton Mifflin Harcourt, 2014.
"Nature is Speaking." *Conservation International.* Accessed July 23, 2016. http://www.conservation.org/nature-is-speaking/Pages/Harrison-Ford-Is-the-Ocean.aspx/.
Peña, John. "Letters to the Ocean." *John Peña Art.* Accessed July 23, 2016. http://www.johnpena.net/letterstotheocean/.
Thoreau, Henry David. *Walden.* New York: Oxford University Press, 1997.

71. Oh, have I died, then?

Barker, Howard. *Arguments for a Theatre.* London: Oberon Books, 2016.
Barker, Howard. *Death, The One and the Art of Theatre.* London and New York: Routledge, 2004.
Barker, Howard. *These Sad Places, Why Must You Enter Them?* London: Impress, 2014.

RELATED WORKS

72. On location and context

Anzaldúa, Gloria, and Cherríe Moraga, eds. *This Bridge Called My Back: Writings by Radical Women of Color.* Watertown, MA: Persephone Press, 1981.
Berardi, Franco "Bifo." "On the Digital Colonization of Human Experience." *Adbusters.* October 9, 2014. Accessed July 23, 2016. http://www.adbusters.org/article/franco-bifo-berardi/.

73. On scale

Adams, George. *Essays on the Microscope.* London: Robert Hindmarsh, 1787.
Chico, Tita. "Minute Particulars: Microscopy and Eighteenth-Century Narrative." *Mosaic* 39, no. 2 (2006): 143–61.
Schikore, Jutta. *The Microscope and the Eye: A History of Reflections, 1740–1870.* Chicago: University of Chicago Press, 2007.

74. Onboard entertainment

Heraclitus. *Fragments.* Translated by T.M. Robinson. Toronto: University of Toronto, 2015.
Kantor, Tadeusz. *A Journey through Other Spaces: Essays and Manifestos 1944–1990.* Edited and translated by Michal Kobialka. Berkeley: University of California Press, 1993.
Serres, Michel. *Angels: A Modern Myth.* Translated by Francis Cowper. Paris: Flammarion, 1995.

75. or, The Whale (For Tess)

Craig, Edward Gordon. *Towards a New Theatre: Forty Designs for Stage Scenes.* New York: E.P. Dutton & Co., 1913.
Cull, Laura. "From *Homo Performans* to Interspecies Collaboration: Expanding the Concept of Performance to Include Animals." In *Performing Animality: Animals in Performance Practices*, edited by Lourdes Orozco and Jennifer Parker-Starbuck, 19–36. Basingstoke and New York: Palgrave Macmillan, 2015.
Goulish, Matthew. *39 Microlectures: In Proximity of Performance.* London and New York: Routledge, 2000.
Deleuze, Gilles and Félix Guattari. *A Thousand Plateaus: Capitalism and Schizophrenia.* Translated by Brian Massumi. Minneapolis: University of Minnesota Press, 1987.
Melville, Herman. *Moby-Dick; or, The Whale.* New York: Harper & Brothers, 1851.
Pour la suite du monde [For the ones to come]. Directed by Michel Brault, Marcel Carrière, and Pierre Perrault. 1963. Montréal: National Film Board of Canada, 2005. DVD.

76. An orogeny

77. Otto's self board meeting

Beckett, Samuel. *Not I.* London: Faber and Faber, 1973.
Harvie, Jen. *Fair Play: Art, Performance and Neoliberalism.* Basingstoke and New York: Palgrave Macmillan, 2013.
Whitman, Walt. *Leaves of Grass: The Complete 1855–92 Editions.* New York: Library of America, 2011.

78. Passenger pigeons

The Civilians' The Great Immensity. Written and directed by Steve Cosson. Music by Michael Friedman. The Public Theater, NY, April–May 2014.
Cole, Adam. "Lonesome George (A Musical Memorial)" *YouTube* video, 3:44. Posted by Skunk Bear: Science from NPR. Accessed July 24, 2016. https://www.youtube.com/watch?v=jmAO44_52vU/.
Rosen, Jonathan. "The Birds, Why the Passenger Pigeon Became Extinct." *New Yorker* 89, no. 43 (2014): 62.
Walcott, Derek. *Remembrance & Pantomime.* New York: Farrar, Straus, and Giroux, 1980.

79. Plant life (excerpt from a play in three acts)

Artaud, Antonin. *Artaud on Theatre*. Edited and translated by Claude Schumacher and Brian Singleton. London: Methuen, 1989.

Beckett, Samuel. *Not I*. London: Faber and Faber, 1973.

The Epic of Gilgamesh. Translated by Andrew George. New York: Penguin Classics, 2003.

Haraway, Donna. "A Cyborg Manifesto: Science, Technology, and Socialist Feminism in the Late Twentieth Century." In *Simians, Cyborgs, and Women: The Reinvention of Nature*, 149–82. London and New York: Routledge, 1991.

Pangean Dreams: A Shamanic Journey. Written and performed by Rachel Rosenthal. Music by Leslie Lashinsky. Los Angeles, CA: Rachel Rosenthal Co., 2010. DVD.

80. Poolside

81. Precipitation

"El Capitan's Dawn Wall: Coverage of the Ascent at Yosemite" *New York Times*. January 14, 2015. http://www.nytimes.com/2015/01/15/sports/el-capitans-dawn-wall-climbers-near-top-yosemite.html?_r=0/.

"Tommy Caldwell Climbing Pitch 15 / The Dawn Wall" Filmed January 14, 2015. *YouTube* video, 3:41. Posted by Patagonia. Accessed July 24, 2016. https://www.youtube.com/watch?v=PLd_c4CjG44/.

82. The previous cry

Cavell, Stanley. *Philosophical Passages: Wittgenstein, Emerson, Austin, Derrida*. Oxford: Blackwell, 1995.

Feynman, Richard. *The Quotable Feynman*. Edited by Michelle Feynman. Princeton: Princeton University Press, 2015.

Hawking, Stephen. "Into A Black Hole." Stephen Hawking Official Website. Accessed July 24, 2016. http://www.hawking.org.uk/into-a-black-hole.html/.

Howe, Susan. "Vagrancy in the Park." *The Nation* 301, no. 18 (2015): 27–35.

Kelleher, Joe. *The Illuminated Theatre: Studies on the Suffering of Images*. London and New York: Routledge, 2015.

Michell, John. "On the Means of Discovering the Distance, Magnitude, &c. of the Fixed Stars, in Consequence of the Diminution of the Velocity of Their Light, in Case Such a Diminution Should be Found to Take Place in any of Them, and Such Other Data Should be Procured from Observations, as Would be Farther Necessary for That Purpose." *Philosophical Transactions of the Royal Society* 74 (1784): 35–57.

83 and 84. Private language argument I and II

Cavell, Stanley. *Must We Mean What We Say?* Cambridge: Cambridge University Press, 1976.

Wittgenstein, Ludwig. *Philosophical Investigations*. 4th ed. Translated by G. E. M. Anscombe, P. M. S. Hacker, and Joachim Schulte. Chichester: Wiley-Blackwell, 2009.

85. Questions for women in prison

Bond, Pat, and Clifford Jarrett. *Gerty Gerty Gerty Stein Is Back Back Back*. Directed by Tom Barnett. 1981. Videocassette (VHS), 60 min.

Elam, Harry, and Robert Alexander, eds. *Colored Contradictions: An Anthology of Contemporary African American Plays*. New York: Plume, 1996.

Fraden, Rena. *Imagining Medea: Rhodessa Jones and Theater for Incarcerated Women*. Chapel Hill: University of North Carolina Press, 2001.

Johnson, E. Patrick, and Ramón H. Rivera-Servera, eds. *Solo/Black/Woman: Scripts, Interviews, and Essays*. Evanston: Northwestern University Press, 2013.
Knight, Keith, Mat Schwarzman, eds. *Beginner's Guide to Community-Based Arts*. San Francisco: New Village Press, 2005.

86. Realism

BBC News. "Hostage-takers 'ready to die'." *BBC News World Edition: Europe*. October 25, 2002. Accessed February 5, 2016. http://news.bbc.co.uk/2/hi/europe/2360735.stm/.
Doyle, Arthur Conan. "A Case of Identity." In *The Adventures and Memoirs of Sherlock Holmes*, edited by Ed Glinert, 27–37. London: Penguin, 2001.
Doyle, Arthur Conan. *A Study in Scarlet*. Edited by Ed Glinert. London: Penguin, 2001.
Loiperdinger, Martin, and Bernd Elzer. "Lumiere's Arrival of the Train: Cinema's Founding Myth." *The Moving Image* 4, no. 1 (2004): 89–118.
Tolstoy, Leo. *Anna Karenina*. Translated by Richard Pevear and Larissa Volokhonsky. London: Penguin, 2001.

87. Remains

Crimp, Martin. *Attempts on Her Life: Seventeen Scenarios for the Theatre*. In *Martin Crimp Plays 2*, 197–284. London: Faber and Faber, 2005.
Magelssen, Scott. *Simming: Participatory Performance and the Making of Meaning*. Ann Arbor: University of Michigan Press, 2014.
Phillips, Lisa, ed. *Chris Burden: Extreme Measures*. New York: Skira Rizzoli, 2013.
Rugoff, Ralph. *Scene of the Crime*. Cambridge: MIT Press, 1997.
Schneider, Rebecca. *Performing Remains: Art and War in Times of Theatrical Reenactment*. London and New York: Routledge, 2011.

88. Rock performance

Bennett, Jane. *Vibrant Matter: A Political Ecology of Things*. Durham: Duke University Press, 2010.
Chen, Mel Y. *Animacies: Biopolitics, Racial Mattering, and Queer Affect*. Durham: Duke University Press, 2012.

89. SHE

Combahee River Collective. "A Black Feminist Statement." In *This Bridge Called My Back: Writings by Radical Women of Color,* 2nd ed., edited by Cherríe Moraga and Gloria Anzaldúa, 210–218. New York: Kitchen Table, Women of Color Press, 1983.
Lorde, Audre. "The Transformation of Silence into Language and Action." In *Sister Outsider: Essays and Speeches,* 40–44. Trumansburg, NY: Crossing Press, 1984.
Moraga, Cherríe, and Celia Herrera Rodriguez. "An Irrevocable Promise: Staging the Story Xicana." In *A Xicana Codex of Changing Consciousness: Writings, 2000–2010,* 34–46. Durham: Duke University Press, 2011.
Shange, Ntozake. "foreword/ unrecovered losses/ black theater traditions." In *Three Pieces,* ix–xvi. New York: St. Martin's Press, 1981.
Shange, Ntozake. "takin a solo/ a poetic possibility/ a poetic imperative." In *See No Evil: Prefaces, Reviews & Essays, 1974–1983,* 26–33. San Francisco: Momo's Press, 1984.

90. Spiked

Burmester, Jörn J., and Feigl, *Burmester + Feigl's Hermetischer Garten* [performances]. Presented at Sophiensæle, Berlin, November 21–23, 2013.

Jay, Ricky. *Learned Pigs & Fireproof Women: Unique, Eccentric and Amazing Entertainers*. New York: Noonday Press, 1998.

91. Stress melody

Alder, Ken. *The Lie Detectors: The History of an American Obsession*. Lincoln, NE: University of Nebraska Press, 2007.
Barad, Karen. "Posthumanist Performativity: Toward an Understanding of How Matter Comes to Matter." *Signs: Journal of Women in Culture and Society* 28, no. 3 (2003): 801–31.
Salter, Chris. "Sound." In *Entangled: Technology and the Transformation of Performance,* 181–220. Cambridge, MA: MIT Press, 2010.

92. Surveillance

Lost Highway. Directed by David Lynch. 1997. Universal City, CA: Universal Studios Home Entertainment, 2008. DVD.
Modern Times. Directed by Charlie Chaplin. 1936. New York: Criterion Collection, 2010. DVD.

93. TALES

Cixous, Hélène. "The Laugh of the Medusa." Translated by Keith Cohen and Paula Cohen. *Signs* 1 (1976): 875–93.
Spector, Michael. "The Gene Hackers." *New Yorker*. November 16, 2015. Accessed February 5, 2016. http://www.newyorker.com/magazine/2015/11/16/the-gene-hackers/.

94. Tectum theatre

Park, Madison, and Paula Hancocks. "Sewol Ferry Disaster: One Year On, Grieving Families Demand Answers." *CNN.com*. 16 April 2015. Accessed July 23, 2016. http://www.cnn.com/2015/04/15/asia/sewol-ferry-korea-anniversary/.
Phelan, Peggy. *Mourning Sex: Performing Public Memories*. London and New York: Routledge, 1997.
Strehler, B.L. "Where is the Self? A Neurological Theory of Consciousness." *Synapse* 7, no. 1 (1991): 44–91.

95. Th'Eater

Benjamin, Walter. *Understanding Brecht*. Translated by Anna Bostock. London: Verso, 1983.
Carême, M. A. *Le Cuisinier parisien, ou, L'art de la cuisine française au dix-neuvième siècle*. 2d ed. Paris, 1828.
Plato. *Plato, the Symposium*. Edited by M.C. Howatson and Frisbee C. C. Sheffield. Cambridge, UK: Cambridge University Press, 2008.
Shakespeare, William. *The Tempest*. Edited by Virginia Mason Vaughan and Alden T. Vaughan. London: Bloomsbury Arden Shakespeare, 2011.

96. Theatre of the Blind (or: description)

Anderson, Patrick. "Colour Blind: Seeing Difference, Performing Sightlessness." In *Performance Politics and Activism*, edited by Peter Lichtenfels and John Rouse, 121–31. Basingstoke and New York: Palgrave Macmillan, 2013.
Kudlick, Catherine, and Susan Schweik. "Collision and Collusion: Artists, Academics, and Activists in Dialogue with the University of California and Critical Disability Studies." *Disability Studies Quarterly* 34, no. 2 (2014): no pag. doi: 10.18061/dsq.v34i2.4251/.

RELATED WORKS

97. The theatre at Calpurnia

Boal, Augusto. *Theatre of the Oppressed.* Translated by Charles A. McBride. New York: Theatre Communications Group, 1993.

George-Graves, Nadine. *Urban Bush Women: Twenty Years of African American Dance Theater, Community Engagement, and Working It Out.* Madison: University of Wisconsin Press, 2000.

States, Bert O. *Great Reckonings in Little Rooms: On the Phenomenology of Theater.* Berkeley: University of California Press, 1987.

Thomas, Lundeana Marie. *Barbara Ann Teer and the National Black Theatre: Transformational Forces in Harlem.* London and New York: Routledge, 1997.

Valdez, Luis. *Luis Valdez Early Works: Actos, Bernabe and Pensamiento Serpentino.* Houston: Arte Publico Press, 1990.

98. Theatre generated by a probabilistic language model, with grammatical artifacts retained

Aeschylus. *Prometheus Bound.* Translated by Joel Agee. New York: New York Review of Books, 2014.

"David Altmejd: Flux." Musée d'Art Moderne de la Ville de Paris. 11 Avenue du Président Wilson, 75116 Paris. 10 October 2014—1 February 2015. http://www.mam.paris.fr/en/expositions/exhibitions-david-altmejd/.

Howe, Daniel C. *RiTa* [Computer software]. 2015. Retrieved from http://rednoise.org/rita/.

Shannon, Claude E., and Warren Weaver. *The Mathematical Theory of Communication.* Urbana: University of Illinois Press, 1963.

Wiener, Norbert. *Cybernetics: or Control and Communication in the Animal and the Machine.* 2d ed. Cambridge, MA: MIT Press, 1961.

99. Theatre of intimacy and abandon

100. The theatre of the town

Orfeo. An Exercise in Dying. Directed by Susanne Kennedy, Suzan Boogaerdt, and Bianca van der Schoot. Zollverein Essen, Ruhrtriennale, August 2015.

101. Theatre/duty

Boal, Augusto. *Theatre of the Oppressed.* Translated by Charles A. McBride. New York: Theatre Communications Group, 1993.

Lee, Chang Rae. *Native Speaker.* New York: Riverhead Books, 1995.

102. A theatrical revenge melodrama with ring-tones

Ellul, Jacques. *The Technological Society.* New York: Vintage Books, 1964.

"Improv Everywhere." *Improv Everywhere.* Accessed February 28, 2016. http://improveverywhere.com/.

Not I, Footfalls, Rockaby. By Samuel Beckett. Directed by Walter Asmus. Performed by Lisa Dwan. Royal Court Theatre, London. Toured 2013–16.

Piepenburg, Erik. "Hold the Phone, It's Patti LuPone." *New York Times.* July 9, 2015. http://www.nytimes.com/2015/07/10/theater/hold-the-phone-its-patti-lupone.html/.

Sack, Daniel. *After Live: Possibility, Potentiality, and the Future of Performance.* Ann Arbor: University of Michigan Press, 2015.

Singer, Ben. *Melodrama and Modernity: Early Sensational Cinema and Its Contexts.* New York: Columbia University Press, 2001.

103. Thee Thy Thou Thine (a fragment)

Brett, Guy, Rose English, and Anne-Louise Rentell. *Abstract Vaudeville: The Work of Rose English.* London: Ridinghouse, 2014.
English, Rose. *Thee Thy Thou Thine.* First performed at the Institute of Contemporary Arts (ICA) London, 18 February, 1986.
Oklahoma! Directed by Fred Zinnemann. 1955. Beverly Hills, CA: Twentieth Century Fox Home Entertainment, 1999.
Plato. "Lysis" and "Euthyphro." In *The Collected Dialogues of Plato,* edited by Edith Hamilton and Huntington Cairns, translated by J. Wright and Lane Cooper, 145–199. Princeton: Princeton University Press, 1961.
di Somi, Leone. "The Dialogues of Leone di Somi." In *The Development of the Theatre: A Study of Theatrical Art from the Beginnings to the Present Day,* edited by Allardyce Nicoll, 252–78. New York: Harcourt Brace, 1957.

104. Then a cunning voice and a night we spend gazing at stars

Fienup-Riordan, Ann. *Yuungnaqpiallerput, The Way We Genuinely Live: Materials of Yup'ik Science and Survival.* Seattle: University of Washington Press, 2007.
Fienup-Riordan, Ann, and Lawrence D. Kaplan, eds. *Words of the Real People: Alaska Native Literature in Translation.* Fairbanks: University of Alaska Press, 2007.
Gould, Janice, and Dean Rader, eds. *Speak to Me Words: Essays on Contemporary American Indian Poetry.* Tucson: University of Arizona Press, 2003.
Wilson, Shawn. *Research is Ceremony: Indigenous Research Methods.* Black Point, Nova Scotia: Fernwood Publishing, 2009.
Womack, Craig. *Art as Performance, Story as Criticism: Reflections on Native Literary Aesthetics.* Norman: University of Oklahoma Press, 2009.

105. Three dramaturgical miniatures (after Nietzsche)

Castellucci, Romeo, Claudia Castellucci, and Chiara Guidi. *Epopea della polvere. Il teatro della Socìetas Raffaello Sanzio 1992–1999.* Milan: Ubulibri, 2001.
de Man, Paul. *Allegories of Reading: Figural Language in Rousseau, Nietzsche, Rilke, and Proust.* New Haven: Yale University Press, 1979.
Nietzsche, Friedrich. *Beyond Good and Evil: Prelude to a Philosophy of the Future.* Translated by Walter Kaufmann. New York: Vintage, 1989.
Nietzsche, Friedrich. *The Birth of Tragedy and The Case of Wagner.* Translated by Walter Kaufmann. New York: Vintage, 1967.
Sloterdijk, Peter. *Thinker On Stage: Nietzsche's Materialism.* Translated by Jamie Owen Daniel. Minneapolis: University of Minnesota Press, 1989.
Wilder, Thornton. *The Collected Short Plays of Thornton Wilder,* Vol II. Edited by A. Tappan Wilder. New York: Theatre Communications Group, 1998.

106. Thresholding

Long, Emma Zurcher. "I am Emma." Accessed July 23, 2016. https://emmashopebook.com/2015/12/.
Manning, Erin. *The Minor Gesture.* Durham: Duke University Press, 2016.
Manning, Erin. *Relationscapes: Movement, Art, Philosophy.* Cambridge, MA: MIT Press, 2009.
Montje, Michael Scott, Jr. "Sense Information/Look for our communications. (An Introduction to Imaginary Friends—Part III)" Accessed July 23, 2016. http://www.mmonjejr.com/2014/06/sense-informationlook-for-our.html.

Yergeau, Melanie. "Clinically Significant Disturbance: On Theorists Who Theorize Theory of Mind." *Disability Studies Quarterly* 33, no. 4 (2013). Accessed July 23, 2016. http://dsq-sds.org/article/view/3876/3405/.

107. Touching touches

Aristotle. *De Anima.* Translated by Mark Shiffman. Newburyport, MA: Focus Publishing/R. Pullins Co., 2011.

Dolan, Jill. *Utopia in Performance: Finding Hope at the Theater.* Ann Arbor: University of Michigan Press, 2005.

Franzen, Jonathan. "Liking Is for Cowards, Go for What Hurts." *New York Times.* May 28, 2011. Accessed March 5, 2016. http://www.nytimes.com/2011/05/29/opinion/29franzen.html.

Kearney, Richard. "Losing Our Touch." *New York Times.* August 30, 2014. Accessed March 5, 2016. http://opinionator.blogs.nytimes.com/2014/08/30/losing-our-touch/.

Sedgwick, Eve Kosofsky. *Touching Feeling: Affect, Pedagogy, Performativity.* Durham: Duke University Press, 2003.

108. Triptych

Beckett, Samuel. *Collected Shorter Plays.* New York: Grove Press, 2010.

Faulkner, William. *As I Lay Dying: The Corrected Text.* New York: Modern Library, 2000.

109. Two dances

Humphrey, Doris. *The Art of Making Dances.* Edited by Barbara Pollack. Princeton: Princeton Book Company, 1991.

Lehmann, Hans-Thies. *Postdramatic Theatre.* Translated by Karen Jürs-Munby. London and New York: Routledge, 2006.

Schechner, Richard. *Between Theater and Anthropology.* Philadelphia: University of Pennsylvania Press, 1985.

110. TwoDoor Drama

Acker, Kathy. "Airplane." In *In Memoriam to Identity,* 99–152. New York: Grove Press, 1990.

Anne of the Thousand Days. Directed by Charles Jarrott. 1969. Universal City, CA: Universal Studios Home Entertainment. DVD.

Aronson, Arnold. "Their Exits and Their Entrances: Getting a Handle on Doors." *New Theatre Quarterly* 20, no. 4 (2004): 331–40.

Chekhov, Anton. "The Seagull." In *The Plays of Anton Chekhov,* translated by Paul Schmidt, 109–164. New York: Harper Perennial, 1999.

Sowerby, Tracey. "The Coronation of Anne Boleyn." In *The Oxford Handbook of Tudor Drama,* edited by Thomas Betteridge and Greg Walker, 386–401. London: Oxford University Press, 2012.

Woolf, Virginia. "Chapter Two." In *A Room of One's Own,* 25–40. New York: Harcourt, Inc., 1989.

111. Universal theatre machine (for Leibniz, Turing, Brecht, and Boal)

Boal, Augusto. *Theatre of the Oppressed.* Translated by Charles A. McBride and Maria-Odilia Leal McBride. London: Pluto Press, 1979.

Brecht, Bertolt. "A Short Organum for the Theatre." In *Brecht on Theatre: The Development of an Aesthetic,* edited and translated by John Willett, 179–205. London: Methuen, 1964.

Leibniz, Gottfried. *Philosophical Papers and Letters: A Selection.* Edited by Leroy E. Loemeker. Chicago: Chicago University Press, 1956.

Russell, Bertrand. *A Critical Exposition of the Philosophy of Leibniz.* London: George Allen & Unwin, Ltd., 1937.

Turing, Alan M. "On Computable Numbers, With an Application to the Entscheidungsproblem." In *The Undecidable: Basic Papers on Undecidable Propositions, Unsolvable Problems and Computable Functions*, edited by Martin Davis, 116–51. Hewlett, NY: Raven Press, 1965.

112. Unstill lives

Cage, John. *Silence: Lectures and Writings*. Middletown: Wesleyan University Press, 1961.

Marranca, Bonnie. "Introduction: Presence of Mind." In *Gertrude Stein, Last Operas and Plays*, edited by Carl Van Vechten, vii–xxvii. Baltimore: Johns Hopkins University Press, 1995.

Stein, Gertrude. *Writings and Lectures, 1909–1945*. Edited by Patricia Meyerowitz. Baltimore: Penguin Books, 1971.

113. Untitled (imaginary theatre #1)

Borges, Jorge Luis. *Collected Fictions*. Translated by Andrew Hurley. New York: Penguin, 1999.

DeLanda, Manuel. *A Thousand Years of Nonlinear History*. New York: Zone Books, 2000. [Schneider]

Deleuze, Gilles, and Félix Guattari. "1227: Treatise on Nomadolagy—The War Machine." In *A Thousand Plateaus: Capitalism and Schizophrenia*, translated by Brian Massumi, 351–423. Minneapolis: The University of Minnesota Press, 1987.

Deleuze, Gilles, and Félix Guattari. "1837: Of the Refrain." In *A Thousand Plateaus: Capitalism and Schizophrenia*, translated by Brian Massumi, 310–50. Minneapolis: The University of Minnesota Press, 1987.

Moebius. *40 jours dans le désert B: ou, la strategie de la démence*. Paris: Editions Stardom, 1999.

114. Untitled (imaginary theatre #2)

de Campos, Haroldo. *Galáxias*. São Paulo: Editora 34, 2011. [Lepecki]

REM. "Nightswimming." *Automatic for the People*. Warner Bros. Records, 1992. [Goulish]

Shakespeare, William. *Romeo & Juliet*. Edited by René Weis. London: Bloomsbury Arden Shakespeare, 2012. [Goulish]

Whitman, Walt. "Children of Adam." In *The Selected Poems of Walt Whitman*, 114–15. Roslyn, NY: Walter J. Black, Inc., 1942. [Goulish]

115. Variations (I–III)

"Advance—Gender Equality in England's Theatres" *Tonic Theatre's Advance Project*. Accessed July 23, 2016. http://www.tonictheatre-advance.co.uk/.

Elam, Diane. *Feminism and Deconstruction: Ms. en Abyme*. New York: Routledge, 1994.

116. Vocabulary

Chaumonot, Pierre Joseph Marie (attribution), Victor Morin, and Prosper Vincent. *[Seventeenth century manuscript, ca. 1640–93; French-Huron Dictionary and Vocabulary]*. John Carter Brown Library, Brown University.

Sagard, Gabriel, and Henri-Émile Chevalier. *Le grand voyage du pays des Hurons: situé en l'Amérique vers la mer douce, ès derniers confins de la nouvelle France dite Canada: avec un dictionaire de la langue huronne*. Paris: Denys Moreau, 1632.

Sioui, Georges E., and Jane Brierley. *Huron-Wendat: The Heritage of the Circle*. Revised ed. Vancouver: University of British Columbia Press, 1999.

117. The waiting room

Baraka, Amiri. *Dutchman and The Slave: Two Plays*. New York: Harper Perennial, 2001.

RELATED WORKS

Fanon, Frantz. *Black Skin, White Masks*. Translated by Charles Lam Markmann. London: Pluto Press, 1967.
Hall, Stuart. "Cultural Identity and Diaspora." In *Colonial Discourse and Post-Colonial Theory: A Reader*, edited by Patrick Williams and Laura Chrisman, 392–403. New York: Columbia University Press, 1994.
McMillan, Michael. "*Brother to Brother*." In *Black and Asian Plays: Anthology*, edited by Cheryl Robson, 137–175. London: Aurora Metro Press, 2000.
Wolfe, George C. *The Colored Museum*. New York: Grove Press, 1988.

118. Wanderspiele

Heddon, Deirdre, and Cathy Turner. "Walking Women: Shifting the Tales and Scales of Mobility." *Contemporary Theatre Review* 22 (2012): 224–36.
Machon, Josephine. *Immersive Theatres: Intimacy and Immediacy in Contemporary Performance*. Basingstoke and New York: Palgrave Macmillan, 2013.
"Syrian Journey: Choose Your Own Escape Route." *bbc.com*. April 1, 2015. Accessed July 24, 2016. http://www.bbc.com/news/world-middle-east-32057601/.

119. What to, where (a poets theatre)

Gómez-Peña, Guillermo. "New World Border." In *The New World Border: Prophecies, Poems & Loqueras for the End of the Century*, 21–47. San Francisco: City Lights, 1996.
Harryman, Carla. "A Sun and Five Decompositions." *Open Box*. New York: Tzadik 2012. CD.
Harryman, Carla. "Third Man." In *The Kenning Anthology of Poets Theater: 1945–1985*, edited by Kevin Killian and David Brazil, 334–44. Chicago: Kenning Editions, 2010.
Hejinian, Lyn, and Barrett Watten. "Symposium on Narrative" and "Poets Theater," *Poetics Journal* 5: Special issue, *Non/Narrative* (May 1985).
Jonson, Ben. *Ben Jonson's Plays and Masques*. Edited by Robert M. Adams. New York: W.W. Norton, 1979.

120. Women & children & an old man Godot

Beckett, Samuel. *Waiting for Godot*. New York: Grove Press, 2011.

121.

Constellations

Note: These numbers refer to the numbers of the imagined theatres and their glosses, not the page number in this book.

CONSTELLATIONS